Management, Gender, and Race in the 21st Century

Margaret Foegen Karsten

UNIVERSITY PRESS OF AMERICA,® INC.
Lanham • Boulder • New York • Toronto • Oxford

Copyright © 2006 by
University Press of America,® Inc.
4501 Forbes Boulevard
Suite 200
Lanham, Maryland 20706
UPA Acquisitions Department (301) 459-3366

PO Box 317
Oxford
OX2 9RU, UK

Library of Congress Control Number: 2005931893
ISBN 0-7618-3275-0 (paperback : alk. ppr.)

Dedication

To my children in their birth order:
John Joseph, Kathryn Anne, and Amy Therese

In thanksgiving for the joy you have brought into my life and
In the hope that the world you inherit will
value each human as a person of inestimable worth.

Contents

Figures and Tables

Acknowledgments

I gratefully acknowledge the University of Wisconsin-Platteville for granting me a sabbatical leave in the fall 2004 semester, during which this manuscript was prepared. Without such a leave, preparation of a book-length manuscript would have been impossible.

I also want to thank the women of Upland Hills Home Health, and Pam White, and Rita Freiburger. Without their help in caring for an immediate family member, this book would not have been written. My appreciation also goes to LaVon M. Blum for modifying tables and assisting with many other tasks, Angela Loeffelholz and Andy Krueger for their help in preparing the figures, Nancy Daniels for her thorough editing, and Melanie Piper for creating the index. Special thanks go to my husband, Randy Karsten, for his patience, not only for the duration of this project, but also for the 25 years of our marriage.

COPYRIGHT ACKNOWLEDGMENTS

Bowden, Valmai. Figure 11.3. *Managing to make a difference.* Copyright © 2000 by Ashgate Publishing, Burlington, VT. Reprinted with permission of Ashgage Publishing,

Cox, Taylor. Change Model for Work on Diversity. *Creating the multicultural organization.* Copyright © 1984 by John Wiley & Sons, Inc., San Francisco, CA. Reprinted with permission of John Wiley & Sons.

Karsten, Margaret Foegen. *Management and gender: Issues and attitudes.* Material from pages 2, 4, 6–7, 58–59, 101–104, 112, 118, 137, 139, 141, 144–48, 158–59. Copyright © 1994 by Margaret Foegen Karsten. Reproduced with permission of Greenwood Publishing Group, Inc., Westport, CT.

Katz, J.H. & Miller, F.A. Figures 2–5 in Building inclusion and leveraging diversity as a way of doing business. 447–72. In Plummer, D.L. Ed. *Handbook of diversity management.* Copyright © 2003 by University Press of America, Inc., Lanham, MD. Reprinted with permission of University Press of America, Inc.

Chapter One

Race, Gender, Class, and Management: An Introduction

OUTCOMES

After studying this chapter, you should be able to:

1. explain how gender differs from biological sex.
2. explain the diversity within the following groups of people: Asian American, Hispanic.
3. define stewardship (with respect to leadership), dispersed leadership, leader-member exchange theory, and the management functions of planning, organizing, leading, and controlling.
4. explain how the constructs of race, gender, and social class may have an impact on those aspiring to top management positions in major U.S. firms.
5. explain similarities and differences between the Managerial Grid and Ohio State Studies.
6. explain servant leadership to someone who is unfamiliar with the concept.
7. compare and contrast transformational and transactional leadership.
8. justify your views regarding whether or not bi- or multi-racial categories should be used in the U.S. census based on pros and cons espoused by supporters and critics.
9. compare and contrast mechanistic and organic organizational structures and a feminist approach to organizations.

Before discussing the impact of race and gender on management of U.S. firms, defining all three terms is important. Some believe divorcing race and gender from social class is impossible, due to the interrelationships among all three. For that reason, social class will be described as well. Other differences

among people that admittedly have affected others' perceptions of their suit-
ability for management and their progress in management careers are beyond
the scope of this book. Likewise, limiting the discussion to U.S. firms is not
an attempt to be ethnocentric but, rather, an acknowledgement of the need to
set parameters.

The concepts of race, gender, and social class are based on societal beliefs,
not on an immutable set of biological or other differences. Though variations
among humans exist, there are more differences *within* groups that have been
characterized as a specific race than between them. In addition, certain people with light skin were not regarded as white in previous eras. At various
times in history, the Irish, southern Europeans, and Jewish people were not
considered white.

This book will integrate content related to the progress of blacks/African
Americans, Hispanics or Latinos/Latinas, Asian Americans, and white, non-
Hispanic American women into topical areas whenever possible. Information
about the experience of Native Americans will be included when it can be obtained. Acknowledging that minority males also have experienced disadvantages and that gender issues affect both males and females is important. For the
sake of relative brevity, however, this work will focus on women's experiences.

The terms *African American* and *black* will be used interchangeably though
some blacks are not African American but have Caribbean or other ancestry.
Similarly, *Hispanic* will refer to a diverse group of individuals of Spanish heritage regardless of their specific country of origin or race. According to the
U.S. census in 2000, Mexicans, also known as Chicana(o), comprise about
two-thirds of all Hispanics, making them the largest subgroup. Others who
are considered Hispanic include Central or South Americans, who make up
about 15%, Puerto Ricans, who make up 9%, and Cubans, who comprise 4%.
The remaining 6% consists of those of mixed racial or ethnic heritage and
other Hispanics, including self-described whites and Europeans (Catalyst,
2003).

Asian American will refer to those whose Asian ancestry or heritage in-
cludes, but is not limited to, those of Chinese, Japanese, Korean, Vietnamese,
Cambodian, Hmong, and other Indochinese ancestry, and Pacific Islanders.
The all-encompassing terms *Native American* or *American Indian* will refer
to the 2.3 million American Indians who live in the U.S. (Walters & Simoni,
2002) and are affiliated with any of the 558 federally recognized tribes
(Champagne, 2001), ranging from the Ojibwa and Iroquois to the Navajo and
Apache. The Equal Employment Opportunity Commission (EEOC) groups
Alaskan natives with Native Americans for reporting purposes.

White will be used instead of *Caucasian* due to the racist roots of the latter
term. At one time, some groups believed that the light-skinned people living

in the Caucasus met the ultimate standard of beauty, and darker skinned individuals compared less favorably.

A controversy has arisen regarding bi-racial or multi-racial identity, which reflects the blending of any two groups but seems most contentious when it involves blacks and whites. Some argue that blurring distinctions among those who have been regarded as members of different races will lead to color-blindness, which they view positively, but many African American leaders opposed the addition of bi-racial or multi-racial categories on data collection forms for the U.S. census in the year 2000. Opposition notwithstanding, respondents to the 2000 census were allowed, for the first time, to indicate that they were of more than one race. About 2.5% did so, and most said that they were white and one additional race (Diversity on the upswing, 2001). Prominent African Americans who are critical of bi- or multi-racial categories say that most individuals with any black heritage identify with the black community. An additional concern is that people who classify themselves as bi- or multi-racial will be ineligible for affirmative action and other programs that were started in the 1960s and 1970s to try to make amends for prior discrimination. Consequently, gains that African Americans and other minority groups have worked hard to achieve over many years could be eroded.

Gender goes beyond the biological differences between males and females. It includes ideas about behaviors that are appropriate for women and men, which have been reinforced through sex role socialization and the sexual division of labor. The latter ensures that some occupations are thought to be acceptable and desirable for one sex and not the other.

Padavic and Reskin (2002) recount the stone soup fable to illustrate the difference between sex and gender. A hungry village newcomer claimed to have a "magic stone" that could be used to make tasty soup. He put the stone in some boiling water and asked for just one carrot, which he told the townspeople would give the resulting stew much more flavor. A villager then agreed to put in a carrot. Similarly, the newcomer coaxed other villagers out of a meat bone, an onion, a potato, and other vegetables, and the stew, ostensibly made with the "magic stone," was delicious. Admitting that they do not "want to push the analogy too far," Padavic and Reskin (2002, p. 5) explain it as follows: "Like the stone, biological sex is the foundation on which societies construct gender. Like the stone, gender depends little on people's biological sex and mostly on how societies embellish it."

Social class can be defined as a stratification that affects a group's access to economic, political, cultural, and social resources (Anderson & Collins, 2003). Wealth, income, and power differentials distinguish among classes. In the U.S., five social classes have been identified: the elite, upper middle-class professionals, middle class, working class, and the poor (Bullock, 2004). Social class may affect access to higher education, which has an impact on occupational level. In turn, occupational level affects income and can affect the accumulation of future wealth.

Though individuals are not presumed to have control over race and gender, they are assumed to be able to change their social class. Often, the challenges associated with such a shift are underestimated. Compelling "rags to riches" stories make it seem as if anyone can achieve economic success in the United States through effort alone. Though that is possible and the idea of "pulling oneself up by the bootstraps" has been engrained in white, middle class culture, those notions minimize the struggles to improve their economic standing of people whose ancestors were poor or members of the working class.

Understandably, the media are more likely to feature stories about people with severe limitations who make outstanding, rather than average, contributions to society. Stories of the Oprah Winfreys and Ronald Reagans, who rose from humble origins to achieve prominence, gain more media attention than those of people who start and remain poor. Viewing as role models those who begin with nothing but end up with wealth may cause more difficulty for poor or working class individuals who fail to attain even middle class standards of economic success despite tremendous effort. Instead of recognizing the obstacles they face, some blame working class or poor people who are unable to move into higher social classes for failing to improve their lot.

How is the interaction of the constructs of race, gender, and class relevant to management? Understanding the impact of one such factor on management without controlling for the effects of the others may not be possible. Only eight women of any race are currently Chief Executive Officers (CEOs) of Fortune 500 firms in the U.S (Hymowitz, 2004). Meaningful conclusions cannot be drawn from a study of such a small group. When more women become CEOs, researchers might want to know the social class of their family of origin to determine whether or not a greater proportion came from mid- or upper class backgrounds.

MANAGEMENT AND LEADERSHIP

Now that race, gender, and class and their interaction have been mentioned briefly, the focus will shift to management and leadership. How have these processes changed since Mary Parker Follett defined the former as the art of getting things done through people, Sayles (1964) compared a good manager to a symphony orchestra conductor, and Henry Mintzberg (1975) discussed

the ten roles that managers enact? How do management and leadership differ, and why has the concept of leadership received so much attention?

Besides leading, other major management functions include planning, organizing, and controlling. These functions, which have been recognized since the early 1900s, will be described briefly in turn, though managers actually perform some of them simultaneously.

Planning involves setting goals and developing strategies and programs to achieve them. Planning may be long-term or short-term; strategic or tactical. Decision making, though necessary in all phases of management, is usually studied as part of the planning function.

Organizing means structuring resources to achieve goals. Resources available to the company include equipment, money, and employees. Departmentalization and centralization or decentralization of authority are issues of concern, as is job design. Staffing, which includes human resource planning, job analysis, recruitment, selection, orientation, and training, is often considered part of the organizing function.

Leading, or directing, is getting employees to work willingly toward organizational goals. It includes communication, motivation, and an ability to deal with formal and informal groups.

Controlling is ensuring that plans are achieved by taking corrective action, if necessary. Ratio analysis and budgets are financial control tools, and performance appraisal is used in human resource control. The word control sometimes has negative connotations because people associate it with overly strict external control rather than self-discipline, which is preferable.

The planning, organizing, and controlling functions have changed in the past decade and have been affected by technological changes that potentially improve their efficiency. Spears, however, questions the value of traditional planning, organizing, and controlling during times of turbulence. The three basic questions, "What is our vision?" "How do we organize resources to achieve the vision that has been translated into a mission?" and "How do we know how well or poorly we have done in achieving the mission?" long considered the "holy grail" of Western management, are losing their currency due to the rapidly changing environment. According to Spears (1995, p. 231),

> No sooner have we set a goal and figured out an action plan than everything seems to change. Consequently, tight control from the center just doesn't work like it used to in large organizations. Those organizations that were unwilling to surrender centralized control . . . have suffered . . . a 'breakdown of the central nervous system.'

The often-recommended solution, empowerment of employees, is only effective if those in various functional areas take a systems approach and examine the impact of their plans on other functions and on the entire organization.

Leadership is the only function that has had "an entire cottage industry" develop around it (Rhode, 2003). In addition to the burgeoning conferences and workshops on the topic, more than 5000 scholarly articles have been written about leadership in the past 25 years (Rhode).

One may be a manager and not a leader or vice versa, though some would argue that it is more difficult to be an effective manager without also being a leader. Leadership has been described as "doing the right things," whereas management is "doing things right" (Bennis, quoted in Loeb, 1994, p. 241).

EVOLUTION OF LEADERSHIP AND CONTEMPORARY APPROACHES

The evolution of the study of leadership has been documented elsewhere. To summarize, until the 1980s, leadership theories were of three major types: trait, behavioral, and situational. The first, which has been discredited, tried to identify a stable set of characteristics to predict which individuals had "the right stuff" to become leaders. Behavioral approaches typically focused on two factors and defined an optimal level of each regardless of the particular circumstances. Two examples are the Managerial Grid and the Ohio State Studies. The Grid, developed by Robert Blake and Jane Mouton, focused on production- and people-oriented leadership and advocated high levels of both. Behaviors known as initiating structure and consideration were described in the Ohio State Studies. Both "production-oriented" leadership and "initiating structure" are task-oriented; the other two emphasize interpersonal skills when relating to people. The most effective leader was thought to be the individual who ranked high on both consideration and initiating structure.

Several theories exemplify the situational approach, including House's Path-Goal theory, Fred Fiedler's contingency theory, and the Hersey and Blanchard model. All indicate that the most effective leadership style depends on situational characteristics; there is no "one best way" to lead.

When studying leadership, Hersey and Blanchard focus on followers' maturity or "readiness" to perform assigned tasks, which includes both ability and willingness. Leaders match their style to subordinates' readiness and move from a task- to a relationship-orientation as subordinates "mature" (Hersey, Blanchard, & Johnson, 2000). Powell and Graves (2003) use gender-related terms corresponding to those that Hersey and Blanchard identify and suggest that leaders adopt styles in this order as followers become increasingly "ready": "masculine" (high task/low relationship), "androgynous" (high on both dimensions), "feminine," (high relationship/low task), and "undifferentiated" (low on both dimensions). The undifferentiated style features total delegation to mature followers, who are able and willing to perform required tasks. Some may object to the use of the words "masculine" and "feminine" to refer to behaviors that anyone can enact.

Contemporary approaches to leadership, which Harvey (2001) calls "normative" include "servant leadership" (Greenleaf, 1977), transformational and transactional styles (Burns, 1978), and dispersed leadership as characterized by stewardship (Block, 1993).

The concept of servant leadership as developed by Greenleaf (1977) appeals to many, but the word "servant" may have a negative meaning. Before rejecting the idea because of its connotation of oppression, Spears asks people to consider the following:

1. The combination of two seemingly opposed terms can lead to creative insights.
2. The notion of servant leadership appeals to many women and people of color. Native Americans seem to view it as consistent with their world view, which emphasizes cooperative, communal, and holistic approaches (Spears, 1995).

Servant leadership requires inversion of the hierarchical organizational pyramid. It is a long-term approach that asks would-be leaders to make service to stakeholders, such as employees, customers, and the community, top priority. It features shared power and a group-oriented approach to decision-making. Success under servant leadership is measured by the degree to which each individual experiences personal growth by becoming wiser, freer, more independent, and more likely to become a future servant-leader.

Many values, skills, and behaviors characterize servant-leaders. They listen actively, reflect on events regularly, accept people and have empathy for them even when their performance or behavior is less than stellar. Servant leaders rely on dialogue and persuasion rather than force and are committed to each person's growth and the development of a sense of community within organizations. They exhibit foresight and a sense of stewardship (Spears, 1995).

Servant-leaders are not "soft." They, along with employees, create a vision, set challenging goals, and provide the support, training, acknowledgement, and rewards to facilitate success for everyone (Lee & Zemke, 1995; Murray-Bethel, 1995). Their behavior reflects Kanter's (1983) idea that good managers should make everyone a hero.

Burns defines *transformational leadership* as a process through which followers learn to become leaders by emulating leaders' good example and cultivating a relationship with them. *Transactional leadership*, on the other hand, emphasizes an exchange of behaviors for rewards or outcomes, focuses on efficiency and fair practice, and advocates management by exception (Bass & Avolio, 1990).

Bass (1985) and Bass and Avolio (1990; 1993) define transformational leadership as leader behaviors marked by charisma, inspiration, consideration for the individual, and intellectual stimulation. Charisma evokes pride and trust as well as articulation of a vision and the importance of an organization's mission. Inspiration means modeling appropriate behavior and exhibiting optimism and excitement about the attainability of the organization's mission. Consideration involves providing individualized attention to each person, treating everyone with respect, offering developmental opportunities to all, and expecting each person to show responsibility. Intellectual stimulation means questioning the status quo and constantly challenging people with new ideas.

Rosener's (1990) definition of transformational leadership features shared information, praise for employees when they do good work, participation in decision making, and a conciliatory approach that enhances mutual respect. Rosener thought that this approach originated in the shared socialization experiences of women entering management in the 1980s. Unlike the "first wave" of managerial women, who believed they had to imitate male executives to be taken seriously, the next generation had more freedom to bring their own "feminine strengths" to the executive suite, according to Rosener. Other authors, perhaps most notably, Sally Helgesen in *The Female Advantage,* (1990) drew similar conclusions. Male executives supposedly view relationships as a means to an end, more like transactions, according to Rosener. They motivate others by providing rewards and punishments contingent on performance and avoid "micromanagement" in favor of involvement in situations only when corrective action is clearly needed.

Rosener's detractors believe her ideas perpetuate stereotypical notions of women's skills and traditional sex role identities associated with management and assume that most females have had similar socialization experiences. Presuming that women have certain strengths could result in detrimental stereotyping, which will be discussed further in chapter 5. Metcalfe and Altman (2001) criticize Rosener for failing to question traditional characterizations of "masculinity" and "femininity" when she equates relationship skills to "feminine" and interaction skills to "masculine" leadership. Critics questioned the wisdom of associating currently popular management behaviors with women.

Dispersed leadership is the idea that employees throughout an organization need to share leadership; it is no longer the purview of management alone. Self-governing teams, the members of which are accountable to each other, epitomize this approach. Also consistent with dispersed leadership is Block's (1993) concept of *stewardship*: leaders should not behave as if they own a position and its accompanying power forever. Instead, they should enact their leadership role temporarily to benefit the entire community. Block eschews traditional leadership, which he believes is built on dependency, self-interest and patriarchy (Harvey, 2001). He believes bonuses for teams that perform well should replace individual performance rating systems, which encourage dysfunctional competition. The ideas underlying stewardship include commitment to the community over self, "partnership instead of patriarchy, empowerment instead of dependency, [and] service instead of self-interest. . ."(Harvey, p. 41).

Traditional—and some contemporary—leadership theories have been censured because they seem to reflect white male perceptions. Those that implicitly assume follower homogeneity may no longer be relevant because of the greater diversity among followers (Chrobot-Mason & Ruderman, 2004).

An approach that considers follower diversity is *leader member exchange theory*. It proposes that each relationship between a supervisor and employee is unique (Chen & Van Velsor, 1996; Scandura & Lankau, 1996). Low exchange relationships focus almost exclusively on job-related communication and are formal. High exchange relationships are characterized by greater openness, informality, and communication about job- and non-job related matters. Though both parties must contribute to the relationship, the supervisor is obliged to cultivate high quality relationships, which have been shown to have a positive impact on work outcomes such as turnover and performance (Gerstner & Day, 1997).

Even leadership theories that extol stereotypically feminine behaviors may not help women who seek top management positions. As Wajcman (1996) points out, due to a remaining double standard, males may be viewed as increasing their repertoire of leader behaviors if they improve their interpersonal skills, which are highly valued in managers. Females may continue to be viewed as possessing *only* such skills and as lacking decision-making skills, which have been stereotypically associated with men.

Many contemporary leadership theories seem consistent with organizations designed to be compatible with various feminist schools of thought, though they have not been described in such terms. Since the late 1980s and early 1990s, concepts compatible with a feminist approach to management have been "mainstreamed." They are based, as Harvey (2001, p. 37) states, on the notion that organizations "must treat workers not merely instrumentally but as moral ends, that capitalist firms are truly communities—makers and defenders of meaning and value for the individuals who compose them."

FEMINISM AND MANAGEMENT

Like management, feminism does not have one universally appealing definition. The term has negative connotations to some, evoking images of leftover
demonstrators from another era. To others *feminism* is a belief that each individual is a valuable human being in his or her own right. Individuals are to be
valued as ends in themselves not simply providers of services or manufactur-
ers of products. Women's lives have intrinsic worth. They are to be valued
simply because they exist, not because of status derived through associations
with men.

Feminist ideologies range from Marxist to women's rights to postmod-
ernist; these have been described elsewhere (Karsten, 1994) and will not be
recounted here. All feminist ideologies question the status quo regarding society and women's roles. Past practices and modes of thinking are not accepted automatically but are scrutinized. As Sheila Ruth states, "Feminism
may be a perspective, a world view, a political theory, a spiritual focus, or a
kind of activism" (1980). It does not revere so-called masculine behaviors,
such as dominance, at the expense of supposedly feminine behaviors such as
compassion. Feminism rejects negative cultural images of women as weak or
incompetent, but affirms their ability to be strong, intelligent, and ethical.
Both sexes can be feminists; the term refers to a belief system rather than to
traits that have been labeled as feminine.

The contemporary feminist movement was rooted in white middle class
experience, which differed markedly from that of women of color and women
who were not privileged based on their social class. Feminist author, bell
hooks, points out that the primarily white mid- to upper class early feminist
movement in the U.S. that viewed paid employment as a means of liberation
from boredom did not resonate with black or working class women who grew
up knowing that they would need to work due to economic necessity (hooks,
2000). Black women felt, and, in some cases, were made to feel unwelcome
at first (hooks). With hindsight, it seems ironic that feminists would have allowed this to happen, given their bias in favor of inclusiveness and dislike of
hierarchy and relationships characterized by unequal power.

Black women thought that some of the leaders of the early feminist movement could not relate to or understand their experiences. Therefore, they
sometimes found it difficult to identify with the goals of the early feminist
movement. This led Livers and Caver (2003) to caution against overstating
the similarities between white and black women. Some majority women who
have not reflected on the way in which women of color might have perceived
the early feminist movement may be surprised that their initial reaction was
lukewarm.

ORGANIC AND MECHANISTIC STRUCTURES AND PROPOSED FEMINIST ORGANIZATION

An organization designed to be consistent with a feminist ideal might have an *organic structure,* characterized by participative decision making, few rules, and lateral communications characterize organic organizations (Burns & Stalker, 1961). Interaction is the preferred method of resolving conflict, and messages communicated are more likely to be advice and counsel than orders. Power is based on expertise and is dispersed throughout the organization. Feminists try to eliminate position-based power distinctions and refer to leaders as facilitators or coordinators who operate at the center of a network, not at the top of a pyramid (Ferguson, 1984). This notion of power is consistent with Block's view of stewardship, which "implies the systematic dismantling of governance structures and the distribution of power" (Harvey, 2001, p. 41).

Features described thus far would appeal to feminists, but the ultimate goal of profitability might not. At one time, abandoning profit as the ultimate criterion against which success is measured might have seemed blasphemous to businesses (Karsten, 1994), but the idea has gained acceptance in new leadership theories including "servant leadership." For example, Greenleaf maintains that employee growth, not profitability, should be the purpose of work. He believes that organizations exist to serve their constituents, not vice versa. In organizations that serve people and make employee development the top priority, "workers then see to it that the customer is served and that the ink on the bottom line is black" (Greenleaf, 1977, p. 145, quoted in Harvey, 2001).

New leadership theories discussed in this chapter reaffirm the notion that firms most likely will be profitable if they produce goods or services for which there is a real need and create a positive work environment in which employees are respected and treated equally. The underlying philosophy, which is consistent with servant-leadership and a feminist approach to management, views profit as a by-product, but financial results may equal or exceed those of firms pursuing profit directly (Karsten, 1994).

Many feminists abhor *mechanistic organizational structures.* At the extreme, mechanistic organizations are the opposite of those that are organic. Authority is concentrated at the top, there are many rules, and downward communication involves giving directions or orders. External controls are imposed, and work is highly specialized. Table 1.1 summarizes features of the organic, mechanistic, and proposed feminist structures.

Ferguson (1984) criticizes the notion that bureaucratic, or mechanistic, organizations are philosophically neutral. She says they view workers as objects and are perverted in the sense that rules set up to facilitate an outcome become ends in themselves. Bureaucracies produce a fragmented work

Table 1.1.   Features of Mechanistic, Organic, and Proposed Feminist Organizational Structures

Features	Mechanistic	Organic	Feminist
Specialization of tasks	*High specialization*	*Low specialization*	*Low specialization*
Power	At the top	Based on skill; wherever competence exists	Based on expertise, not position
Conflict Resolution	By superior	By interaction	By interaction
Rules	Many	Few	Few
Type of Communication	Downward	Upward, downward,	Upward, downward, lateral lateral
Content of Communication	Directions, orders	Advice, counsel	Advice, counsel
Decision making	Unilateral, at the top	Participative	Participative
Control*	External	Internal	Internal, self
Role of profit*	Ultimate goal	Ultimate goal	By-product
Loyalty	To organizational System	To work group	To work group
Appropriate environment	Stable	Dynamic	Any environment

*Feature not mentioned in the original work by Burns and Stalker

process, isolated workers, and depersonalization of remaining communication channels. Individual deficiencies, rather than factors inherent in the structure of the institution, are thought to cause employee problems, according to Ferguson.

The feminist preference for organic structures already has been explained. If feminists advocate these structures in all situations, they would contradict contingency principles, which state that the best organizational structure, or leadership style, depends on the situation. Organic structures are considered more effective in dynamic, turbulent environments. Mechanistic or bureaucratic structures might be preferable in stable, predictable environments.

Besides organizational structure, other aspects of hypothetical feminist organizations should be considered. They would offer leaves of absence for legitimate reasons as well as flexible schedules and benefits to allow employees to integrate work and personal life. Such entities would emphasize cooperation and teamwork but treat people as unique individuals (Karsten, 1994).

Dysfunctional win-lose competition, in which coworkers vie for a limited number of rewards, would be discouraged. Instead, competition with oneself would be encouraged. There would be less need for external controls under a system of genuine worker self-management (Ferguson, 1984). If discipline were necessary as part of the control function, it would be corrective, not punitive.

Ferguson (1984) discusses the importance of moving toward a vertical division of labor in which each person is responsible for both the creative and the mundane. She says, "A feminist restructuring of work entails rejection of the hierarchical division of labor . . . and a reintegration of planning and performance of tasks."

This reintegration resembles *job enrichment,* which gives workers more responsibility for both preparatory and decision making activities, adding tasks at different responsibility levels. *Job enlargement,* on the other hand, adds activities requiring similar types of skills. Enrichment is a vertical division of labor, whereas enlargement is horizontal. Many organizations use both techniques to increase employee satisfaction, but feminists would prefer enrichment.

Feminists might be receptive to skill-based compensation, in which employees are paid for their knowledge instead of their activities. This encourages workers to learn more about their own job, co-workers' jobs, and the total process involved in providing a good or service. Employers who have tried skill-based pay believe it gives them a more flexible workforce (Kanter, 1987).

The feminist approach assumes that most employees are motivated by needs such as esteem or self-actualization. Further, it presumes that employees like to work and want to do their best. This perspective may not address problems of motivating employees who view work as a necessary evil and whose main concern is to earn enough money to satisfy basic survival and security needs.

Race, gender, and class have been defined, the way in which those terms will be used in this book have been explained, and new theories related to the function of leadership have been summarized. It is now time to shift focus to explore the progress of women and minority groups in achieving management or executive positions in major U.S. businesses. Chapter 2 will discuss their accomplishments since World War II, remaining challenges that they face, and possibilities for overcoming them.

REFERENCES

Anderson, M.L. & Collins, P. H. 2003. *Race, Class, and Gender: An Anthology,* 5th ed. Belmont, CA: Wadsworth.

Bass, B.M. 1985. *Leadership and performance beyond expectations.* New York: Free Press.

Bass, B.M. & Avolio, B.J. 1990. *Manual for the multifactor leadership questionnaire.* Palo Alto, CA: Consulting Psychologist Press.

Bass, B.M. & Avolio, B.J. 1993. Transformational leadership: a response to critiques. In M.M. Chemers & R. Ayman. Eds. *Leadership theory and research: Perspectives and Directions.* New York: Academic Press.

Block, P. 1993. *Stewardship: Choosing service over self-interest.* San Francisco: Berrett-Koehler.

Bullock, H. 2004. Class diversity in the workplace. 224–42. In M. Stockdale & F. Crosby, Eds. *The Psychology and management of workplace diversity.* Malden, MA: Blackwell Publishers, Ltd.

Burns, T. & Stalker, G. 1961. *The management of innovation.* London: Tavistock.

Burns, J.M. 1978. *Leadership.* New York: Harper & Row.

Catalyst. 2003. *Advancing Latinas in the workplace: What managers need to know.* New York: Author.

Champagne, D., Ed. 2001. *The Native North American Almanac,* 2nd ed. Farmington, MI: Gale Group.

Chen, C.C. & Van Velsor, E. 1996. New directions for research and practice in diversity leadership. *Leadership Quarterly, 7*(2). 285–302.

Chrobot-Mason, D. & Ruderman, M.N. 2004. Leadership in a diverse workplace. 100–121. In M. Stockdale and F.J. Crosby, Eds. *Psychology and management of workplace diversity.* Malden, MA: Blackwell Publishers, Ltd.

Diversity in U.S. on upswing as America grows. 2001, Mar. 13. *Pensacola News-Journal.* 8A.

Ferguson, K. 1984. *The feminist case against bureaucracy.* Philadelphia: Temple University Press.

Gerstner, C.R. & Day, D.V. 1997. Meta-analytic review of leader-member exchange theory: Correlates and construct issues. *Journal of Applied Psychology, 82.* 827–44.

Greenleaf, R.K. 1977. *Servant leadership: A journey into the nature of legitimate power and greatness.* New York: Paulist Press.

Harvey, M. 2001. The hidden face: A critique of normative approaches to leadership. *SAM Advanced Management Journal, 66*(4). 36–47.

Helgesen, S. 1990. *The female advantage: Women's ways of leadership.* New York: Doubleday.

Hersey, P., Blanchard, K.H., & Johnson, D.E. 2000. *Management of organizational behavior: Utilizing human resources.* 8th ed. Englewood Cliffs, NJ: Prentice-Hall.

hooks, bell. 2000. *Feminist theory: From margin to center.* 2nd ed. Cambridge, MA: South End Press.

Hymowitz, C. 2004, Nov. 8. Through the glass ceiling. *The Wall Street Journal.* R1, R3.

Kanter, R.M. 1983. *The change masters.* New York: Simon and Schuster.

Kanter, R.M. 1987, Jan. From status to contribution: Some organizational implications of the changing basis for pay. *Personnel.* 12–37.

Karsten, M.F. 1994. *Management and gender: Issues and attitudes.* Westport: Greenwood Publishing Group, Inc.

Lee, C. & Zemke, R. 1995. The search for spirit in the workplace. In L.C. Spears, Ed. *Reflections on leadership.* New York: John Wiley & Sons, Inc.

Livers, A.B. & Caver, K.A. 2003. *Leading in black and white: Working across the racial divide in corporate America.* San Francisco: John Wiley & Sons, Inc.

Loeb, M. (1994, September 19). Where leaders come from. *Fortune.* 241.

Metcalfe, B. & Altman, Y. 2001. Leadership. In Wilson, E., Ed. *Organizational Behaviour. Reassessed.* Thousand Oaks, CA: SAGE Publications.

Mintzberg, H. 1975, July/Aug. The manager's job: Folklore and fact. *Harvard Business Review.* 49–61.

Murray-Bethel, S. 1995. Servant-leadership and corporate risk taking: When risk taking makes a difference. In L.C. Spears, Ed. *Reflections on leadership.* New York: John Wiley & Sons, Inc.

Padavic, I. & Reskin, B. 2002. *Women and men at work.* 2nd ed. Thousand Oaks, CA: SAGE Publications.

Powell, G. N. & Graves, L.M. 2003. *Women and men in management.* 3rd ed. Thousand Oaks, CA: SAGE.

Rhode, D., Ed. 2003. *The difference 'difference' makes: women and leadership.* Stanford, CA: Stanford University Press.

Rosener, J. 1990, Nov./Dec. Ways women lead. *Harvard Business Review.* 119–125.

Ruth, S. 1980. *Issues in women's studies.* Geneva, IL: Houghton Mifflin.

Sayles, L. 1964. *Managerial behavior.* New York: McGraw-Hill.

Scandura, T.A. & Lankau, M.J. 1996. Developing diverse leaders: A leader-member exchange approach. *Leadership Quarterly, 7*(2). 243–63.

Spears, L. 1995. Servant leadership and the Greenleaf Legacy. In Spears, L.C. Ed. *Reflections on leadership.* New York: John Wiley & Sons, Inc.

Wajcman, J. 1996. Desperately seeking difference: Is management style gendered? *British Journal of Industrial Relations.* 34(4). 333–49.

Walters, K.L. & Simoni, J.M. 2002. Reconceptualizing Native women's health: An "indigenist" stress-coping model. *American Journal of Public Health, 92*(4). 520–24.

Chapter Two

Women and Racial and Ethnic Minorities in Management: Overcoming Challenges

OUTCOMES

After studying this chapter, you should be able to:

1. define class action lawsuit, glass ceiling, glass walls, concrete ceiling, reverse discrimination, career ladder, narrow band of acceptable behavior, homo-social reproduction, miasma, biculturalism, colorism, tempered radicalism.
2. explain the impact of World War II on the participation of white and black women in management.
3. explain how social, legal, and political changes in the 1960s and 1970s set the stage for advancement of women and minorities in management.
4. compare the educational levels of women, men, and minorities in the U.S.
5. explain why equity in the overall percentages of women and men in management does not necessarily indicate parity.
6. explain why relatively few women of color (black, Native American, Asian American, Hispanic) or white women are in top management positions of major U.S. firms.
7. compare and contrast barriers that women of color and women in general face in their pursuit of upper level management positions.
8. explain several actions organizations can take to deal with unsupportive organizational structures and practices, also called "systemic barriers," which hinder career progress of women and minorities.
9. compare factors contributing to managerial success of women of color and women in general.

10. explain factors contributing to miasma among African Americans who advance in managerial careers.
11. explain special challenges that many Native American women and Latinas experience that may hinder their progress in management.
12. explain five specific changes in human resource practices that will improve women's and minorities' chances of career advancement.
13. determine how actions that individuals can take to increase their chances of managerial advancement could be applied in a real or hypothetical organization.
14. justify your beliefs about whether rewarding team, rather than individual, performance helps or harms upwardly mobile managerial women.

OVERVIEW OF POST WORLD WAR II PROGRESS OF WOMEN AND MINORITIES IN MANAGEMENT

During World War II, white women started moving into positions from which they had been excluded previously, including supervision, due to a labor shortage. Many men and some women joined the armed services to support the war effort. The irony of the fact that African Americans could risk their lives to defend their country in war but were treated as second class citizens in the job market otherwise was not lost on the black community.

After the war, women were urged to return to the home. Some lost their jobs to returning members of the armed services. Others enjoyed being in the workforce and did not want to leave. For that reason, World War II became a turning point in terms of the participation of white women in the paid labor force. They believed Rosie the Riveter's wartime slogan, "You can do it," and there was no turning back.

Nevertheless, the immediate postwar growth in the percentage of women in management was slow. Only 5% of all first-line supervisors were women in 1947, and in the 1950s, the number in high ranking positions could be counted on one hand. They included Dorothy Shaver, President of Lord & Taylor, Oveta Culp Hobby, publisher of the *Houston Post* and former colonel and cabinet member, Bernice Fitz-Gibbon, Advertising Executive at Macy's and Gimbel's, and Elsie Murphy, President of S. Stroock & Company, a textile firm (Hamill, 1956). No women of color were among their ranks.

Decades would pass before diversity was tolerated, much less thought to provide a competitive edge. The title of a 1965 *Harvard Business Review* article, "Are Women Executives People," (Bowman, Worthy & Greyser) summarized the facts of organizational life in the 1950s. Organizations were not receptive to those who failed to fit the corporate mold.

Others have eloquently described the significance of the seminal 1954 U.S. Supreme Court decision, *Brown v. Board of Education,* which required an integrated public school system. Though it was only the first step on a long path to educational equity, future actions that resulted from it paved the way for people of color to eventually enter many occupations that previously had been closed to them, including management.

A milestone for women pursuing management was their admission to a Harvard-Radcliffe undergraduate business program for the first time in 1959. Radcliffe, however, still issued their diplomas. In1963, women were admitted to the Harvard MBA program, which was important because graduation from a prestigious MBA program provided entrée into management jobs in major corporations (Karsten, 1994).

Social and legal changes in the 1960s led to greater participation of women and minorities in higher level positions including those in business. The Equal Pay Act of 1963 was passed as an amendment to the 1938 Fair Labor Standards Act, and Title VII of the Civil Rights Act, which dealt with equal opportunity in employment, was passed in 1964. These and other relevant federal laws will be discussed in chapter 3.

In 1960, only one-third of white women were in the paid workforce, (Amott and Mattheai, 1996), and they were regarded as "casual" employees who would leave when they married and had children, which was the expectation, or when they no longer needed supplemental household income. As it had been in the 1950s, domesticity was the norm for most white women in 1960. Forty percent of black women were in the labor force in that year, mainly in service or domestic occupations. They participated at a higher rate than their white counterparts because black males' long-term earnings were insufficient (Amott & Mattheai, 1996). In 1960, the percentages of black and Hispanic managers were only 1.7% and 1%, respectively, and most were in education or government (Thomas & Gabarro, 1999).

Historians have detailed events of the turbulent 1960s, which will be summarized here to show how they set the stage for later career advancement of women and minorities. In addition to increasing concern about the Vietnam War toward the end of the decade, lack of responsiveness to African Americans' quest for civil rights led to unrest. Hispanics, Asian-Americans, and Native Americans also began to make demands. Mexican Americans formed a political party, La Raz Unida, and sponsored the National Chicano Moratorium March in Los Angeles (Thomas & Gabarro, 1999). Asian Americans mobilized to end the exploitation of garment workers. In the 1970s, they advocated equal education for non-English speaking Chinese students in *Lau v. Nichols*, which led to mandated bi-lingual education nationwide (Thomas & Gabarro, 1999). Like other minorities, Native Americans began to demand college curricula to address experiences and perspectives of their ethnic groups. At the same time, the few white women in business grew dissatisfied with externally imposed limits on their career advancement, and the women's movement gained strength, at least among white mid- to upper class females.

By 1970, a mere 1.4% of employed black women and 3.9% of their white counterparts had managerial or administrative positions, most of which were in the public sector (Amott & Matthei, 1996). Sex and race segregation were the norm, and the full impact of 1960s legislation to end employment discrimination was not felt until the mid to late 1970s, when the Equal Employment Opportunity Commission (EEOC) began to win lawsuits against major U.S. employers. *Class action* lawsuits benefit not only the individual who files suit but also any others who are "similarly situated." For example, if a firm is found guilty of denying an applicant a position based on race or ethnicity, others of the same ethnic or racial heritage who were qualified for a similar position but were not hired also may be entitled to monetary damages.

Despite the fact that the percentage of female college graduates rose steadily during the 1970s, white women still were steered to secretarial positions. A woman who graduated from a university business program "with highest honors" was offered a clerical job in a consumer products manufacturing firm though she had applied for a managerial position. Unfortunately, that was fairly common. As Bell and Nkomo (2000) point out, it is ironic that women, who were excluded from secretarial posts when males held them in an earlier era, were directed to such jobs when they became female dominated, low-paying support positions to male executives.

African American women, on the other hand, did not gravitate to secretarial positions; they were not particularly welcome in such posts in the early 1970s. College educated black females were encouraged to become teachers or social workers; their parents and relatives discouraged them from pursuing business or management careers. Instead, the growing black middle class directed their daughters to careers in law, medicine, or education because the elders perceived relatively fewer barriers to entry in those professions (Bell & Nkomo, 2000).

Affirmative action plans will be discussed in chapter 3, but a basic definition is that they are ongoing, results-oriented programs designed to identify job categories in which women and minorities are underutilized and take specific, action-oriented steps to rectify that situation. President Kennedy first used the term "affirmative action" in the employment context in 1961. Executive Order 11246, passed in 1967, required *affirmative action plans* of government contractors and subcontractors with at least 50 employees and $50,000 in contracts each year.

Early affirmative action plans had no "teeth," however. For practical purposes, they were voluntary until the early 1970s, when an order issued by the

Nixon Administration provided for enforcement. Thomas and Gabarro (1999) indicated that affirmative action plans had a "profound effect" on the career progress of women and minorities in the 1970s.

By the late 1970s, corporations added new positions to oversee equal opportunity and affirmative action compliance. Racial/ethnic minorities and women were the logical candidates to fill those positions. African Americans and Hispanics were hired to manage units with a large percentage of minority employees and became assets in the employment division due to their ties with historically black and Hispanic colleges. Positions in recruitment and EEO were steppingstones to further advancement for racial and ethnic minorities (Thomas & Gabarro, 1999).

By the end of the 1980s, minority groups' middle class expanded, perhaps due to the improved economy. Political forces at the beginning of the decade did not help minorities; officials in the Reagan administration viewed affirmative action unfavorably and relaxed reporting requirements. Major surveys by Fernandez (1981) showed that Americans believed discrimination in the U.S. had diminished from 1972 to 1976, but Fortune 500 managers and administrators thought it rose from 1976 to 1986. Nevertheless, minority males became top executives of a few well-known firms, such as Beatrice Foods, the Equitable Company, and TIAA-CREF, a large pension fund, in the 1980s (Thomas & Gabarro, 1999).

The 1978 *Regents of the University of California v. Bakke* case and economic woes in the early 1980s fueled allegations of "reverse discrimination" and backlash against affirmative action. Despite the fact that quotas were illegal, companies were accused of hiring applicants who were ostensibly less qualified than white males to achieve the quotas. Affirmative action goals were thought to hurt the best and brightest female and minority applicants, who had to work twice as hard to counter the stigma that they were only hired to meet a numerical mandate.

Workforce 2000: Work and Workers for the 21st Century (Johnston & Packer, 1987) changed the nature of the discussion. Because of a predicted labor shortage, the report argued that full utilization of all human talent was essential regardless of the way it was "packaged." Thus, the "business case" for diversity was born. In many instances, the same individuals who opposed what they perceived as affirmative action "quotas" strongly favored efforts to make the workplace more inclusive.

By the late 1980s and 1990s, many women and minorities seemed to have done "all the right things" to advance. A record number earned bachelor's and master's degrees in business, including MBAs; women and minorities gained business experience and tried to find mentors and create time to expand their networks. Due to larger, systemic issues, individual efforts were insufficient, and women and minorities encountered obstacles, to be discussed later in this chapter, which seemed intractable at first.

An appropriate education is necessary, but not sufficient, for those aspiring to top management posts today. Lack of education can be a "show stopper," as it has been for certain minority groups, such as Native Americans, who also have relatively low labor force participation and a high poverty rate (Champagne, 2001). Underlying issues related to economic self sufficiency must be addressed before conditions are ripe for larger numbers of Native Americans to move into management.

Overall, the percentage of females earning baccalaureate and master's degrees in the U.S exceeded the percentage of males earning them in 2002. Fifty-seven percent of bachelor's degrees and 58% of master's degrees were awarded to women in that year (U.S. Department of Education, 2002a & b). Males earned 59% of business master's degrees awarded in 2002 compared to 41% for females, but the overall percent of males and females earning undergraduate business degrees was about equal (U.S. Department of Education, 2002a & b).

As Figure 2.1A shows, though some differences were minimal, a greater percentage of women in all racial/ethnic groups except whites and nonresident aliens earned an undergraduate business degree than their male peers. A higher percentage of black and Asian females earned a master's degree in business than did males in the same racial groups, as illustrated in Figure 2.1B. The percentage of business master's degrees earned by male and female Hispanics and American Indians was extremely close. A higher proportion of male whites

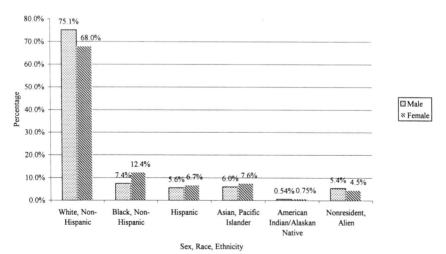

Figure 2.1A.   Percentage of Bachelor's Degrees in Business Awarded in 2002 Based on Sex, and Race or Ethnicity

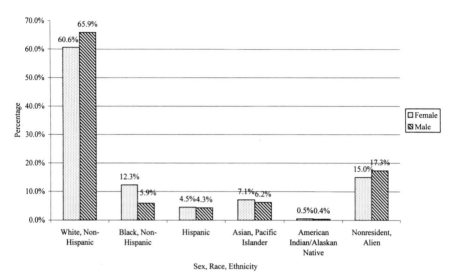

Figure 2.1B.   Percentage of Master's Degrees in Business Awarded in 2002 Based on Sex and Race or Ethnicity

and nonresident aliens than females in those groups earned master's degrees in business. Native Americans of both sexes combined made up less than 1% of those awarded bachelor's degrees and only one-half of 1% of those who earned master's degrees in 2002. Only 1% of all residents of the U.S. were Native Americans in that year, however (U.S. Census Bureau, 2002). Comparing percentages of minority groups with the group numerically in the majority over time is difficult. Consistent data may not have been maintained for each group until fairly recently due to their relatively small representation in management. In other instances, data for particular groups are spotty or difficult to obtain. Agencies collecting relevant data define management occupations in different ways, contributing to inconsistency.

Though they are still underrepresented in the most powerful positions in Fortune 500 firms, the percent of women in management has increased substantially since 1970, as Figure 2.2 shows. The percentage of the total number of women who are employed who chose managerial, administrative, or executive positions also has climbed steadily over 35 years. Powell and Graves (2003) indicate that management is now a sex-neutral occupation. Overall, the percentages of women and men in management are quite similar, but this convergence may mask disparities at the highest levels.

The percentage of African Americans in managerial and professional specialties, which is a broader category than managerial, administrative, and executive positions, slowly rose from 3.6% in 1977 to 6% in 1986 (Davidson, 1997). From 1986 to 1996, the absolute numbers of African Americans in

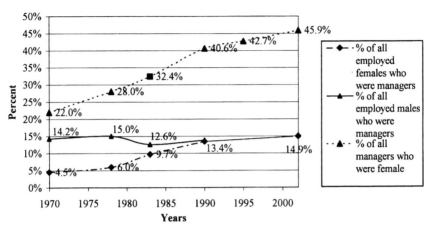

Figure 2.2. **Percentage of All Employed Who are Managers by Sex and Women as Percent of All Managers, Selected Years, 1979–2002**

managerial and professional occupations grew from 900,000 to 1.6 million, representing a 79% increase (U.S. Department of Labor, 1997). Livers and Caver (2003) reported that the percent of black women in managerial or professional occupations surpassed the percent of black men in the same occupations in 1990 and 2000. The percentages climbed in that decade from 19.5 to 25.2 for black females and from 13.2 to 17.7 for black men.

Figure 2.3 depicts percentages of officials and managers by sex and race/ethnicity in 1998 and 2002 based on data that the EEOC maintains. The Commission's definition of officials and managers seems more restrictive

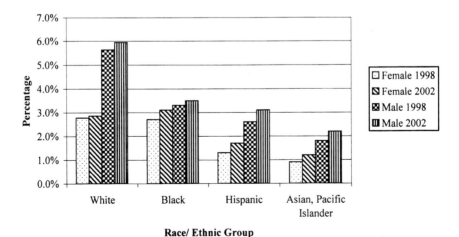

Figure 2.3. **Percent of Officials and Managers by Sex and Racial or Ethnic Group:1998 and 2002**

than a widely used and reported definition of executives, managers, and administrators, so data are not comparable to those in Figure 2.2. According to the EEOC (2002), the percent of officials and managers who were female in 2002 was only 35%; a more commonly cited percentage of female executives, managers, and administrators in that year was 45.9%. The variation can be explained by the difference in the inclusiveness of the definition of managers.

The low percentages of officials and managers who were from various minority groups in 2002 according to EEOC data indicate the need for additional progress. The percent of officials and managers who were Native American remained at .1 in 2002, the same as in 1998. The percent who were Native American men dropped from .3 in 1998 to .2 in 2002 (EEOC, 2002).

As of the second quarter of 2004, the percentages of Asian Americans and whites who were managers in the labor force approximated the percent of all those employed who were in executive or managerial occupations, which was 10.5. Again, smaller percentages of blacks and Hispanics (5.8 and 4.9%, respectively) were represented in the managerial ranks.

PROGRESS OF WOMEN AND MINORITIES
IN TOP MANAGEMENT

Percentages do not tell the entire story. The percent of women and racial/ethnic minorities is rising, but they tend to be concentrated in lower level positions rather than in those with clout. Fewer than 5% of senior managers in major U.S. corporations were women in 1990; that percentage rose to 6.2 by 2000. Of senior executives in Fortune 500 firms, 6% were female in 2002. Over 95% of senior managers, male or female, in major U.S. firms are non-Hispanic whites.

Besides being concentrated in lower management levels, in the late 1990s, racial and ethnic minorities faced a problem that women encountered earlier. They were likely to be found in staff positions outside the business mainstream. According to Thomas and Gabarro (1999, p. 7), "such jobs, while important in their own right, seldom lead to the CEO position. . ."

At this point, a digression may be in order to examine the concept of success as used in this book. The reader already may have questioned the admittedly narrow notion that makes vertical movement in organizations synonymous with success. Individuals' conceptions of success vary. Not everyone aspires to top management; many believe that satisfying work, intellectual challenge, a chance to "make a difference," and time to enjoy and maintain high quality relationships are more important. Those more inclusive definitions of success are eminently valid, but this book's purpose is to focus on women and minority group members who aspire to lead large organizations and the processes that help or hinder them. Vertical movement is necessary to enable them to lead major U.S. corporations and perhaps modify their organizations' definitions of success after they reach the top.

Progress of women of color in corporate officer positions from 1999 to 2002 was minimal, increasing only from 1.3 to 1.6%. Over a seven year span beginning in 1995, the overall percent of women who were corporate officers jumped from 8.7 to 15.7% (Catalyst, 2002).

In 1980, Katharine Graham of the *Washington Post* was the only female CEO of a major U.S. corporation, and she obtained her position only after the death of her husband, who previously ran the company. Ms. Graham followed the only path open to U.S. women who were interested in business in prior eras. They had to become widows or adult "orphans" with no male relatives before they could inherit a business. The fact that most women who became owners or managers in this way successfully ran their businesses was immaterial; if their fathers or husbands had not died, business management would not have been an option. By 1990, Marion Sandler of Golden West Financial Corporation and Linda Wachner or Warnaco had joined Katharine Graham as CEOs of Fortune 1000 firms (Billard, 1990).

In Fortune 500 Corporations, there were two female CEOs in 2000; five in 2001 (Padavic and Reskin, 2002), and eight in 2004 (Lublin, 2004). Catalyst (2000) predicts that 20% and 27% of corporate officers in Fortune 500 firms will be women by 2010 and 2020, respectively. More progress is needed before that prediction becomes reality.

Andrea Jung, CEO of Avon, is about the only woman of color to lead a Fortune 500 firm. Born in Toronto, she is of Asian ancestry.

As of 2002, no African American females were CEOs of Fortune 500 firms. Oprah Winfrey, CEO of Harpo, was ranked tenth on *Fortune's* list of 50 top black business executives (Daniels, 2002) and sixth on its list of 50 top female executives in 2004 (Harrington & Bartosiewicz, 2004). Ann Fudge, who joined the advertising firm, Young Rubicam, at a top level after leaving an executive position at Kraft Foods, previously was mentioned as a managerial African American woman with the potential to be a CEO, but she was excluded from the *Fortune* list of the top 50. Myrtle Potter, an African American female who was President of Commercial Operations at Genentech, made the list. She aspires to a CEO position and is thought to have a good chance of achieving it (Daniels, 2002).

The men who occupied the top three ranks among the 50 most powerful African American executives in 2002 were Stanley O'Neal, COO at Merrill Lynch, and two CEOs, Ken Chenault of American Express and Dick Parsons of AOL Time Warner. In an interview for *Fortune,* Ella L.J. Edmondson Bell, professor at the Tuck School of Business at Dartmouth, referred to the list of 50 most powerful blacks as the "brothers' list" and admitted that, though African American women want to support achievements of black men, doing so is difficult because the women "have been made invisible" in corporate America (Daniels, 2002).

Among Native Americans who have excelled, women are more likely to hold leadership positions in education, government, or in the tribe. One of the most well-known female Native American leaders may be Wilma Mankiller, chief of the Cherokee nation from 1985 to 1995. Mankiller's position as tribal leader differs markedly from a CEO's position in a Fortune 500 firm. Unless a leader is solely a figurehead, however, he or she most likely will perform major management functions or supervise those who do. The two male Native Americans who were listed as corporate executives in *The Native North American Almanac* (Champagne, 2001) were Steven Stallings, senior vice president and director of Native American Banking Services for Wells Fargo Bank and William R. Ernisse, vice president of sales operations and marketing for the Western Operations of Xerox Corporation.

According to Padavic and Reskin (2002), women are more likely to reach the top in businesses in the service industry. Higher percentages of women typically are employed in that industry, but numbers alone do not guarantee upward mobility as evidenced by the discredited *pipeline theory* that predicted it would be only a matter of time before women would be represented proportionally in top management.

The business and leadership index developed by the Committee of 200 (C200), which measures women's business clout, shows evidence of slow but steady progress toward the executive suite. On a scale ranging from one to ten, ten represents parity with men, and in 2004, the C200 business leadership index was 4.66, up from 3.95 in 2002 and 4.28 in 2003 (Llewellyn-Williams, 2004). At this rate, 2019 is the earliest when total parity between women and men on factors measured by the index may be reached (Llewellyn-Williams, 2004). Another estimate indicates that it will take an additional 475 years before gender parity is reached at the upper echelons of business (Corsun & Costen, 2001). Compared to the Committee of 200's projection that parity in the ten factors comprising the business leadership index may be reached by 2019, this seems quite pessimistic.

The C200 index is a weighted aggregate of ten factors. They include the percent of women serving as members of boards of directors or corporate officers of Fortune 500 firms, the percent of organizations led or owned by women, their access to venture capital and enrollment in top MBA programs, the size of women-run firms, the gender wage gap, and the percent of women who are honorary fundraising chairs at the ten largest U.S. charities that have such posts and percent who are keynote speakers at prestigious annual business conferences (Llewellyn-Williams, 2004).

Prospective members must be invited to join the Committee of 200. They include "the world's most successful women entrepreneurs and corporate leaders who are dedicated to fostering growth and increasing opportunities for the next generation of women business leaders" (Llewellyn-Williams, 2004, p. 33).

WOMEN AND MINORITIES ON CORPORATE BOARDS

In the 1970s, 6% of newly elected corporate board members were women, and by the mid-1980s, women represented 4% of members of corporate boards of directors of major U.S. firms (Hellwig, 1992). Though the percentages have grown, they remain low. In 2001, females comprised 10.9% of corporate boards of Fortune 1000 firms (Babcock, 2003), and by 2002, that figure had risen to 13.6% (Catalyst, 2002). Nearly 84% of Fortune 500 firms had at least one female member on their board of directors in 2000, however. (Padavic & Reskin, 2002). The percentage of Hispanics on corporate boards of Fortune 1000 firms has grown about 10% per year since 1993. In 2002, they held about 2% of board positions at Fortune 1000 companies (Placencia, 2002).

Different selection criteria for board members may explain the shortage of women on corporate boards according to Daily and Dalton (2003). They believe that criteria applied to women who wish to be board members are more restrictive than those applied to men and that active recruitment of women and minorities to serve on boards has several advantages. These include pleasing external constituents, adding new perspectives, and sending a signal that the organization is committed to career progress of nontraditional groups, which could aid in employee recruitment. Further, Daily and Dalton (2003) indicate that board diversity is "good for the bottom line."

CHALLENGES TO ASPIRING TOP EXECUTIVE WOMEN

Statistics regarding the progress of women and minorities have been presented. It is now appropriate to examine hindrances, which, if unchallenged, may continue to interfere with their ascent to the executive suite.

Some authors emphasize success strategies and refuse to discuss obstacles to advancement to avoid stressing negative elements. People gravitate toward objects on which they focus, according to Gallagher and Golant (2000). For example, drivers who try to avoid an object when their car spins may increase their chances of hitting it by concentrating on it. Similarly, examining impediments to career success may cause people to see more of them than they might otherwise (Gallager & Golant, 2000). To provide a balanced view of the situation, however, both aids and hindrances to career progress of women and minorities must be considered.

Beginning in the 1970s, studies of women in management falsely assumed that all women's experiences were similar, regardless of their race or ethnicity. Because so few women of color were managers at that time, color was disregarded as a variable. Though unfortunate, this parallels pre-1960 studies of managers that focused exclusively on white males. In those days, corporate management was a white male bastion, and the one or two females or minority males who happened to achieve executive ranks were regarded as anomalies. Much has changed in the past 30 years, but studies of women's progress in management that lump all women together still reflect issues encountered by white women, which may differ from those faced by African American or Asian American women or Latinas. Therefore, obstacles faced by women in general will be discussed first. Hindrances that are common to African American, Asian American, and Hispanic women will be discussed next.

An arguably overused visual image that explains the cumulative effect of all the detractors to career advancement for women is the *glass ceiling*. First defined in 1987, the term refers to a transparent, impermeable barrier that prevents women from being promoted to the top jobs in America's major corporations. It has spawned other terms such as the *concrete ceiling*, a barrier so strong that the women of color who encounter it cannot see the top of the organization. *Glass walls* prevent moves from staff to line positions or lateral transfers designed to better prepare women for top posts, and *squishy floors* keep African Americans stuck in jobs with little opportunity for career progress, according to Thomas and Gabarro (1999).

Frankforter (1996) suggests that a series of glass ceilings exists through which women must pass to reach the top. As soon as they crack one, another appears in its place.

Meyerson and Fletcher (2000) believe that the glass ceiling, a symbol of the situation prospective executive females faced in the 20th century, should be replaced with imagery more appropriate for the new millennium. They compare the challenges of women and minorities in management to those that tall people would encounter in a world created for shorter individuals. Tall people might need to bend — or occasionally walk on their knees — to fit in this world.

Enlightened short people might restructure doorways to make it easier for the tall people to pass through them. Alternatively, short individuals might emphasize advantages of having a few tall people around. In one last concession to the glass ceiling imagery, Meyerson and Fletcher (2000, p. 136) conclude, "It's not the ceiling that's holding women back; it's the whole structure of the organization in which we work: the foundation, the beams, the walls, the very air."

Though the issues that limit aspiring women are pervasive, they are more subtle than in the 1970s. The situation is not hopeless, according to Meyerson and Fletcher (2000), who advocate a "small wins" approach for dealing with an environment that limits aspiring women.

The top three hindrances to the careers of managerial women in 1996 and 2003 were lack of appropriate experience, exclusion from networks, and stereotypes and perceptions of others. In 1996, stereotypes ranked number one in a list of impediments to managerial women; by 2003 it had dropped to third place (Catalyst, 2003c).

Padavic and Reskin (2002) claim that women generally have fewer years of experience to prepare them for top management than men and that experience is necessary, but insufficient, for upward mobility. A survey conducted by Catalyst, an organization dedicated to women's career progress, showed that the percent of upper level executive women who thought aspiring females had not been in managerial positions long enough to be CEOs dropped from 29% in 1996 to 10% in 2003.

Line management with responsibility for profit and loss is crucial for prospective chief executives. Until recently, fewer women than men have been responsible for operations. For example, Padavic and Reskin (2002) report that women have only recently been able to gain experience in commercial lending, which they must have to reach top posts in banking. Previously, women were more likely to end up in staff positions and were less likely than their male counterparts to be assigned to start a division or to gain troubleshooting or turnaround experience. International assignments are now critical proving grounds for would-be top executives, and women face more challenges than men in being chosen for those assignments.

Forty-one percent of upper tier female executives said that exclusion from the informal organization was a major problem in 2003, as compared to 49% who said so in 1996. Forty-three percent were either dissatisfied or neutral about their opportunities for networking in 2003 (Catalyst, 2003c). Men are more likely to take another man, rather than a woman, 'under their wing' and help him reach the executive suite (Bell & Nkomo, 2000). To the extent that applicant pools at top levels are drawn from several networks of which the hiring managers are a part, women may be at a disadvantage (Padavic & Reskin, 2002). Some executive women still believe they do not receive the coaching, sponsorship, or political advice to the same extent men do, though some progress has been made (Karsten, 1997).

Lack of networking may relate to both stereotyping and lack of appropriate line management experience. Some may falsely assume that most women lack time to develop informal social contacts due to other obligations. This may be true for some executive females, but not for others. To the extent that women are "out of the loop," they miss professional opportunities and may not be considered for highly visible, important assignments (Rhode, 2003).

Executive women whom Gallagher and Golant (2000) interviewed are skeptical of the career benefits of networking. They disapprove of the superficiality of networking relationships and the idea that networking involves "using" others. Some complain that networking wastes their time, but they are open to the development of more meaningful "alliances" with others. Perhaps their negative views of networking reflect a misunderstanding of the process.

Stereotypes and the perceptions and expectations of others still have a profound influence on careers of upwardly mobile business women. The stereotype that equates management skills with men cannot be debunked easily. Job competence is not always assumed of managerial women as it typically is for men (Rhode, 2003). Specific stereotypes that cause problems for women will be discussed in chapter 5. One to be discussed here is the "double bind" that women face due to a *"narrow band of acceptable behavior"* (Morrison, 1992). The "narrow band" is the area common to two overlapping circles. Stereotypically feminine qualities appear in one circle and stereotypically masculine qualities in the other. Female executives are expected to limit their behavior to the area where the circles overlap. For example, they must be decisive but not overbearing, compassionate but not "soft," and assertive but not pushy. If their behaviors stray from the area of overlap, executive women face censure, as did some high-ranking women who were thought to be "too aggressive." To keep their jobs, they had to attend a training session for "bully broads" (Babcock & Laschever, 2003).

Until recently, some assumed that women were uninterested in top corporate positions. A study reported in 2004 reveals that 55% of women and 57% of men want to be CEOs and women with and without children have similar aspirations (Lublin, 2004).

Only one item seemed more likely to be a career obstacle for managerial women in 2003 than in 1996; that was a commitment to personal or family responsibilities. Twenty-six percent listed this factor among the top three barriers to executive women pursuing top positions in 2003 as compared to 18% who considered it a major impediment in 1996 (Catalyst, 2003c). In 2003, there was no difference in the views of this factor among women regardless of their parental status. Even women without children may be affected by stereotypes about their likelihood to have family or other responsibilities that interfere with work.

There are many ways to categorize factors that detract from women's career advancement in corporations. Table 2.1 presents a framework that was modified because one original factor, "inhospitable organizational culture and climate," dropped from fourth to eleventh place between 1996 and 2003 in a list of barriers to women's career advancement (Catalyst, 2003c). Some studies still refer to items that were considered manifestations of an inhospitable climate. They include difficulty finding mentors, homo-social reproduction, discrimination and harassment, and constant performance pressure. Another factor formerly in that category that has diminished in importance since the late 1990s is white male backlash.

Though white women, but not women of color, supposedly obtained mentors at about the same rate as men by the late 1990s (Karsten, 1997), only 23% of executive females surveyed in 2003 were satisfied with the availability of mentors (Catalyst, 2003c). Sixty percent had no mentor. Though some are alarmed that a majority of managerial women lack mentors, Gallagher and Golant (2000), say it is a myth that women need a mentor to succeed. Rather, they recommend cultivating advocates, influencers, and role models.

Kanter (1977) described *homo-social reproduction* as a tendency of decision makers to promote people who were similar to themselves. In an environment characterized by uncertainty, this was considered less risky than promoting someone considered "different." When the decision makers were recruiters, however, Powell & Graves (2003) found inconsistent support for the idea that applicants were evaluated more favorably simply because they were of the same sex as the recruiter.

Even if decision makers do not promote people who are similar to themselves, the psychological principle that small groups tend toward homogeneity

Table 2.1.   Hindrances to the Careers of Managerial Women in General

➢ Lack of Appropriate Experience
➢ Exclusion from Networking
➢ Stereotypes and Others' Perceptions and Expectations
➢ Real or Perceived Commitment to Personal or Family Responsibilities
➢ Inhospitable Culture or Climate
  • Difficulty Finding Mentors
  • Homo-social Reproduction
  • Discrimination and Harassment
  • Constant Performance Pressure
➢ Unsupportive Organizational Structures and Processes
  • Recruitment and Selection
  • Performance Management
  • Promotion Criteria
  • Career Support and Training
  • Accountability for Diversity Management
  • Use of Employee Benefits

Adapted from Karsten. 1997. Women in management. In Tierney, H., Ed. *Women's Studies Encyclopedia.* G-P. Westport, CT: Greenwood Publishing Co., Inc.

may cause problems. Group members who are similar are generally more comfortable with each other. For this reason, white male CEOs tend to be more comfortable with other white males. This may harm women or minorities who want to join the top ranks. In the executive suite, competence is assumed and "fit," an inherently subjective term, carries more weight.

Though many believe that overt discrimination no longer occurs, in the 1990s, male chief executives ranked it as the number one reason why there are not more women in top management (Fisher, 1992). A casual perusal of *The Wall Street Journal* clearly shows that discrimination still exists. Some headlines in June and July 2004 were, "Judge Certifies Wal-Mart Suit As Class Action: Up to 1.6 Million Could Join Sex Discrimination Case: Company Plans to Appeal" (Zimmerman, 2004) and "Morgan Stanley Settles Bias Suit for $54 Million" (Kelly and DeBaise, 2004).

Countless examples, some of which will be discussed in chapter 3, from the Navy's Tailhook scandal to office strip tease shows to which a female Morgan Stanley trader was subjected in the early 2000s, illustrate that harassment, a form of sex discrimination, remains an issue. According to Schneider, Fitzgerald, and Swan (1997), an inverse relationship exists between *any* sexual harassment and the upward mobility of women.

The last obstacles to be discussed as manifestations of an inhospitable culture and climate are performance pressures and the fact that women often are held to a higher standard than men. Regarding the former, others' constant challenge of the credentials of upper level executives is exhausting and requires them to expend more energy than their male peers just to do their jobs. Men earn more and have higher status positions in six different occupations including those related to business, according to Valian (1998). Many factors explain the disparity, but "gender always explains an additional portion" because the standard for women is set higher (Valian, 1998).

White male backlash and reverse discrimination are not the barriers they were in the mid to late 1990s. At that time, those who would abhor the notion that they might have benefited from unearned privilege felt relatively disadvantaged and used the term "white male backlash." Some tried to end affirmative action, a program designed to give a temporary advantage to members of a group that experienced discrimination in the past. Though the two U.S. Supreme Court cases decided in 2003, *Gratz v. Bollinger* and *Grutter v. Bollinger*, required that the University of Michigan modify its admissions procedures, they left affirmative action intact. Until the economy improved, some white males may have been angry because women and minorities were filling jobs they believed they would have had otherwise. When jobs are scarce, healthy competition may turn dysfunctional. On the other hand, when the economy is improving and "all boats are rising," backlash tends to decline. Fewer executive women thought their male colleagues were concerned about *reverse discrimination* in 2003 than in 1996. The percentage who believed men thought it was a problem declined from 40 to 25 in those seven years (Catalyst, 2003c). Reverse discrimination occurs when those trying to eliminate unfair treatment of women and minorities take actions that place majority group members at a disadvantage.

The final category of obstacles can be called *unsupportive organizational structures and practices,* or systemic barriers. They include sex segregation of jobs and ineffective human resource practices in terms of recruitment and selection, performance management, promotion criteria, career encouragement and training, accountability for diversity management, and use of employee benefits, such as flexible scheduling and leaves of absence. Discussion of these barriers is anathema to some, such as Deemer and Frederickson (2002) who, in *Dancing on the Glass Ceiling,* advocate "finding the solution within yourself." Such advice seems to blame women for their lack of success when the true cause might be institutional in nature. According to Kanter (1990, p. 11),

> The whole social system must be changed if women in general, not just a hardy pioneering few, are to gain economic power. The apparent openness of American society to the overachiever from an underprivileged minority group who can pull herself up by the pantyhose and succeed makes it too easy to assume that the problems and solutions are all individual ones. It makes it easy for those in power to point to the token overachiever as an example.

Women's overrepresentation in jobs with short career ladders is a manifestation of sex segregation of jobs and a factor that contributes to their turnover and lower wages as compared to men. *Career ladders* are paths for transfer or promotion between lower and higher level jobs. According to Padavic and Reskin (2002, p. 109), "employers designed many traditionally female jobs, such as teacher, without job ladders in order to encourage turnover, thereby keeping wages low." Ambitious women reach the top of the ladder fairly quickly and may then leave an organization to find a better position elsewhere or to start their own businesses. Compared to smaller firms, large corporations usually have job ladders with many steps. This is less helpful to women than to men, because women are concentrated in non-profit and small for-profit organizations (Padavic & Reskin).

Sex segregation of jobs also is apparent not only when women hold few of an organization's highest managerial positions but also when they are underrepresented in non-managerial positions in firms that rely heavily on promotion-from-within to fill supervisory jobs. Under such circumstances, few women typically have managerial positions (Cohen, Broschak & Haveman, 1998; Reskin & McBrier, 2000).

Selection interviewers are perceived to favor applicants of the same sex. Studies in the early 1980s showed that female, but not male, interviewers were more likely to view *male* candidates favorably. When repeated in the early 1990s, female interviewers favored female applicants. Again, male interviewers showed no bias (Powell & Graves, 2003). Women tend to support, rather than disparage, other women when status differences between males and females are small (Powell & Graves). That may explain female recruiters' better treatment of female candidates in the 1990s compared to the 1980s and the relative extinction, during about the same time frame, of *Queen Bees*, women who attribute success exclusively to their own merits and refuse to help other females advance.

Recruiters' personalities affect their decisions. Those with "traditional" ideas about gender roles are more likely to discriminate against women applying for positions in which males dominate numerically. Those who reject "traditional" gender roles and stereotypes tend to discriminate *in favor* of women applying for such jobs (Gallois, Callan & Palmer, 1992).

Short selection interviews resulted in unintentional bias against female candidates in an investment firm and resulted in initial frustration about not being able to hire more women. When the firm's partners analyzed the problem in retrospect, they thought they might have inadvertently relied on first impressions when making their hiring recommendations because the interview was so short. They extended the interview from 30 to 45 minutes and modified questions to ask about relevant skills and abilities that people of various backgrounds might have developed. Previous inquiries dealt with "deal making," which disadvantaged many female candidates, since men were more likely to have had such experience as investment bankers (Meyerson & Fletcher, 2000).

Different promotion criteria for women and men are problematic. Men are more likely to be promoted based on potential; women advance based on past performance. Women must have a solid record of achievement to move up, but men with less-than-stellar records get the nod simply because a decision maker believes they have potential (Karsten, 1997).

Career encouragement and training are important for all who aspire to top management, and the lack thereof may be especially detrimental to females. Women who are supported in their careers are more likely to seek training opportunities than those who are not; encouragement or lack of it does not seem to affect men (Therenou, Latimer & Conroy, 1994). Stroh, Langlands & Simpson (2002) contend that prospective female top executives need even more training than similarly situated men because they tend to have fewer developmental job responsibilities and experiences. Evidence about whether or not managerial females get additional training is mixed (Simpson & Stroh, 2002; Keaveny & Inderrieden, 1999).

Accountability for results of diversity management essentially invokes the control function. It involves monitoring components of diversity management, comparing them to agreed-upon benchmarks, diagnosing the reasons for gaps between the goals and the result, and recommending corrective action. In a Center for Creative Leadership Study, Morrison, Schreiber and Price (1995) note that lack of incentives for diversity management and lack of accountability are associated with relatively low numbers of women or minorities in management.

Useful, constructive feedback is the hallmark of an effective performance management system. As recently as the mid-1990s, managerial women were less likely to get performance feedback than their male counterparts. Perhaps this was due to some male CEOs' relative discomfort with female colleagues. If so, it is time to move beyond that. Anyone will have trouble succeeding without specific formal and informal feedback that reinforces positive behaviors and creates a mutual plan for shoring up areas of deficiency.

To be perceived as evenhanded, performance appraisal systems must be based on specific, job-related criteria that are communicated to those whose performance is to be assessed before the evaluation period begins. Some subjectivity is inherent in the nature of appraisal systems. Decision makers who wish to create an environment conducive to the promotion of previously disenfranchised groups should avoid vague, unclear performance review systems, however. Some use factors that are so subjective that decision makers may be influenced by subconscious bias without realizing what is happening. Sometimes, decision makers purposely treat employees differently. For example, one rater refused to clarify the meaning of an evaluation factor in a performance appraisal system. This lack of clarification allowed the rater to shift standards and apply the factor differentially to ratees. In this instance, though a woman was disadvantaged, most likely due to her "outsider" status, this was based on her area of expertise, not gender.

Performance appraisals pose additional challenges for African Americans. Their performance success is likely to be attributed to external causes and failure to internal causes (Greenhaus & Parasuraman, 1993). External causes of behavior are those outside one's control, such as luck and effort. Internal causes are those within a person's control, such as skill and ability. Behavior that is inconsistent with an established "scheme," or perceptual categorization mechanism, is assumed to have an external cause and vice versa (Jackson, Sullivan & Hodge, 1993). Studies have shown consistently that blacks are rated lower than whites on performance appraisals and that this difference reflects blacks' "systematic disadvantage" in leadership positions, not lack of ability (Knight et al., 2003).

Rhode (2003) identifies a gap between policy and practice regarding the use of employee benefits such as flexible schedules and leaves. Such benefits improve quality of life for all employees, but unfortunately some view them as ways to help women cope with *their* assumed dual job and domestic responsibilities. In reality, some women may have few domestic obligations; some men may have more than "average."

The notion that involved parenting is incompatible with the demands of leadership roles (Rhode, 2003, p. 15) is a barrier that must be overcome. To that end, Vinnecombe and Bank (2003) advocate a change in the culture of "long hours." The notion that those who are not present at the workplace for an unlimited amount of time lack commitment must be discredited and replaced by a more realistic notion that values results more than "face time."

CHALLENGES TO WOMEN OF COLOR WHO WISH TO BE TOP MANAGERS

In 1998 and 2001, Catalyst (2002) studied women of color, defined as African American, Hispanic, and Asian American women who sought top executive positions in U.S. firms. The top four barriers the women faced remained the same and were lack of: 1) a mentor or sponsor, 2) informal networking, 3) role models from their racial or ethnic group, and 4) high visibility assignments. Lack of a mentor was the top barrier for Hispanics (Catalyst, 2003a), and Asian American women indicated that a lack of key professional relationships was their major obstacle to achieving high ranking positions (Catalyst, 2004).

African American women were more likely than Hispanic or Asian American women to say that chances for members of their group to advance to top management decreased from 1998 to 2001. Thirty-seven percent of black women surveyed believed they faced declining opportunity to enter the executive suite compared to 24% of Latinas and 23% of Asian American women. They attribute this to discrimination even in firms that give lip-service to diversity. One disillusioned woman indicated that in her company, diversity meant opportunity for white females and males born outside the United States (Catalyst, 2002). African American females were not the only women of color who thought diversity management programs needed to be improved. Hispanics believed they were relatively ineffective (Catalyst, 2003a), and Asian American women felt overlooked by such programs (Catalyst, 2003b).

An important challenge that African Americans encounter as they advance in managerial careers is *miasma*, defined as fog of misperceptions and distortions (Livers & Caver, 2003). Other racial and ethnic minorities also may experience this phenomenon, but Livers and Caver use the term to refer specifically to African Americans. Miasma may result from the following:

1. stereotypes leading to low targets for minority advancement,
2. assumptions of white managers and coworkers that white is the norm and should not be perceived as a color,
3. expectations that one African American's opinions reflect those of all blacks,
4. African Americans' uncertainty about their acceptance in workplace teams, which leads to guardedness in social interactions, and their feelings of being undervalued at work, and
5. Blacks' visibility coupled with others' expectations that their racial identity should remain invisible in the workplace.

Each factor contributing to miasma will be discussed in turn.

Thirty-two percent of African American women think their white colleagues believe the stereotype that blacks are under-qualified for their current position. In comparison, only 22% of Hispanic and 14% of Asian American women believe white coworkers think they are under-qualified (Catalyst, 2003). The same bias leading to low expectations for African Americans' career progress helps create the "squishy floors and revolving doors" that exclude them from top management and contribute to excess turnover (Thomas & Gabarro, 1999). The "floors and doors" are considered greater impediments to the advancement of African Americans than glass ceilings.

Fifty-six percent of the African American women responding to Catalyst's survey (2004) say that many stereotypes about women of their race/ethnicity persist in the workplace. This is higher than the percent of Hispanic or Asian American women who think workplace stereotypes are prevalent. Latinas also believe stereotypes harm their upward mobility (Catalyst, 2003a), and Asian American females cite as barriers cultural values that make them uncomfortable challenging the status quo or promoting themselves (Catalyst, 2003b).

Assuming that white skin color is the norm sets the stage for racial misunderstandings. Whites who believe that their color is transparent may not understand why African Americans and other minorities believe it is important to maintain their identity as people of color.

In general, whites do not have to deal with *biculturalism*—living, behaving, and speaking as if they are in one cultural world at work and in another at home. They have not experienced accusations of "selling out" to another race if they emulate that group's style of speech and mannerisms or of not "fitting in" at a place of employment that has adopted the norms of middle class whites. Though people of any race or ethnicity may feel unable to be themselves occasionally, they typically do not feel as if they must wear a mask to work each day. Having to act and speak differently at work than at home or with friends creates added strain that most mid- to upper class whites do not experience. Other blacks may judge African Americans harshly as "not black enough" if they use precise language and adopt hairstyles and clothing that help them gain acceptance in a predominantly white workplace.

Some African Americans may behave guardedly in social situations because they are unsure about their white coworkers' or supervisors' racial attitudes (Davidson, 1997). Many promotion decisions are heavily influenced by informal relationships, and people who are afraid to let others get to know them could be at a disadvantage.

African Americans may be asked to explain the actions of prominent or infamous blacks when the only commonality is race. To understand what this might be like, white Americans should consider how they would react if they were asked to explain the actions of other whites accused of torturing Abu Ghraib prisoners during the war between the U.S. and Iraq that began in 2003. Most would have no special insight, nor should they be expected to have additional knowledge simply due to their race and nationality.

Kanter discussed the increased visibility associated with numerical tokenism in *Men and Women of the Corporation* (1977). *Tokenism*, to be discussed in chapter 7, occurs when fewer than 15% of an organization's members belong to a group with "outsider" status. Many disadvantages are associated with token status. Visibility, like biculturalism, however, can be an advantage, particularly in an international assignment. It also creates added pressure.

African Americans are more likely than white women to believe that they must prove themselves (Livers & Caver, 2003). This can become wearing. Fifty-one percent of African American business professionals indicated that their mistakes at work could affect other blacks. They believe that their behavior is scrutinized due to their visibility and, therefore, experience extreme pressure not to fail (Thomas & Gabarro, 1999). On a more positive note, over 90% think that their job success would cause other African Americans to be viewed more favorably (Livers & Caver, 2003).

Identity is defined as the interaction between the way others perceive an individual and the way that person perceives him- or herself (Livers and Caver, 2003). Because the importance of identity issues may not be acknowledged in the workplace, some African Americans feel as if they must leave their racial identity at the door and assimilate into the dominant culture. Over 50% of African Americans surveyed believe they must give up part of their racial identity just to do their jobs (Livers & Caver).

If all African Americans experience miasma, black women face additional obstacles due to their "double outsider" status based on both race and gender. Effects of a "double disadvantage" should not be assumed to be additive; detrimental effects may multiply when discrimination based on both race and gender occur.

Bell and Nkomo (2000) identify six barriers to success in their study of black women in management. Some such obstacles also may apply to black men, but they were not subjects of the research. Two challenges already have been discussed, namely the expectation that African Americans must keep their racial and ethnic identities invisible and difficulties created by their exclusion from informal networks, which all women of color, and to a lesser extent, white women, face. Remaining obstacles include daily doses of racism, higher standards and the belief that they must work twice as hard as others to achieve them, constant challenges to their authority, and a superficial, insincere commitment to the advancement of minorities.

Another obstacle unique to African Americans is *colorism*, or discrimination based on the shade of their skin. A Catalyst study (2004) focusing exclusively on managerial African American women reveals that lighter-skinned females with fewer ethnic facial features are more satisfied with their opportunities to get ahead than are their darker-skinned counterparts who have more ethnic facial features.

Additional challenges that African Americans must deal with that other minorities also might experience are others' assumptions that they are experts on minority issues and their own feelings of being undervalued or not taken seriously due to their race or ethnicity (Davidson, 1997). Regardless of their knowledge of or interest in racial issues, some African Americans are incorrectly presumed to have expertise simply because of their race. Such a presumption is inappropriate.

A challenge that Hispanics are more likely than other women of color to mention as a barrier to management success relates to their responsibility toward the extended family, which may include adult siblings, grandparents, or other relatives. A greater percentage of Latinas than other women of color have elder care responsibilities, and some coworkers do not understand the importance of relationships with extended family members to Hispanics. A Latina who rejected a coworker's repeated requests to have lunch or stay late at work was told that she didn't have a family and that her excuse that she had family obligations was "getting old." Her response: "Yes, I do. It's my brothers, my sisters, my parents, my cousins, my aunts, my uncles." Reflecting on her coworker's reaction, the Hispanic woman said, "Your extended family is as high priority as your children and your husband" (Catalyst, 2003a, p. 12).

Unwritten rules about guests at company sponsored events sometimes cause problems for Latinas. A single woman who wanted to invite her extended family to a company event did not do so because she thought others would frown on it. She also was afraid she would be stereotyped as a single woman "out scouting" if she went alone (Catalyst, 2003a).

Saying that Native Americans, particularly the women, face extreme challenges in obtaining positions that may eventually lead to management is no exaggeration. Relatively few complete a bachelor's degree, which has increasingly become necessary to be hired as an entry level manager. Native Americans have a relatively low labor force participation rate, and very few hold management positions. For these reasons, they have been ignored in most scholarly studies of management. They do, however, perform management functions and hold tribal leadership positions. In this respect, the situation of Native American women resembles that of colonial American women, who planned, organized, directed, and controlled but would never have been called managers nor given credit for their management activities (Karsten, 1992).

A miniscule number of Native Americans have become managers. Their communities have disparaged some such individuals for failing to maintain cultural connections with their tribes. The concern is that they may be using their minority status to gain advantages though they do not identify themselves as Native Americans otherwise (Burns, 2004).

Now that challenges women and minorities face have been explored, the following questions will be addressed:

1. Who are the women and minorities who made it to the top of business organizations?
2. What factors have helped them succeed?
3. What can organizations and individuals do to increase the percentage of women and minorities at the top of major U.S. corporations?

CHARACTERISTICS OF EXECUTIVE WOMEN OF VARIOUS RACES AND ETHNICITIES

Table 2.2 summarizes characteristics of executive women of various races gleaned from several studies over three years. Nearly four-fifths of the 200 executive women Gallagher and Golant (2000) studied and the 875 black and white executive women responding to Bell's and Nkomo's national survey (2000) have earned graduate degrees. Catalyst studies of all executive women (2003c) and of women of color (2002) show a greater racial divide than the

Bell and Nkomo research between those who have and have not earned a graduate degree and between the percent who have attended four or fewer years of college. A larger percent of women of color than of all women had four or fewer years of higher education. Some of this disparity can be explained by the fact that two years elapsed between the study of women of color and that of women in general. At any rate, those who wish to become top executives are more likely than in the past to have earned a graduate degree.

Women of color seem less likely than all women to be married (Catalyst 2002, 2003c), and the same is true of black as compared to white women (Bell & Nkomo, 2000). Compared to their white counterparts, a larger proportion of black executive females never married. Gallagher and Golant (2000) report a much larger percent of married executive females than either of the other two studies.

Slightly over 50% of executive women of color and all executive women have children currently living with them (Catalyst 2002, 2003c). Of the 55% of respondents to Gallagher's and Golant's study (2000) who have children, only 11% had three or more. Nkomo and Bell report that only 30% of the black women and 38% of the white women they surveyed have children. Given the time-consuming nature of both child care and executive work and the fact that women still have a disproportionate share of the responsibility for child care in the U.S., it is not surprising that fewer executive women than men have children.

Hewlett (2002) found that 81% of male "ultra-achievers," defined as those who earned $100,000 or more in 2001, were parents compared to only 51% of their female peers. For many of the women, remaining childless was not a conscious choice but, rather, a "creeping non-choice" attributable to "the brutal demands of ambitious careers, the asymmetries of male-female relationships, and the difficulties of bearing children late in life" (Hewlett, 2002, p. 66). Of high achievers 41 to 55 years old, two-thirds of the women and three-fourths of the men had children. Forty-two percent of the corporate women whom Hewlett (2002) surveyed were childless.

In terms of type of position held, 38% of all executive women have either line or line/staff assignments as compared to 51% of the women of color (Catalyst, 2003c, 2002). As Table 2.2 shows, Bell and Nkomo (2000) indicate that white managerial women are more likely than black executive females to have line positions.

A major discrepancy exists between the percentage of women of color and women in general who hold positions within two levels of the CEO. Only 12% of the former group is in that category compared to 76% of the latter (Catalyst 2002, 2003c.) The percent of white women in top management is more than twice the percent of black women in that category in Bell's and

Table 2.2. Characteristics of Executive Women

	Nkomo & Bell (2000) Black	White	Catalyst (2003) All	(2002) Women of Color	(2004) African American	(2003) Hispanic	(2004) Asian American	Gallagher (2000)
EDUCATION								
4 yrs. college or less	12%	12%	22%	39%				19%
Grad./professional study	11%	8%	15%	15%	52%	38%	59%	
Graduate degree	76%	80%	62%	46%				81%
MARITAL STATUS								
Single/Never Married	43%	25%	8%					
Married[1]	44%	60%	81%	61%	52%	65%	70%	90%
Separated/Divorced	13%	14%	10%					
Widowed	1%	2%	1%					
CHILDREN								
Yes	30%	38%	51%[4]					55%
No	71%	62%	49%					
AGE[2]	42	41	47	43	40	39	38	x̄ = 44
TYPE OF CURRENT POSITION								
Line	61%	70%	19%	24%	27%	27%	21%	
Staff			62%	49%				
Both line & staff			19%	27%				
Reporting within levels of CEO[3]								
Two levels	14%[2]	32%	76%					
Three levels				12%	13%	12%	6%	

[1]Catalyst study of "all" executive women used the category, "Married/Partnered." [2]median values unless noted otherwise [3]Bell & Nkomo referred to these women as being in "top management" but did not specify the number of levels of their position from the CEO. [4]Catalyst study of "all" executive women reported the percent of women who had dependent children living with them currently.

Nkomo's national survey (2000). Though more likely than other women of color to earn a graduate degree, Asian American women are less likely to hold a position within three levels of the CEO (Catalyst, 2003b).

Some demographics about white women and women of color who aspire to top management have been presented, but the factors to which women—and those who have studied them—attribute their success are more informative than statistical data.

FACTORS THAT HELP MANAGERIAL WOMEN AND MINORITIES AT THE TOP: ORGANIZATIONAL ACTIONS

Catalyst (2003c, 2002) indicates that women in general and women of color said that exceeding performance expectations and completing visible assignments are among the five most important factors in their quest for highest level positions. Having an influential sponsor or mentor is the third most important factor for women of color but seventh for all women. Significantly fewer executive women in the 2003 study said obtaining a mentor was crucial to their career success than in 1996 in the overall sample; the percentage declined from 37% to 29%. The importance of networking to women of color increased from 29% to 49% from 1998 to 2001 but was ranked as the fifth most crucial factor in both of those years. In the study of all women, networking was ranked as the tenth most important factor leading to upper management.

Two factors that the sample of all women, but not women of color, consider instrumental in achieving top management are "successfully managing others" and "developing a style with which male managers are comfortable" (Catalyst, 2003c). The factor, "successfully managing others" was added to the Catalyst survey of all executive women in 2003. It may not have been listed as an option on the survey of women of color in 2002. Alternatively, women of color may have deemed it less crucial in facilitating career progress than other strategies.

The importance of "developing a style with which managers are comfortable" dropped significantly from 1996 to 2003 in the Catalyst sample of all women, but it remained the number three strategy. That women of color would omit this from their top advancement strategies is not surprising. White women mention being "taken under the wing" of white, male managers and being treated as if they were daughters, perhaps due to their racial similarity. Not one black woman had this experience (Bell & Nkomo, 2000).

Besides finding a mentor, which the Catalyst studies discussed, Vinnecombe and Bank (2003) indicate that the success of the small sample of executive females she studied may be attributable to early career challenges.

These gave the women a chance to prove themselves and gain confidence and a wide range of experiences.

In the 1990s, an early move from staff to line positions was considered crucial for would-be executive women. Though "gaining line experience" was listed as a factor in the 2003 Catalyst survey, it was ranked eighth most important and was selected by only 28% of the survey respondents. Chief executive officers, however, ranked line experience as the third top factor leading to the executive suite; 50% of those surveyed said it was important (Catalyst, 2003c).

A contentious issue is whether women and minorities who wish to advance or the organizations that employ them are responsible for increasing their representation in top management: Meyerson and Fletcher (2000) note that managers who try to deal with underutilization of females in management by "fixing women" may reinforce the erroneous belief that women are deficient. Other authors have asked how groups that still have relatively less power, authority, and influence at the upper echelons can be expected to rectify a problem that has been created over hundreds of years. Yoder, a psychologist, says, "Relying on women themselves to compensate for structural inequities is inherently unfair" (2001, p. 819).

Philosophical argument aside, the combined efforts of organizations and individuals are needed to open top levels to greater numbers of women and minorities. Recommended actions by organizations to help women in general, which, unfortunately, usually means white women, will be discussed as will recommendations for particular subgroups. Then steps that individuals can take will be suggested.

ORGANIZATIONAL ACTIONS TO ACHIEVE TOP POSITIONS

The words used by those who recommend revamping the organization to be more hospitable to previously disenfranchised groups are instructive. Ruderman (2002) advocates "remodeling" the organization, whereas Meyerson and Fletcher (2000) suggest "reinventing" it. Either term is consistent with *tempered radicalism* (Bell & Nkomo, 2000), an incremental approach to change.

An alternative approach to incremental change rests on the premise that corporations are based on hierarchical, bureaucratic processes, which are oppressive by nature. According to this view, managers in such organizations resemble those described in William F. Whyte's *The Organization Man* in 1956. Trappings may have changed, but the underlying values regarding the overriding importance of work and a high regard for competition, individual achievement, rationality, and dominance have not (Ruderman, 2002).

Overall recommendations for organizations that wish to be more inclusive of women and minorities at all levels including the top are as follows:

1. Take a comprehensive, ongoing approach to cultural change and diversity management beginning with an assessment and cultural audit. Benchmark best practices, develop specific, targeted programs based on results of the assessment, monitor progress toward goals, ensure accountability for results, and make corrections as needed.
2. Examine human resource practices and modify them if desirable. Monitor the results, while recognizing that conducting a controlled experiment is impossible due to constant shifts in other relevant variables.

Both recommendations represent major, long-term changes and require support from both top management and the supervisors charged with their implementation (Powell & Graves, 2003). The first suggestion will be discussed in detail in chapter 4. For now, it is important to understand that advocates of the "business case for diversity" must base their arguments on research findings.

Nearly every human resource management function should be scrutinized in a serious attempt to improve the chances for advancement of women and minorities. The structure of jobs and career paths, internal selection and retention, training and development, monetary and non-monetary rewards, employee benefits such as flexible schedules and work/life integration or balance, performance appraisal, and employee relations should be examined. Conceivably, employee safety and health could be analyzed to determine how to reduce the extra workplace stressors that women and minorities in management face. The first suggestion, dealing with cultural change and diversity management, could fit under the human resource umbrella.

Jobs should be structured to facilitate internal transfers, which can be valuable ways to gain a variety of experience, including line management, trouble-shooting, and turnaround assignments. Multiple career ladders should be longer, rather than shorter, to facilitate upward internal mobility instead of turnover.

Beyond avoiding discrimination in consideration of internal candidates for promotion, top managers should actively recruit minorities and women to high-level leadership positions. They should stress the developmental aspects of top positions instead of emphasizing their time-consuming nature and inevitable hassles (Catalyst, 2003c).

Democratic, participatory approaches are typically associated with more adaptable organizations (Catalyst, 2003c). These approaches also are important in internal recruitment and are aided by an open job posting system that makes information about vacancies widely available so interested candidates can identify themselves. Previously disenfranchised groups will be disadvantaged if top managers disseminate information about vacancies only to those they think might be interested instead of publicizing it widely.

In training and development, managers should clarify the link between employees' personal goals and those of the organization and the tie between employee growth and business strategy. Top managers interested in more diverse successors must ensure that all employees are considered for visible, challenging assignments and leadership development programs. Those who take part in the latter benefit not only from the content but also from the chance to develop networks and contacts with those at upper levels that could lead to mentoring relationships. Women of color, in particular, could benefit from multiple mentors (Catalyst, 2002). Top managers should support networks for women of color and should sponsor forums at which they will have exposure to others at the top.

In addition, specific skills training for all managers should be ongoing. This can help them improve in many areas including their ability to motivate, actively listen to, and resolve conflicts in a diverse workforce.

Both performance evaluation and rewards can be used to modify employee behavior. Monitoring monetary rewards by race and gender and tying rewards to contributions as assessed through performance appraisal can help ensure that pay disparities do not encourage excess turnover. Non-monetary rewards, such as access to informal information networks, recognition, and status symbols can be made contingent on outcomes, not "face time." Employee benefits, such as those that aid work/life balance or integration, and flexible schedules facilitate success for previously disenfranchised groups, particularly women.

Ruderman (2002, p. 202) advocates supplementary, team-based rewards to recognize the unheralded work necessary to maintain connections within organizations, which she believes is done primarily by women. She acknowledges challenges associated with rewarding teamwork within a hierarchical system but states that "many women—and some men—prefer working in partnerships and teams and claiming less individual credit for their accomplishments."

Babcock and Laschever (2003, p. 109) however, advocate rewarding individuals, not teams. They believe that "women do better and suffer less harm from negative stereotypes about their competence when they are evaluated for their individual work products rather than for their contributions to the work of a team." This is because a female member is unlikely to get credit for her team's success (Babcock & Laschever, 2003).

Specific performance criteria that are communicated to employees before the beginning of the evaluation period can reduce ambiguity and decrease the likelihood that ratings will be made based on vague generalities and stereo-typical assumptions. Ideally, employees should participate in developing mutually acceptable criteria. Managers must give informal and formal performance feedback to all employees in a way that makes them receptive to changing their behavior as necessary. Performance review results must be monitored for subgroups including women and minorities to avoid inadvertent bias. Some managers seem unwilling to promote women of color out of their units because of a negative impact on their own unit's equal employment or affirmative action goals or because they consider it riskier to recommend someone who is not a member of the majority group (Catalyst, 2002).

As recently as the mid-1990s, CEOs were less likely to give performance feedback to executive women than to men. Perhaps the CEOs, most of whom were male, felt somewhat less comfortable with managerial women than with their male peers (Morrison, Schreiber & Price, 1995). When women receive performance feedback from male managers, it tends to focus on their current position. Male managers are more likely to discuss strategies to achieve the next promotion with male subordinates (Catalyst, 2002), and this difference could affect women negatively. For that reason, executives should offer to help all employees set goals that will take them to the next level.

A flexible schedule may mean the difference between burnout and successful coping to employed parents, those dealing with their own or a loved one's serious or chronic health condition, and others who must juggle multiple responsibilities. Technology can allow greater flexibility, but there is a danger that it may set the stage for conscientious workers to become workaholics. Many people are more than willing to take the risk. One couple with children appreciates the freedom to leave their respective workplaces early two or three days per week to watch their children's after-school sports events. They make up lost work time using a personal computer with an Internet connection later in the evening when their household is relatively calm.

Chapter 10 will address balance or integration between work and personal life and will mention differences among various racial/ethnic groups. Having programs to address quality of life issues is ineffective if executives are afraid to use them. The stigma associated with taking a leave to provide care for a loved one must end, and work/life integration must not be viewed as a "women's issue." A good way to eliminate the stigma is for current executives of both sexes to serve as role models by using options the organization provides to better manage life and work. Careers of those who avail themselves of flexible schedules, leaves of absence, and other programs for a period of time should not be sidetracked. When they are ready, they should again be offered opportunities to advance. It is also important to avoid resentment of employees who have flexible schedules or take leaves. This can be done by making sure those who work standard schedules and eschew leaves are not overburdened due to their coworkers' schedule flexibility.

Executives must go out of their way to establish positive individual and collective employee relations. Their efforts are invaluable in creating a motivating environment and retaining a diverse workforce. They should develop trust by getting to know each employee—not just those in the majority—as a person. Executives must seek opportunities to highlight excellent performance of African American, Hispanic, and Asian American employees and of other underrepresented groups as a way to boost their credibility. Attempts to undermine their authority should not be tolerated, and assumptions based on stereotypes should be challenged immediately (Catalyst, 2004).

ACTIONS INDIVIDUALS CAN TAKE TO ACHIEVE TOP POSITIONS

Though some argue that organizations and powerful individuals within them must bear the main responsibility for advancing women and minorities, others might interpret exclusive reliance on organizations as anathema to empowerment. Many believe that this is a mutual responsibility of members of groups who were previously excluded from management who wish to progress and the organizations employing them. The mindset that urges the disenfranchised to take charge of their career advancement appeals to rugged individualism that is prevalent in white middle class America and in some other ethnic groups. It may not resonate with others. It has, however, spawned publication of many self-help books for women who aspire to the executive suite. Though a few include women of color tangentially, most assume, incorrectly, that all women face similar challenges. Most books of this genre are based on at least one research study, but generalizations may or may not be warranted. A summary of behaviors that these books urge women who wish to move into top management to adopt appears in Table 2.3.

Most of the advice in Table 2.3 is self-explanatory. Changing companies as a way to achieve one's dreams deserves additional clarification. According to Bell and Nkomo (2000), black and white women who encounter barriers to advancement or have supervisors whose behavior is racist or sexist make *outspiraling moves*. That is, they change employers. The top three reasons why roughly one-quarter of women of color left their 1998 employers were because they wanted more money, a promotion, or a chance to develop additional skills. Leaving was a good strategy, because by 2002, those who had quit working for prior employers received bigger raises and more promotions and were at higher levels than those who stayed with the firms that employed them in 1998 (Catalyst, 2002).

Table 2.3.   Summary of Advice to Women Who Wish to Advance to Top Management in Major U.S. Firms

1. Cultivate and maintain confidence and competence.

2. Know yourself and apply that self-knowledge to the career planning process.
   - Know what you enjoy, want to, and can do; then make plans to do it.
   - Choose organizations that are well-known for welcoming and supporting diversity.
   - Know how fast or slow you want your career to progress, and know how to avoid getting stuck.
   - Be willing to turn down opportunities that do not fit with your strategy right now—or ever.
   - View yourself as a legitimate "player."
   - Aim high and promote yourself. Let key people know what you want to do.

3. Have a dream, and make plans to achieve it.
   - Never lose sight of the vision or the "big picture."
   - Make decisions without all of the information you would like.
   - Solve problems instead of complete tasks.
   - Set "stretch goals" and make plans to achieve them.
   - Strive for excellence, but avoid perfectionist tendencies.
   - Do not be overly-attached to one outcome.
   - Take calculated risks.
   - Change companies if necessary

4. Develop positive internal and external relationships.
   - Cultivate several advocates who will recommend you for various opportunities.
   - Share information with others.
   - Be willing to collaborate with those in power.
   - Know when you need support and take steps to get it.

5. Cultivate intellectual, emotional, and physical stamina.

Sources: (Gallagher, C. & Golant, S.K. 2000; Gilberd, P. 1998; Ruderman, M.N. & Ohlott, P.J., 2002; Zichy, S. & Kellen, B. 2000).

The fourth and fifth most important reasons for turnover among women of color between 1998 and 2002 were difficult supervisors and a desire to find a more supportive environment, respectively. Conversely, those who stayed did so because of positive relationships with supportive supervisors who facilitated their development, were committed to diversity, and fostered an open environment (Catalyst, 2002).

SUMMARY

This chapter begins with a historical overview of the progress of women and minorities in management since World War II and explains some legal, social, and political changes in the 1960s and 1970s that set the stage for their later career progress. It presents information about challenges and factors enhancing the success of upwardly mobile women and minorities in management. Steps that organizations can take and actions individuals can pursue to assist the advancement of women and racial/ethnic minorities are discussed.

REFERENCES

Amott, T. & Matthaei, J. 1996. *Race, gender, and work: A multicultural economic history of women in the United States.* Boston: South End Press.

Babcock, L. & Laschever, S. 2003. *Women don't ask: Negotiation and the gender divide.* Princeton, N.J.: Princeton University Press.

Bell, E. & Nkomo, S. 2000. *Our separate ways: Black and white women and the struggle for professional identity.* Cambridge, MA: Harvard Business School Press.

Billard, M. 1990. Women on the verge of being CEO. *Business Month.* 26–47.

Bowman, G., Worthy, N., & Greyser, S. 1965, July–Aug. Are women executives people? *Harvard Business Review.* 15–28, 164–78.

Burns, T. Conversation on July 14, 2004 with UW-Platteville professor, former chair of Ethnic Studies Program Council and Department of Humanities.

Catalyst, 2000. *Census of women corporate officers and top earners.* New York: Author.

Catalyst. 2002. *Women of color in corporate management: Three years later.* New York: Author.

Catalyst. 2003a. *Advancing Latinas in the workplace: What managers need to know.* New York: Author.

Catalyst. 2003b. *Advancing Asian women in the workplace: Catalyst's new guide for managers.* New York: Author.

Catalyst. 2003c. *Women in U.S. corporate leadership.* New York: Author.

Catalyst, 2004. *Advancing African American women in the workplace: What managers need to know.* New York: Author.

Cohen, L.E., Broschak, J.P. & Haveman, H.A. 1998. And then there were more? The effects of organizational sex composition on hiring and promotion. *American Sociological Review.* 64. 711–27.

Collins, S. 1997. *Black corporate executives: The making and breaking of a black middle class.* Philadelphia: Temple University Press.

Corsun, D.L. & Costen, W. M. 2001, Mar. Is the glass ceiling unbreakable? Habitus, fields, and the stalling of women and minorities in management. *Journal of Management Inquiry.* 10(1). 16–25.

Daily, C.M. & Dalton, D. R. 2003. Women in the boardroom: A business imperative. *The Journal of Business Strategy.* 24(5). 181–86.

Daniels, C. 2002. July 22. The most powerful black executives in America. *Fortune.* 146(2).

Davidson, M.J. 1997. *The black and ethnic minority woman manager: Cracking the concrete ceiling.* London: Paul Chapman Publishing, Ltd.

Deemer, C. & Fredericks, N. 2002. *Dancing on the glass ceiling.* New York: McGraw Hill.

Equal Employment Opportunity Commission. 2002. Occupational employment in private industry by race/ethnic group/sex, and by industry, United States. Retrieved July 21, 2004 from http://www.eeoc.gov/stats/jobpat/2002/us.html.

Fernandez, J.P. 1981. *Racism and sexism in corporate life; Changing values in American business.* New York: Lexington Books.

Fisher, A.B. 1992, Sept. 21. When will women get to the top? *Fortune.* 44–45, 47, 52, 56.

Frankforter, S.A. 1996. The progression of women beyond the glass ceiling. In Crandall, R. Ed. Handbook of gender research. Special issue. *Journal of Social Behavior and Personality.* 11(5).

Gallagher, C. with Golant, S.K. 2000. *Going to the top: A road map for success from America's leading women executives.* New York: Viking Penguin.

Gallois, C., Callan, V.J. & Palmer, J.M. 1992. The influence of applicant communication style and interviewer characteristics on hiring decisions. *Journal of Applied Social Psychology.* 22. 1041–60.

Gilberd, P. 1998. *The 11 commandments of wildly successful women.* New York: John Wiley & Sons.

Greenhaus, J. H., & Parasuraman, S. 1993. Job performance attributions and career advancement prospects: An examination of gender and race effects. *Organizational Behavior and Human Decision Processes.* 55. 273–97.

Hamill, K. 1956. Women as bosses. *Fortune.* 53(6). 104–108, 214–16, 219–20.

Harrington, A. & Bartosiewicz, P. 2004. Who's up? Who's down? *Fortune.* 150(8). 8–9.

Hellwig, B. 1992, Sept./Oct. Executive female's breakthrough 50. *Executive Female.* 43–46.

Hewlett, S.A. 2002. Executive women and the myth of having it all. *Harvard Business Review, 80*(4). 66–74.

Jackson, L. A., Sullivan, L. A. & Hodge, C. N. 1993. Stereotype effects on attributions, predictions, and evaluations: No two social judgments are quite alike. *Journal of Personality and Social Psychology.* 65. 69–84.

Johnston, W.B. & Packer, A.H. 1987. *Workforce 2000.* Indianapolis, IN: Hudson Institute.

Kanter, R.M. 1977. *Men and women of the corporation.* New York: Basic Books.

Kanter, R.M. 1990, Spring/Summer. Foreward: Special issue on women and economic empowerment. *New England Journal of Public Policy, 6.* 11–14.

Karsten, M.F. 1992. *Gender issues in management.* Madison: Author. 23.

Karsten, M.F. 1994. *Management and gender: issues and attitudes.* Westport: Greenwood Publishing Group, Inc.

Karsten, M.F. 1997. Women in management. 882–86. In H. Tierney, Ed. *Women's Studies Encyclopedia.* Westport, CT: Greenwood Publishing Group, Inc.

Keaveny, T. J. & Inderrieden, E.J. 1999. Gender differences in employer supported training and education. *Journal of Vocational Behavior. 54.* 71–81.

Kelly, K. & DeBaise, C. 2004, July 13. Morgan Stanley settles bias suit for $54 million. *The Wall Street Journal.* A1.

Knight, J.L., Hebl, M.R., Foster, J.B. & Mannix, L.M. 2003, Winter. Out of role? Out of luck: The influence of race and leadership status on performance appraisals. *Journal of Leadership & Organizational Studies. 9*(3).

Livers, A.B. & Caver, K.A. 2003. *Leading in black and white: Working across the racial divide in corporate America.* San Francisco: John Wiley & Sons, Inc.

Llewellyn-Williams, M. 2001–2004. *The C200 business leadership index 2004: Annual report on women's clout in business.* Chicago: The Committee of 200.

Lublin, J.S. 2004, June 23. Women aspire to be chief as much as men do. *The Wall Street Journal.* D2.

Meyerson, D. & Fletcher, J. 2000, Jan./Feb. A modest manifesto for shattering the glass ceiling. *Harvard Business Review.* 117–36.

Morrison, A., Schrieber, C. & Price, K. 1995. *A glass ceiling survey: Benchmarking barriers and practices.* Greensboro: Center for Creative Leadership.

Morrison, A., White, R., Van Velsor, E. & The Center for Creative Leadership. 1987. *Breaking the glass ceiling.* Reading, MA: Addison-Wesley.

Morrison, A. 1992. Leadership diversity and leadership challenge. *Issues and observations, 12*(3). 1–4.

Padavic, I. & Reskin, B. 2002. *Women and men at work.* 2nd ed. Thousand Oaks, CA: SAGE Publications .

Placencia, W. 2002, May. Breaking the board ceiling. *Hispanic. 15*(5).

Powell, G. N. & Graves, L.M. 2003. *Women and men in management.* 3rd ed. Thousand Oaks, CA: SAGE.

Reskin, B.F. & McBrier, D. 2000. Why not ascription? Organizations' employment of male and female managers. *American Sociological Review. 25.* 335–61.

Rhode, D., ed. 2003. *The difference 'difference' makes: women and leadership.* Stanford, CA: Stanford University Press.

Ruderman, M. N. & Ohlott, P.J. 2002. *Standing at the crossroads: Next steps for high-achieving women.* San Francisco: Jossey-Bass.

Schneider, K.T., Fitzgerald, L.F. & Swan, S. 1997. Job-related and psychological effects of sexual harassment in the workplace: Empirical evidence from two organizations. *Journal of Applied Psychology 82*, 3. 401–15.

Simpson, P.A. & Stroh, L.K. 2002. Revisiting gender variation in training. *Feminist Economist. 9.* 3.

Snipp, C.M. 2001. Economy. In Champagne, D., Ed. *The Native North American Almanac,* 2nd ed. Farmington, MI: Gale Group.

Stroh, L.K., Langlands, C.L. & Simpson, P.A. Shattering the glass ceiling in the new millennium.147–67. In M.S. Stockdale & F.J. Crosby, Eds. *The psychology and management of workplace diversity.* Malden, MA: Blackwell Publishing, Ltd.

Tharenou, P., Latimer & Conroy, D. 1994. How do you make it to the top: An examination of influences on women's and men's managerial advancement. *Academy of Management Journal. 37*(4). 899–932.

Thomas, D.A. & Gabarro, J. 1999. *Breaking through: the making of minority executives in corporate America.* Boston: Harvard Business School Press.

U.S. Census Bureau. 2002. USA statistics in brief: population—race, Hispanic origin. Retrieved July 21, 2004 from http://www.census.gov/statab/www/poprace.html.

U.S. Department of Education, National Center for Education Statistics, Digest of Education Statistics. 2002. Table 268: master's degrees conferred by degree granting institution, by racial/ethnic group, major field of study, and sex of student,

2001–02. Retrieved July 21, 2004 from http://www.nces.edu.gov/programs/digest/d02/tables/dt265.asp.

U.S. Department of Education, National Center for Education Statistics, Digest of Education Statistics. 2002. Table 265: bachelor's degrees conferred by degree granting institution, by racial/ethnic group, major field of study, and sex of student, 2001–02. Retrieved July 21, 2004 from http://www.nces.edu.gov/programs/digest/d02/tables/dt265.asp.

U.S. Department of Labor, Women's Bureau. 1997. *Update.* Washington, D.C.: U.S. Department of Labor.

Valian, V. 1998. *Why so slow? The advancement of women.* Cambridge, MA: MIT Press.

Vinnecombe, S. & Bank, J. 2003. *Women with attitude: lessons for career management.* London: Routledge.

Wei, W. 1994. *The Asian American movement.* Philadelphia: Temple University Press.

Yoder, J. 2001. Making leadership work more effectively for women. *Journal of Social Issues. 57*(4). 815–28.

Zichy, S. & Kellen, B. 2000. *Women and the leadership Q: Revealing the four paths to influence and power.* New York: McGraw-Hill.

Zimmerman, A. 2004, June 23. Judge certifies Wal-Mart suit as class action. *The Wall Street Journal.* A1.

Chapter Three

Equal Employment Opportunity and Harassment

Margaret Foegen Karsten and Frank P. Igou

OUTCOMES

After studying this chapter you should be able to:

1. define reverse discrimination, bona fide occupational qualifications (BFOQ), disparate impact discrimination, disparate treatment discrimination, affirmative defense and tangible employment action (as related to sexual harassment), sexual harassment, sex-based harassment, racial harassment, affirmative action plan, underutilization, and relevant labor market
2. explain why managers should understand equal employment opportunity laws and regulations.
3. explain how comparable worth differs from equal pay required by the Equal Pay Act.
4. state and refute two arguments that have been presented to justify the pay gap between women and men.
5. explain the impact of any three U.S. Supreme Court cases dealing with employment discrimination.
6. explain steps organizations should take to prevent liability for sexual harassment.
7. explain what an organization can do to reduce its liability when a workplace romance ends.
8. restate provisions of the Pregnancy Disability Act of 1978
9. compare and contrast provisions, coverage, and penalties of Title VII of the Civil Rights Act of 1964 and Executive Order 11246.
10. explain three provisions of the Civil Rights Act of 1991.

11. justify whether or not you believe affirmative action plans remain useful based on common arguments for and against them.

IMPORTANCE OF AN UNDERSTANDING OF EEO LAWS

Familiarity with equal employment opportunity (EEO) laws is important for employees and managers alike. To make sure their organizations fulfill legal requirements, managers must be knowledgeable about them. Employees must understand EEO laws and regulations to safeguard their rights and deal with employment discrimination effectively, if it occurs.

Chapter 3 focuses on federal EEO laws that ban gender and race-based job discrimination, including harassment. Laws dealing with employment unfairness based on other factors will be discussed only if they concern gender and race discrimination. Romantic workplace relationships will be covered as they pertain to harassment.

EQUAL PAY ACT

The Equal Pay Act of 1963 predates Title VII of the Civil Rights Act by one year. Technically an amendment to the Fair Labor Standards Act of 1938, known as the overtime and minimum wage law, the Equal Pay Act requires males and females to be compensated equally for jobs done under similar working conditions that have equivalent skill, effort, and responsibility requirements and are similar in content. Incentives and employee benefits also are covered by this law. It applies only to gender based pay differences, not to differentials based on race or ethnicity.

When the Equal Pay Act was passed, many employers thought lower compensation for women than men was acceptable. They justified differential pay based on stereotypes—the beliefs that men are family breadwinners and women are less committed to the workforce because most will bear children. In 1997, however, almost 67% of employed women said they contributed at least half of their total household income (AFL-CIO, 2005). The need to keep pace with rising costs and increasing career expectations of women, fueled by higher education levels and the women's movement, helped dispel these myths, to a certain extent.

Two landmark court cases further defined and strengthened the Equal Pay Act. The Third Circuit U.S. Court of Appeals in *Schultz v. Wheaton Glass Co.* (1970) decided that jobs must be "substantially similar" but need not be identical to be protected. Thus, employers were prohibited from making minor changes to job descriptions or titles to justify paying females less than males. In *Corning Glass Works v. Brennan* (1974), the U.S. Supreme Court ruled that it was unacceptable to pay men more than women because males refused to work at the low rates females earned. Conversely, paying women less than men simply because females traditionally received lower wages based on the "going market rate" was illegal.

A few lawful exceptions to the Equal Pay Act exist. Males and females may be paid different rates for the same work based on any legitimate factor other than their sex. Incentives related to production, piece rate incentives, or bona fide seniority or merit systems may justify compensation variations.

COMPARABLE WORTH AND PAY EQUITY: EXPLANATION AND PROS AND CONS

The Equal Pay Act requires the same pay for jobs alike in content whether performed by women or men, but *comparable worth* advocates the same pay for women and men who do dissimilar jobs that are deemed of equal value to an organization. A classic example compares custodians with public health nurses. Historically, males have been numerically dominant in custodial positions whereas females predominate as public nurses. Public health nurses argued that their positions were at least—if not more—valuable than custodian positions based on skill, effort, responsibility, and working conditions, yet they were often paid less. They believed this was an ethical issue that needed to be addressed.

Pay equity, as now understood, proposes that dissimilar jobs of equal value to an organization should be paid the same whether whites or racial or ethnic minorities perform them.

Originally, pay equity involved compensating jobholders equally if they held jobs in which one sex predominated that were different in content but deemed of equal value to the company. For example, a pay equity rather than a comparable worth standard would apply if jobs of tax accountants and engineers were judged of equal worth and 70% of incumbents in both job categories were male. This use of the term pay equity is no longer common.

Persistence of gender pay disparities more than 40 years after the Equal Pay Act was passed and compensation discrepancies based on race and ethnicity set the stage for emergence of concern about comparable worth and pay equity. In 1963, women, overall, made about 59% of men's earnings in the U.S. This percent rose to 74% in 1992 but only increased another 3% in the next 10 years. From 2002 to 2003, it declined from 77% to 76%. In 2002, when white women took in 77% of white men's earnings, black women earned 70% and Latinas 58%. Asian and Pacific Islander women fared better, but they made only 84% of the pay of white males in 2002 (AFL-CIO, 2005). From 1979 to 2002, white women's earnings grew 30% after adjustment for inflation; comparable figures for Latinas and black women were 10% and 22%. Inflation adjusted earnings of Hispanic males fell during the same time frame; those of black males remained constant, and white males posted only a 2.6% gain (U.S. Department of Labor, 2003).

The wage gap between white and racial or ethnic minority women is less than the disparity between their respective male peers. For example, white women's median weekly earnings were nearly 39% more than Latinas and almost 16% more than black women's in 2002. By comparison, white men's median weekly earnings were 56% more than male Hispanics' and 34% higher than black men's in the same year (U.S. Department of Labor, 2003).

Salary inequities are not limited to lower level positions. Even in management, gender based differences exist. The U.S. General Accounting Office (2001), in its comprehensive research of executive posts in several industries that collectively employ nearly three-fourths of females in the labor force, reported that the compensation gap between executive women and men grew from 1995 to 2000.

Progress in pay equity has been made in the past 50 years, but striking disparities remain, particularly among racial and ethnic minorities. These represent ethical issues that must be addressed. Comparable worth or pay equity provides mechanisms for doing that. To implement either, organizations must equate jobs differing in content. Job evaluation plans are available for this purpose: since the early 1900s, they have been used to rank jobs according to their value (Karsten, 1994). All such plans require subjective judgment; they should not be considered cure-alls. Also, various job evaluation systems may yield different results when determining job value, which may explain why comparable worth claims relying on job evaluation have not always fared well in the courts.

Even if totally objective job evaluation systems existed and firms relied on them to set wages based on a comparable worth standard, such companies might have trouble retaining good workers. Employers typically use money to discourage employee turnover, but this would be impermissible under a comparable worth standard. For example, if, as an inducement to stay, a private high school wanted to raise the pay of a math teacher who had been offered a higher salary by a business, the school also would have to increase the compensation of teachers in other disciplines, such as foreign language and physical education, assuming teaching positions in all disciplines had been deemed of equal value. Raising the pay of all other teachers to retain those in a field for which demand is high would be impossible for most schools.

On the other hand, perhaps companies could compete on factors other than wages. Employers could emphasize espirit de corps, exceptional benefits packages, and their high quality of work life (Karsten, 1994).

Some argue that implementing comparable worth involves comparing apples and oranges. Others maintain that this is relatively easy when fruits can be analyzed in terms of fiber, vitamins, and other measures of nutritional value. It is not so different from job evaluation procedures that analyze jobs in terms of skill, effort, responsibility and working conditions.

Another argument is that increasing women's wages, which may be required to implement comparable worth, could raise unemployment in traditionally female jobs. According to traditional market economics, employers would demand fewer workers as their wages rose, thereby aggravating unemployment and perhaps encouraging displaced employees to consider other careers in the long-run. Some would consider this desirable.

A perceived negative aspect of comparable worth or pay equity is its effect on costs. Yet pay adjustments to implement comparable worth in Minnesota were only 3.7% of total payroll costs and were phased in over four years (National Committee on Pay Equity, 2004–2005). Proponents maintain that this is a small price to redress wage discrimination, which they believe is required ethically.

POSSIBLE EXPLANATIONS FOR GENDER AND RACE BASED PAY DISPARITIES

Some arguments to justify compensation differentials are not persuasive. Three common explanations in this category to be discussed are that:

1. Pay disparities are due, totally, to differences in experience and education, or human capital
2. Women choose certain low-paying occupations that are highly flexible because skills are expected to deteriorate slowly in them.
3. Women are more likely than men to take breaks from the workforce to care for children or other family members.

In response to the first argument, considering differences in education and experience still leaves no explanation for 25% to 50% of the pay gap (National Committee on Pay Equity, 2004–2005). In support of arguments 2 and 3, Taff (2003) believes that employees who are also primary caregivers to children or elders may choose occupations in which "human capital" does not erode rapidly due to leaves of absence or extended part-time employment. The National Committee on Pay Equity (2004–2005), however, indicates that jobs heavily populated by women are not necessarily more flexible. In addition, occupations filled with women and people of color tend to have lower compensation than those filled with white males.

In support of argument 3, women are assuming a disproportional responsibility, compared to men, for providing care for aging relatives. The National Committee on Pay Equity (2004–2005) counters that leaving the workforce temporarily to care for family members should be considered acceptable for either males or females. The majority of women do not do this, however. As evidence, the National Committee on Pay Equity indicates that 65% of females with children under six are in the work force, and over 50% work full time.

If common explanations for the pay gap are inaccurate, why else might it persist? Occupational crowding, in which supply exceeds demand for workers and depresses wages, may be a factor. Crowding suggests that child-care employees' pay would rise due to a chronic shortage, but that has not happened. Another explanation relates to a movement away from well-defined pay structures to flexible systems emphasizing merit and incentive pay, which began in the 1990s. In the former systems, top managers made compensation decisions in consultation with human resource specialists using fixed criteria. Now, given more decentralized, flattened structures with "empowered teams," team members or immediate supervisors may make pay decisions. As compensation policies become less formal and require more interpretation by immediate supervisors, unconscious gender bias may be activated (Reskin, 2000; Rudman, 1998; Gomez-Meija & Balkin, 1992).

Comparable worth court cases, such as *County of Washington v. Gunther* (1981) and *AFSCME v. State of Washington* (1985), emerged in the 1980s. In the *Gunther* case, which really dealt with sex discrimination, the U.S. Supreme Court allowed for the possibility of future comparable worth cases. It clarified that Title VII bans compensation discrimination even among jobs that are not identical. As a result of the *AFSCME* case, the state of Washington settled by paying over $400,000 to women employees determined to have been underpaid by a compensation survey taken in the 1970s. The state had failed to correct wage disparities unrelated to job content that the survey identified between jobs dominated by women and men.

STATE AND PROPOSED FEDERAL PAY EQUITY LEGISLATION: PRESENT AND FUTURE

Currently, about 20 states have adopted comparable worth or pay equity standards for state employees. Only Maine's statute applies to its private as well as public sector employees. Unlike Washington, which did not implement comparable worth until it was forced to do so, Minnesota, a leader in comparable worth, adopted it in 1982. The state rated its jobs according to the required level of education or training, responsibility, customer or client contact, and work conditions or stress. Positions of registered nurses and vocational education teachers were found to be of equal value, but the nurses, who were mainly women, were paid about $500 less per month than the teachers, who were mainly men. To correct this inequity, the state of Minnesota raised the registered nurses' wages.

In 1998, a national comparable worth law, The Paycheck Fairness Act, was soundly defeated in the U.S. Senate. The proposed law was to be enforced by the Department of Labor and was intended as a framework for laws covering private and public sector employment. Because legislators in this era hesitate to impose more regulation on business, similar legislation is unlikely to be introduced in the near future.

Though the quest for pay equity seems like an uphill battle, the future looks brighter for the elimination of noticeable gender based wage distinctions than for pay differences based on race or ethnicity. Wide racial disparities exist, but women are earning more baccalaureate and master's degrees than men. Women may gain from the shift from a manufacturing based economy favoring males, especially those with lower levels of formal education, to a knowledge-based economy that rewards higher level skills. They also should benefit from the ongoing shift to the service industry.

DISCRIMINATION: A DEFINITION

Defining the term discrimination is necessary before discussing Title VII of the Civil Rights Act, a monumental law dealing with employment discrimination. Discrimination means classifying objects or people into groups. Thus, workplace discrimination may be viewed as rational if it distinguishes among individuals based on job-related qualifications. In the 21st century, however, the term has become synonymous with unfair, irrational differentiation among employees that was unrelated to job performance. Two distinct types of discrimination that are banned under Title VII will be discussed in the context of the U.S. Supreme Court decisions that determined they were illegal.

TITLE VII OF THE CIVIL RIGHTS ACT OF 1964

A fairly inclusive federal employment discrimination law, Title VII of the Civil Rights Act bans job unfairness in recruitment, hiring, discharge, compensation and benefits, selection for training or any other term of employment based on race, color, religion, sex, or national origin. Those obliged to comply with Title VII include private employers with 15 or more employees, labor unions with at least 15 members, public and private educational institutions, employment agencies, and state and local governments.

When first introduced, Title VII did not bar sex discrimination. The word "sex" was added as a protected class by the law's opponents to guarantee its defeat. According to their logic, few lawmakers who favored outlawing race discrimination would support the idea of banning bias against women. In the end, however, the amended version of Title VII, which prohibited sex discrimination, passed (Deckard, 1983, as cited in Karsten, 1994).

Courts may punish organizations violating Title VII in various ways. They may issue injunctions to stop discriminatory acts or order the reinstatement of employees who were fired or denied promotion unfairly (Karsten, 1994). Such employees are entitled to *back pay*, which is remuneration they would have earned had they not experienced discrimination, for up to two years. They may receive *forward pay*, or the estimated future earnings lost due to an illegal practice. A court-ordered affirmative action plan is another possible penalty. Firms are not required to develop a plan automatically simply because they must comply with Title VII, but if they are found guilty of discrimination, courts may order them to do so (Karsten). The Civil Rights Act of 1991, an amendment to Title VII, provides additional sanctions, which will be discussed later in this chapter.

Bona Fide Occupational Qualification Under Title VII

In certain narrowly defined circumstances, Title VII permits discrimination based on sex, religion, race, or national origin. This is called the *bona fide occupational qualification* (BFOQ) exception, and a BFOQ is a characteristic, such as sex, national origin, or religion, that is necessary for the normal operation of a business. Employers may defend themselves against discrimination charges by showing that failing to hire solely members of a particular sex, race, ethnicity, or religion would harm the essence of their business (*Dothard v. Rawlinson,* 433 U.S. 321, 323, 1977). For example, a firm could lawfully refuse to employ women to portray male characters or vice versa for authenticity reasons. A Lutheran school could require its religion teachers to be Lutherans in good standing.

Hooters Restaurant's claim that being a female was a BFOQ for servers, bartenders, and hosts was rejected in *U.S. v. Hooters* (1992). Seven males who were not hired as servers based on their sex filed discrimination charges. Hooters tried to defend its practice of employing only women in certain jobs by claiming that it provided "vicarious sexual recreation," but this was not persuasive. If the essential nature of the firm had been entertainment, perhaps being female would have been a BFOQ for servers and other front-of-the house staff, but Hooters depicts itself to the public as a restaurant. Male complainants received $2 million in a settlement of this class action suit, and Hooters had to pay $1.75 million in attorneys' fees and establish three gender neutral jobs. The restaurant may restrict wait staff jobs to women, but "Hooters' Persons," who assist the servers, must be hired with no consideration of gender.

Gender may be a BFOQ when privacy concerns arise, such as in locker rooms or lavatories used exclusively by males or females, or in certain medical settings. Though men or women can perform the tasks, limiting employment to those of one sex may be justifiable if employing both males and females would violate community moral standards or cause discomfort due to privacy issues.

Berman (2000, p. 750), however, believes that the privacy BFOQ has been interpreted too broadly in medical settings. In her words, "existing law permits sex-based employment policies with respect to nurses, nurses' aides, janitors, child care specialists at psychiatric hospitals, and prison guards because these jobs sometimes require employees to view the naked bodies of patients or inmates." She points out inconsistencies of policies that allow males to be obstetric gynecologists but not nurses in labor and delivery units. Such rules also may permit female nurses to care for male patients but bar male nurses from dealing with female patients.

Denying employment to women or racial minorities based on gender or racial stereotypes or assumptions about client, customer, or coworker preferences violates Title VII; it does not qualify as a BFOQ exception. Similarly, having to provide separate restrooms or other facilities is not a valid justification for refusing to hire women unless the cost is extremely high (Karsten, 1994).

The Equal Employment Opportunity Commission (EEOC), the agency that enforces Title VII, has five members who must be approved by the President and confirmed by the Senate. It has developed detailed procedures for filing discrimination charges, which appear on its web page. Until 1971, when the EEOC received resources and legal authority to investigate the act and ensure that its provisions are carried out, the agency was relatively powerless.

A Sample of Precedent-Setting Title VII Court Cases

A few of the many U.S. Supreme Court cases dealing with Title VII will be summarized here. These include *Griggs v. Duke Power,* which established disparate impact discrimination and *McDonnell Douglas v. Green,* which first explained the concept of disparate treatment discrimination. Two early and two relatively recent "reverse" discrimination cases will be discussed as will *Autoworkers v. Johnson Controls*, dealing with fetal protection. Other cases to be highlighted are *U.S. v. Virginia, Dukes v. Wal-Mart,* and *Morgan Stanley v. U.S.* The cases, *General Electric v. Gilbert* and *Wards Cove Packing v. Atonio*, will be mentioned only as they relate to the Pregnancy Discrimination Act of 1978 and the Civil Rights Act of 1991, the laws they prompted.

Cases Establishing Disparate Impact and Disparate Treatment

The first U.S. Supreme Court case dealing with issues that Title VII raised was *Griggs v. Duke Power* (1971). It considered race discrimination and established three precedents, namely that unintentional discrimination may be illegal, that employment practices must be job related, and that the employer has the burden of proof to demonstrate that they are. The idea that unintentional discrimination is still illegal underlies the notion of *disparate impact discrimination.*

In this type of discrimination, non-job related, seemingly neutral factors that are applied to all in similar circumstances exclude a greater percentage of women or racial minorities from employment or promotion. Unless the employer can demonstrate that using such factors is a "business necessity," it is unlawful to do so. For example, mandating that all workers including laborers must have a high school diploma may seem fair. If, however, a much smaller percent of racial minorities than non-minorities in the recruiting area has completed secondary education, it may not be. If laborers can perform their jobs adequately without a high school education, then requiring it is unjustifiable unless the employer can prove it is a business necessity.

In the U.S. during the 1950s and 1960s, a greater percent of whites than blacks living in the south had graduated from high school. Thus, requiring a high school education for a position as coal handler, which was Duke's practice, excluded a much greater percent of minorities than whites. This statistical comparison could result in claims of disparate impact discrimination regardless of the employer's intent.

Other examples illustrate successful challenges to disparate impact sex discrimination. Before the U.S. Supreme Court case, *Dothard v. Rawlinson* (1977), prison guards in certain locations were required to be at least 5'2" tall and weigh 120 pounds. Though appearing neutral, this requirement disproportionately excludes women and some racial minorities from consideration for prison guard positions. Therefore, it was struck down. Female construction workers in the 1970s challenged lifting requirements successfully. Being able to lift from 80 to 100 pounds was not a business necessity; equipment could be used to help employees lift such heavy loads. Such a requirement had an unfair impact on women and was banned, benefiting all workers.

Adverse (disparate) impact does not always signify illegal discrimination. If a selection procedure is deemed job-related and the only other process an employer can find with less adverse impact sacrifices job-relatedness, then using the first procedure is legally defensible, although it has adverse impact.

Because it is simple and understandable, the EEOC adopted the *4/5ths, or 80%, rule* to determine whether or not an employment practice has an adverse impact on women or racial minorities. If the hiring or promotion rate for women or minorities is less than 80% of the rate for men or whites, evidence of possible adverse impact exists, according to this rule.

Before *Griggs,* workers had to prove that another type of discrimination, called disparate treatment, took place. This entailed showing that the employer intended to discriminate against them and that they were treated differently due to their race, color, religion, sex, or national origin. Proving that disparate impact discrimination occurred is more difficult for employees than demonstrating that an employer's action resulted in disparate impact discrimination (Karsten, 1994).

McDonnell Douglas v. Green (1973), another race discrimination case, outlines the most common way to show that an employer has engaged in disparate treatment during its selection process. Consider the following scenario: A black candidate is not offered a job for which he or she is qualified and the employer is seeking applicants. The job stays open and the employer continues searching for applicants. In this situation, the employer must prove that job-related reasons exist for refusing to hire the black applicant. An employer who can do this meets the required burden of proof.

Reverse Discrimination Cases

The next two sets of high court cases, *University of California v. Bakke* and *Steelworkers v. Weber,* decided in the 1970s, and *Gratz v. Bollinger* and *Grutter v. Bollinger,* decided in 2003, involved an issue dubbed reverse discrimination. The first two dealt with race discrimination but set precedents that courts consider when deciding sex discrimination cases. *Gratz* dealt with race and *Grutter* with sex discrimination, and all but *Weber* involved admission to an undergraduate or graduate university program.

Understanding the controversial nature of "reverse discrimination" is necessary before discussing these cases. As mentioned in chapter 2, *reverse discrimination*, as generally understood, occurs when majority group members are treated unfairly because decision makers have gone "too far" to try to make up for past discrimination minorities experienced (Karsten, 1994). Those who support this definition of reverse discrimination maintain that fair policies must be "colorblind" and should disregard factors such as race, color, sex, and national origin. Unchangeable, non-job-related characteristics should be ignored, according to this logic. Considering such factors insults females and people of color who wish to be evaluated based on competence (Karsten).

Title VII's legislative history, including statements from politicians on both sides of the aisle, is used to justify this interpretation of reverse discrimination. For example, Hubert Humphrey, a Democratic U.S. Senator from Minnesota, said "he would eat a copy of the bill if anyone could show him words in it justifying discrimination in favor of blacks" (Barone, 2004, A10).

In his dissent to *Steelworkers v. Weber* (1979), Justice Rehnquist said:

> Not once during the 83 days of debate (about Title VII) in the Senate did a speaker, proponent or opponent, suggest that the bill would allow employers voluntarily to prefer racial minorities over white persons. In light of Title VII's flat prohibition on discrimination against any individual . . . because of such individual's race, such a contention would have been . . . too preposterous to warrant response . . .

The notion of reverse discrimination would be defined out of existence by another idea that declares fairness the converse of discrimination. If the opposite of discrimination is fairness and "reverse" means opposite, then "reverse discrimination" has no meaning (Jones, 1981, cited in Karsten, 1994). Others claim the term is unnecessary because Title VII bans discrimination people of *any* race or national origin.

Regardless of opinions about the term, managers and peers must deal with workers who are disgruntled by what they regard as reverse discrimination. Allowing them to vent may be wise, but they need to know that respecting diverse coworkers and cooperating to achieve the organization's goals is a job expectation (Karsten, 1994).

Though it has been used in the employment context since the 1960s, affirmative action still is widely misunderstood. For that reason, employees, especially those who are concerned about reverse discrimination, must receive accurate information about it. Affirmative action is designed to provide a temporary advantage to women and racial or ethnic minorities to make up for past discrimination. It remains controversial, and arguments for and against its use appear later in this chapter.

In *Bakke* (1978), the first of the earlier reverse discrimination cases to be discussed, the U.S. Supreme Court held that inflexible quotas to achieve racial balance are impermissible. Race or sex may not be the determining factor but may be considered when making admissions or hiring decisions as part of voluntary affirmative action plans. In this case, Allan Bakke, a white male, was denied admission to medical school though he had higher medical college admission test scores than blacks who were accepted. Sixteen percent of the medical school seats were reserved for blacks, and the high court ruled that this practice constituted "reverse discrimination." In its decision in favor of Bakke, the Court forced the University of California-Davis' medical school to accept him into the program.

In *Steelworkers v. Weber* (1979), the Supreme Court ruled in favor of the United Steelworkers of America (USWA). In that case, Brian Weber, a white male, was not admitted to a training program though he had more seniority than the black employee who was chosen. Weber's denial of admission was due to a voluntary affirmative action plan between the USWA and Kaiser Aluminum. The Supreme Court upheld the legality of the affirmative action plan because it was "designed to eliminate conspicuous racial imbalance in traditionally segregated job categories" (443 U.S. 193 [1979]). Rules for distinguishing between acceptable and impermissible affirmative action plans were not provided by the Court in *Weber*, but later interpretations indicated that such plans must be voluntary and temporary and must not suppress majority interests unnecessarily (Twomey, 1990). They also must be set up to break down old hierarchical patterns and allow women and minorities entry into occupations from which they had been excluded previously (Twomey).

Gratz v. Bollinger (2003) involved two white high school students, Jennifer Gratz and Patrick Hamacher, who applied for undergraduate admission to the College of Literature, Science, and Arts at the University of Michigan. Despite their good grades and test scores, Gratz and Hamacher were not admitted. The admissions process automatically added 20 points (of a total of 100) to applications of African Americans, Hispanics, and Native Americans as a way to increase diversity of students enrolled, which was considered important for educational purposes at the University of Michigan. The two white students claimed that if they had received 20 extra points, they would have been admitted.

Though some justices appreciated the desire to increase diversity, the Supreme Court struck down the practice of automatically adding points to applications from racial and ethnic minorities. Siding with Gratz and Hamacher, they said this violated the equal protection clause of the U.S. Constitution. Applications had to be considered individually.

A different outcome occurred in *Grutter v. Bollinger* (2003). Barbara Grutter, who was white, applied for and was refused admission to the University of Michigan Law School though racial minorities with lower test scores were admitted. Each application was considered individually, and race could be used as a "plus factor" to achieve diversity goals. In this case, the U.S. Supreme Court agreed with the University of Michigan, implicitly endorsing affirmative action.

Gratz and *Grutter* indicated that being a member of an underutilized group may be the deciding factor in selection, whether for university admission or a position in a private firm, after applicants have been deemed qualified. Numerical points may not be added if a scoring process is used, however. Membership in a protected class may merely be used as a "plus factor" or "tiebreaker" when candidates are considered equally qualified.

Gender Discrimination Case-Fetal Protection

In the past decades, complying with equal opportunity laws has been challenging when they do not conflict with other requirements. Employers may be caught in a vicious circle when they do, as is the case when sex discrimination laws and fetal protection policies collide.

The Supreme Court decided, in *United Auto Workers v. Johnson Controls* (1991), that Title VII as amended by the Pregnancy Discrimination Act, bans sex-specific fetal protection policies that are not justifiable as BFOQ exceptions. Therefore, most sex-specific fetal protection policies prohibiting fertile women from jobs requiring contact with hazardous substances are illegal (Sprotzer & Goldberg, 1992). As a result, employers may be liable for both disparate impact discrimination and potential fetal injury.

This risk can be reduced, but not eliminated, through education and training. Employers must fully inform employees of all potential health risks and train them to handle toxic materials properly. Even if employees who wish to do work involving exposure to hazardous substances sign a waiver, however, it will not apply if employers fail to take other "good faith" steps to minimize toxicity. One such step would be to use technology to reduce toxic agents in the workplace. For example, closed systems for chemical processing and better ventilation systems might be helpful. Filter masks, protective clothing, or other personal protective devices, some of which the Occupational Safety and Health Administration (OSHA) may require, also are recommended. Some have suggested using urine or blood tests to screen employees who are at risk for health problems due to exposure to toxic agents and transferring them to safer work environments, if necessary. Employers should be cautious about doing this and may wish to seek legal counsel to avoid violating privacy rights or raising issues related to discrimination based on medical or genetic information.

Gender Discrimination Cases-Military Academy, Retailer, Investment Firm

The three remaining court cases to be addressed here concern gender discrimination in admission to a military academy, promotion and pay at a major retailer, and treatment of women employed in a Wall Street investment firm. In 1996, the Supreme Court struck down the male only admission policy at the Virginia Military Institute in *U.S. v. Virginia* (518 U.S. 518). At a state-supported entity, this policy violates the 14th Amendment to the U.S. Constitution.

Dukes v. Wal-Mart became a class action suit in June 2004. It applies to as many as 1.6 million present and former female employees at Wal-Mart since 1998 and alleges that women were paid less than men despite having more seniority and higher performance ratings. The EEOC also found disparate impact in promotion rates between women and men at many stores throughout the U.S. Women who had similar qualifications to men took much longer to be promoted to store manager, which was often the only full-time position with benefits in a store.

At Morgan Stanley, female and male employees were treated differently, and women were subjected to lewd comments and coarse behavior from male supervisors and coworkers. Most of the 340 plaintiffs in *Morgan Stanley v. U.S.* (2004) were in the institutional stock division. They were held back from promotions and pay raises and excluded from sales outings to golf resorts with clients. Morgan Stanley lost this case, had to pay $54 million in damages, and was ordered to hire an outside consulting firm to monitor its selection, promotion, and compensation policies for the next 10 years.

Morgan Stanley v. U.S. is one of many workplace sexual harassment cases. The history of this age-old problem, its pervasiveness and nature, events that increased the public's awareness of it, and other types of harassment that are illegal under Title VII will be discussed next.

SEXUAL HARASSMENT: HISTORICAL EXAMPLES, EVOLUTION, PERVASIVENESS, AND COMPLAINTS

Sexual harassment has occurred for thousands of years. A Bible story involving Potiphar and Joseph illustrates the problem's ancient roots. Potiphar, the wife of an Egyptian pharaoh, only had power because of her husband's position. The notion that women obtain power through association with men is repugnant to contemporary feminists, but it was the norm even in Western societies until recently. Today, the idea that women enjoy power in their own right is a given in most Western cultures. Potiphar used her power to harass Joseph. She asked him to sleep with her, but when Joseph rebuffed her advances, Potiphar dishonestly said that he had propositioned her. Based on a false accusation, Joseph served a prison term (Karsten, 1994).

Skipping to the 1800s, Louisa May Alcott, a well-known U.S. author of that era, spoke of a "personal dilemma." This was a euphemism for harassment. The brother of an older woman, for whom Alcott was employed as a companion, made unwanted sexual overtures toward her (Biles, 1981 cited in Karsten, 1994).

Moving rapidly to the 1960s, Title VII of the Civil Rights Act of 1964 banned sex discrimination including sexual harassment. Concern about harassment gained some momentum after the EEOC issued guidelines in 1980, but claims skyrocketed eleven years later following the October 1991 Senate confirmation hearings of Supreme Court Justice, Clarence Thomas. Oklahoma law professor, Anita Hill, alleged that Thomas had created an offensive environment when she reported to him at the Equal Employment Opportunity Commission, which he chaired in the early 1980s. Hill claimed Thomas made unwanted sexual remarks to her, showed pornographic films, and boasted of his sexual prowess. Thomas strongly denied all charges, which resulted in a standoff and his eventual confirmation to the U.S. Supreme Court (Karsten, 1994). Regardless of one's beliefs about the truthfulness of Hill or Thomas, the nationally televised, live confirmation hearings increased awareness of workplace sexual harassment as nothing had done before. In the last half of 1991, sexual harassment charges filed with the EEOC jumped 71% compared to the previous year (Meyer, 1992).

Another 1991 event that publicized sexual harassment was the Las Vegas Tailhook Convention. In a motel hallway, male aviators passed women, some of whom were naval officers, down a gauntlet, tore their clothes, and grabbed and pinched them (Karsten, 1994).

The trend toward increased awareness of sexual harassment continued through the 1990s and beyond as other branches of the military, such as the Army and Air Force, confronted it as did private sector firms, including Mitsubishi and Wall Street investment firms. A notable investment firm case in the 1990s involved Smith Barney, infamous for its "Boom Boom Room," a basement party area at its Long Island, NY office, where some male employees engaged in crude behavior directed toward women (Norton, 2005).

Political figures were not immune from harassment claims. Senator Robert Packwood of Oregon was dogged by sexual harassment charges that finally forced his resignation, and Bill Clinton faced charges stemming from conduct when he served as governor of Arkansas. Though Clinton's acknowledged inappropriate relationship with Monica Lewinsky was not regarded as harassment because Lewinsky did not find the conduct unwelcome, the power disparity between the parties was a concern to those trying to prevent workplace sexual harassment.

In 1981, the year after the EEOC issued guidelines on sexual harassment, 3,661 charges were filed. Over the next two decades, the number of formal complaints rose dramatically. In 1991, 5,644 formal complaints were made.

Sexual harassment claims received by the EEOC (2004c) topped 13,450 in 2003, and an additional 6,180 racial and 2,365 national origin charges were filed that year. The number of sexual harassment charges dropped to 13,136 in 2004 (EEOC, 2005).

From 57% to 88% of employees had been sexually harassed in the 1970s and 1980s, according to surveys taken then (Ford & McLaughlin, 1988). More recent studies reported by Equal Rights Advocates (2005) put that percentage between 40% and 90%. Though the percentage of males filing sexual harassment charges topped 15% in 2004 (EEOC, 2005), up from 9% in 1992 (EEOC, 2004b), most of those subjected to unwanted sexual attention on the job are female. Foy (2000, p. 58) states, "while most men aren't harassers, most harassers are men." Nevertheless, 19% of male federal employees surveyed had been sexually harassed between 1991 and 1993 (MSPB, 1995); in 21% of the cases, other males were the perpetrators (MSPB).

Besides being female, other risk factors for sexual harassment are relative youth, low job status, marital status, sex-based occupational segregation, and race. Those who are harassed tend to be under 35 years old (MSPB), and "the most likely targets . . . are those who are lower on the rungs of status and power" (Jackson & Newman, 2004, p. 707). Foy (2000, p. 58) believes that "Organizations that appear most susceptible to breeding sexual harassment consist of older men in positions of power and younger women who have considerably less hierarchical power. Law firms, public accounting firms, the military, and the U.S. Congress are a few types of organizations that fit this profile." Being married seems to deter harassment of females and males alike. (Jackson & Newman), but the incidence of sexual harassment is higher if occupational segregation exists (Schultz, 1998). This occurs when more than 70% of those in an occupation are of one sex. African American women are particularly susceptible to sexual harassment, according to Muliawan and Kleiner (2001), due to their economic vulnerability and stereotypes about their sexual availability.

ILLEGAL HARASSMENT:
DEFINITION AND NATURE OF THE PROBLEM

Sexual harassment may be the most well-known form of illegal harassment under Title VII of the Civil Rights Act, but other forms of severe, repeated non-sexual annoyance of employees based on gender, race, color, or national origin also constitute unlawful hostile environment. Harassment based on disability and age (if over 40) are unlawful but are banned by other federal laws so will not be discussed here. Sex-based and racial harassment will be explained later in the chapter.

Retaliation for complaints about harassment and other illegal discrimination is prohibited. Nevertheless, Wendt and Slonaker (2002), who conducted a 15–year longitudinal study on sexual harassment claims in Ohio, estimate that nearly half result in retaliation, the most common form of which is discharge.

Harassers or those being harassed may be male or female; same sex harassment has been illegal since the U.S. Supreme Court settled that issue in *Oncale v. Sundowners* (1998). Besides supervisors and coworkers, non-employees such as customers or clients, suppliers, or vendors who harass employees can create liability for their employers.

According to the EEOC's 1980 guidelines, sexual harassment includes requests for sexual favors, unwanted sexual advances, and other sexually oriented verbal or physical conduct when 1) acceptance of that conduct is made a term or condition of a person's employment either directly or indirectly, 2) employment decisions are based on an individual's compliance with or refusal of such conduct, or 3) the conduct unreasonably interferes with a person's work performance or creates an intimidating, hostile, or offensive work environment.

Parts 1) and 2) of the EEOC definition explain the "quid pro quo" form of sexual harassment. The Latin phrase means "this for that" and refers to an exchange of favors. For example, perhaps the supervisor promotes or raises the pay of employees who comply with requests for sexual favors. Perhaps employees who turn down sexual advances are demoted or are assigned undesirable tasks (Karsten, 1994). To be considered "quid pro quo," the harassment must result in a tangible positive or negative employment action.

Part 3) of the definition deals with environmental sexual harassment. Whether or not this type has occurred is decided on a case-by-case basis considering all relevant circumstances. Behavior contributing to illegal hostile environment may include unfulfilled threats or a workplace atmosphere that interferes with employees' ability to work because it is charged with explicit sexual comments or behavior (Karsten, 1994).

Sexual harassment represents an abuse of power that harms another person. It is more closely related to dominance and power than to sexuality (Karsten, 1994).

Behavior constituting sexual harassment lies on a continuum. Mild forms include unwelcome sexually oriented jokes and remarks that poison the environment. Rape and attempted rape are at the opposite end of the spectrum. Examples of behaviors between those extremes include unwanted sexual touching and explicit displays of material of a sexual nature (Karsten, 1994). Sexual harassment regulations are not designed to mandate a civil workplace, however. Teasing and occasional questionable remarks typically do not subject employers to liability unless they are part of a pattern contributing to an offensive work environment (EEOC, 2004a).

Receivers' perceptions determine whether or not harassment occurred, regardless of the harasser's intentions. Courts also will consider how a "reasonable person" in a similar situation would perceive it. This approach seems to have evolved from a "reasonable woman" standard, adopted by *Ellison v. Brady* (1991). Before 1991, courts had applied a "reasonable man" standard to males and females for more than 150 years (Karsten, 1994). A "reasonable woman" standard was adopted based on evidence showing that, when presented with an identical scenario, 75% of women considered it sexual harassment but 75% of the men thought it was flattery (Hayes, 1991). Because of the divergence in perceptions of males and females, the Court deemed the "reasonable woman" standard is more appropriate in cases in which women experience sexual harassment.

FIRST U.S. SUPREME COURT CASE DEALING WITH SEXUAL HARASSMENT: MERITOR V. VINSON

A case "so steamy it could germinate orchids" (Greene, 1986), *Meritor v. Vinson* (1986) focused on an intimidating environment. A male supervisor exposed himself to Vinson, his female direct report, chased her into a restroom, and had intercourse with her several times over a period of years. The outcome of *Vinson,* the first U.S. Supreme Court case considering sexual harassment, hinged on the fact that the supervisor's behavior was unwelcome. Vinson said her supervisor's behavior definitely had been unwanted though she did not refuse his advances. The supervisor had neither threatened tangible job-related harm nor promised Vinson job benefits due to the sexual relationship. In a unanimous decision, the U.S. Supreme Court said that, irrespective of any economic impact, serious, pervasive, unwanted sexual behavior violates Title VII of the Civil Rights Act.

Meritor Savings Bank tried to deny liability due to its written policy banning discrimination. This attempt failed for two reasons. First, it directed employees to make sexual harassment complaints to their immediate supervisor and provided no bypass if the supervisor is the harasser, as he was in *Vinson*. Secondly, Meritor's policy did not specifically prohibit sexual harassment.

EMPLOYER LIABILITY: FARAGHER AND ELLERTH

In *Vinson,* the Supreme Court made no conclusive ruling on employer liability. Employers were found absolutely liable for supervisors' behavior in quid pro quo cases but not in hostile environment cases (Karsten, 1994). This ambiguity set the stage for clarification attempts in two 1998 decisions, *Faragher v. City of Boca Raton* and *Burlington Industries v. Ellerth.* In those cases, the Court tried, not completely successfully, to explain its new position regarding employer liability and the definition of supervisor. Because *Faragher* and *Ellerth* dealt with similar issues, only *Faragher* will be described at length.

In *Faragher v. City of Boca Raton,* a female lifeguard, Faragher, was employed during the summers and part-time during the rest of the year as a lifeguard for the Marine Safety Division in Boca Raton, FL. A male lieutenant and captain, both of whom reported to a male chief, Bill Terry, directly supervised Faragher. The lieutenant and captain gave daily assignments and oversaw training; the chief made hiring, firing, and disciplinary decisions (Blackman, 2001). The chief directed vulgar gestures and derogatory comments at the women lifeguards and touched them sexually without their consent. One of Faragher's direct supervisors behaved similarly. Faragher told her other direct supervisor about the offensive conduct. She did not view this as a formal complaint; apparently he did not, either, because he did nothing. The City had a sexual harassment policy, but it had not been distributed to the Marine Safety Division.

Faragher alleged quid pro quo and hostile environment harassment, but the City tried to avoid liability by claiming that harassing behaviors of Terry and his male underlings were "outside the scope of their employment" (Blackman, 2001, p. 137). The U.S. Supreme Court rejected that argument, broadening the definition of supervisor to include anyone who has immediate or successively higher authority over an employee. Under this definition, team leaders, who typically have informal position without much authority, could create employer liability by harassing team members. Previously, supervisors were defined as those with authority to make recommendations that would carry weight in hiring, firing, disciplinary, and other decisions having an impact on employees' status and work assignments.

In *Faragher,* the Supreme Court also stated a new standard for employer liability for sexual harassment. Employers were to be strictly and automatically liable for supervisors' illegal harassment in both quid pro quo and hostile environment cases. They could assert an *affirmative defense*, which, if proved, would absolve them of liability in intimidating environment cases, but not in the quid pro quo type.

The first part of the affirmative defense is that employers must take reasonable care to prevent or end workplace sexual harassment. Secondly, employees alleging harassment must "unreasonably" fail to avail themselves of employers' mechanisms for dealing with harassment or averting other injury

(Blackman, 2001). If those two elements can be proved, employers may avoid liability in a hostile environment case. In cases in which employees experience tangible actions, such as demotion, promotion denial, or unfavorable assignments, due to refusal to cooperate with requests for sexual favors or obtain pay raises or promotions for compliance, the affirmative defense is not available. Employers are strictly liable in such situations.

The U.S. Supreme Court settled the controversy about whether or not constructive discharge is a tangible employment action in *Pennsylvania State Police v. Suders* (2004). Constructive discharge occurs when employees feel their only choice is to quit their job due to intolerable conditions. Some lower courts argued that constructive discharge was a tangible employment action. If that view had prevailed, employers would have been subject to strict liability for sexual harassment without recourse to an affirmative defense. The high court ruled in favor of employers in *Suders* and said that they can assert an affirmative defense to protect themselves from liability stemming from constructive discharge.

THIRD PARTY SEXUAL HARASSMENT AND PARAMOUR PREFERENCE

The following scenario illustrates one form of illegal third party sexual harassment: Chris is better qualified for a promotion than Kim, but Kim receives it because her supervisor is sexually harassing her. Chris may file a harassment charge against the firm even if Kim makes no claim. Or the company could face simultaneous suits from Kim for sexual harassment by the supervisor and from Chris for third party harassment.

Employees who feel uncomfortable with the sexually explicit banter their coworkers consensually engage in at work also may file a third party sexual harassment claim. Another example of third party harassment involved a female operating room nurse in California. She was offended when male doctors repeatedly grabbed other nurses in front of her at work and filed a lawsuit to get them to stop (Hayes, 1991 cited in Karsten, 1994).

Third party harassment differs from paramour preference, which is legal. *Paramour preference* occurs when a consensual sexual liaison exists between a supervisor and employee. The boss then promotes the employee with whom he or she is having an affair. This sort of favoritism is linked to many human resource problems but is legal. Other employees who are denied the promotion lack a claim "because all of the individuals, whether women or men, are not disadvantaged because of their gender but because of the intimate relationship the manager enjoys with one favored person" (Wagner, 1992).

COSTS OF SEXUAL HARASSMENT

Sexual harassment is costly to individuals and organizations. It increases distress and contributes to physical problems from headaches and sleep problems to gastrointestinal disorders. Harassment affects employees psychologically and may lead to loss of self-esteem, anxiety, depression, and undeserved self-blame. For example, a woman in her 20s who was uncomfortable when a high-ranking male manager put his arms around her waist at a company event blamed herself for having worn a skirt with a slit in the back (Karsten, 1994). Sexual harassment harms careers of those who have been subjected to it. Even if they do not lose their jobs, which may happen as the result of being harassed, their job satisfaction and morale decline. Damaged work relationships may never recover (Equal Rights Advocates, 2005). Each year, federal employees, collectively, lose $4.4 million and use 973,000 hours of unpaid leave to deal with sexual harassment (Equal Rights Advocates).

Besides harming individuals, sexual harassment has negative consequences on organizations. Declining morale and job satisfaction may affect absenteeism and turnover, causing productivity to suffer. In Fortune 500 firms, absenteeism and turnover costs an average of $282 per employee annually (Equal Rights Advocates, 2005), or $6.7 million per company each year. The U.S. Department of Defense estimates losing over $43 million annually in absenteeism, turnover, additional recruiting costs, and productivity losses attributable to sexual harassment (U.S. Marine Corps, 1998).

Though difficult to quantify, the opportunity cost of sexual harassment is no small matter. It siphons time and energy from other pursuits.

Mounting a legal defense against charges of sexual harassment charges is pricey. Six-figure legal fees are not uncommon. Losing a lawsuit hurts a firm's bottom line, but settling a case is not cheap either. It cost ASTRA USA $10 million (Foy, 2000) and Mitsubishi $34 million (EEOC, 1998) to settle, excluding effects of adverse publicity, which undoubtedly damaged the reputation of both firms.

Foy (2000) believes that sexual harassment is the top financial risk factor for today's firms. Tarnishing a publicly traded firm's reputation, a likely result of a case of pervasive sexual harassment, may cause its market value to slip from five to 30% (Foy).

SEXUAL HARASSMENT PREVENTION:
ACTIONS OF ORGANIZATIONS AND INDIVIDUALS

Employers who are concerned about liability for harassment can take several steps to protect themselves. They must write an understandable policy, which must be distributed to all employees, explaining behaviors constituting harassment and prohibiting them. Training should be conducted covering suggestions for dealing with harassment, internal reporting mechanisms, the investigation process, and discipline to be administered in proven cases of harassment. Firms with Employee Assistance Programs (EAPs) should explain how they can be used to help employees being harassed and perpetrators. EAPs are essentially mechanisms to refer employees to appropriate social service or other agencies to deal with problems ranging from financial mismanagement to substance abuse. They will be discussed again in chapter 11.

Several ways to report harassment complaints should be established. Being able to discuss these concerns with others besides supervisors is important, because supervisors may be the harassers. Human resource managers and others known for fairness and sensitivity could serve as complaint intake personnel. They must be able to refer employees to other units for more assistance, if needed (Karsten, 1994).

Employees' harassment allegations must be taken seriously and investigated promptly, objectively, and as confidentially as possible. Additional specific recommendations for investigating sexual harassment charges are available on the EEOC web page. Incontestable evidence of sexual harassment should result in discipline commensurate with its severity. For example, repeated verbal harassment contributing to an offensive environment might result in a written warning. First degree sexual assault might be punished by immediate discharge. Demotions, suspensions, and pay cuts are examples of other possible penalties (Karsten, 1994).

When proving harassment is impossible, both parties should be told that the company seriously considered the charge. Alleged victims should be informed that their sincerity is not in question and that they are encouraged to report retaliation or additional harassment. Alleged harassers should be told that they have been cleared because insufficient evidence exists to take action but that future complaints will be considered seriously and investigated thoroughly (Segal and Schiller, 1991 cited in Karsten, 1994).

Ignoring sexual harassment typically does not eliminate it. Direct, open, assertive communication with the harasser may be effective, and, unless it is so severe that it causes them to fear for their safety, recipients of unwanted sexual attention are usually expected to let perpetrators know that their advances are unwelcome and must stop. Those who have been harassed must be specific and focus on the offensive conduct, not the person. Doing this is easier when harassing behavior has been on the mild end of the continuum. For example, Pat could say, "Jaime, your constant attempts to give me backrubs in the office make me uncomfortable. I want to maintain a professional working relationship with you, so please stop." If the backrubs continue, Pat should write Jaime a letter restating this request and indicating that she will follow the organization's formal procedures if the offensive conduct does not end. If no in-house procedures are available, Pat should state her willingness to file a charge with the EEOC. Generally, employees should exhaust company policies before pursuing legal remedies (Karsten, 1994).

Documentation is crucial if formal charges of sexual harassment are filed, so victims should record details regarding dates and times of incidents and what was said or done. They should also indicate names of any witnesses.

Employees who have been harassed need to know how to respond; those who want to avoid being accused also can benefit from some guidelines. The American Management Association offered suggestions in the 1990s that remain useful. People should ask themselves if they would say or do the same thing in the presence of their parents, spouse or partner, children, or same-sex peers. They should then think about how they would feel if their words were repeated or behavior exposed in the media or on the Internet. If they would feel comfortable doing or saying the same things, then the statements or actions probably would not be misinterpreted as harassment. If not, avoiding such statements or behavior would be wise (Meyer, 1992 cited in Karsten, 1994).

WHEN WORKPLACE ROMANCE SOURS: THE LINK TO SEXUAL HARASSMENT

In the 1980s employers were urged to deal with workplace romance if it affected performance. Just as they would intervene if some other problem contributed to a productivity decline, poor morale, or low quality work, managers were urged to deal with the "sticky but troublesome issue" of romantic involvement at work (Anderson & Hunsaker, 1985).

Over the next two decades, romantic workplace relationships flourished as people worked longer hours and the office became a primary meeting place. In that environment, employers wanted to respect privacy rights, and many adopted an informal non-interference approach to intimate workplace relationships. Such an approach seemed effective if romances were not between supervisors and subordinates and were handled discreetly without reducing morale or performance. A problem surfaced when romantic relationships ended, however. With their demise came the possibility of retroactive sexual harassment charges. The jilted party could claim that the relationship was never consensual. On the other hand, the party responsible for the break-up might say that the former lover's attempts to rekindle the romance constituted sexual harassment.

Some firms now address such situations proactively by asking employees involved in romantic relationships to identify themselves and sign "love contracts" (Schaefer & Tudor, 2001). These are legal documents in which the parties state that they are voluntarily involved in a consensual relationship and will not file a sexual harassment charge if it ends. Theoretically, this allows the parties to continue their personal relationship and absolves the employer of liability.

Sometimes when romantic relationships are damaging productivity and morale, employers might decide to transfer, demote, or fire one of the parties. If this seems necessary, employers must use extreme caution to avoid disparate impact discrimination. A policy that demotes the employee with less seniority or the lower position seems neutral but may have a disproportionately negative impact on women and may need to be avoided for that reason.

SEX-BASED, TRANSGENDER, AND RACIAL HOSTILE ENVIRONMENT HARASSMENT

Sex-based hostile environment harassment, which is sometimes called gender harassment, also is illegal. It is not sexual in nature but disparages individuals based on their sex. An atmosphere emphasizing or relying on sex role stereotypes contributes to sex-based harassment, and women or men may engage in this behavior targeting either sex. Mitzrahi (2004) argues that Title VII also bans conduct in which women systematically undercut and undermine other females based on sex because the law was designed to remove obstacles to career progress of women and minorities and reduce occupational segregation.

An egregious example of sex-based harassment involved male construction workers who disliked having female coworkers. Urinating in the gas tank of a female worker's vehicle, refusing to repair a dangerous condition in a truck their women peers needed to drive, and failing to unlock the door of a restroom the women needed to use were among their most blatant harassing acts (*Hall v. Gus Construction Co.* cited in Karsten, 1994).

Transgender harassment is a relatively new form. It may occur when an employee who is changing his or her sex gradually through surgery and other treatments is disparaged to the extent that the work environment becomes hostile. Employers should monitor lawsuits dealing with this rapidly evolving, volatile topic. So far, lower court rulings been inconsistent.

Racial harassment occurs when stereotypes, putdowns, and slurs belittling employees based on race create an offensive environment making it difficult for employees to do their jobs. "Graffiti, vandalism, actions to avoid someone, suggestion of unpleasant smell . . . comments and imitations of people's language with the intention to make fun, refusal to work with or train someone because of ethnic background" are examples of racial harassment (Milos & Kleiner, 2000, p. 20). Depending on the context, incidents may only need to occur once to be legally actionable.

From 1990 to 2001, racial harassment complaints rose 100% (Bernstein, 2001). Hispanics and Asian Americans filed more charges, but blacks filed the most (Bernstein). Major U.S. firms such as the FBI, Pizza Hut, Filene's in Boston, St. Louis-based May Department stores, and Macy's either received complaints or were named as defendants (Milos & Kleiner). These are in addition to highly publicized cases involving Boeing, Texaco, and Lockheed.

Perhaps, as Bernstein (2001) believes, the increased number of cases could be a positive sign, reflecting minorities' increased faith that their claims will be taken seriously and that flagrant harassment will not be tolerated. Finding anything positive in the rising number of racial harassment cases involving nooses reminiscent of lynching is impossible, however. During the 18 months ending in July 2001, the EEOC dealt with 25 such cases in locations from Marietta, GA to racially diverse urban centers such as Detroit and San Francisco (Bernstein).

Just as they must cope with double jeopardy discrimination based on race and sex, women of color face harassment based on both factors. The slavery legacy is relevant in explaining racial and sexual harassment that African American women experience. In early studies, African American women believed that white supervisors who harassed them would not be punished. That attitude is reminiscent of the subjugation associated with colonization and slavery (MacKinnon, 1979 cited in Muliawan & Kleiner, 2001).

In the past, African American women were reluctant to complain about sexual harassment. They did not want to jeopardize their position as indispensable wage earners in their families and had little faith in the legal system. In addition, they were aware of common stereotypes about their promiscuity, which they feared would be used against them. Changes in stereotypes and in the perceptions of the legal system held by African American women made them and other women of color more willing to come forward.

Though the percent of racial harassment cases has grown tremendously, most harassment cases are based on conduct that is sexual in nature, and most sexual harassment still is directed toward women. Pregnancy discrimination, a form that affects women exclusively, will be discussed next.

PREGNANCY DISCRIMINATION ACT OF 1978

Outrage over a U.S. Supreme Court case, *General Electric v. Gilbert* (1976), led to passage of the Pregnancy Discrimination Act of 1978 (PDA), which amended Title VII. *Gilbert* allowed firms to exclude pregnancy-related disabilities from their temporary disability insurance programs. Other non-job related injuries that men experienced were covered, and the public would no longer tolerate this double standard. Some covered injuries, they argued, disrupted a business more than pregnancy related disability, which could sometimes be anticipated. The PDA required pregnancy to be treated as a temporary disability in existing insurance plans but did not mandate employers without such programs to offer them to cover pregnancy-related disability.

The other more widely known provision of the PDA regards discrimination based on pregnancy, childbirth, or related medical conditions as illegal sex discrimination under Title VII. Women must not be refused employment due to pregnancy or related conditions if they can perform essential job functions. They must be treated the same as other applicants or employees with similar limitations and abilities and must not be fired based on the gender stereotype that the job will become secondary to family concerns after the child's birth. Refusal to hire also may not be based on prejudices of customers, clients, or coworkers.

The Pregnancy Discrimination Act often is confused with the Family and Medical Leave Act, passed much later in 1993. Provisions of the FMLA will be explained in chapter 10.

CIVIL RIGHTS ACT OF 1991

Just as the Pregnancy Discrimination Act was passed in response to *General Electric v. Gilbert,* the Civil Rights Act of 1991, also an amendment to Title VII, came about due to reaction to another U.S. Supreme Court case, *Wards Cove Packing v. Atonio* (1989). *Wards Cove,* a race discrimination case, gutted the concept of disparate impact discrimination, which had been used since it was discussed in *Griggs v. Duke Power* in 1971.

From 1971 until the *Wards Cove* case in 1989, workers filing discrimination suits had to demonstrate that an employment practice that seemed neutral had an adverse impact on women or minorities. In response, employers had to show that maintaining the questionable practice was a "business necessity." Statistical proof of a disproportionately negative effect on women or minorities was insufficient evidence of discrimination, according to *Wards Cove.* Until the Civil Rights Act of 1991 was passed, employers did not need to prove that the challenged practice was a business necessity. Instead, the burden of proof shifted to employees if employers could provide a legitimate reason for the practice. Employees had to demonstrate that it was not business-related, which was extremely difficult to do. Because of this, few employees won discrimination suits from 1989 until 1991 (Karsten, 1994).

The burden of proof standards established in *Griggs* were reinstated with the passage of the 1991 law. Statistical evidence that a neutral practice had a disproportionately negative impact on women or minorities once again established a presumption of discrimination. To successfully counter that assumption, employers were required to justify that the "neutral" practice was a "business necessity" (Karsten, 1994).

Besides making it easier for employees to win discrimination suits, the Civil Rights Act of 1991 contained several other provisions. Perhaps most notable are those permitting compensatory and punitive damages where they were not allowed before, providing for jury trials, and banning race norming. The Act also set up a Glass Ceiling Commission to make recommendations to aid career advancement of managerial women.

Punitive damages are awarded to deter future discrimination and punish those who engaged in it. Previously, those harmed by race discrimination could collect unlimited punitive damages, but sex discrimination and harassment victims who won lawsuits were eligible for only court costs and back pay. The 1991 Civil Rights Act allowed punitive damages in sex, age, and disability discrimination cases but capped them based on the size of the organization being sued. Damages ranged from $50,000 for firms with 15 to 100 employees to $300,000 for companies with more than 500 employees (EEOC, 1997). Women's groups were unhappy about the caps imposed on punitive damages in sex discrimination suits because unlimited punitive damages were permitted in race discrimination suits.

Race norming means adjusting cut-off scores by racial group when testing. For example, perhaps Hispanics applying for a position would need to score 80% on a job-related, valid test to proceed to the interview phase but African Americans would need to score only 70%. The Civil Rights Act of 1991 made this practice illegal.

PROPOSED FEDERAL LEGISLATION TO BAN DISCRIMINATION BASED ON SEXUAL ORIENTATION

Several states and cities prohibit employment discrimination based on sexual orientation, and federal legislation to do that was first introduced in the 1970s. Two attempts to pass the Employment Non-Discrimination Act, which would bar workplace unfairness based on sexual orientation, failed in the 1990s, and another unsuccessful attempt occurred in 2002.

EXECUTIVE ORDER 11246 AND AFFIRMATIVE ACTION

Unlike Title VII, Executive Order 11246, as amended, is a presidential decree. Executive orders are edicts issued by the president that are enforced as law unless Congress or the federal courts overturn them. The purpose and protected classes under Executive Order 11246 and Title VII are identical. The order bans discrimination based on race, color, religion sex, and national origin in hiring, firing, selection for a training program, compensation, and any other terms or conditions of employment.

Title VII is more widely applicable than Executive Order 11246. The latter applies to firms that are contractors or subcontractors with the federal government or to entities with federally assisted contracts, such as states receiving matching federal funds for a public works project. Two levels of compliance exist. Companies receiving at least $10,000 in government contracts must make a written commitment to equal employment opportunity. In addition, a written affirmative action plan, including hiring and promotion goals and timetables for their achievement for any protected group in the company that is underutilized, is required of firms with at least 50 employees and $50,000 in annual contracts.

An *affirmative action plan* is a results-oriented, ongoing process to identify underutilization of racial and ethnic minorities and women in employment and take steps to correct the problem. To assure accountability, a high ranking executive, who has top management's full support, should be in charge of implementing the affirmative action plan.

The firm must maintain records indicating the number and percent of women and minorities in each of several job categories. In a procedure called a "stock analysis," these data are compared to percentages of females and minorities who are both qualified for certain job categories and available in the geographic area from which the organization usually recruits for that job type. This geographic area is called the relevant labor market, and it varies based on the job class to be filled. For example, a company may recruit nationally or internationally for a specialized engineering position or for a chief executive. The relevant labor market for a clerical position, on the other hand, might be the county in which the office where the clerical employee will work is located. Generally, the relevant labor market is a larger area for highly paid jobs requiring advanced education and a smaller area for jobs demanding fewer skills (Karsten, 1994).

Underutilization occurs if the percent of women and minorities a firm employs is less than the percent of women and racial or ethnic minorities qualified for a job class in the relevant labor market. In 2002, about 47% of U.S. managers were women. Assuming a national labor market for managers, about 47% of the firm's executives should have been women in that year. If only 2% of its managers were women, females would have been underutilized in that job class. In each job class where underutilization exists, the organization must have written goals to raise percentages of minorities and women and timeframes for their achievement (Karsten, 1994). In the situation involving underutilization of women in managerial jobs, an appropriate affirmative action goal might be to increase the percent of managerial women from 2% to 6% over the next five years.

Goals must be realistic, specific, and achievable for at least two reasons. First, goals meeting these criteria are more likely to be viewed as sincere, and thus reachable, by internal and external constituents evaluating them subjectively. Constituents are not impressed by goals that are nearly impossible to achieve or by those that were set primarily to placate members of protected groups. Secondly, the agency enforcing Executive Order 11246, employees, and the community will view practical, precise goals more favorably than those that are unrealistic if unforeseen circumstances preclude attainment of targets. A company that sets achievable goals is more likely to be viewed as having made good faith efforts to address workforce disparities than one with unrealistic goals.

A firm must develop action plans to rectify underutilization. Specific steps that are expected vary based on the company's financial resources and whether it expects to hire or lay off employees. If workforce expansion is predicted, the firm might consider starting internship programs with colleges enrolling a large percentage of students who are racial or ethnic minorities. The company might be able to hire some of these interns after they graduate (Karsten, 1994). Other examples of possible action steps are focus interviews with target group members to gather input regarding reasons why their group is underutilized and use of alternative recruitment sources or new ways to announce job vacancies. If, on the other hand, the company expects to cut its labor force, certain action steps involving recruitment may be impossible and would not be expected.

A company must monitor affirmative action data periodically as part of an audit to ensure that minorities, women, and men are considered equally when selection and promotion decisions are made. If any goals are not met in a timely manner, the person designated to implement the affirmative action plan must try to establish the reasons (Karsten, 1994).

The Office of Federal Contract Compliance Programs in the U.S. Department of Labor, which enforces Executive Order 11246, may penalize companies that are required to have an affirmative action plan but do not. Injunctions, suspension or cancellation of current government contracts, bans from future contracts, and proceedings for filing false information are among the penalties. Non-complying firms may have their names published on a list designed to use public pressure to force compliance (Karsten, 1994).

Though affirmative action plans have been used to rectify employment inequities since the 1960s, they remain controversial, partly due to misunderstanding. Evans (2003, p. 129) claims that people who understand the details of affirmative action plans are more likely to see them as fair than those who do not. He concludes by saying that such plans "must not only be represented accurately" but "must also be practiced faithfully."

Misperceptions of affirmative action plans may stem from the fact that four different levels of programs exist. Kovach, Kravitz, and Hughes (2004) identify them, in order of strength, as equal opportunity, opportunity enhancement, "tiebreak," and strong preferential treatment. Equal opportunity, the weakest plan, tries to stamp out overt discrimination in hiring and in pay and promotion processes. Examples of opportunity enhancement, a form of affirmative action plan highly recommended by the OFCCP, are cultivation of new recruitment sources to produce a more diverse applicant pool, mentoring programs, and validation of tests and other procedures used to make employment decisions. "Tiebreak" programs allow an advantage to be given to females or racial/ethnic minorities when they and majority group candidates are equally qualified. Referring to three U.S. Supreme Court cases decided in the 1980s and 1990s, Kovach, Kravitz, and Hughes (2004) indicate that tiebreak plans must be flexible, temporary, and "narrowly tailored" to "address [compelling] interests." Also, they cannot hurt others disproportionately. A form of affirmative action plan that is illegal unless ordered by a court after a firm is found guilty of discrimination is called strong preferential treatment. This may entail passing up better qualified majority group members to hire qualified members of a target group. Kovach, Kravitz, and Hughes recommend avoiding strong preferential treatment plans because defending them is difficult.

Common arguments for and against affirmative action appear in Table 3.1. Most are self-explanatory; those to be explained further are argument 5 favoring affirmative action and argument 1 opposing it. By 1995, 6,000,000 white and minority women had advanced in the workplace due to affirmative action (Reverse discrimination, 1995), a clear indication of its effectiveness, as mentioned in argument 5. Affirmative action never required organizations to hire unqualified organizations; doing so would constitute an abuse of the program and would rightfully result in discrimination charges by qualified majority group members who were overlooked.

Though some have anticipated affirmative action's demise for years, it has survived. Even the 1996 California Civil Rights Initiative, otherwise known as Proposition 209, has not spread rapidly to other states as some feared and

Table 3.1.   Common Arguments For and Against Affirmative Action

For Affirmative Action:

Affirmative Action . . .
1. "Levels the playing field" in a society in which women and ethnic or racial minorities were systematically placed at a disadvantage in the past.
2. Draws women into occupations for which they may have talent but never considered.
3. Helps create a society in which all people's talents are used optimally.
4. Helps break down stereotypes.
5. Is effective in helping women and racial or ethnic minorities gain access to positions from which they were excluded in the past.
6. Is still necessary because workplace equality is not a reality yet; sociological phenomena such as discrimination, which have developed over millennia, take a long time to eliminate.

Against Affirmative Action:

Affirmative Action . . .
1. Promotes hiring of unqualified workers due to pressure to fulfill "quotas."
2. Leads to "reverse discrimination:
3. Stigmatizes intended beneficiaries; others may perceive that they obtained their positions due to affirmative action rather than ability and effort.
4. Reduces self-esteem of women and racial and ethnic minorities
5. Is ineffective. Equality in the workplace has not been achieved after two generations of affirmative action; it's time to try something else.
6. Has outlived its usefulness; organizations have moved beyond affirmative action and are now more interested in managing diversity effectively.

others hoped. That referendum was passed to repeal what were considered excesses of affirmative action. It prohibits the state; local governments; public universities, colleges, and schools; and other governmental agencies from discriminating against or giving preferential treatment to individuals or groups based on race, color, sex, ethnicity, or national origin in public education, employment, or contracting. Proposition 209 allows the use of BFOQs and compliance with Executive Order 11246, which is needed to obtain government contracts (Jung, 2004).

Some argue that Proposition 209 is logical for California, given its shifting demographics, and soon will make sense for other states. After all, affirmative action's main purpose was to redress past discrimination. As of the 2000 census, with whites just under 50% of the population, California had no numeric majority group. Hispanics, Asian, and African American populations have grown significantly in the state. If majority group status were determined solely based on numbers, this argument might carry some weight. Majority group status is, however, determined by power and wealth and their accompanying "perks."

If current demographic trends continue, however, changes in California's workforce and population will appear in the rest of the U.S. around the middle of the 21st century (U.S. Census Bureau, 2002). The federal government may, at some point, allow states to regulate and enforce affirmative action. Even if a few states decide to end affirmative action, organizational commitment to workplace equity will remain in the form of diversity management, which is the topic of chapter 4.

SUMMARY

Federal equal employment opportunity legislation such as the Equal Pay Act and Title VII of the Civil Rights Act of 1964 as amended by the Pregnancy Discrimination Act of 1978 and the Civil Rights Act of 1991 were discussed in this chapter as was Executive Order 11246 and the nature of affirmative action plans, which it required. Precedent-setting discrimination cases spanning more than three decades were presented. New standards in prosecuting harassment cases, most notably the affirmative defense, which employers can use to protect themselves if no tangible employment action was taken as a result of their behavior, were presented. Though the scenario of an older male sexually harassing a younger female remains common, other forms, such as same-sex and non-sexual gender harassment, and racial harassment occur and are illegal. Once again, women of color experience double jeopardy with respect to harassment.

Voices heralding the demise of affirmative action proved premature. Concern that measures such as California's Proposition 209 banning affirmative action would be passed in a majority of states was exaggerated. Two Michigan cases, *Gratz* and *Grutter* left affirmative action plans intact but clarified which features are and are not permissible.

EEO INCIDENTS

Suggestions for responding to questions raised by the following incidents: Do not indicate that making a decision is impossible due to insufficient information. Managers must make decisions based on incomplete information daily. Also, realize that there may be several different acceptable approaches to incidents that occur.

Best Qualified?

Joe is a white manager of a non-profit organization located in an area where few ethnic or racial minorities live. He is interviewing two finalists for an administrative assistant position. The two candidates are Sue, a Native American woman who looks to be in her 50s, and Brandi, a white woman who appears to be in her 20s. Both meet or exceed job qualifications. Sue has been described as an "awesome administrative assistant" and has excellent word processing and database management skills. She is eager to learn and has 15 years of experience in secretarial positions. Her references are impeccable. Brandi has two years of secretarial experience and is very reliable. She, too, has excellent references and very good word processing and database management skills. Joe has decided to offer Brandi the position because he believes he can save money by paying her less than he could have offered Sue. "Besides," he says, "Brandi is easy on the eyes." What concerns, if any, does Joe's decision raise? Would your response regarding concerns raised differ if Brandi were Hispanic, African American, Asian American or Native American? If so, how?

Hugh's Search Committee

Hugh, a white, middle-aged Vice President at a private university chaired a search committee for a position important to the entire campus. The newly hired individual would report directly to Hugh. Two white women and an African American man were finalists for the position. Committee members prepared interview questions, which Hugh summarized and distributed to the members. He told committee members participating in the 45–minute interviews that, during the interview of each candidate, they could choose the questions they wanted to ask on an impromptu basis from among about 25 on the summary sheet. Both female candidates were asked a question regarding an area in which they could improve, but the male candidate was not asked that question. The committee decided that one female finalist lacked sufficient experience for the position. The remaining female and the male applicant both were considered qualified, and an offer was made to the female candidate. She accepted. What aspect of this selection process, if any, could have equal employment opportunity implications? Explain.

REFERENCES

AFL-CIO. 2005a. It's time for working women to earn equal pay. Retrieved March 25, 2005 from http://www.aflcio.org/issuespolitics/women/equalpay/index.cfm?RenderForPrint=1

AFL-CIO. 2005b. Fact sheet: Equal pay for women of color. Retrieved March 25, 2005 from http://www.aflcio.org/issuespolitics/women/equalpay/FactSheetEqualPay_F_W_O_C.cfm

Anderson, C. & Hunsaker, P. 1985, Feb. Why there's romancing in the office and why it's everybody's problem. *Personnel.* 57–63.

Barone, M. 2004. July 2. A very civil act. *The Wall Street Journal,* A10.

Berman, J.B. 2000. Defining the 'essence of the business': An analysis of Title VII's privacy BFOQ after *Johnson Controls, 67*(3). 749–75.

Bernstein, A. 2001, July 30. Racism in the workplace: In an increasingly multicultural U.S., harassment of minorities is on the rise. *Business Week.* 37–43, 64–67.

Biles, G. 1981, June. A program guide for preventing sexual harassment in the workplace. *Personnel Administrator.* 49–56.

Blackman, S.A.H. 2001. The Faragher and Ellerth problem: Lower courts' confusion regarding the definition of 'supervisor.' *Vanderbilt Law Review, 54*(1). 123–64.

Deckard, B. 1983. *The women's movement.* New York: Harper and Row.

Equal Employment Opportunity Commission. 1997. The Civil Rights Act of 1991. Retrieved April 30, 2005 from http://www.eeoc.gov/policy/cra91.html

Equal Employment Opportunity Commission. 2004a. Enforcement guidance: Employer liability for unlawful harassment by supervisors. Retrieved on April 22, 2005 from http://www.eeoc.gov/policy/docs/harassment.html

Equal Employment Opportunity Commission. 2004b. Sexual harassment charges EEOC & FEPAs combined: Fy 1992–fy 2003. Retrieved January 20, 2005 from http://www.eeoc.gov/stats.harass.html

Equal Employment Opportunity Commission. 2004c. Trends in harassment charges files with the EEOC. Retrieved April 17, 2005 from http://www.eeoc.gov/stats/harassment.html

Equal Employment Opportunity Commission. 2005. Sexual harassment. Retrieved April 17, 2005 from http://www.eeoc.gov/types/sexual_harassment.html

Evans, D.C. 2003. A comparison of the other-directed stigmatization produced by legal and illegal forms of affirmative action. *Journal of Applied Psychology, 88*(1). 121–30.

Ford, R, & McLaughlin, F. 1988. Sexual harassment at work. *Business Horizons, 31*(6). 14–19.

Foy, N.F. 2000. Sexual harassment can threaten your bottom line. *Strategic Finance, 82*(2). 56–61.

Gomez-Meija, L.R. & Balkin, D.B. 1992. *Compensation, Organizational Strategy, and Firm Performance.* Mason, OH: South-Western Series in Human Resources Management, South-Western Publishing.

Greene, R. 1986, June 16. A pattern of fornication. *Forbes.* 66.

Hayes, A. 1991, Oct. 11. How the courts define harassment. *The Wall Street Journal.* B1.

Jackson, R.A. & Newman, M.A. 2004. Sexual harassment in the federal workplace revisited: Influences on sexual harassment by gender. *Public Administration Review, 64*(6), 705–17.

Jones, J. 1980, Fall. Lecture in equal employment law course. University of Wisconsin-Madison.

Karsten, M.F. 1994. *Management and Gender: Issues and attitudes.* Westport: Greenwood Publishing, Inc.

Kovach. K.A., Kravitz, D.A., & Hughes, A.A. 2004. Affirmative action: How can we be so lost when we don't even know where we are going? *Labor Law Journal, 55*(1). 53–61.

MacKinnon, C.A. 1979. *Sexual harassment of working women: A case of sex discrimination.* Westford, MA: The Murray Printing Co.

Meyer, A. 1992. Getting to the heart of sexual harassment. *HRMagazine, 37*(7). 82–84.

Milos, E. & Kleiner, B.H. 2000. New developments concerning racial harassment in the workplace. *Equal Opportunities International, 19*(6/7). 20–23.

Mizrahi, R. 2004. 'Hostility to the presence of women': Why women undermine each other in the workplace and the consequences for Title VII. *The Yale Law Journal, 113*(7). 1579–1621.

Muliawan, H. & Kleiner, B.H. 2001. African-American perception of sexual harassment. *Equal Opportunities International, 20*(5–7). 53–58.

National Committee on Pay Equity. 2004–2005a. Questions and answers on pay equity. Retrived February 2, 2005 from http://www.pay-equity.org/info-Q&A.html

National Committee on Pay Equity. 2004–2005b. Handling the arguments against pay equity. Retrieved February 2, 2005 from http://www.pay-equity.org/info-opposition.html

Norton, J.M. 2005, April 1. Lawsuit claims Smith Barney discriminates against women. Law.com. Retrieved April 28, 2005 from http://www.law.com/jsp/article.jsp?id=1112263513444

Reskin, B.F. 2000. Getting it right: Sex and race inequality in work organizations. *Annual Review of Sociology, 26.* 707–710.

Reverse discrimination of whites is rare, labor study reports. 1995, March 31. *New York Times.* A23.

Rudman, L.A. 1998. Self-promotion as a risk factor for women: The costs and benefits of counter-stereotypical impression management. *Journal of Personality and Social Psychology, 74*(3). 629–46.

Schaefer, C.M. & Tudor, T.R. 2001. Managing workplace romances. *S.A.M. Advanced Management Journal, 66*(3). 4–10.

Schultz, V. 1998. Reconceptualizing sexual harassment. *Yale Law Journal, 107*(6). 1683–1805.

Segal, T. & Schiller, Z. 1991, Oct. 28. Six experts suggest ways to negotiate the minefield. *Business Week.* 33.

Sprotzer, I. & Goldberg, I.V. 1992. Fetal protection: Law, ethics, and corporate policy. *Journal of Business Ethics, 11*(10). 731–36.

Taff, H.P. 2003. Tmes have changed? IABC Research Foundation's 'The velvet ghetto' study revisited. *Communication World, 20*(2).10–12.

Twomey, 1990. *Equal employment opportunity law.* Chicago: South-Western Publishing.

U.S. Census Bureau, Population Projections Program, Population Division. 2002. Total population by race, Hispanic origin, and nativity, 2050–2070. Retrieved April 30, 2005 from http://www.census.gov/population/projections/national/summary/np-t5–g.txt

U.S. Department of Labor. 2003, September. *Highlights of Women's Earnings in 2002.* Report 972. Washington, D.C.: U.S. Government Printing Office.

U.S. Government Accounting Office. 2003, October. *Women's earnings: Work patterns partially explain difference between men's and women's earnings.* GAO-04–35. http://www.gao.gov/cgi-bin/getrpt?GAO-04-35.

U.S. Marine Corps. 1998, July. Marines awaiting training program, student handout, sexual harassment. p. 6. Retrieved April 22, 2005 from www.tecom.usmc.mil/downloads/mat/102–sh.doc 1998

U.S. Merit Systems Protection Board (MSPB). 1995. *Sexual harassment in the federal workplace: Trends, progress, continuing challenges.* Washington, D.C.: U.S. Government Printing Office.

Wagner, E. 1992. *Sexual harassment in the workplace.* New York: Creative Solutions, Inc.

Wendt, A.C. & Slonaker, W.M. 2002. Sexual harassment and retaliation: A double-edged sword. *S.A.M. Advanced Management Journal, 67*(4). 49–57.

Chapter Four

Diversity Management:
From Melting Pot to Mosaic

OUTCOMES

After studying this chapter, you should be able to:

1. define monolithic culture, pluralistic organization, multicultural organization, the "business case" for diversity, systems approach, alternation approach to diversity, synergy.
2. Justify whether a more or less inclusive definition of diversity management would be preferable in an organization with which you are familiar.
3. Compare and contrast Thomas' and Ely's three diversity paradigms with the three approaches to diversity developed earlier by consultant, R. Roosevelt Thomas.
4. Compare and contrast equal employment opportunity and diversity management.
5. Explain several reasons why concern for workforce diversity and diversity management emerged when it did.
6. Justify whether or not you believe the benefits of diversity management outweigh the drawbacks in an organization with which you are familiar.
7. Explain how the diversity models developed by Taylor Cox and Allen & Montgomery are similar and different.
8. Explain the Katz & Miller Breakthrough/Inclusion Diversity Model to someone who is unfamiliar with the concept of diversity management.

As diversity management evolved over the past 30 years, imagery developed to illustrate a definition of the term that emphasized inclusiveness and each employee's contributions toward the achievement of the organization's goals, not in spite of, but because of individual differences. The melting pot, which supported assimilation, gave way to images of the diverse workforce as a salad bowl or a mosaic. If a stew in a melting pot simmers long enough, eventually the individual ingredients lose their identity, and the remaining liquid is less flavorful than it might have been otherwise. The overcooked stew is an example of the assimilation strategy that is inconsistent with an approach that values differences. A diverse workforce can be thought of as a salad with identifiable ingredients including greens and various vegetables. As each ingredient adds its own taste, each employee brings unique insights and skills to an organization. The salad bowl as an illustration of workforce diversity breaks down, however, because people's varying tastes cause disagreements regarding whether a particular vegetable enhances or detracts from the flavor. The mindset that values diversity insists that all differences add something beneficial to the organization. Another image that better illustrates the importance of valuing diversity is a mosaic. As each piece contributes to the picture, every employee has a unique role in the organization. If one piece of the mosaic is missing, the resulting picture is incomplete. Likewise, if one person does not contribute fully to the organization's goals due to the belief that his/her contributions will not be valued, the organization's performance may suffer.

Diversity management has been the topic of a flurry of books and articles, and the Society for Human Resource Management declared it the top issue in the field (Kersten, 2000). As of 1998, 75% of Fortune 500 firms had diversity management programs (SHRM releases new survey, 1998), and in the 1990s, 67% of large firms and 26% of medium sized firms had such programs (Brotherton, 2001). The number of empirical studies on diversity has quadrupled (Hays-Thomas, 2004) since the 1980s, and the number of diversity trainers has risen fourfold since 1990 (VonBergen, Soper & Foster, 2002). Because of the burgeoning information, covering the topic comprehensively in one chapter is impossible. For that reason, material in this chapter provides highlights of the literature. First, the controversy about the definition of diversity management will be summarized. Then reasons why diversity management evolved when it did, its similarities to and differences from equal employment opportunity, and its proposed advantages will be explained. Real and perceived drawbacks of diversity management will be discussed next, followed by a synopsis of representative approaches.

DIVERSITY MANAGEMENT: DEFINITIONS

Various perspectives exist regarding the most appropriate way to define diversity management. Some focus on voluntary programs to value each employee's unique contributions to an organization and embrace a wide variety of differences, whereas others advocate recognition of only differences that have caused inter-group inequality and resulting economic hardship. Consistent with the first approach, Loden and Rosener (1991) define *primary differences*, which they say cannot be changed at will, as gender, race, ethnicity, age, physical and mental abilities, and sexual orientation. They categorize religion, marital status, education, work background, military experience, and other variations as *secondary differences*. Other researchers do not distinguish between primary and secondary differences and include social class, income, personality traits, cultural worldviews, ideas, norms, traditions, job level, and job functions in their lists of factors on which humans may differ.

Many others have developed inclusive definitions of diversity management (Ely & Thomas, 2001; Cox, 2001; Kersten, 2000). Thomas and Ely (1996, p. 80) view diversity as the "varied perspectives and approaches to work that members of different identity groups bring." Cox (2001, p. 3) focuses on "understanding the effects" of "the variation of social and cultural identities among people existing together in a defined employment or market setting" and "implementing behaviors, work practices, and policies that respond to them in an effective way." Moving beyond social identities, Kersten (p. 236) describes diversity management at the organizational level as a "process of systemic cultural transformation designed to eliminate any further forms of exclusion."

Instead of focusing on diversity management, Strauss and Connerly (2003) study a construct called universal diverse orientation, which Milville et al. (1999, p. 291) define as "an attitude of awareness and acceptance of . . . similarities and differences that exist among people." They argue that an understanding of both similarities and differences is necessary to effectively manage diversity, and their research reveals a significant relationship between agreeableness, a personality dimension, and all aspects of universal diverse orientation. Agreeableness is defined as courteousness, tolerance, selflessness, and cooperation.

Overman's (1991) seemingly paradoxical definition of diversity couples "an acute awareness" of features that typically characterize a majority of the members of a group with the simultaneous treatment of each group member as an individual. Initially, this might seem like trying to walk forward and backward at the same time, but it is possible.

In the early 1990s, Elsie Cross (2000), the CEO of a highly respected diversity consulting firm, became concerned that the expansive definitions of diversity, which she claimed were developed to gain support of white males, would detract from underlying problems of sexism and racism. Linnehan and Konrad (1999) also believe that a broad definition may make diversity management meaningless. If it includes all differences, it could lose focus. Linnehan and Konrad argue that diversity should concentrate on the acceptance of differences in gender, race, ethnicity, and sexual orientation, which, when devalued in the past, caused economic harm.

The purpose of diversity management efforts as stated by various authors differs markedly. Linnehan and Konrad (1999) insist that it must be to "reduce inter-group inequality" and resulting power disparities. Others believe the purpose should be to "create a positive work environment for all employees" (VonBergen, Soper, & Foster, 2002, p. 239) so the organization's goals can be achieved or to "create greater inclusion of all individuals into informal social networks and formal company programs" (Gilbert, Stead, & Ivancevich, 1999, p. 61).

Because diversity management programs are so different, challenges in describing them are similar to those that a person who is blindfolded would experience when trying to explain the nature of an elephant by touching one part of the animal. The description would vary depending on whether the blindfolded individual touched the elephant's trunk or side.

Besides differing levels of management commitment to them, their degree of comprehensiveness, and specific techniques used, diversity management efforts vary in approach, the level at which they are implemented, and the culture of the organization in which they are introduced. For example, diversity may be addressed at the individual, group, or organizational/systemic level in cultures that are monolithic, pluralistic, or multicultural (Cox, 1991). R. Roosevelt Thomas (1990), a pioneer in the field and President of the American Institute for Managing Diversity, identifies affirmative action, affirming diversity, and diversity management as three approaches to diversity management. D. Thomas and Ely (1996) explain three paradigms for dealing with diversity, namely discrimination and fairness, access and legitimacy, and creation and maintenance of a learning organization. The levels at which diversity is implemented are self-explanatory; the cultures and paradigms merit additional discussion.

A *monolithic* culture has a homogeneous labor force comprised mainly of white males. Bias against minorities exists, but inter-group conflict is minimal because everyone is similar. Cox (1991) maintains that this culture is untenable for large employers. A *pluralistic* organization, typical of large organizations in the 1990s, features majority and minority cultures that adopt some of each other's norms. The labor force is more heterogeneous in a pluralistic than in a monolithic culture, but racial minorities remain concentrated at lower levels. An attempt is made to include racial and ethnic minorities in informal aspects of organizational life, but diverse employees are expected to repress their cultural identities to fit with the majority. Cox (1991) indicates that a pluralistic culture, characterized by high inter-group conflict and majority backlash, is consistent with an "affirmative action mentality." Few firms in the 1990s exemplified the ideal of a *multicultural* organization, which fully integrates majority and minority groups in all positions and informal groups, values, rather than tolerates, diversity, and has no bias and low inter-group conflict (Cox, 1991).

R. Roosevelt Thomas' *affirmative action* approach focuses on recruiting and hiring women and minorities. *Valuing diversity* is concerned with improving interpersonal relations among people with varying backgrounds, whereas *diversity management*, a term coined by Thomas, refers to overall, systemic change, which is necessary to realize long-term cultural benefits of employing people with divergent backgrounds and ideas.

Thomas and Ely (1996) expand on Thomas' ideas in their diversity paradigms. *Discrimination and fairness,* the first they describe, assumes colorblindness and leaders who pride themselves on due process and equal treatment. All employees must be treated with respect, but no attempt is made to capitalize on their differences. Sameness is valued, and achievement of recruitment and retention goals is paramount. Those who differ from the majority are expected to adopt the majority's culture. The U.S. military exemplifies this approach, which goes beyond numbers to include career planning and mentoring for women and minorities, but still reflects an affirmative action mentality. The importance placed on recruitment and hiring of women and minorities is similar to Thomas' affirmative action approach (1990), but Thomas and Ely's emphasis on retention and their other ideas expanded on Thomas' earlier proposal.

Access and legitimacy, the second paradigm, arose in the competitive business climate of the 1980s and 1990s when it was popular to "celebrate differences." Workforce diversity was considered advantageous when dealing with various clients, customers, and job applicants (Thomas & Ely, 1996). Firms wanted access to all customer niches and labor pools and legitimacy when dealing with them. Diverse employees were not integrated throughout the organization but were concentrated in customer service positions dealing with demographically similar clients. This reinforced an emphasis on differentiation of workers based on unchangeable characteristics. Some felt "used" because they were not welcome in all positions; others feared that they would lose their jobs during downsizing. Thomas and Ely (1996) said that the access and legitimacy paradigm resulted in career paths that were "tenuous and untenable." Cross (2000), agreed and noted that re-engineering and diversity management were incompatible.

Full integration of diverse individuals throughout the organization is the goal of the *learning and effectiveness* paradigm, later renamed the *integration and learning* approach. This perspective maintains that "we are all are on the same team *with* our differences, not despite them" (Ely & Thomas, 2001, p. 51). It infuses diverse ideas into the organization and urges employees to use knowledge and specific cultural skills gained outside the workplace to solve organizational problems. An example involved a Chinese woman employed as a chemist by an organization making soup in the food industry. A Chinese soup did not taste just right, but the woman hesitated to use her cultural knowledge about the taste of Chinese food and her culinary expertise because she feared being stereotyped based on ethnicity and gender and being perceived as less professional. She put those initial concerns aside for the good of the company and solved the problem (Thomas & Ely, 1996). If the learning and effectiveness model had been operating fully, she would have shared all of her skills initially regardless of how she had gained them.

The learning and effectiveness model opposes domination that might inhibit employees' contributions to the organization. It urges re-examination of the organization's main tasks, which could require the mission, markets, or products and services to be redefined based on perspectives of employees of differing backgrounds (Thomas & Ely, 1996). In its analysis of the entire organization, the learning and effectiveness model resembles what Thomas (1990) called managing diversity.

Critics of the learning and effectiveness approach argue that it stereotypically assumes that women and minorities have different perspectives as a result of their gender, race, or ethnicity. In this view, Thomas' and Ely's paradigm advocates "a way of thinking which perpetuates the impression that knowledge of how to do work is automatically different if one is a man, a woman, or from one ethnic origin rather than another" (Lorbiecki, 2001, p. 355). Others spurn the idea that "some extrinsic and essential content to any identity, defined either by a common origin (e.g. place of birth, racial heritage) or a common structural experience" (Lorbiecki, p. 356) exists.

Studying diversity is difficult because of the lack of consensus on the definition, the sensitivity of the topics that must be investigated, and the fear of lawsuits. In addition, until recently, tools available to measure other aspects of management effectiveness were not used to analyze diversity efforts. Unless diversity initiatives are studied systematically, however, evaluating their effectiveness will be impossible.

REASONS FOR DIVERSITY MANAGEMENT

Demographic trends predicted in *Workforce 2000* (Johnston & Packer, 1987) and *Workforce 2020* (Judy & D'Amico, 1997) spurred the growth of diversity management programs in the 1990s. Other contributing factors were a desire to go beyond equal employment opportunity and affirmative action, a move which was designed to increase support of white males in powerful positions, lawsuit avoidance, a growth in acquisitions and mergers, the importance of the service economy, and globalization. Kelly and Dobbin (1998) suggested another explanation—job security for diversity trainers.

The net increase to the labor force of white, male entrants who were born in the U.S. was predicted to be only 15% from 1988–2000 (Johnston & Packer, 1987), but because they represented 47% of the labor force at the beginning of the period, a relatively low net gain left a workforce comprised of 41% white males at the end of that time frame (Hays-Thomas, 2004). Overall, in the 1990s, the workforce grew at a slower pace than it had previously, a trend that may continue (Judy & D'Amico, 1997). Forty-three percent of new entrants in the 1990s were immigrants or racial and ethnic minorities from the U.S.; the remaining 42% were white women (Johnston & Packer, 1987).

One-third of the population of the U.S. consists of ethnic minorities; collectively, they will comprise over half the population by 2010 (Neukrug, 1994). Sixty-five percent of the population between the ages of 16 and 64, who are most likely to be in the labor force, are expected to be non-Hispanic whites, 28.4% will be Hispanics of any race or blacks, 5.4% will be Asians or Pacific Islanders, and less than 1% will be Native Americans by 2015 (Populations Projections Program, 2000). The Hudson Institute estimates that one-third of the workforce in 2020 will be made up of ethnic and racial minorities (Judy & D'Amico, 1997), which is consistent with predictions regarding percentage breakdowns by race and ethnicity in the entire population. Further, the workforce is expected to continue to age through 2020, at which point a large percentage of the baby boomers, those born between 1946 and 1964, will retire.

What implications do these trends have for diversity management? Slower labor force growth among white males makes it imperative for business to recruit, retain, and fully utilize the talents of women and minorities in all positions. Ethnic and racial minorities will make up a huge proportion of the consumer market and may prefer to buy products and services from organizations that demonstrate that they value diversity. To retain a workforce and appeal to a wide range of customers, organizations must deal with diversity effectively.

Diversity management can be described as an outgrowth of equal employment opportunity, which was legislated in the 1960s, and affirmative action, which began to affect employment after former President Nixon issued Revised Order Number 4 in 1972. Many practitioners distinguish diversity from

EEO and affirmative action, to the consternation of some diversity consultants and experts (Cross, 2000; Linnehan & Konrad, 1999). Linnehan and
Konrad (1999) describe the distancing of diversity management from equal
employment opportunity as "unfortunate" because it will detract from the reduction of inter-group inequality.

Due to misunderstandings or distortion of affirmative action requirements,
a stigma some intended beneficiaries felt, and instances of poor implementation of the plans, some wanted to make sure that diversity initiatives were not
considered affirmative action plans by another name (Yakura, 1996). Efforts
to distinguish the two have not been completely successful, however.

Table 4.1 presents similarities and differences between equal employment
opportunity/affirmative action and diversity management. Equal employment
opportunity is an ideal that allows everyone a chance to get a job and be promoted based on qualifications, not on factors beyond their control, such as
race and gender. Firms must not discriminate, but, other than that, no extra
steps are required. Affirmative action, on the other hand, requires employers
to be proactive. They must seek and hire qualified women and minorities in
the geographic area from which they usually recruit for specific positions and
consider them for promotion.

Misunderstandings about affirmative action that alienate majority group
members include confusion about or distortion of the meaning of goals and
quotas and the mistaken belief that affirmative action requires employers to
hire unqualified individuals due to their race or gender. *Affirmative action
plans* require organizations to set achievable, numeric goals to increase the
percentage of women and minorities with the requisite skills in job categories
where they have been determined to be underrepresented compared to their
availability. Employers must make "good faith efforts" to reach goals, which
must *not* be seen as rigid quotas. The latter always have been illegal. Some
have ignored that important distinction.

Though poor implementation practices may have given a different impression, affirmative action plans require firms to hire only applicants who are qualified for positions they seek. Employers may have had to justify certain job requirements to make sure that they are necessary job related skills rather than a
pretext for discrimination, however. For example, a bachelor's degree in accounting is essential for some positions because the knowledge and skills gained
are vital to job performance. For other positions, accounting skills and knowledge acquired through experience and training may suffice. Requiring a college
degree in accounting for the latter positions might be a pretext for discrimination
if it excludes people who would have performed the job satisfactorily.

Because whites are currently in the majority in the U.S., most do not consider race to be an important status. As do most privileged groups, they take

Table 4.1.   Similarities and Differences between Equal Employment Opportunity and Diversity Management

Similarities:

Underlying purposes for both are to improve utilization of people whose talents have not been fully used in the past and to improve their workplace conditions

Ethics and social responsibility were among the original motivating factors for development of both.

Quantitative assessment of each is emphasized currently.

Some implementation strategies are similar.

Factor	*Differences*	
	Equal Employment Opportunity	Managing Diversity
Purpose	Avoid discrimination	Value & use contributions of all
Coverage	"Protected classes" under Title VII of the Civil Rights Act, Americans with Disabilities Act, Age Discrimination in Employment Act etc. (narrower)	All employees and prospective employees
"Ownership" of Issue	Human resource managers	All managers and employees
Focal Point	Organizational Entry (recruitment and selection)	Upward mobility and full utilization
Motivating Factors	Legal compliance; avoidance Lawsuits	Business reasons—to obtain competitive advantage, deal with demographic shifts, increase innovation
Acculturation	Assimilation	Integration
Duration	Temporary	Ongoing; continuous
Historical Measurement/Assess.	Quantitative change	Qualitative change

their race for granted and consider it "normal." Because of this, mid- to upper class whites may hotly contest the notion that they have been recipients of unearned privilege. They may believe in meritocracy and attribute success to their own efforts. For this reason, they may perceive reductions in unearned privilege that are necessary to promote workplace equality for previously disenfranchised groups as losses and, therefore, oppose affirmative action. Linnehan and Konrad (1999) believe that such perceptions by the majority may be unavoidable. They suggest including white males in diversity management programs because they hold most top positions and, therefore, must approve diversity initiatives and because they may be asked to change their behavior as part of such efforts. These authors believe diversity initiatives should avoid focusing too much attention on white males, because, as a group, they remain quite powerful.

Diversity efforts instigated to avoid lawsuits have not always achieved that goal. Initiatives that backfired and led to legal action they were intended to prevent will be discussed later in this chapter along with other potential drawbacks of diversity management.

In addition to the factors already described, changes ranging from a soaring number of mergers and acquisitions in the 1990s to the ongoing globalization of business contribute to enthusiasm for diversity management programs. Such initiatives also are relevant when different corporate or social cultures must coexist. For example, contributions of employees from an acquired firm must be valued to avoid a mass exodus of talented individuals. Sometimes, one group with the same functional expertise in a merged unit seeks dominance and tries to devalue the talents of those who are skilled in other fields. Without plans to effectively manage all skills represented in the combined unit, morale may deteriorate and other negative consequences may follow.

Globalization has made it increasingly important for employers not only to minimize cultural errors but also to understand and work with people of various backgrounds. Widespread electronic communication allows even small entrepreneurs in rural areas to do business globally, but they must be adept in dealing with cultural differences without the nonverbal cues that face-to-face communication provides.

Kelly and Dobbin (1998) think that EEO/AA practitioners' self-interest influenced the timing of the emergence of diversity management. Because they wished to remain employed and were concerned about threats to affirmative action that began in the 1980s, these specialists "transformed themselves into diversity managers" and "repackaged" components of affirmative action plans as diversity initiatives (Kelly & Dobbin, p. 963). CEOs who publicly resolved in the 1980s to continue using quantitative goals and timetables to track the progress of women and minorities regardless of any legal requirements "resisted the dismantling of EEO/AA programs . . . because the specialists . . . that administered them had become integral to the management team" (Kelly & Dobbin, p. 970).

Most of the major reasons why diversity initiatives flourished beginning in the 1980s have been explained. Perceived and empirically supported benefits of diversity management to organizations and associated challenges and drawbacks will be addressed next.

POTENTIAL BENEFITS

The "business case" for diversity suggests that effective management of differences increases profits due to a competitive advantage gained by being a leader in attracting and retaining employees in a slowly growing labor pool. The time to realize such an advantage may have passed, however, because so many companies already have begun diversity initiatives. Organizations without processes to guarantee that all workers' talents are used fully will be at a disadvantage in the labor market.

A workforce that is demographically similar to customers might provide a competitive advantage if employees are more knowledgeable about customers who resemble them. Clients might feel more comfortable with company representatives who share demographic characteristics. This argument has drawbacks, however, because it could cause racial and ethnic minority employees with many talents to be pigeonholed in customer service and not offered other opportunities, thereby underutilizing them. There might be a tendency for customers to want to deal exclusively with employees who are like them, which was an unacceptable reason for employment discrimination in the 1970s. At that time, companies claimed that they had to hire men because their customers or clients refused to deal with women in certain positions. This was not a valid excuse for sex discrimination in decades past, and a desire to deal only with employees of one's own ethnic group remains objectionable today.

Diversity management may enhance profits through reduction of turnover and absenteeism, increased productivity on complex tasks, enhanced problem solving, greater creativity and innovation due to the synergistic effects provided by many different perspectives, and decreased lawsuits and penalties due to discrimination. Besides boosting profits, diversity management may lead to other desirable outcomes such as improved employee morale, satisfaction, and commitment to the organization's goals, reduction of interpersonal conflict and formal grievances, enhanced teamwork, and improved communication. Managing differences successfully may allow more energy to be directed toward other organizational opportunities and create a flexible system that reacts to environmental changes quickly.

In the aftermath of accounting and mutual fund scandals that were exposed after 2000, ethical conduct was re-emphasized. In an environment characterized by renewed concern about ethics, diversity management may demonstrate a firm's ethical commitment to reduce inter-group inequality. Some organizations may start or continue diversity management programs as evidence of their social responsibility.

At the end of the 1990s, researchers called for empirical studies to examine whether or not the touted advantages of diversity exist and, if so, the circumstances in which they will materialize. A need for additional empirical research remains. Tools have been developed to measure the effects of diversity management, which must be done to verify the impact on the organization's performance. Hubbard's (2003) Diversity Return on Investment is an example of one such tool.

Some studies have verified a link between successful diversity efforts and sales and productivity. In terms of productivity, profit, and reduced absenteeism, branches of a bank with diverse employees outperformed those with a homogeneous workforce (Ng & Tung, 1998). In a study of 63 banks, a firm's growth strategy moderated the impact of diversity on productivity. Richard (2000) found that productivity, sales, market share, and profits rose in racially diverse firms that were expanding. Association does not necessarily indicate causality, however, and other variables may have been responsible for such increases. In one study from 1988 to 1992, firms that were ranked in the lowest one-fifth for recruiting minorities and women were eight percentage points behind the stock market, whereas those in the highest one-fifth were two points ahead of the market (Equal Opportunity Pays, 1993).

Gilbert and Stead (1996) replicated an earlier study (Heilman, Block, & Lucas, 1992) showing that organizations that valued diversity considered female employees to be more qualified for their positions than firms that did not. This was referred to as a "positive spillover effect" of concern for workplace diversity (Gilbert, Stead, & Ivancevich, 1999).

POTENTIAL DRAWBACKS

Separating drawbacks associated with inappropriate or inadequate implementation strategies and/or the superficiality of some diversity management programs from their underlying concepts is difficult. Some have derided diversity management as "too simplistic" (Kersten, 2000; Kochan et al., 2003). Employees in diverse units may not necessarily be more satisfied or committed to their firms or have higher performance levels than those in homogeneous units (Jackson et al, 1995; Millikin & Martins, 1996; Williams & O'Reilly, 1998). According to Kersten (2000), diversity programs have not even demonstrated effectiveness in eliminating employment discrimination. Only one-third of firms that completed diversity training indicated that their efforts were successful; nearly one-fifth indicated the initiative was unsuccessful (Rynes & Rosen, 1995). Specific training could have been considered ineffective due to poor implementation, which includes unskilled trainers.

Though some consultants are worth every cent, as in any potentially lucrative, unregulated field, a few unqualified individuals have done more harm than good. The conduct of a diversity trainer at the University of Cincinnati was egregious—even cruel. He told a white, male graduate student who recently lost his father that the death had removed one more racist influence from the student's life (Von Bergen, Soper, & Foster, 2002).

Some might argue that confrontational tactics have a place in diversity training, but they can create resistance where none exists otherwise. For example, a middle aged white woman whose family volunteers regularly at an inner city organization to assist a particular racial/ethnic minority was offended by a diversity consultant's approach at a mandated training seminar. At the beginning of the session, the consultant arbitrarily walked over to a few participants, looked them in the eye, and said "You are racist." The middle-aged woman thought she had been stereotyped based simply on race.

Besides using questionable methods, Von Bergen, Soper, & Foster (2002) list other mistakes diversity trainers commonly make. These include:

1. the expectation that only one group needs to change or that the trainees are "the problem,"
2. "too little" training which is done too late or in response to a crisis,
3. an appearance of "political correctness" that, ironically, can put off those with differing views,
4. narrow—or no—definitions of terms,
5. outdated materials, and
6. selection of trainers based primarily on their minority group membership.

Remaining drawbacks of diversity management relate to increased dysfunctional conflict, resistance, backlash, and lawsuits, which properly managed diversity initiatives are supposed to reduce. Efforts that focus on demographic changes alone to improve the organizational climate also may be ineffective.

A thorough discussion of all the types of conflict that could be associated with diversity management is beyond the scope of this book. Interpersonal conflict and emotional/relationship inter-group conflict may lead to greater understanding and constructive resolution of problems if handled properly. If not, they might result in avoidance of coworkers. Thomas, Mack, and Montagliani (2004) found that emotional/relationship conflict may cause absenteeism, turnover, and lowered satisfaction of employees but uncovered no evidence that these consequences impede work group performance (Pelled, Eisenhardt, & Xin, 1999).

Diversity management programs that produce creativity and innovation might simultaneously increase conflict and turnover (Williams & O'Reilly, 1998). Kersten (2000, p. 246) argues that much racial conflict has gone underground and that diversity efforts that do not substantively affect organizational structure or power relations "have not altered, but merely diverted the location and expression of the conflict."

Avoiding the diversity training mistakes mentioned earlier might lessen resistance to diversity efforts and backlash from both majority and minority group members. Still, Lorbiecki (2001, p. 354) reports that Gordon's studies (1995) document instances of "white rage and political correctness as well as a sense of frustration and disappointment from women and ethnic groups who feel that diversity has failed to deliver its promise of greater equality."

Diversity training is supposed to lessen the incidence of lawsuits, but Lucky Stores and Texaco faced legal action due to misinterpretation that occurred during a diversity workshop. A common technique to dispel race- and gender-based myths involves asking participants to list such stereotypes so their inaccuracies can be discussed. When managers at Lucky Stores, a food store chain in California, mentioned stereotypes during a workshop when they were asked to do so, offended participants submitted notes from the session as evidence against the company, and it was found guilty of discrimination and fined $90 million in damages (Von Bergen, Soper, & Foster, 2002).

In another misunderstanding, an audiotape of a Texaco executive's conversation which was secretly recorded was submitted as evidence of discrimination against African Americans. When taken out of context, the executive's remarks sounded like racial slurs, but they referred to an analogy used in diversity training. Nevertheless, as Von Bergen, Soper, and Foster (2002, p. 247) pointed out, "the incredible result was that MORE diversity training was recommended as a solution to the problem—which was caused by diversity training in the first place."

CONTEXT-DEPENDENT RESULTS OF DIVERSITY MANAGEMENT

Results of some diversity initiatives are positive or negative depending on the type of diversity and the context. For example, gender diversity is positively linked to bonuses in groups only in units that have "a people-oriented organizational culture, diversity-focused human resource practices, and customer-oriented business strategy" (Kochan et al., 2003, p. 10). In units with competitive organizational cultures, growth oriented business strategies, and human resource practices focused on training, but not in other contexts, racial diversity is negatively associated with performance (Kochan et al.).

DIVERSITY MANAGEMENT THEORIES AND MODELS

Additional paradigms for diversity management besides the earlier models Cox (1991) and Thomas and Ely (1996) developed have been proposed. The earlier models typically included three approaches to diversity on a continuum ranging from reactive to proactive, and organizations were urged to adopt proactive approaches (Agars & Kottke, 2004). Golembiewski's (1995) model defines five methods ranging from "diversity under duress" to "managing diversity" and identifies factors driving each. For example, the need to solve a specific problem is the motivating factor in "diversity under duress," and the achievement of organizational goals motivates behavior in the "managing diversity" approach.

Though Cox's (2001) revised approach is practitioner-oriented and Allen and Montgomery's (2001) model is theoretical, both view diversity management as an overall, ongoing change process, which takes years, not months, to implement. These models appear in Figures 4.1.A and 4.1.B. An underlying feature of Cox' model is the *systems approach*, or the idea that each element has an impact on every other element and on the entire organization. Allen and Montgomery, on the other hand, explicitly show how diversity management fits into the organizational change process popularized by Lewin (1951). The Leadership and Research & Measurement phases of Cox's model, collectively, seem similar to the Unfreezing stage of the Allen and Montgomery model. Techniques listed under Research & Measurement by Cox could provide data to create a "felt need for change," which would be important in the Unfreezing stage (Allen & Montgomery, 2001). Education, as described by Cox (2001), could be an important means for implementing the Moving phase in the Allen and Montgomery model. Items in the "Aligning Management Systems" phase (Cox, 2001) could relate to Moving or Refreezing (Allen and Montgomery). Allen and Montgomery did not address systematic follow-up, but that might be because they emphasized theory rather than practice. Nevertheless, items in the Alignment of Management Systems phase (Cox, 2001) that Allen and Montgomery excluded from the Moving phase are consistent with their Refreezing stage. Allen and Montgomery depart from their theoretical bent in the last part of their model, which they call "Competitive Advantage." Rather than a phase, this is a list of advantages of managing diversity effectively.

Agars and Kottke (2004, p. 67) developed a *full integration model,* which "identifies diversity change management as a multi-level, systems-based, three-tier process." Except for the fact that *full integration* is practitioner oriented, there could be a one-to-one correspondence between its three main phases, issues identification, implementation, and maintenance, and the phases of Unfreezing, Moving, and Refreezing in the Allen & Montgomery model. Unlike Allen & Montgomery, however, Agars and Kottke examine the impact of four perceptual processes which can facilitate or derail diversity initiatives. These are perceptions of threat, utility, and justice, and social perceptions, which include stereotypes or social identities. Perceived threat may

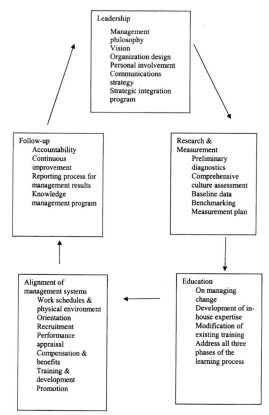

Figure 4.1A.   Practitioner-Oriented Model of Diversity Management

lead to rigid, closed responses that could stymie diversity endeavors. Utility refers to financial benefits or gains and justice to the perceived fairness of diversity management to all organization members. Social perceptions can influence thought processes to make them either receptive or hostile to greater organizational inclusiveness. Perceptions of utility are crucial to manage in the issues identification phase to avoid stagnation of diversity initiatives; the other perceptions are considered crucial in the implementation phase for the same reason (Agars & Kottke, 2002).

Agars and Kottke (2004) summarize the ecosystems view (Mor-Barak, 2000) and alternation (LaFromboise, Coleman, & Gerton, 1993), other approaches to diversity, and discuss additional factors that could affect the relative success of diversity initiatives. The ecosystems view proposes that organizations, as members of society, should incorporate responsibility to their communities in diversity efforts. In alternation, members of minority groups

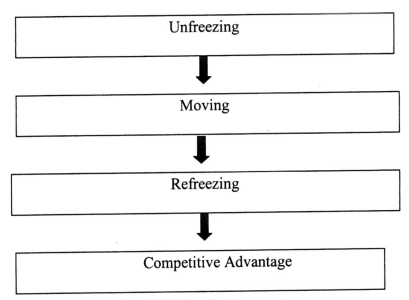

Figure 4.1B. Theoretical Model of Diversity Management

expand their repertoires to include cultural behaviors associated with majority and minority cultures. They enact the behavior that seems most appropriate in a particular situation. Though majority group members also might benefit from learning new behaviors associated with minority cultures, the alternation model does not ask them to do so.

Though not as elaborate as the Cox or Allen and Montgomery models, other research findings have implications for diversity management. For example, Schneider and Northcraft (1999) show that decisions people make when they believe outcomes will inevitably conflict are influenced by their social identities. Knowing this might help diversity educators and managers understand reasons for resistance to diversity and develop strategies to overcome them. Similarly, leaders of diversity efforts should understand that the level of group diversity and members' tolerance for new experiences will affect group performance through their impact on thought processes, as Austin (1997) demonstrated.

PHASES OF DIVERSITY MANAGEMENT INITIATIVES

Diversity initiatives should not be reduced to a series of "how to" steps. Progress in managing diversity effectively may not proceed linearly, and setbacks may occur. One author has compared the implementation of diversity management to a trip in a car with a small child, who asks, repeatedly, "Are we there yet?" With respect to diversity management, the answer is "no." Just as automobiles traveling to the same destination may be at different points after a few hours based on their rate of speed, their route, and the number and length of stops they made, organizations aiming for greater inclusiveness are at different points on the journey depending on several factors (Saunders, 2003).

Unlike a journey with a fixed destination, diversity management, as an ongoing process, has no endpoint. Progress can be made, but there always will be room for improvement. Firms with diversity practices against which other organizations compare their efforts include AT&T, Corning, Xerox, and U.S. West. Even these firms are likely to continue to evaluate diversity efforts and hold managers accountable for their implementation. This constant monitoring enables them to deal with diversity-related challenges before they become major problems.

Diversity management is a comprehensive, long-term commitment to organizational change in which the unique contributions of each worker are valued and inter-group inequality is reduced. It is beyond the scope of this book to teach individuals how to become successful diversity educators or consultants, but examining common stages that occur after organizations decide to embrace diversity and recognizing that standardized programs are ineffective is instructive. Suggestions regarding diversity education must be tailored to the characteristics of the organization seeking to better manage differences.

A Breakthrough/Inclusion model (Katz & Miller, 2003) proposes four phases for implementing diversity management, which appear Table 4.2. They rarely proceed linearly but must be depicted that way due to the limitations of the printed page.

The Breakthrough-Inclusion model is based on four principles, which are:

1. development of linkages, or *synergy*, so that the "whole is greater than the sum of the parts,"
2. leadership at all levels,
3. continuous learning that considers mistakes part of the process instead of calamities, and
4. leverage points, which are cultivated to gain the largest payoff from each diversity activity by concentrating on those who are receptive to the message.

Phase I, Building the Platform for Change, combines elements in two stages of Cox' change model (2001), namely *Leadership* and *Research & Measurement.* Convincing the organization's leaders of the "business case" for diversity is part of this phase. Though diversity management is considered socially responsible, it should not be undertaken for that reason alone. Leaders must understand the reasons, which were explained earlier in this chapter, why they must deal effectively with diversity.

Diagnosis and communication of the current situation are critical to Phase I. Powell and Graves (2003) and Thomas and Ely (1996) recommend a cultural audit, which the former define as a "snapshot of the culture as experienced by employees." Without effective diagnostic tools, setting goals for improvement is impossible. Tools must be chosen considering the characteristics of the organization. Cox (2001) advocates *triangulation*, which means using several tools to approach a phenomenon from different angles. Plummer (2003) lists commonly used tools in diversity diagnosis, namely questionnaires, interviews, observation, focus groups, benchmarking, and diversity dialogue sessions.

To have credibility, a team that leads a diversity initiative must include members from a variety of backgrounds and functional areas. For that reason, only one or two human resource managers should be on the team.

Top management support is necessary but insufficient for effective diversity initiatives (Powell & Graves, 2003; Cox, 2001). Supervisors and managers at all levels must understand the importance of dealing effectively with customer, employee, and labor force diversity. This commitment by all leadership levels must start in Phase I and continue indefinitely. Nothing is more likely to cause diversity efforts to stagnate than a loss of support from the senior levels. In the 1990s, Cox (2001) experienced this while working with a mid-sized insurance company and an engineering and research firm. In both organizations, a CEO who was committed to diversity left and was replaced by someone who was less dedicated to the concept. This led to de-emphasis of diversity and predictably lackluster results.

In Phase II, Creating Momentum, Katz and Miller promote an initial 12–18 month strategy for implementing the organizational change that diversity management represents, followed by a long-term strategic plan developed in Phase III. Cox (2001) argues that these time frames are too short for most large organizations. Instead, he proposes planning horizons of two to three years because he believes it will take six to nine years for many organizations to meet their benchmarks, which is consistent with estimates that creating lasting changes in an organization's culture takes seven to ten years. Cox admits that cultural change may occur more quickly in smaller organizations because of their greater flexibility.

Education efforts begun in Phase I will be expanded in Phase II. Cross (2000) indicates that consultants in her firm develop clients' "internal capacity" to manage diversity with the goal of eventually putting themselves out of

Table 4.2.   Breakthrough/ Inclusion Model

		Recommended Actions		
Phase 1: Building the platform for change	Position effort to be a way of life; establish the organizational imperative for the culture change	Undertake organizational assessment, i.e., "giving voice" sessions; begin education and alignment of senior leaders	[Conduct] feedback session with learning partners; identify internal identify internal leadership for the change effort	Take immediate actions in areas that need attention and/or "make a statement" about the commitment to the culture change
Phase 2: Creating momentum	Develop initial 12-to-18-month plan	Implement aggressive efforts to engage, inform and enroll the people of the organization; develop a critical mass of agents of change	Begin education to create new competencies for senior leaders, managers, individual contributors; create processes to address blatant or subtle discrimination/barriers	[Create] support networks, mentoring, coaching and buddy systems; identify and begin work in "pockets of readiness"
Phase 3: Making diversity and inclusion a way of life	Expand the initial plan to a long-term strategic plan that integrates and partners with all change initiatives	Formalize accountability for living the competencies in the new culture (scorecards & other tools); [Integrate building inclusion . . . and] leveraging diversity into all training and [educational] programs	Implement incentives and rewards to support the culture change and to create organizational pull; enhance performance feedback systems to support the new culture	Involve stakeholders (e.g.: suppliers, joint ventures, a community, board members, acquisitions)
Phase 4: Leveraging learning	Reassess organization to identify progress and gaps; reassess how the work of the organization is done	Communicate accomplishments and successful practices internally and externally	Identify and address areas that will support higher performance	Continuously improve the change process

Source: (Katz & Miller, 2003, pp. 455, 460, 465, 468 Figures 1, 2, 3, 4)

business. Any properly motivated person can become a diversity educator according to Cross (p. 140), but she thinks self-knowledge and understanding of the following are essential:

1. historical, social, and political realities related to oppression and discrimination.
2. how to help adults learn
3. ways in which organizations and systems operate and change and
4. one's relationships to others in terms of race, gender, and other differences

In addition, diversity educators should be skilled, sensitive communicators who know how to encourage constructive conflict while defusing its dysfunctional aspects. They should understand the organizational change process and the levels at which change must occur, "certainly at the individual awareness level, where prejudice resides, but also at the group level, where prejudice results in discrimination, and at the system level, where discrimination is embedded in every aspect of the organization's norms and practices" (Cross, 2000, p. 56). Diversity educators also should be familiar with theories of adult development and learning.

Despite Lucky Stores' and Texaco's legal problems that resulted from trying to debunk stereotypes, Linnehan and Konrad (1999) favor diversity education that includes a discussion of cultural differences to counter the trend toward assimilation. Ford Motor Company followed this advice at its Dearborn, Michigan plant, which employs hundreds of Arab-Americans. After the 2001 bombing of the World Trade Center in New York, Ford offered sessions where Muslim and non-Muslim workers could learn the facts and misconceptions about Islam in a non-threatening environment (Nixon & West, 2000).

Remaining Phase II tasks are developing interest- and identity-based networks that are open to all to prevent isolation, encouraging mentoring, coaching, and career planning, creating processes to deal with overt discrimination, changing human resource practices, and capitalizing on "pockets of readiness" (Katz & Miller, 2003). Mentoring and networking are discussed in chapter 9, and modifications in human resource practices such as recruitment and appraisal were addressed in chapter 2.

A five-year career planning effort was central to an effort at Inland Steel, which has been described as "one of the more celebrated diversity programs" in a U.S. firm. Employees at the 100–year-old manufacturing company were urged to "shift their [career] expectations from who they are to who they can become" (Nixon & West, 2000, p. 7).

Katz and Miller's suggestion that organizations create processes to deal with blatant discrimination is similar to Meyerson and Fletcher's (2000,

p. 131) "small wins" strategy, which they describe as a "persistent campaign of incremental changes that discover and destroy the deeply embedded roots of discrimination." Increasing the length of an interview from 30 to 45 minutes to allow sufficient time to move beyond often stereotypical first impressions is an example of a small wins strategy mentioned in chapter 2.

There is a tendency to spend excess time and effort persuading those who are most resistant to diversity of its benefits. Instead, Katz and Miller (2003) argue that diversity change agents should direct their efforts toward those who are receptive to their message. Concentrating on such individuals will create a "critical mass" of supporters relatively quickly and might result in a model unit that others could be urged to emulate.

Nixon and West (2000) make a suggestion that might be most appropriate to consider in Phase II. They believe a pilot diversity program should be tested on a unit in the organization prior to full-scale, long-term implementation.

Phase III, Making Diversity and Inclusion a Way of Life, (Katz & Miller, 2003) includes features such as accountability and feedback, which Cox (1991) mentioned explicitly as part of Follow-up, and involvement of stakeholders, which he did not address. Accountability is necessary to make sure that all employees and managers are serious about diversity initiatives. It ties monetary and non-monetary rewards and consequences to managers' full development of all employees' talents. Shareholder involvement could include partnership agreements with distributors and suppliers affirming the value of each individual employed by the partner organizations and denouncing harmful behaviors, such as harassment.

Phase IV, Leveraging Learning and Challenging the Status Quo, involves constant reassessment of the organization and the way its work is done, using the same tools as in the initial diagnosis. Other features are fairly self-explanatory. Katz and Miller (2003, p. 470) think it is necessary to ask questions such as "What do we need to next . . . to be more inclusive?" and "How can we leverage a wider range of differences for even higher performance?" to reinforce and maintain diversity gains.

Katz and Miller (2003, p. 471) admit that organization-wide adoption of the Inclusion/Breakthrough model is rare. They believe subunits may be more likely to use it, and when they do, the "real power of human diversity" provides "a foundation for higher performance, for greater productivity, and for all to grow and develop."

Though she has no illusions about how long it will take to rid society of the "isms" that prevent people and organizations from achieving their full potential, Cross (2000) believes their harmful effects can be lessened. Her hope rests on the fundamental similarity in the response of all to prejudice, injustice, and abuse and on a common temptation induced by the trappings of power "to forget our common humanity and to look for rationalizations of 'difference' to justify our advantage." The U.S. will function as a real democracy only when all of its citizens recognize their true equality, according to Cross. She concludes, "When our leaders gain the skills and find the courage to begin to manage to this end, we will all be able to hold our heads a little higher, as fellow citizens of the world's most promising democracy" (Cross, 2000, p. 165). When implemented effectively, diversity management can go a long way toward creating an environment in which people feel courageous enough to act based on their convictions without fear of retribution.

SUMMARY

This chapter presented various definitions of diversity management and factors precipitating greater concern about it by organizations. Advantages and potential drawbacks of diversity management were covered as was a discussion of its similarities to and differences from equal employment opportunity. Several comprehensive diversity management models were explained.

CASE STUDY: ALMA REYNOSO AND LYNDALL IMPORTS BY CONSUELO S. FERNANDEZ

Lyndall Imports is an equal opportunity employer with 750 employees in its Houston, Texas headquarters and a total of 30 employees in its Bakersfield, California, and Dayton, Ohio, field offices. Lyndall executives are David G. Feldman, Wayne P. McCord, Darrell Johnson, John Lewis, and Henry Sullivan. Their titles appear in the organizational chart on p. 114.

The company recently lost a joint venture opportunity with a prominent South American corporation, which would have established Lyndall Imports as an innovative, cosmopolitan firm. Though Lyndall Imports employs minorities, it has been slow to develop effective training programs to promote and retain them in positions beyond the clerical and lower administrative levels. Women represent the majority of the hourly and contract positions at Lyndall. Formal mentoring programs are nonexistent, though executives share annual hunting trips with clients and prospective junior executives. Some think that this practice adds to the growing disparity between the executive level and various minority subgroups.

One of Lyndall's competitors, Quintana Industries, a Hispanic-owned firm with strong community involvement, has aggressively recruited an increasing number of women and Hispanic employees away from Lyndall. This fueled

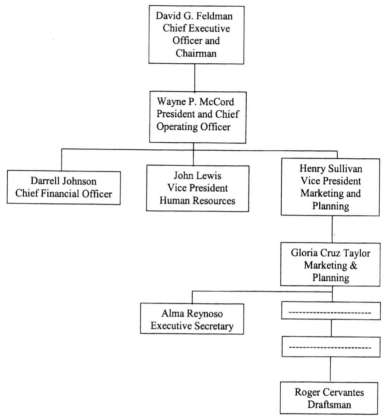

Figure 4.2. Organizational Chart for Lyndall Imports

rumors of job discrimination at Lyndall. Negative press in the business community, partly because of this, has finally led Lyndall to retain the services of Monroe and Stephens, a Los Angeles-based consulting firm specializing in helping corporations implement cultural diversity programs.

Alma Reynoso, a Mexican-American who was hired twelve years ago as a clerk-typist, has proved to be an ambitious, dedicated employee who has consistently excelled in every position she has assumed. Alma has a strong work ethic and juggles her position at Lyndall with night classes at her local community college. She remains confident that she will be the first in her family to earn a college degree. Currently Alma is Executive Secretary to Gloria Cruz Taylor, Marketing and Planning Coordinator, who reports directly to Henry Sullivan. Gloria shares Alma's cultural heritage and has been a strong motivational influence in terms of Alma's career choices with Lyndall. Although Alma considers Gloria to be a confidante and close friend, she is aware of some reluctance of her boss to discuss some topics. Gloria seems to prefer not to talk about the increasing lack of promotion opportunities for women and minority employees, the anticipated effect of Monroe and Stephens' recommendations on Lyndall's current structure, and the fact that minorities have left Lyndall for Quintana Industries. Gloria's tenure with Lyndall is shorter than Alma's; she was hired three years ago to replace Edgar Martinez. Alma had not worked with Edgar but had heard of his dissatisfaction with Lyndall and rumors that he had been planning to file a job discrimination complaint when Quintana made him an offer.

Lately Alma has found it more difficult to come to work focused and motivated. When she received a phone call from friend and coworker, Roger Cervantes, to "grab lunch and talk about the things going on at Lyndall," she eagerly accepted. Though Roger, a Senior Draftsman supervising two contract workers, considers himself more Puerto Rican than American, he has shared Alma's career ambitions and had hoped to retire with Lyndall. Now, away from the office, Roger and Alma pour out their concerns.

Alma started, "Roger, I'm so glad you called. I've been dying to talk with someone. Gloria is keeping to herself these days. So how are you doing? It seems you've been putting in a lot of overtime lately."

"Yeah, well, the venture project was dominating every waking hour for us. We were jumping through hoops to meet deadlines, and I've had to be creative to keep my temps motivated. Just when things seemed to be going well, we heard the rumors that negotiations were stalling," said Roger.

"Then they were discussing so-called legal issues," he continued.

"At the end, we stopped hearing about things altogether, but we surmised that it had to do with Lyndall's image. What a waste of time and staff! Now, this . . . consulting firm from L.A. What's the name?"

"Monroe and Stephens," Alma replied.

"Yeah, M.S., we're calling them. They're supposed to fix everything and make Lyndall a more Hispanic-friendly company," said Roger, with a trace of cynicism in his voice.

"Well, what's so bad about that?" Alma asked. "If Lyndall needs help to revamp and become more culturally aware, maybe this Monroe and Stephens is a good thing," she said.

"I don't know," said Roger. "How come it's taken Lyndall this long to figure out they're behind the times? They should have done their homework before trying to set up a joint venture with a South American firm. It's embarrassing!"

"I know what you mean," said Alma, "but it isn't as if everyone at Lyndall has had their head in the sand. I know that Henry Sullivan and John Lewis have actively worked on getting a formal mentoring program established, and I heard that Mr. Lewis had contacted Monroe and Stephens last summer when

Quintana Industries started recruiting on television. He was really upset about our falling minority headcount. And . . ."

"Yeah," Roger interrupted, "I heard the same things: something about unless drastic measures were implemented to retain and recruit minorities, Lyndall would fall behind in the multicultural environment. Look, I know Lyndall's trying to make things right. I just don't know if I can afford to stick around and wait until they do."

"Are you thinking of going off to Quintana?" Alma asked.

"You know that they have an aggressive management trainee program and a strong policy about promoting from within. None of this preferential treatment like what happened when you were overlooked for promotion a few years ago because some close friend of John Lewis just happened to be available," said Roger.

On a roll, he continued, "Quintana seems to be more aware of the Hispanic community, too. Did you know Quintana is involved in the Junior Achievement for Latinos Program and a couple of at-risk school programs? I don't know. I've got a lot of time invested with Lyndall, and I really like the people in my department. Still, I'm keeping my resume updated. Hey, I'm doing all the talking here. What about you? You can't tell me you haven't considered bailing out."

"Well, actually, Roger," Alma began, "I'm not real sure what to think. Yesterday everything was going so well. Lyndall seemed to be on the move. I was already preparing myself for my new position as Assistant to the Vice President of South American Affairs.

"You deserved it," commented Roger, "It should have been yours for the asking."

"Well, that's history," said Alma. "Now, I'm not sure where I stand. Everything's happening so fast, and so much seems to be out of everyone's control. I see everybody breaking off into small groups, congregating at the break rooms, taking early lunches. I don't like what I'm hearing about Lyndall. I used to like coming to work. I was proud of my work and where I work. Now, I don't know. I've reached a plateau, and to make matters worse, I'm not sure whether Gloria will stick around to help me sort things out."

"What!" exclaimed Roger, "Is she leaving too? I thought things were going well for her, since she's next in line to the V.P."

"You really think so?" asked Alma. "It's hard because you don't see yourself as different until they make you feel different. I hate to be so negative, but it's the truth. Gloria is a very competent, intelligent woman who has paid her dues repeatedly, but I don't see her advancing any higher than her current position. If management doesn't wake up, I wouldn't blame her if she's the next one knocking at Quintana's door."

"So where does that leave you?" asked Roger.

Alma replied, "I have to sit down and reevaluate my priorities and goals and prepare for the worst. Like it or not, Lyndall is going to change, hopefully for the better. There are a lot of unknowns, and that is scary. Monroe and Stephens could come in and recommend that we start over with a brand new management team."

"That may not be so bad," responded Roger.

"Maybe," replied Alma. "But a lot of us have worked hard and stuck it out—maybe because we hoped Lyndall was doing something right even though we saw a lot that was wrong. It's going to be chaotic around here for a while, and I'm afraid we'll see a lot more attrition before this is over."

Analyze this case by responding to the following:

1. Identify the most critical current problem.
2. Identify the most crucial underlying problem. (What is the root cause of the most critical current problem?)
3. Provide three non-overlapping alternatives to either the most critical current problem or the most crucial underlying problem. Indicate which problem you are addressing.
4. State at least two criteria on which you will evaluate all of the alternatives. Criteria are factors on which you can compare the alternatives, such as cost, advancement potential, etc. If evaluating an alternative based on one criterion does not make sense, then a different criterion should be used instead.
5. Select one alternative (not a combination) as the solution to the problem. Explain your reasons for choosing one alternative rather than the others.

REFERENCES

Agars, M.D. & Kottke, J.L. 2004. Models and practice of diversity management: A historical review and presentation of a new integration theory. 55–77. In M.S. Stockdale & F.J. Crosby, Eds. *The Psychology and management of workplace diversity.* Malden, MA: Blackwell Publishers, Ltd.

Allen, R.S. & Montgomery, K.A. 2001. Applying and organizational development approach to creating diversity. *Organizational Dynamics, 30.* 149–61.

Austin, J.R. 1997. A cognitive framework for understanding demographic influences in groups. *International Journal for Organizational Analysis, 5.* 342–59.

Brotherton, P. 2001. Diversity update: How is corporate America dealing with diversity? *Diversity Career Opportunities and Insights, 3*(1). 20.

Cox, T. 1991. The multicultural organization. *Academy of Management Journal, 5*(2).

Cox, T. 2001. *Creating the multicultural organization.* San Francisco: John Wiley & Sons, Inc.

Cross, E.Y. 2000. *Managing diversity: The courage to lead.* Westport, CT: Quorum Books.

Diversity in U.S. on upswing as America grows. 2001. *Pensacola News-Journal,* March 13. 8A.

Ely, R.J. & Thomas, D.A. 2001. Cultural diversity at work: The effects of diversity perspectives on work group processes and outcomes. *Administrative Science Quarterly, 46.* 229–73.

Equal Opportunity Pays. 1993, May 4. *The Wall Street Journal.* 1.

Fletcher, B.R. 2003. Diversity: A strategy for organizational change and success. In D.L. Plummer, Ed. *Handbook of diversity management.* 223–42. Lanham, MD: University Press of America, Inc.

Gilbert, J.A. & Stead, B.A. 1996. Stigmatization revisited: Does diversity management make a difference? Unpublished manuscript.

Gilbert, J.A., Stead, B.A. & Ivancevich, J.M. 1999. Diversity management: A new organizational paradigm. *Journal of Business Ethics, 21*(1). 61–76.

Golembiewski, R. 1995. *Managing diversity in organizations.* Tuscaloosa: University of Alabama Press.

Gordon, L. 1995, May. Different from what? Diversity as a performance issue. *Training,* 25–33.

Harrison, D., Price, K. & Bell, M.P. 1998. Beyond relational demography: Time and the effects of surface- and deep-level diversity on work group cohesion. *Academy of Management Journal, 41.* 96–107.

Hays-Thomas, R. 2004. Why now? The contemporary focus on managing diversity. 1–30. In M.S. Stockdale & F.J. Crosby, Eds. *The Psychology and management of workplace diversity.* Malden, MA: Blackwell Publishers, Ltd.

Heilman, M.E., Block, C.J. & Lucas, J.A. 1992. Presumed incompetent? Stigmatization and affirmative action efforts. *Journal of Applied Psychology, 77.* 536–44.

Hubbard, E.E. 2003. Assessing, measuring, and analyzing the impact of diversity initiatives. In D.L. Plummer, Ed. *Handbook of diversity management.* 271–306. Lanham, MD: University Press of America, Inc.

Jackson, P.B., Thoits, P.A. & Taylor, H.F. 1995. Composition of the workplace on psychological well-being: The effects of tokenism on America's black elite. *Social Forces, 74*(2). 543–57.

Johnston, W.B. & Packer, A.H. 1987. *Workforce 2000.* Indianapolis, IN: Hudson Institute.

Judy, R.W. & D'Amico, C. 1997. *Workforce 2020: Work and workers in the 21st century.* Indianapolis, IN: Hudson Institute.

Katz, J.H. & Miller, F.A. 2003. Building inclusion and leveraging diversity as a way of doing business. 447–72. In D.L. Plummer, Ed. *Handbook of diversity management.* Lanham, MD: University Press of America, Inc.

Kelly, E. & Dobbin, F. 1998. How affirmative action became diversity management. *The American Behavioral Scientist, 41*(7). 960–85.

Kersten, A. 2000. Diversity management: Dialogue, dialectics, and diversion. *Journal of Organizational Change Management, 13*(3). 235–49.

Kochan, T., Bezrukova, K., Ely, R. et al. 2003. The effects of diversity on business performance: Report of the diversity research network. *Human Resource Management, 42*(1). 3–21.

LaFromboise, T., Coleman, H. & Gerton, J. 1993. Psychological impact of biculturalism: Evidence and theory. *Psychological Bulletin, 114.* 395–412.

Lewin, K. 1951. *Field theory in social science.* New York: Harper Row.

Linnehan, F. & Konrad, A.M. 1999. Diluting diversity: Implications for inter-group inequality in organizations. *Journal of Management Inquiry, 8*(4), 399–415.

Loden, M. & Rosener, J.B. 1991. *Workforce America! Managing employee diversity as a vital resource.* Homewood, IL: Business One Irwin. 196–200.

Lorbiecki, A. 2001. Changing views on diversity management: The rise of the learning perspective and the need to recognize social and political contradictions. *Management Learning, 32*(3). 345–62.

Meyerson, D. & Fletcher, J. 2000, Jan./Feb. A modest manifesto for shattering the glass ceiling. *Harvard Business Review.* 117–136.

Milliken, F.J. & Martins, L.L 1996. Searching for common threads: Understanding the multiple effects of diversity in organizational groups. *Academy of Management Review, 21.* 402–33.

Milville, M.L., Gelso, C.J., Pannu, R. et al. 1999. Appreciating similarities and valuing differences: The Milville-Guzman universality diversity scale. *Journal of Counseling Psychology, 46.* 291–307.

Mor-Barak, M.E. 2000. The inclusive workplace: An ecosystem approach to diversity management. *Social Work, 45.* 339–52.

Neukrug, E.S. 1994. *The Journal of Intergroup Relations, 21*(2). 3–11.

Ng, E.S. & Tung, R.L. 1998. Ethno-cultural diversity and organizational effectiveness: A field study. *International Journal of Human Resource Management, 9.* 980–95.

Nixon, J.C. & West, J.F. 2000. American addresses workforce diversity. *Business Forum, 25*(1/2), 4–10.

Overman, S. 1991. Managing the diverse workforce. *HRMagazine, 36*(4). 32–36.

Pelled, L.H., Eisenhardt, K.M. & Xin, K.R.1999. Exploring the black boss: An analysis of work group diversity, conflict, and performance. *Administrative Science Quarterly, 44.* 1–44.

Plummer, D.L. 2003. Diagnosing diversity in organizations. 243–70. In D.L. Plummer, Ed. *Handbook of diversity management,* Lanham, MD: University Press of America, Inc.

Population Projections Program. 2000. Population Division, U.S. Census Bureau, Washington, D.C. Retrieved January 8, 2005 from http://www.census.gov/population/projections/nation/summary/np-t4–d.pdf.

Powell, G. N. & Graves, L.M. 2003. *Women and men in management.* 3rd ed. Thousand Oaks, CA: SAGE.

Richard, O.C. 2000. Racial diversity, business strategy, and firm performance: A resource-based view. *Academy of Management Journal, 4.* 164–77.

Rynes, S. & Rosen, B. 1995. A field survey of factors affecting the adoption and perceived success of diversity training. *Personnel Psychology, 48,* 247–71.

Saunders, L.M. 2003. Momentum and internal relationship building: On the road from exclusion to inclusion. 323–62. In D.L. Plummer, Ed. *Handbook of Diversity Management.* Lanham, MD: University Press of America, Inc.

Schneider, S.K. & Northcraft, G.B. 1999. Three social dilemmas of workforce diversity in organizations: A social identity perspective. *Human Relations, 52.* 1445–67.

SHRM releases new survey of diversity programs. 1998. *Mosaics, 4*(4). 1.

Strauss, J.P. & Connerly, M.L. 2003. Demographics, personality, contact, and universal-diverse orientation: An exploratory examination. *Human Resource Managemen. 42*(2). 59–74.

Thomas, R. R., Jr. 1990, March-April. From affirmative action to affirming diversity. *Harvard Business Review.*

Thomas, D.A. & Ely, R. 1996. Making differences matter: A new paradigm for managing diversity. *Harvard Business Review, 74*(5). 79–90.

Thomas, K.M., Mack, D.A. & Montagliani, A. 2004. The arguments against diversity: Are they valid? 31–51. In M.S. Stockdale & F.J. Crosby, Eds. *The Psychology and management of workplace diversity.* Malden, MA: Blackwell Publishers, Ltd.

VonBergen, C.W., Soper, B. & Foster, T. 2002. Unintended negative effects of diversity management. *Public Personnel Management, 31*(2). 239–52.

Yakura, E.K. 1996. EEO law and managing diversity. 25–50. In E.E. Kossek & S.A. Lobel. Eds. *Managing diversity: Human resource strategies for transforming the workplace.* Cambridge, MA: Blackwell.

Williams, K.Y. & O'Reilly, C.A., III.1998. Demography and diversity in organizations: A review of 40 years of research. 79–140. In B. Staw & L.L. Cummings, Eds. *Research in organizational behavior.* Greenwich, CT: JAI Press.

Chapter Five

Stereotyping and its Impact on Perceptions of Leadership

OUTCOMES

After studying this chapter, you should be able to:

1. define stereotype, cumulative effect of stereotyping, prescribed and proscribed behavior, stereotype threat, social context, androgynous management, "model minority, "men's movement"
2. explain why people apply stereotypes to others.
3. present evidence to debunk common gender stereotypes.
4. present evidence to debunk common racial/ethnic stereotypes and those applied to specific groups of women of color.
5. explain the effects of social context on gender stereotypes.
6. state the circumstances in which original work created by women has been assessed less positively than that developed by men.
7. explain reasons why "masculinity" continues to be associated with leadership and management, despite evidence to the contrary.
8. give examples of intensified and relaxed gender-related prescriptions for and proscriptions on behavior.
9. explain the typical consequences for violation of relaxed and intensified gender related prescriptions for and proscriptions on behavior in a real or hypothetical organization.
10. explain why stereotypes are so difficult to eradicate.
11. evaluate actions and approaches of supervisors and managers designed to reduce the harmful effects of stereotyping at the organizational level.

STEREOTYPE: A DEFINITION

The word stereotype was first used in 1798 when European printers coined the term to describe a new procedure they invented to permanently copy images (Lhamon, 2002; Chang & Kleiner, 2003). Stereotyping means applying an assumed set of "typical" characteristics and behaviors of a group to an individual based solely on knowledge of that individual's membership in the group. A given individual may actually exhibit a few, none, or most of the characteristics that typify the simplified picture of the entire group. For example, if the only thing a student knows about a female professor is that she teaches courses that are included in the Women's Studies curriculum, the student might assume knowledge about that professor's beliefs regarding other issues and her political beliefs that could be mistaken.

WHY ARE STEREOTYPES USED?

Stereotyping simplifies the perceptual process by classifying the millions of stimuli that constantly bombard people. It helps them organize thoughts about individuals by trying to fit them into categories in the same way that having compartments for shoes, sweaters, and other items in a closet helps people organize that space. Unlike the clothing that usually fits into a drawer, however, people do not always fit into predetermined categories. Forcing them to do so creates problems not only for those who are stereotyped but also for people who believe the stereotypes and for organizations employing both. Relying on stereotypes to simplify thought processes and provide a convenient way to categorize may seem relatively benign. The use of negative stereotypes to justify dislike of others (Carr-Ruffino, 1999) is more problematic.

STEREOTYPING RESEARCH:
EMPHASIS ON DOMINANT GROUP

Most research has focused on stereotypes that dominant groups (in terms of power and numbers) have of less powerful groups. Less powerful groups typically must be more concerned with the idiosyncrasies and stereotypes of more powerful factions because the latter may exert more control over the former (Hyde, 2001). Various racial/ethnic groups have stereotypes of each other and of other members of their own group. For example, blacks may stereotype other African Americans as "too white" or "too black" (Livers & Caver, 2003) Racial/ethnic groups that are in the minority statistically also stereotype the more prevalent Euro-Americans (whites). To illustrate this point, stereotypes that Hispanics have of non-Hispanic whites appear in Table 5.1. Also, as will be discussed later in this chapter, black and white women have developed stereotypical images of each other.

Little research has been done on the gender stereotypes of African American managers, but as management becomes more diverse, knowing about their stereotypes and those of managers from ethnic/racial groups that have been in the minority statistically will be increasingly important. McRae (1994) shows that male and female black managers do not differ in their sex-role stereotypes. Neither group makes hiring decisions based on an applicant's sex, but both try to avoid assigning black males to female sex-typed tasks. No similar hesitance exists about having a black female perform male sex-typed tasks. McRae opines that black managers may want to ensure that males of the same race/ethnicity have positions that are perceived as powerful, which are those involving male sex-typed tasks. This may reflect sensitivity to the disparagement black males have experienced historically and a desire to counteract it by assigning them power-enhancing tasks.

Distinguishing between stereotypes and gender, ethnic, or cultural differences that may be presented as part of diversity training is important. *Stereotypes* are sweeping generalizations that may have been based on a kernel of truth at one time. Studies of cultural or gender differences are systematic and more nuanced; they are clear about the existence of individual differences and exceptions and may qualify their findings based on contextual factors.

This chapter will address features of stereotypes and concepts associated with stereotyping, selected race/ethnic- and gender-based stereotypes with emphasis on those that are relevant to positions of leadership and management, drawbacks of reliance on them to various parties, reasons why stereotypes persist, and ways in which stereotypes can be made less harmful to the careers of organizational members.

FEATURES OF STEREOTYPES

Stereotypes may be positive or negative, but even constructive labels can be detrimental. If a group is thought to have certain skills, a member who does not possess them may be viewed unfavorably. On the other hand, that individual's unique skills in other areas could be overlooked due to the stereotype.

Besides describing behavior thought to be characteristic of a group of which people are members, stereotypes also may prescribe behavior. *Prescriptive stereotypes* create an expectation of "appropriate" behavior for a person of one's gender, racial/ethnic heritage, or other identity group, which may contribute to a self-fulfilling prophecy and lead to consequences for violation. College professors have observed that students tend to live up or down to professors' expectations. For that reason, having high, but realistic, expectations is important. Likewise, people of whom not much is expected may contribute less than they would otherwise. Thomas (2005, p. 105) states that "lower expectations for members of minority groups can result in reduced performance" and refers to Taylor Cox' belief (1994) that prejudice damages performance the most because it creates self-fulfilling prophecies.

Although negative stereotypes may not be intentional, they are, nevertheless, simplistic and disempowering (Holmes, Burns et al., 2003). Researchers have reached different conclusions about the circumstances in which stereotypes are likely to be activated but agree that they are enduring, may have a cumulative effect, and are influenced by social context. The durable nature of stereotypes will be discussed in the section of this chapter dealing with their elimination; other features will be addressed in the following paragraphs.

Devine (1989) surmises that stereotypes are over-learned during socialization and are therefore automatically, unintentionally activated at the sight of a member of the group about which the stereotype is held. People who have low prejudice levels vary in their reactions to group members. Their beliefs conflict with negative stereotypes of a group. Even so, those who are low in prejudice must suppress stereotypes actively to avoid having them sway their decisions. Otherwise, stereotyping will influence their decision-making as much as it affects that of highly prejudiced individuals (Collier & Shaffer, 1999).

The notion of automatic stereotype activation in the presence of a representative of a group about which the stereotype is held has been criticized by researchers such as Gilbert and Hixon (1991). They show that the state of being "cognitively busy," or having many mental tasks to complete in a short time, reduces the activation of ethnic stereotypes.

Collier and Shaffer (1999) tested whether or not 80 male students who had previously taken the Modern Racism Scale to determine their degree of prejudice would be influenced by two common stereotypes about black males when selecting the "best" candidate as linebacker coach and a general manager in a professional football organization. Their results support Gilbert and Hixon's (1991) theory. Only students who had plenty of time to review applications and think about their own race-based stereotypes favored a black candidate as linebacker coach and a white candidate as general manager. Further, Collier and Shaffer (1999, p. 2301) reported that "participants' levels of prejudice in no way influenced these significant racial trends."

Collier and Shaffer (1999) also distinguished between attitudes and stereotypical beliefs; they propose that attitudes have a greater impact on decisions that must be made in a short time and deal with personal preferences. Beliefs, on the other hand, are more influential when decision makers have much time and must achieve a specific goal for which criteria related to candidates' abilities and qualifications exist. Stereotypical beliefs about aggressiveness and relative intelligence, not attitudes, may have been operative in the study of the selection of a linebacker and coach (Collier & Shaffer). If attitude had been a factor, whites would have been preferred for both the linebacker coach and general manager position because most whites, regrettably, have less favorable attitudes toward blacks than toward other whites. That did not happen. Collier and Shaffer indicate that an unfavorable attitude, or feeling, toward a group almost always results in a decision unfavorable to members of that group, but a negative cognitive belief about a group, though faulty, may not. Although aggressiveness is generally considered negative, decision-makers who had enough time to think about their beliefs viewed black candidates for the linebacker coach position as more qualified than their white counterparts due to a stereotype that black males are aggressive.

Stereotyping when making one decision may not result in long-term harm but may have a *cumulative effect*, meaning that the damage it causes compounds and worsens over time. Agars (2004) demonstrates this cumulative effect statistically and urges more researchers to study issues related to the effects of gender stereotyping on performance evaluation. Until now, researchers have not been interested because gender effects have been small.

In addition to the cumulative effect, another concern is *stereotype threat.* This is a fear that people will be judged according to—or will actually conform to—negative global generalizations about their group (Steele, 1997). Those striving to succeed in occupations inconsistent with gender role expectations, such as women who aspire to top executive positions, experience this threat as do individuals about whom there are widespread, false mindsets about capabilities of those of similar ethnic or racial backgrounds. Perceived stereotype threat reduces performance by causing a person to focus more on the implications of being evaluated based on a stereotype or on avoidance of behavior that might seem to verify a stereotype than on the task itself (Roberson et al., 2003). For example, a female business student who accompanied two graduate students on a visit to a major manufacturer to gather data for a project was chagrined when she realized that her attire marked her as a stereotypical young, female college student rather than a serious business professional. The mistake in attire was exacerbated by her realization that she had inadvertently ignored advice of the "dress for success" genre with which she had recently become familiar. Her self-consciousness about how others would view her undermined her performance and led her to behave in ways that made the stereotype a self-fulfilling prophecy.

SELECTED STEREOTYPES BASED ON RACE AND ETHNICITY

Selected stereotypes of various ethnic/racial groups, some of which apply to one gender or another within the ethnic/racial group, are presented in Table 5.1. Unless noted otherwise, these reflect mainly the views of whites of western European ancestry. To be included in this table, stereotypes had to appear in at least two sources. Though not intended to be comprehensive, Table 5.1 provides a representative sample of existing stereotypes. All portray some unflattering characteristics; those of African Americans, Hispanics, and Native Americans are almost exclusively negative. In addition to the general stereotypes of African Americans, males of that group are portrayed as angry and predisposed to violence (Gilbert, Carr-Ruffino, et al., 2003). If decision makers believed the caricatures of Asian American women and Latinas, as depicted in Table 5.1, they would be unlikely to select them for managerial positions in the U.S.

Some items in Table 5.1 require additional explanation and "debunking." These include the "Mammy" and "Sapphire" stereotypes of African American women, the portrayal of Asian Americans as the "model minority," the double standard that accuses Hispanics of being "too family oriented," similarities among stereotypes of African Americans, Asian Americans, and Hispanics, and views of American Indians that demonstrate regrettable ignorance of their actual circumstances. However, assuming that disconfirming information will eliminate stereotypes quickly is unrealistic. Such information must be repeated often to make an impact because stereotypes are so engrained (Powell, Butterfield, & Parent, 2002).

In the past, white women had notions that black women fit the "Mammy" or "Sapphire" stereotypes (Bell & Nkomo, 2000). The "Mammy" epitomized the devoted, self-sacrificing caregiver and is derived from Civil War-era literature about the South when a loyal servant was trusted implicitly to care for the master's family and the plantation. Bell and Nkomo indicate that Oprah Winfrey, who is known for her empathy and concern for others' problems, seems to have an image consistent with the "Mammy" stereotype. "Sapphire," on the other hand, is the assertive, brassy, impudent woman who speaks out against injustice and sometimes exhibits anger and rage. Whoopi Goldberg supposedly illustrates this stereotype (Bell & Nkomo).

At first, the "model minority" stereotype of Asian Americans might not seem to be a problem. Those who wish to excel in management might appreciate being seen as productive, intelligent, and hard working high achievers who are "driven." In the aggregate, Asian Americans are better educated than whites. They have been successful economically and hold positions in various occupations. The fact that they are labeled as a minority instead of ac-

Table 5.1. Selected Stereotypes of Various Ethnic/Racial Groups

Racial/Ethnic Group	African American Women	African American	Asian Americans	Asian American Women	Euro-Americans (held by Hisp.)	Latinas	Hispanic/Latino	Native-American
Stereotypes	Strong Independent Striving Assertive More stable & cooperative than African Amer. men "Mammy" "Sapphire" "Welfare queen"	Lazy Unintelligent Irresponsible Superstitious Criminal Athletic Troublemaker Rhythmic Hostile Loud Tend to blame others for problems	"Model Minority" Technically superior Productive Thrifty Punctual Hard-working Obedient to authority Submissive	Childlike Obedient Content with lower level assembly jobs "Timid Asian Flower" Erotic	Cold Insensitive Impersonal Remote Plain, no "flavor" Too driven Take themselves too seriously	Submissive Easily-intimidated Lacking in power & influence	Illegal immigrants Lazy Lacking in ambition Criminal Foreign Poor Uneducated Too emotional and excitable	Alcoholic Lazy Homogeneous Stoic, lacking sense of humor Childlike Superstitious Successful at gaming Less willing to be self-sufficient than Euro-Americans

(continued)

Table 5.1. (*continued*)

Racial/Ethnic Group	African American Women	African American	Asian Americans	Asian American Women	Euro-Americans (held by Hisp.)	Latinas	Hispanic/Latino	Native-American
		Less willing to be self-sufficient than Euro-Americans Relatively poor	Passive Stoic Intelligent High achiever Intense, driven Sneaky Deceitful Unwilling to mesh with Euro-Amer. culture. Hard workers. Martial arts experts. Have communic. difficulties; Not loyal to U.S.		Value career over family		Hot-tempered Unorganized Too-family oriented Do not value time; late Have difficulty with English language	Receive govt. $$ for being Native American Devalue women

Sources: (Bell & Nkomo, 2000; Carr-Ruffino, 1999; Chang & Kleiner, 2003; Davidson, 1997; Devine & Elliott, 1995; Gilbert, Carr-Ruffino, Ivancevich & Lownes-Jackson, 2003; Job, 1998; Mihesuah, 996; Oakley, 2000; Nash, 1998; Oyserman & Sakamoto, 1997; Tan & Lucht. 1997)

cepted as successful Americans is a problem to those who see the labeling as an attempt to marginalize Asian Americans (Oyserman & Sakamoto, 1997). If powerful groups single out Asian Americans as worthy of emulation, other minority groups might resent them, which could cause organizational conflict. High expectations of all Asian Americans might create unrealistic standards for those of Asian ancestry who are average in terms of skills and ambitions. Finally, the model minority stereotype might cause challenges facing relatively recent Asian immigrants, such as the Hmong, to be overlooked (Carr-Ruffino, 1999).

The assumption of technical superiority has created what has been dubbed a "bamboo ceiling" for Asian Americans. They are overrepresented in technical positions but underrepresented in management (Gilbert et al., 2003) and may be regarded as "too compliant and polite" to succeed as managers (Carr-Ruffino, 1999).

In an era when organizations tout their support of families as a recruitment and retention tool, assuming that they can agree on a definition of 'family," it is ironic that Hispanics are criticized for being "too family oriented." Perhaps this is because their definition of "family" is more inclusive than that of many whites, as was discussed in chapter 2.

Some view African Americans, Native Americans, and Hispanics as lazy, less likely to be self-sufficient than whites (Chang & Kleiner, 2003; Job, 1998), or dependent on government assistance. Job (1998) believes that the notion that Hispanics—and, by extension, members of other minority groups—are lazy is derived from the belief that many are poor. Whites, or others who emphasize individualism and self-help, may assume that those who are poor must be lazy. Otherwise, so the thinking goes, they would be more successful. This mindset obscures the fact that government policies make escaping poverty difficult for most people. For example, a seriously disabled poor person was not allowed to save for a purchase because the amount of money he would have, by virtue of saving, would exceed the maximum allowable limit, making him ineligible for essential medical assistance. This person, however, was told that he could finance the item he wished to buy, which would have forced him to pay several times its actual cost.

African Americans and Native Americans are portrayed as dependent on welfare. Despite the U.S. government's responsibilities to Native Americans based on negotiated treaties with tribal governments, the public typically does not distinguish between assistance to American Indians and to any other poor people. Despite the economic progress of many African Americans, the stereotype of the "welfare queen" persists. For Hispanics, the stereotype is not dependence as much as a lack of willingness to be self-sufficient as compared to non-Hispanic whites.

Asian Americans, Native Americans, and Hispanics are thought to be less patriotic or loyal to the United States than whites. Though many are third and fourth generation U.S. citizens with no ties to another country, some Asian Americans and Hispanics may be viewed this way based on appearance. Carr-Ruffino (1999, p. 155) believes the "exotic, perpetual foreigner myth" about Asian Americans lingers because they are considered to be "from a culture and lifestyle that is just too different for comfort."

Job (1998) describes the assumptions made by a colleague of "Fred," a real estate firm employee who is a second generation Mexican-American. In casual conversation, the colleague indicates his belief that "Fred" probably does not celebrate Thanksgiving because it is an "American holiday." At that point, "Fred" tells the co-worker that he plans to celebrate Thanksgiving, as he does each year, by attending a large dinner hosted by his grandmother.

Thanksgiving is a holiday that some Native Americans who are aware of their cultural heritage might wish to skip. According to Mihesuah (1996, p. 83), "Indians have no problem with giving thanks for what they have, but why celebrate the American 'Thanksgiving' when Pilgrims proceeded to massacre the Wampanoags who helped them survive after they arrived on the shore of Narragansett Bay?" Similarly, Mihesuah (1996) sees no reason for Native Americans to celebrate Columbus Day to honor an individual whom he considers an invader who treated indigenous people poorly. Not all American Indians agree, but Mihesuah (1996, p, 79) believes that celebrating many holidays that are taken for granted by whites, including the Fourth of July, is "tantamount to celebrating the Massacres at Sand Cree, Wounded Knee . . . the mass hanging of the Santee Sioux, and numerous other conflicts that are thoroughly chronicled." In summary, Mihesuah believes that if Native Americans are less patriotic than other groups, they have good reasons.

Refutations of stereotypes regarding Native Americans

Several common stereotypes about Native Americans with their refutations appear in Table 5.2. Chapter 2 mentioned the diversity of the tribal nations that are collectively known as Native Americans. They differ in cultural and religious practices, style of dress, language and social structure. Though references tend to categorize Native Americans according to the geographic region where they reside, physical proximity is unrelated to similarity. In addition, assuming that all American Indians are similar is as fallacious as thinking that all Europeans are the same, whether they hail from Italy or Sweden (Mihesuah, 1996).

Tribal nations recognize that alcoholism is a problem among its members. Its severity and prevalence differ among individuals and nations as in other populations, however (Mihesuah, 1996).

Ashley and Jarratt-Ziemski (1999) deplore proposals that require "means testing" of Native Americans to determine their eligibility for government assistance. Treating American Indians like any other group in the U.S. that has a percentage of poor members needing aid ignores crucial facts. First, the federal government has a fiduciary responsibility to the tribes, which are regarded as domestic, dependent nations with higher status than any state. Secondly, binding treaties require the federal government to provide health and educational assistance and protect remaining land as partial payment for tribal land that was taken. Native Americans are not getting a "handout;" they are being repaid according to the terms of negotiated agreements with the federal government. Some argue that they can never truly be repaid.

Success at gaming has been overrated as the solution to issues facing Native Americans. Some, like the large Navajo nation, are not involved in gaming, and not all are as successful as those that have received publicity. Tribal nations that have prospered due to gaming have been asked to help other nations that have been less successful, but "asking successful Indian nations to 'share the wealth' is akin to asking California to bail out Texas when oil prices fall—it is ludicrous!" (Ashley & Jarrett-Ziemski, 1999).

Most Indian cultures respect and value women; they had much authority in most tribal nations (Karsten, 1986). Iroquois and Cherokee children became members of the mother's clan and lived with her family, and chiefs of those

Table 5.2.   Stereotypes and Truths about Native Americans

Native Americans . . .
1. Are a homogenous group.
   Truth: The federal government has recognized over 500 tribes.
2. Are alcoholic.
   Truth: Though alcohol abuse is a problem, it varies among individuals and tribes as it does among Euro-Americans.
3. Receive government aid simply because they are American Indians.
   Truth: In exchange for tribal land ceded, sometimes involuntarily, treaties oblige the federal government to protect remaining Indian land and provide health and educational aid
4. Are all successful at gaming.
   Truth: Some tribal nations including one of the largest, the Navajo, are not involved in gaming.
5. Do not value women.
   Truth: Women were chiefs in some tribal nations; in others, the woman's line was dominant. Females lost power in tribes after male Native Americans were influenced by Euro-American traders and missionaries.
6. Are stoic and lack humor.
   Truth: Native Americans have as much of a sense of humor as any other group.

Sources: (Ashley & Jarrat-Ziemski, 1999; Chang & Kleiner, 2003; Mihesuah, 1996.)

nations were selected from the mother's side Mihesuah, 1996). Shawnee women were eligible to become chiefs in their own right (Karsten, 1986).

Just as the dominant culture sometimes portrays Asian American as submissive or erotic and African American women as caretakers or "welfare queens," it depicts American Indian women as overworked squaws or princesses. In reality, tasks assigned to women were no more arduous than those given to men (Karsten, 1994). Disney's Pocahontas is a good example of the princess stereotype. That characterization of Native American females is ironic because indigenous cultures did not bestow titles of royalty on their leaders. Europeans who came in contact with American Indians used terms familiar to them, such as princess or king, to clarify power relationships within a tribal nation, which they found confusing (Mihesuah, 1996).

The misconception that American Indians have no sense of humor may have developed because they are rarely shown smiling in historical photographs. Mihesuah (1996) provides a logical explanation. Most photographs were taken after the Native Americans had been captured or had been pressured into signing treaties which did not necessarily favor their interests. Their serious expressions in old photos should not be interpreted as lack of a sense of humor today.

Minority Stereotypes of the Dominant Culture

A few stereotypes not listed in Table 5.1 should be mentioned. These are labels that African American women have for white women and mindsets of white males, which they sometimes apply to others of similar heritage and gender.

If white women typecast black counterparts as "Mammy" and "Sapphire," black women regarded White peers as "Miss Anne," "Snow Queen," or the "Femme Fatale" (Bell & Nkomo, 2000). "Miss Anne" was a "proper," stylish woman who could be callous. Her power was derived from her association with white men. Dependent and submissive to them, she presented the views of white men and defended them. Bell and Nkomo claim that Hillary Clinton was labeled a "Miss Anne," although she would undoubtedly find the adjectives "dependent" and "submissive" offensive as well as inaccurate.

The "Snow Queen" used to be called a "Queen Bee." As mentioned in chapter 2, she was a pioneer who had to be tough to achieve her current position and who refused to assist other women who would follow her. She believed her accomplishments were won through her own efforts. Ambitious and controlling, this woman sacrificed relationships in her single-minded pursuit of goals. She had a big ego and was considered unfriendly and insensitive (Bell & Nkomo, 2000). The media turned Jill Barad, former CEO of Mattel, into a "Snow Queen" after she had been depicted previously as a "warm, charming marketing guru and team player" (Bell & Nkomo, 2000, p. 249).

The stereotype of using one's sexuality to achieve career goals is one of the oldest. This was the idea behind the "Femme Fatale" image, which also included flirtation and innuendo. The career of a promising Harvard MBA, Mary Cunningham, was irreparably harmed due to her alleged involvement with the CEO of Bendix Corporation, Bill Agee, soon after she finished graduate school and accepted a position at Bendix in 1979 (Bell & Nkomo, 2000).

Viewing anyone as an "object" is inappropriate, but some argue that if majority culture women have been treated as "sex objects, as in the "Femme Fatale" stereotype, their male counterparts have been treated as "financial objects." Being viewed as financially successful is positive, however, whereas being considered a sex object typically is not.

Just as they apply stereotypes to other groups, white males may label others who are similar to themselves. As will be discussed later, they may assume that all men desire upward career mobility.

Another mindset is that men should avoid taking extended family and medical leave though they are eligible for it. These stereotypes hurt individual males, but because they have not harmed powerful white males, collectively, eradicating them is not seen as important.

GENDER STEREOTYPES

In the 1960s and 1970s, shortly after the passage of civil rights laws affecting employment, additional stereotypes besides those that appear in Table 5.3 were prevalent. Though evidence could be presented to refute them, calling attention to old gender myths, vestiges of which some still believe, might reinforce them. A summary article by Merrick (2002) provides more information about gender stereotypes of 30–40 years ago for those who are interested. Other good sources include those by L.K. Brown (1979) and R. Dipboye (1975).

Most gender stereotypes in Table 5.3 are self-explanatory and will be mentioned as related to other topics associated with stereotyping. Stereotypes of women that require additional explanation include the belief that they lack a sense of humor and are not skilled in giving directives. Holmes, Burns et al. (2003) find that women chairing meetings contribute more humor than male chairs do, which provides evidence to dispel the notion that managerial women lack humor. This stereotype, along with those that women do not run meetings or give directives well "could be laughed out of court as ludicrous if they were not so pervasive and so potentially damaging," according to

Table 5.3. Gender Stereotypes

Women	Men
Possess more communal qualities— Supportive, kind, tactful	Possess more agentic qualities— Assertive, daring, competitive, courageous
Are "other-oriented," interpersonally-focused	Are "self-oriented," task-focused
Are process and relationship-oriented	Are outcome and instrumentality- oriented
Lack humor	Are unemotional, objective, active, logical, worldly, self-confident
Lack skill in providing directives, running meetings, challenging views with which they disagree	Are aggressive, ambitious, analytical, consistent, emotionally stable, forceful, well-informed, independent
Are aware of others' feelings	
Are cheerful, creative, helpful, intuitive, modest, Sophisticated	Desire responsibility
Have humanitarian values	Have no desire for friendship
Are more committed to family than to career	Are more committed to career than to family
Are less capable if physically attractive	Are strong and muscular
Are less self-confident, analytical, emotionally stable, and consistent than men	

Sources: (Diekman, Goodfriend & Goodwin, 2004; Merrick, 2002; Powell, Butterfield & Parent, 2002).

Holmes, Burns et al. (p. 414). Executive women are likely to use an array of direct and indirect methods to get others to complete assignments. Specific methods vary with contextual factors such as power and social distance, but women have no trouble giving direct orders when that is appropriate (Holmes, Burns et al, 2003). Some men do not wish to behave in ways consistent with gender stereotypes but may not be vocal about this for fear they will be derided. Males who accept gender stereotypes may find it challenging to adhere to them.

Reactions to both gender stereotypes that harmed men and to the women's movement led some males to seek more information about or join the "men's movement," popularized by Bly (1992) in *Iron John*. The men's movement concentrates on two crucial but typically mismanaged transitions, which are separation from the mother and entrance to the male world. Mishandling of the latter transition results in "father hunger," which causes men to become "soft males," who are out of touch with their feelings and inner selves and lack conviction. The remedy was to get in touch with the "wild men" within them, who are not brutal or macho but have deep convictions and can be spontaneous. To help them get in touch with their inner selves, make up for any deprivation due to their fathers' detachment while they were growing up, and communicate with other men on important rather than superficial topics, the men's movement organized male bonding retreats. At those meetings, which were held throughout the U.S., topics such as cars, jobs, and sports were banned (Karsten, 1994).

Men's studies courses exist in some colleges and universities. The interest in the men's movement seems to have waned since the early 1990s, however.

REAL GENDER DIFFERENCES OR STEREOTYPES?
THE ROLE OF SOCIAL CONTEXT

Are assumptions about gender variations stereotypes or real differences supported by research evidence? Different schools of thought focus either on innate differences related to biological sex or on diverse socialization experiences, in general, of males and females. Those who favor the socialization explanation believe that few biologically-based distinctions exist. Studies support both views. For example, Eagly (1995) concluded that gender differences exist, but Hyde (1996) found none after both examined the same meta-analyses.

Yoder and Kahn (2003) proposed an overriding framework to explain potentially confusing results of studies on gender differences. According to these authors, determining conclusively whether or not gender distinctions exist is impossible because they are affected by another phenomenon, *social context*. Citing Ross and Nisbett (1991), Yoder and Kahn (2003, p. 283) define that term broadly as "any element in a person's social environment that can produce or constrain behavior." It exists at the individual, group, and organizational levels.

Power and status are notable elements of social context at the organizational level because they can be confounded with gender and with other variables related to social identity. When this occurs, the part of the difference due to gender cannot be separated from the part due to power or status. For example, women are considered to be more sensitive to interpersonal cues than men, but those in subordinate roles also have greater sensitivity to interpersonal cues. So if women in high level positions have relatively low sensitivity to interpersonal cues and men in low level positions have high sensitivity, the context (status of position) may have been "confounded" with gender (Riedle, 2004).

To add more complexity, contexts that seem similar may differ if various groups perceive and experience them differently. For example, studies of similarities and differences among males and females in an occupation are considered credible despite the fact that there could be huge differences in the ways others perceive males and females and the ways the sexes experience the situation depending on the gender balance within the occupation. Kanter (1977) argues that when women comprise less than 15% of a work group, they are tokens and will experience negative consequences. She studied tokenism pertaining to gender, not race, but Bell and Nkomo (2000) contend that black women experience "double tokenism," which also has been called double jeopardy.

Gender- and race-based tokenism will be discussed more thoroughly in chapter 7. For now, realizing that a woman or minority group member in an occupation or organization with few other females or minorities may have a different experience than one in a situation characterized by balance is important.

Males could be statistical tokens, but some would argue that the consequences would be less harmful. In fact, males who are statistically in the minority often are presumed to desire career advancement regardless of their true wishes. This, too, is a stereotype. Males in the historically female-dominated occupation of nursing hold leadership posts in disproportionate numbers (Lane & Piercy, 2003). Male therapists employed in hospitals may be assumed to hold the higher status position of physician due to gender stereotypes.

Gender differences indicating that men are more likely than women to be aggressive (Eagly & Steffen, 1986), help or rescue strangers (Eagly & Crowley, 1986), and excel in mathematical performance (Stumpf & Stanley, 1998) and mental rotation tasks (Voyer, Voyer, & Bryden, 1995) are minimized when factors in the social context are considered. For example, Powell (1988) shows that women are as aggressive as men under certain circumstances: when provoked and when engaged in marital conflict. Women and men are equally aggressive in a simulation when they cannot be identified, but women report less aggression, presumably because they do not want to deviate from their gender stereotype (Yoder & Kahn, 2003). Sex differences in helping strangers drops when women are not concerned about safety; women and men are equally likely to help in response to a request, but men are more likely to offer unsolicited assistance (Eagly & Crowley, 1986). Parents' perceptions of their daughters' math abilities influence their performance (Eccles & Jacobs, 1986), and women and men perform equally well in mathematics when women reject the stereotype about men's superior mathematical skills (Steele, 1997; Cheryan & Bodenhausen, 2000).

The difference with the strongest research support is that men's spatial ability is better than women's. Social context changes modify even that difference. Males' performance declined when spatial tasks concerned interior design and improved when the situation in which they were applied involved a naval ship (Sharps, Price & Williams, 1994). Further, with respect to mental rotation skills, "men hearing masculinized instructions outperformed the other groups; men exposed to feminized instructions performed comparably to women" (Yoder & Kahn, 2003, p. 284).

Examples thus far have shown how social context can minimize gender differences that research supports; when context is considered, gender differences that did not seem to exist previously can be found. Studies show no gender differences between task- or relationship-oriented behavior (Eagly & Johnson, 1990) and assessment of original work (Swim, Borgida & Maruyama, 1989), and minimal variations in self-disclosure and autocratic versus democratic leadership style (Eagly & Johnson). Women are slightly more likely to exhibit the latter style. However, more pronounced gender-related variations in both task- and relationship- and autocratic/democratic style occur when the composition of followers, the consistency between a person's leadership role and his or her gender stereotype, and the study's setting are considered. Women are more likely to use an autocratic style if they have mainly male subordinates; both men and women are more task-oriented when their roles are consistent with stereotypes associated with their gender, and stereotypical differences are more prevalent in laboratory studies than in those conducted in work settings (Yoder & Kahn, 2003).

Though they acknowledge the importance of context, after reviewing the evidence, Powell and Graves (2003, p. 150–51) disagree with Yoder and Kahn. They conclude that the sex difference in democratic leadership style is not situational and state unequivocally that "women . . . are higher in democratic decision-making style than men in all types of studies," whether of "actual leaders, non-leaders [or] participants in laboratory experiments."

Context can lead to differences in the way original work is perceived based on the gender of the developer. For example, original work that women create is evaluated less positively than that produced by men when:

1. little information about the developers is available (Yoder & Kahn, 2003),
2. women work in groups of predominantly men even when both sexes were equally qualified in terms of education, experience, and ability (Sackett, DuBois & Noe, 1991), and
3. the "original work" consists of a resume or job application (Lott, 1985).

The variation in self-disclosure between males and females depends on contextual factors including the relationship between the parties, the sex of the person to whom the disclosure is made, and whether it is self-reported or observed (Yoder & Kahn, 2003). As this finding and others in the preceding paragraphs illustrate, evidence shows that social context influences perceptions of the existence and extent of gender differences. Just as factors in the social context can be confounded with gender; race and gender can be confounded. When that happens, addressing gender issues without considering race can lead to inappropriate solutions. For example, both black and white female fire-fighters report differential job treatment. Due to stereotypes about African American women's strength and ability to work hard, they are overburdened on the job. White women, on the other hand, are stereotyped as "fragile" and therefore are overprotected and under-worked. Due to stereotype threat, they feel as if they must disguise real illnesses or weaknesses. In this case, it is important to understand the underlying reason for the differential treatment based on race to be able to deal with the problem effectively.

WHY DOES THE STEREOTYPICAL NOTION ASSOCIATING MANAGEMENT WITH MASCULINITY PERSIST?

Upon closer examination of the context, some gender differences evaporate. Nevertheless, though variations supported by research diminish in the presence of moderating variables, a belief that has not declined over more than three decades is the notion that good managers are masculine, if not male. This idea, and the underlying gender stereotypes that support it, could undermine the progress of women who aspire to top executive positions.

Bem (1974) argues that "feminine" and "masculine" behavior should be regarded as separate dimensions. To measure them, she developed the Bem Sex Role Inventory, which was later shortened in response to criticism that the items labeled as "feminine" were not desirable for any adult. Previously, "feminine" and "masculine" behavior had been considered opposite ends of one continuum, and both males and females were pressured to adopt "appropriate" behaviors and avoid those considered improper for their gender. Powell and Graves (2003) indicate that notions of "masculinity" and "femininity" on the shortened BSRI reflect beliefs of most whites and approximate those of Hispanics but fail to capture those of African Americans.

Bem also developed the concept of *androgynous management*, an ideal style in which leaders expand their repertoire of behaviors and apply them flexibly. The word *androgyny* is derived from two Greek words, *andr,* which means man, and *gyne-,* which means woman. Androgynous managers apply "masculine" or "feminine" behavior according to the demands of specific situations.

Over time, female undergraduates in the U.S. have become more androgynous. Their scores on "masculine" characteristics and behaviors on the BSRI have risen, but their scores on "feminine" characteristics have not changed. Though the BSRI scores of male U.S. undergraduates have increased slightly, the change is insufficient to make them more androgynous overall (Powell & Graves, 2003). Female college students, some of whom will become managers, are now more likely than ever to be able to enact both so-called "masculine" and "feminine" behaviors. Interpersonal skills, open communication, and flexibility, previously viewed as more prevalent in women than men, have been repeatedly touted as essential for managers of the twenty-first century. Nonetheless, research studies spanning three decades during which time the proportion of women in management jumped from slightly over one-fifth to nearly one-half, shows a widespread tendency for a majority in the U.S. to view managers as "masculine."

Powell and Graves (2003, p. 138) summarize as follows:

> . . . Men and women at different career stages, including undergraduate business students preparing to enter the workplace, part-time MBA students preparing for managerial careers, and practicing managers, described a good manager as higher in stereotypically masculine traits than stereotypically feminine traits. Support for the masculine stereotype of the good manager has diminished somewhat over time but remains strong. Support for the stereotype of men as more suited for the leader role than women is also strong, except in the views of U.S. women.

Readers interested in the specifics of studies conducted in 1976–77, 1984–85, and 1999 are urged to consult chapter 6 in *Women & Men in Management* by Powell and Graves (2003).

Neither stereotypically "feminine" nor "masculine" behavior is likely to increase managers' effectiveness (Powell & Graves, 2003) despite similarities between some aspects of transformational leadership and the feminine stereotype. Leader effectiveness is thought to result from either high concern for both people and production or enactment of behavior considered appropriate to the given situation.

Self-selection, organizational selection, and socialization processes perpetuate the belief that "good managers are 'masculine' (Powell, Butterfield, & Parent, 2002), however, as does the fact that stereotypes resist extinction. Resistance to extinction will be discussed later in this chapter. In the past, women who thought their skills and behaviors were consistent with the "feminine" stereotype may have hesitated to choose a career that they believed required behaviors consistent with the "masculine" stereotype. This reluctance, if it remains, has undoubtedly diminished. The fact that more U.S. women now regard themselves as androgynous and able to enact behaviors formerly labeled "masculine" and "feminine" equally well could counteract the trend to avoid careers still considered "masculine." Those selecting candidates for entry-level management positions may subconsciously view candidates high in behaviors and characteristics dubbed "masculine" more favorably than others.

Top executives set the tone regarding acceptable organizational behavior, and newcomers are socialized in the ways of those who are most powerful. Powell, Butterfield and Parent (2002) contend that the fact that top managers are still mainly white males may mean that women will not have an impact on gender stereotypes until large numbers of them reach top management. That view seems stereotypical because it assumes that top executive women, but not men, will esteem behaviors such as open communication, delegation, and concern for people, which have been referred to as "feminine." CEOs who are concerned about the bottom line and ethical behavior will want to use effective behaviors, regardless of the gender stereotype, just as they will want to fully use talents of all employees regardless of race, ethnicity, gender, and other immutable factors. Powell and Graves (2003) indicate that further increases in the percentage of women in management are unlikely to reduce gender stereotypes; to have an impact, changing sex ratios must occur at the highest management levels.

Though no evidence shows that men make better leaders or that good managers are masculine (Powell & Graves, 2003), managerial women must contend with such beliefs. Their sweeping effects extend to subordinates' views about working for executive females. A 1965 *Harvard Business Review* survey (Bowman, Worthy, & Greyser) replicated in 1985 (Sutton & Moore) showed that the percentage of men who would feel comfortable reporting to an executive female rose from 27 to 47% over 20 years. Seventy-five percent of those earning at least $75,000 in the early 1990s said that the supervisor's gender was immaterial, however (Karsten, 1994).

Regardless of their increased comfort, 50% of females and 45% of males in a Gallup poll of people in 22 nations indicated a preference for a male boss in 2000 (Powell & Graves, 2003). They might prefer to work for a man because they believe gender stereotypes about leader effectiveness or because they perceive men as more powerful than women. Kanter (1977) maintains that a preference for male bosses reflects, not gender bias, but a distaste for working for anyone who has little clout to secure needed resources. Another study (Ragins & Sundstrom, 1990) shows that subordinates of both sexes regard supervisors with the same positions as having equivalent power. If able to be generalized, those findings could cause Kanter's contention to be questioned. Bhatnagar and Swamy (1995) indicate that subordinates respond similarly to male and female supervisors with whom they have actually worked, but Heilman et al.'s work (1989) contradicts that finding. Subordinates who are satisfied with work-related exchanges with their female bosses are likely to view managerial women more favorably than those who are not.

Because gender stereotypes are strongly held, those who violate them may be censured. The nature and severity of the response depends on whether stereotypes are *prescribed*, or expected for a particular sex, or *proscribed*, which means prohibited for that sex. Prentice and Carranza (2002) propose that stereotypes of women and men are not mirror images of each other. Instead, certain behaviors are expected or discouraged for each sex to varying degrees. Both prescriptions for and prohibitions of gender related behavior may be classified as "intensified or "relaxed." In their study, Prentice and Carranza regard friendliness, warmth, and kindness as socially desirable, intensified prescriptions for women and "controlling" and "arrogant" behaviors, though undesirable for anyone, as intensified proscriptions for females. Relaxed prescriptions are less desirable for one sex but not more desirable for the other than they would be for any person, male or female. For example, it is considered "less desirable for a woman but not more desirable for a man . . . to have common sense and a good sense of humor . . . than it was for a person to have these qualities" (Prentice & Carranza, 2002, p. 272).

Relaxed proscriptions are undesirable for anyone but are perceived as less negative for one sex than the other (Prentice & Carranza, 2002). For example, "rebellious" and "domineering" are adjectives describing behavior for which there is a relaxed proscription for males. Though undesirable for anyone, such behaviors are considered less objectionable for males than for females in the U.S. Table 5.4 provides examples of relaxed and intensified prescribed and proscribed behavior for women and men.

Prentice and Carranza (2002) justify the complexity of their model because it can enhance understanding of ways in which various parts of gender role stereotypes result in different types of discrimination. Their model also helps explain different penalties for violations of gender stereotypes.

The *descriptive* part of gender stereotypes explains how males and females are thought to be, based on gender alone. The *prescriptive* part tells how males or females "should" behave. Descriptive stereotyping exerts pressure to conform to what is considered one's nature based on one's gender. As explained in chapter 3, *disparate impact* discrimination occurs when a neutral standard has a disproportionately negative effect on a protected group. The neutral standard here is the belief that each sex, by nature, is unsuited for occupations stereotypically associated with the other sex. Women may be assumed unfit for "masculine" jobs and may still feel subtle social pressure to avoid them. Similarly, men may be viewed as unsuited for "feminine" jobs (Prentice & Carranza, 2002), but women's exclusion from "masculine' jobs may do more economic harm if such jobs command higher pay rates.

Prentice and Carranza (2002) believe another type of discrimination, which they call *disparate standards discrimination,* may occur when women disregard

Table 5.4. Relaxed and Intensified Prescriptions and Proscriptions for Females and Males

	Valued more in females than males	Valued less in females than males	Valued more in males than females	Valued less in males than females
Desirable for any U.S. adult	Warm and kind Friendly Sensitive	Intelligent High self esteem	Business sense Athletic ability	Happy Enthusiastic Helpful
Prescribed Behaviors	*Gender intensified prescription*	*Gender relaxed prescription*	*Gender intensified prescription*	*Gender relaxed prescription*
	Tolerated/accepted more in females than males	**Tolerated/accepted less in females than males**	**Tolerated/accepted more in males than females**	**Tolerated/accepted less in males than females**
Undesirable for any U.S. adult	Yielding Emotional Childlike	Rebellious Intimidating Stubborn, Cynical Controlling	Rebellious Domineering Promiscuous	Emotional Shy Impressionable
Proscribed Behaviors	*Gender relaxed proscription*	*Gender intensified proscription*	*Gender relaxed proscription*	*Gender intensified proscription*

(Source: Adapted from Riedle, 2003)

Row 2 lists desirable behaviors for any U.S. adult, male or female. Of these generally desirable behaviors, being warm, kind, and friendly are especially prized in women. Being intelligent and mature, though valued in any U.S. adult, have been less valued in women than in men. Having business sense and being enthusiastic and happy are generally valued in any U.S. adult. Business sense has been seen as more valuable for men than women, whereas being happy and enthusiastic are less valued in men than women, though they are desirable characteristics overall. Row 4 lists undesirable behaviors for any U.S. adult. Being emotional or yielding, though undesirable behaviors for any U.S. adult, are slightly more acceptable in women than men. Rebellious or intimidating women totally violate their gender stereotype. Though U.S. society does not value rebellious or intimidating behavior in any adult, society views such behavior in women as far less acceptable than in men. Emotional and shy behaviors are not valued in any U.S. adult, but men who exhibit such behaviors totally violate their gender stereotype. Such behaviors are deemed far less acceptable in men than in women.

relaxed prescriptions for or proscriptions on behavior. Achievement-related behaviors are prescriptions that are relaxed for women but intensified for men, and females in the U.S. are "not held to equally high . . . standards of agency and achievement" (p. 280) as males. Though differential standards may not inevitably lead to unequal treatment of men and women, they are, nonetheless, harmful. The fact that accomplishment-related behaviors are considered relaxed prescriptions for women is no advantage in an achievement-oriented culture. "Instead, it reflects 'the soft bigotry of low expectations' " (Prentice & Carranza, 2002, p. 280, quoting George W. Bush's description of the way minority students are treated in schools), which can become a self-fulfilling prophecy and damage advancement prospects.

Prentice and Carranza give no examples of disparate standards discrimination that men experience when violating relaxed prescriptions for and proscriptions on behavior. Determining whether or not these researchers believe that men are harmed when they ignore relaxed prescriptions and proscriptions in the same way that women are disadvantaged is not possible.

A typical response to those who violate intensified gender stereotypes is pressure to conform to the stereotype. Those who flout relaxed gender prescriptions or proscriptions may experience discrimination based on different standards as mentioned previously. Alternatively, they may be rewarded. Instead of being considered "deviants," they may be seen as flexible individuals who have adopted an androgynous management style. For example, achievement-oriented women will be viewed favorably as long as they still are perceived as modest and nurturing (Prentice & Carranza, 2002). Likewise, people will respond positively to creative, optimistic men who continue to be goal-oriented and rational.

Violators of intensified prescriptions or proscriptions may be punished harshly. They can expect to be isolated and disliked and to experience negative job consequences such as lower performance evaluations, minimal pay raises, and reduced chances for promotion. Women who succeed in domains previously dominated by men or labeled "masculine" may experience social rejection and other adverse consequences that women who do well in gender-neutral or "feminine" typed occupations do not face (Heilman, Wallen, et al., 2004). For example, Ann Hopkins (1989) was punished for violating intensified gender stereotypes. Her performance was excellent, and she had more billable hours than male peers but was initially denied partnership in the accounting firm not due to any performance deficits or failure to get along with clients, but because she was deemed "not feminine enough." Hopkins was told she might benefit from attending "charm school." She was vindicated in the U.S. Supreme Court case, *Price Waterhouse v. Hopkins* (1989).

NEGATIVE CONSEQUENCES OF STEREOTYPING ON INDIVIDUALS AND ORGANIZATIONS

Stereotyping has negative consequences to those who are pigeonholed, those who label others, and the organization employing them. Those who are stereotyped exhibit some similar responses, but each person's coping mechanisms are unique. Some eventually accept the situation reluctantly; others rail against it, try to change it, or use a combination of tactics over time depending on the situation. Some may question themselves and start to act in ways that are consistent with stereotypes that have been drummed into them. They may feel insecure and become sensitive (Carr-Ruffino, 1999), which may result in feelings of being misunderstood or disregarded when majority group members accuse them of being "overly sensitive." Other passive responses include disengagement or withdrawal from the organization, the most extreme example of which is leaving. Resistance-oriented responses include rebelling against or attacking the majority group or trying to discredit the stereotype by changing behavior. Unless one's group comprises at least 15 to 35% of the organization, defined as a "critical mass" (Kanter, 1977), the latter is more likely to result in being labeled an "exception."

Insecurity has been described as a consequence of stereotyping that those who are typecast experience. It may also be a reason for prejudice and stereotyping. Individuals develop prejudices for many reasons including their socialization experiences, fear of competition from those in the group they stereotype, frustration due to lack of career progress and the resulting need for a "scapegoat," and difficulty dealing with new people or situations (Carr-Ruffino, 1999). Needs to feel superior or to conform with or gain the approval of the majority, which also are reasons for prejudice, may stem from insecurity. Those who stereotype others might feel smug initially if they believe they have demonstrated their superiority. This may give way to negativity, which leaves little mental energy for other more positive beliefs and behaviors (Carr-Ruffino, 1999).

Those who stereotype others might develop prejudices. *The American Heritage Dictionary* (1979) defines prejudice as "an adverse judgment or opinion formed beforehand or without knowledge or examination of the facts." Stereotypes are used to "prejudge" many people based only on the fact that they are members of a certain group. Other specific information about them is unknown. Those whose personalities are "highly authoritarian" and who see issues as "right" or "wrong" are more likely to have prejudices than those who are more tolerant and flexible, according to over 1000 studies dating from 1950 (Carr-Ruffino, 1999). Though prejudice does not inevitably cause harmful behavior, people may act on their prejudices through overt or subtle discrimination. As explained in chapter 3, employment discrimination against members of protected classes is illegal, and most also regard it as unethical.

Arguably the most damaging consequences of stereotyping to organizations are underutilization and misallocation of human talent. Always serious ethical issues, these problems compound when demand for professional and technical employees and workers with specialized expertise exceeds supply. To the extent that stereotyping leads to prejudice which results in discrimination, the impact on organizations is predictable and dangerous. Selection processes and opportunities to participate in training programs will be affected. Executive women whom Larwood and Wood interviewed (1995) think stereotyping has a major impact on whether males or females receive certain types of training.

Stereotyping may affect the first two phases of group development, forming and storming, which can stymie the functioning of work groups or teams. In the forming stage, group members get to know each other, learn about one another's strengths and behaviors, assess what various members can do, and choose a leader. In the storming stage, the group sets goals and establishes interaction patterns. Bass, Tomkiewicz et al. (2001) studied the stereotypes that 102 black graduating seniors majoring in business at a school accredited by the Association for the Advancement of Collegiate Schools of Business (AACSB) have of Hispanics, non-Hispanic whites, and other blacks. The blacks in the study saw themselves as extremely able leaders, and their positive view of members of their own racial/ethnic group precluded favorable views of any other group. Bass, Tomkiewicz et al. (2001, p. 267) thought this might reduce their motivation to get to know diverse others and that "self-managed work groups under such circumstances would exist in name only." The researchers suspected that groups might have difficulty moving beyond the storming stage if one formed a clique and considered itself superior to those of other ethnic/racial origins. In addition, the African American subjects might not seek input regarding group priorities from those who are ethnically different because of their assumption of their own superiority, which Bass, Tomkiewicz et al. (2001) dubbed "affirmative exclusivity."

If organizations develop a bad reputation, perceptions of a negative workplace culture may create recruitment and retention difficulties. Dysfunctional conflict and stress may increase due to stereotyping. Productivity may decline due to reduced performance of individuals who face stereotype threat.

ELIMINATION OF STEREOTYPES

Why is it so difficult to eradicate stereotypes? How can their destructive effects be minimized if they cannot be eliminated? Social and mental processes reinforce the stability of stereotypes, which are over-learned during early so-cialization. The self-fulfilling prophecy has been discussed as a cognitive explanation for the persistence of stereotypes. People may be more likely to notice those who seem to fit a preconceived mold and then use such observa-tions to reinforce stereotypes. On the other hand, they will view those who do not match stereotypes as exceptions, or "deviants" (Kanter, 1977). This process allows them to retain the stereotypes.

Though collective attitudes toward groups that have been labeled in the past have shifted, stereotypes, which represent the status quo, resist change. Highly prejudiced individuals might be persuaded to stop discriminatory behavior based on changes in cues indicating that such actions are no longer socially desirable (Devine & Elliott, 1995). Whether or not behavioral change will lead them to reject negative stereotypes is another matter. Belief changes may not herald a re-duction in the pervasiveness of stereotypes. It is possible to have knowledge of a stereotype that totally conflicts with one's beliefs. This is the situation of indi-viduals who are low in prejudice. Stereotypes are not erased from their memory; in fact, stereotypical responses can be accessed easily and compete with re-sponses based on beliefs while the stereotype reduction process is occurring (Devine & Elliott, 1995). Deliberate attempts to suppress stereotypes could make them more available (Macare, Bodenhausen, et al., 1994), and even highly motivated people with little prejudice must expend much effort to eliminate them (Devine & Elliott). Racial and gender stereotypes are especially resistant to extinction. The former are infused throughout the dominant culture in the U.S. Gender stereotypes resist elimination and "have remained essentially stable over time in different cultures, even as attitudes about women's rights and roles have changed"(Powell, Butterfield, & Parent, 2002, p. 178).

Stereotypes may change suddenly, as in the "conversion" model, or gradu-ally, as in the "bookkeeping" approach (Rothbart, 1981). Conversion occurs after a breakthrough in thinking, which results from presentation of relevant, crucial data that makes it nearly impossible to ignore that a stereotype is false. New information confirming or refuting stereotypes can cause people to mod-ify them over time, according to the "bookkeeping" approach. A steady stream of contradicting information is needed before stereotypes are rejected.

REDUCING HARMFUL INFLUENCE OF STEREOTYPING: ORGANIZATIONAL RESPONSE

Supervisors and managers have a crucial role in reducing the harmful conse-quences of stereotyping. By appreciating each employee's unique contribu-tions, they help create an environment in which members of groups value themselves. That must occur before they can value other groups (Kohatsu et al., 2000).Supervisors must understand the human tendency to resort to stereotyping, ways in which the process injures individuals and the organization, and the content of stereotypes that groups in the workforce and community hold about each other. Supervisors and managers must guard against relying on stereotypes themselves.

Because people's stereotypes do not necessarily disappear the first time they encounter disconfirming information, supervisors should take every opportunity to dispel myths about other groups. Human resource departments could assist them by providing information to debunk stereotypes, which they could disseminate to employees who report to them as a regular follow-up to diversity training. Alternatively, clips from the Society for Human Resource Management's *Mosaics* or similar diversity-related newsletters could be shared with employees. Employees may be more likely to seriously consider information that their supervisors, rather than human resource managers, give them because supervisors can provide or withhold workplace rewards.

Instead of ignoring statements that reflect stereotypes, managers throughout the organization should confront them in ways that avoid diminishing people who made the statements. Without directly asking people to change deeply held beliefs, middle and upper level managers should encourage subordinates and other employees to consider other views. Those demonstrating a willingness to do so must be respected regardless of whether or not they eventually change underlying beliefs.

Managers must focus on workplace behavior, not beliefs. They should state that respectful treatment of co-workers, clients, customers, and suppliers is a non-negotiable job requirement and assure that failure to meet it has consequences.

Stereotypes should be addressed in diversity training, but care must be taken to assure that this does not result in legal liability, as it did for Texaco and Lucky Stores. Before stereotypes can be debunked, they must be acknowledged, but prudent organizations should consult with legal counsel regarding the portion of diversity training dealing with stereotypes prior to conducting it.

Though hiring consultants is not necessary, selecting only those who have had training in successful ways to conduct diversity workshops as facilitators of such sessions is crucial to avoid having the training backfire. The skills such trainers should possess were discussed in chapter 4.

Discussions of stereotypes may proceed more smoothly if trainers begin by asking participants to think about situations in which they—or others they know well—felt as if they did not fit in a group. Feeling like the "other" is an almost universal experience, and asking people to recall their affective reactions to such a situation might help them understand—and perhaps develop empathy for—individuals who must contend with such feelings regularly due to circumstances beyond their control. Such an activity could help avoid polarization that sometimes occurs if one group thinks it is being unfairly blamed for difficulties experienced by another. This approach might facilitate a transition between a discussion of the general experience of feeling like the "other" and the differences among employees that are most relevant or problematic in a particular organization.

To avoid chronic anger and maintain a positive outlook, members of groups that are stereotyped are urged to view stated assumptions or questions about themselves as opportunities to educate others. For example, people who require interpreters or attendants due to physical disabilities experience situations in which others address the interpreter or attendant instead of them. Others might incorrectly assume that those with physical disabilities also are cognitively impaired. Assertively and calmly indicating that the conversation and questions should be directed to them, not to their assistants, may be an appropriate response. Though preferable to an angry reply, this gets wearing and time-consuming if the same stereotype must be debunked repeatedly, another example of an extra burden not faced by the majority. As information to refute stereotypes is repeated and society becomes more knowledgeable about differences, perhaps stereotypes will be more widely recognized for what they are. When that occurs, members of groups that have been stereotyped may gladly relinquish their educational roles.

SUMMARY

In this chapter, the term "stereotype" has been defined, and characteristics such as cumulative effect and stereotype threat have been explained. Stereotypes based on race/ethnicity, gender, and both have been discussed, and evidence has been presented to discredit them. Reasons for the persistence of gender stereotypes of leadership, despite evidence to the contrary, have been explored as has the role of social context in clarifying results of studies on gender differences. Explanations for the difficulty of eradicating stereotypes have been offered, and the chapter concluded with a discussion of constructive approaches organizations and individuals can take to minimize dysfunctional consequences of stereotypes that cannot be eliminated.

REFERENCES

Agars, M.D. 2004. Reconsidering the impact of gender stereotypes on the advancement of women in organizations. *Psychology of WomenQuarterly, 28.* 103–111.

American Heritage Dictionary of the English Language. 1979. Morris, William, Ed. Boston: Houghton-Mifflin. p. 1033.

Ashley, J.S. & Jarrat-Ziemski, K. 1999. Superficiality and bias. *American Indian Quarterly, 3*(3/4). 49–63.

Bass, K., Tomkiewicz, J., Adeyemi-Bello, T., Vaicys, C. 2001. Workgroup productivity: The implications of African-Americans' racial stereotypes for cooperative job designs. *Work Study, 50* (5/6). 263–69.

Bell, E. & Nkomo, S. 2000. *Our separate ways.* Cambridge: Harvard Business School Press.

Bem, S.L. 1974. The measurement of psychological androgyny. *Journal of Consulting and Clinical Psychology, 42.* 155–62.

Bhatnagar, D. & Swamy, R. 1995. Attitudes toward women as managers: Does interaction make a difference? *Human Relations, 48.* 1248–1307.

Bowman, G., Worthy, N. & Greyser, S. 1965, July-Aug. Are women executives people? *Harvard Business Review.* 15–28, 164–78.

Brown, L.K. 1979. Women and management: Review essay. *Signs, 5*(2). 266–88.

Bly, R. 1992. *Iron John: A book about men.* New York: Random House.

Carr-Ruffino, N. 1999. *Diversity success strategies.* Boston: Butterworth-Heinemann.

Chang, S.H. & Kleiner. B.H. 2003. Common racial stereotypes. *Equal Opportunities International, 22*(3). 1–9.

Cheryan, S. & Bodenhausen, G. 2000. When positive stereotypes threaten intellectual performance: The psychological hazards of the 'model minority' status. *Psychological Science, 11.* 399–402.

Collier, C.A. & Shaffer. D.R. 1999. Activation and use of racial stereotypes in personnel decisions: A test of two theories. *Journal of Applied Psychology, 29*(11). 2292–2307.

Cox. T.H., Jr. 1994. *Cultural diversity in organizations: Theory, research, & practice.* San Francisco: Berrett-Koehler.

Davidson, M.J. 1997. *The black and ethnic minority woman manager: Cracking the concrete ceiling.* London: Paul Chapman Publishing.

Devine, P.G. 1989. Stereotypes and prejudice: Their automatic and controlled components. *Journal of Personality & Social Psychology, 56.* 5–18.

Devine, P.G. & Elliott, A.J. 1995. Are racial stereotypes really fading? The Princeton trilogy revisited. *Personality and Social Psychology Bulletin, 21*(11). 1139–50.

Diekman, A.B., Goodfriend, W. & Goodwin, S. 2004. Dynamic stereotypes of power: Perceived change and stability in gender hierarchies. *Sex Roles, 50*(3/4). 201–215.

Dipboye, R. 1975, May/June. Women as managers: Stereotypes and realities. *Survey of business.* 22–6. Eagly, A.H. 1995. The science and politics of comparing women and men. *American Psychologist, 50.* 145–58.

Eagly, A.H. & Crowley, M. 1986. Gender and helping behavior: A meta-analysis. *Psychological Bulletin, 100.* 283–308.

Eagly, A.H. & Johnson, B.T. 1990. Gender and leadership style: A meta-analysis. *Psychological Bulletin, 108.* 233–56.

Eagly, A.H. & Steffen, V.J. 1986. Gender and aggressive behavior: A meta-analytic review of the social psychological literature. *Psychological Bulletin, 100.* 309–30.

Eccles, J.S. & Jacobs, J.E. 1986. Social forces shape math attitudes and performance. *Signs, 11*. 367–80.

Gilbert, D. & Hixon, G. 1991. The trouble of thinking: Activation and application of stereotypical beliefs. *Journal of Personality & Social Psychology, 60*. 509–17.

Gilbert, J. N. Carr-Ruffino, Ivancevich, J.M. & Lownes-Jackson, M. 2003. An empirical examination of inter-ethnic stereotypes: Comparing Asian-American and African-American employees. *Public Personnel Management, 32*(2). 251.

Heilman, M., Block, C., Simon, M. & Martell, R. 1989. Has anything changed: Current characterizations of men, women, and managers. *Journal of Applied Psychology, 74*. 935–42.

Heilman, M.E., Wallen, A.S., Fuchs, D. & Tamkins, M.M. 2004. Penalties for success: Reactions to women who succeed at male gender-typed tasks. *Journal of Applied Psychology, 89*(3). 416–27.

Holmes, J., L. Burns, Marra, M., Stubbe, M. & Vine, B. 2003. Women managing discourse in the workplace. *Women in Management Review, 18*(8). 414.

Hyde, J. 1996. *Half the human experience.* 5th ed. Lexington, MA: Heath.

Hyde, J. 2001. Psychology of Women & Gender. In J.S. Halonen & S.F. Davis, Eds. *The many faces of psychological research in the 21st century.* Published by The Society for the Teaching of Psychology. Retrieved September 3, 2004 from http://teachpsych.lemoyne.edu/teachpsych/faces/text/.

Job, J.R. 1998. *Just because I'm Latin doesn't mean I mambo: A success guide for Hispanic Americans.* New York: The Ballantine Publishing Group.

Kanter, R.M. 1977. *Men and women of the corporation.* New York: Basic Books.

Karsten, M.F. 1986. *Women in Management.* Course guide for U216–334. University of Wisconsin Extension. Independent Study-Business and Economics. Madison, WI: Board of Regents of the University of Wisconsin.

Karsten, M.F. 1994. *Management and gender: Issues and attitudes.* Westport: Greenwood Publishing Group, Inc.

Kohatsu, E.L., Dulay, M., Lam, C., Concepcion, W., Perez, P., Lopez, C. & Euler, J. 2000. Using racial identity theory to explore racial mistrust and interracial contact among Asian Americans. *Journal of Counseling & Development, 78*. 334–42.

Lane, N. & Piercy, N.F. 2003. The ethics of discrimination: Organizational mindsets and female employment disadvantage. *Journal of Business Ethics, 44*(4). 313–25.

Larwood, L. & Wood, M. 1995. Training women for management: Changing priorities. *The Journal of Management Development, 14*(2). 54–65.

Lhamon, W.T. Jr. (n.d.) Racial stereotypes. Retrieved September 3, 2004 from http://www.africana.com/research/encarta/tt_285.asp.

Livers, A.B. & Caver, K.A. 2003. *Leading in black and white: Working across the racial divide in corporate America.* San Francisco: John Wiley & Sons, Inc.

Lott, B. 1985. The devaluation of women's competence. *Journal of Social Issues, 41*(4). 43–60.

Macare, C.N., Bodenhausen, G.V., Milne, A.B. & Jetten, J. 1994. Out of mind but back in sight: Stereotypes on the rebound. *Journal of Personality & Social Psychology, 36*. 929–40.

McRae, M.B. 1994. Influence of sex role stereotypes on personnel decisions of black managers. *Journal of Applied Psychology, 79*(2). 306–09.

Merrick, B.G. 2002. The ethics of hiring in the new workplace: Men and women managers face changing stereotypes discover correlative patterns for success. *Competitiveness Review,12*(1). 94–115.

Mihesuah, D.A. 1996. *American Indians: Stereotypes and realities.* Atlanta: Clarity Press, Inc.

Oakley, J.G. 2000. Gender-based barriers to senior management positions: Understanding the scarcity of female CEOs. *Journal of Business Ethics, 27*(4). 321–35.

Nash, K. 1998. Gender bias: Do outdated domestic stereotypes still haunt women at work? *EEO Bimonthly, 29*(1). 36.

Oyserman, D. & Sakamoto, I. 1997. Being Asian American: Identity, cultural constructs, and stereotype perception. *The Journal of Applied Behavioral Science, 33*(4). 435–54.

Powell, G.N. 1988. *Women and men in management.* Newbury Park, CA: SAGE.

Powell, G.N., Butterfield, D.A. & Parent, J.D. 2002. Gender and managerial stereotypes: Have the times changed? *Journal of Management, 28*(2). 177–93.

Powell, G.N. & Graves, L.M. 2003. *Women and men in management.*3rd ed. Newbury Park, CA: SAGE. Prentice, D.A. & E. Carranza. 2002. What women and men should be, shouldn't be, are allowed to be and don't have to be: The contents of prescriptive gender stereotypes. *Psychology of Women Quarterly, 26.* 269–81.

Prentice, D.A. & Carranza, E. 2002. What women and men should be, shouldn't be, are allowed to be, and don't have to be: The contents of prescriptive gender stereotypes. *Psychology of Women Quarterly, 26.* 269–81.

Price Waterhouse v. Hopkins. 1989. 490 U.S. 228. FindLaw for Legal Professionals. Retrieved September 3, 2004 from http://caselaw.lp.findlaw.com/scripts/getcase .pl?court=US&vol=490&invol=228.

Ragins, B. & Sundstrom, E. 1990. Gender and perceived power in management-subordinate relationships. *Journal of Applied Psychology, 63.* 273–87.

Riedle, J.E. 2004. Chapter 6. Gender and race-based socialization processes. In M.F. Karsten, Ed. *Management, Gender, and Race in the 21st Century.* Lanham, MD: University Press of America, Inc.

Riedle, J.E. 2003, March 10. Modern stereotypes. Lecture notes for PSYC/WMST 2530 *Psychology of Women.* University of Wisconsin-Platteville.

Roberson, L., Deitch, E.A., Brief, A.P. & Block, C.J. 2003. Stereotype threat and feedback seeking in the workplace. *Journal of Vocational Behavior, 62.* 176–188.

Ross, L. & Nisbitt, R.E. 1991. *The person and the situation: Perspectives of social psychology.* New York: McGraw Hill.

Rothbart, M. 1981. Memory processes and social beliefs. In D.L. Hamilton. Ed. *Cognitive processes in stereotyping and intergroup behavior.* Hillsdale, N.J.: Erlbaum.

Sackett, P.R., DuBois, C.L. & Noe, A.W. 1991. Tokenism in performance evaluation: The effects of work group representation on male-female and White-Black differences in performance ratings. *Journal of Applied Psychology, 76.* 263–67.

Sharps, M.J., Price, J.L. & Williams, J.K. 1994. Spatial cognitions and gender: Instructional and stimulus influences on mental image rotation performance. *Psychology of Women Quarterly, 18.* 413–26.

Steele, C.M. 1997. A threat in the air: How stereotypes shape intellectual identity and performance. *American Psychologist, 52.* 613–29.

Stumpf, H. & Stanley, J.C. 1998. Stability and change in gender-relatd differences on the college board advanced placement and achievement tests. *Current Directions in Psychological Science, 7.* 192–96.

Sutton, C. & Moore, K. 1985, Sept./Oct. Executive women 20 years later. *Harvard Business Review.* 43–46.

Swim, J.K., Borgida, E. & Maruyama, G. 1989. Joan McKay versus Jon McKay: Do gender stereotypes bias evaluations? *Psychological Bulletin, 105.* 409–29.

Tan, A., Fujioka, Y. & Lucht, N. 1997, Summer. Native American stereotypes, TV portrayals, and personal contact. *Journalism & Mass Communication Quarterly, 74(2).* 265–84.

Thomas, K.M. 2005. *Diversity dynamics in the workplace.* Belmont, CA: Thomson Wadsworth.

Thomas, K.M., Mack, D.A. & Montagliani, A. 2004. The arguments against diversity: Are they valid? In M.S. Stockdale & F.J. Crosby, Eds. *The psychology and management of workplace diversity.* Malden, MA: Blackwell Publishers, Ltd.

Voyer, D., S. Voyer & Bryden, M.P. 1995. Magnitude of sex differences in spatial abilities: A meta-analysis and consideration of critical variables. *Psychological Bulletin, 117.* 250–70.

Yoder, J.D. 2003. *Women and gender: Transforming psychology.* 2nd ed. Upper Saddle River, N.J.: Prentice-Hall.

Yoder, J.D. & Kahn, A.S. 2003. Making gender comparisons more meaningful: A call for more attention to social context. *Psychology of Women Quarterly, 27.* 281–90.

Chapter Six

Gender and Race-Based Socialization Processes

Joan E. Riedle

OUTCOMES

After studying this chapter, you should be able to:

1. define sex-typed behavior, eligibility pool hypothesis, schema
2. explain how Margaret Mead's studies of three New Guinea societies contradict the notion that gender roles are static and determined by nature.
3. explain how parents, caregivers, peers, play behavior, and the media contribute to the gender role socialization of children in the U.S.
4. identify the three analytic processes of gender role socialization that occur in early childhood.
5. explain how the gender schema lead to preferences for gender-typed activities.
6. justify whether or not you believe it is desirable to avoid teaching children to differentiate the world in terms of gender.
7. explain how apparent gender differences may really result from status differences between women and men.
8. compare and contrast the gender, job, and integrated models that relate gender and work.
9. explain how racial socialization can be used to develop and promote worldviews about race and ethnicity that benefit minorities.
10. explain the impact of the media on race-role and sex-role socialization.
11. explain how stereotypes and socialization based on gender and race are related to each other and to power differences and workplace discrimination.

SOCIALIZATION PROCESSES: AN OVERVIEW

The content of gender and race-based stereotypes was discussed in chapter 5. We know what is believed, but why do we believe it? And if those beliefs are largely unfounded, why do they persist? Theories differ in how they answer these questions. Essentialist theories basically argue that biology is the source of gender differences; some essentialist theories address female weakness and others argue for female superiority, but all downplay the importance of culture and learning. Feminist theories are more likely to argue that the gender differences which actually exist are much smaller than might be anticipated and are largely (if not completely) acquired. The information presented in this chapter will support the perspective that some innate cognitive tendencies contribute to the process of stereotyping, but that the specific content of our stereotypes is acquired and highly flexible and that observed gender differences are largely a result of socialization.

Rosalind Barnett and Caryl Rivers (2004) explore various explanations for gender differences that essentialists have proposed. They argue that beliefs about the appropriateness of gender-related role distinctions, with men striving for success outside of the home and through careers and women striving for success within the home and through relationships, are often justified as rooted in men's early roles as hunter and warrior. They describe this position in a nutshell as:

> . . . meat-eating males were responsible for the development of our capacity to stand upright, make tools for hunting, develop speech to facilitate the group hunt, and bring back provisions to women and children. Males skilled at warfare and hunting came quickly to dominate the environment around them. Hunting in particular, they say, equipped males with a distinct advantage that still plays out in the workplace today, giving men an edge in jobs from piloting airliners through the sky to governing the state. (p. 127)

While this image of our early ancestry is probably familiar to us all, Barnett and Rivers point out that it largely originated in the 1950's, and had the effect of both trivializing women's contributions to our society and providing justification for the existing disparities in women's and men's roles. Since that time, multiple scientific findings have brought the hunter-warrior image of our male ancestors into question. Barnett and Rivers (2004) cite anthropological evidence that ancient men and women did not live in fixed locations with women huddled around the campfire waiting for men to provide; that early skeletal evidence of war is now considered to be evidence of attacks by carnivorous animals rather than skilled warriors; that big game hunting is actually a rather recent development (fifth century, B.C.) and not likely to be the source of evolutionary differences in skills and abilities; that women also hunted and trapped game, usually with nets; and that while war may be a more recent invention than previously thought, many women served as warriors. They suggest that women's less extensive role in combat may actually be a result of society's greater need for women than men:

> Rather than women's weakness, we believe, the fragility of the human infant and the extended human childhood lay at the root of the historical taboo of women in combat. A single male could produce enough sperm to repopulate a tribe. But it took one female years to bear and nurse each child. Women simply could not be spared for combat. When parents could expect only half of their children to make it to adulthood, large families helped ensure the survival of the tribe and the species. (p. 143).

In the modern world, with medical and technological advances and the greatly decreased infant mortality rate, Barnett and Rivers predict that age-old restrictions on women's roles will continue to fall away.

But, while the biological necessity for gender-role distinctions may be fading, psychological forces continue to resist change. We "know" this is how women and men are meant to be. Change would be unnatural and wrong. Change is frightening. Change would take away privileges from some and power from others and thus is resisted. Stereotypes, and the socialization practices that perpetuate them, have served as powerful mechanisms to maintain the status quo. Thornton, Chatters, Taylor, and Allen (1990) state: "through the process of socialization, individuals acquire an understanding of recognized statuses, roles, and prescribed behaviors and locate themselves and others in the social structure" (p. 401). Indeed, many argue that the stereotypes we currently associate with men and women, and with whites and minorities, are actually the stereotypes of the powerful and the powerless (or less powerful). We may be confusing gender with status, or race with status, and as status differences disappear so may many of the things that we presume to "know" about the sexes and the races. In a slight variation of the status theme, some argue that we are confusing gender with differences in roles (such as homemaker and employee), and that as the presence of the sexes becomes more equal in those roles the perceived differences between the groups will lessen (Eagly & Steffen, 1984; Hoffman & Hurst, 1990).

In this chapter, the perpetuation of stereotypes through cultural practices will be explored, as will various misconceptions about group difference. Our discussion will include psychological theories and findings relevant to:

1. Gender-based socialization processes;
2. Contextual effects;

3. The meaning of "difference";
4. Gender-based socialization and work;
5. Racial socialization;
6. Media contributions to socialization;
7. Discrimination, socialization, and power.

GENDER-BASED SOCIALIZATION PROCESSES[1]

We tend to believe that what is true of our culture is true of every other. Further, when consistency across cultures is discovered, we tend to believe that the patterns observed are innately determined. For example, we may assume that what is true of women's and men's roles in our Western culture is true throughout the world and, in being true throughout the world, that the gender roles must be genetically determined. One of the most dramatic examples of the fallacy of these beliefs comes from the studies of Margaret Mead (1935; 1963).

Mead studied the gender roles evidenced in three societies from northeastern New Guinea. She found that each had developed a very different conceptualization of the "natural" roles for women and men (none of which match those of our culture). The first two tribes differed from each other, but in each men and women displayed the same temperaments. In the mountain-dwelling community of the Arapesh, Mead found both men and women to display a warm and maternal temperament. She described the Arapesh women and men in terms that our culture considers feminine: nurturant, gentle, unaggressive, and responsive to the needs of their community. The river-dwelling Mundugumors were cannibals and headhunters. Both Mundugumor men and women were hostile and competitive, traits we consider masculine. In the third tribe, the lake-dwelling Tchambuli, Mead found the traditional Western gender roles to be reversed. Tchambuli women were hardworking and reliable, running the business of the community, while the men were emotionally and economically dependent and primarily concerned with self-adornment, the arts, and ceremonial life.

The development of such different cultural styles, within such a restricted geographic area, flies in the face of beliefs that gender roles are constant and set by nature. Rather, gender roles may be culturally determined, with Mead's findings vividly illustrating that all cultures do not teach the same patterns of behavior. Through what processes are gender-related cultural belief systems disseminated? Can such beliefs be modified?

Gender-Role Acquisition

Weitzman (1979) divides gender role learning during early childhood into *three analytic processes*:

1. to *distinguish* between men and women and between boys and girls, and to know what kinds of behavior are characteristic of each;
2. to express appropriate gender role *preferences* for himself or herself; and
3. to *behave* in accordance with gender role standards.

Cognitive social psychology, gender schema theory, and social learning theory may each contribute to our understanding of how these processes are accomplished.

Analytic Process 1: Distinguishing Groups. Cognitive social psychology extends basic findings about human cognitive processes (i.e., how our mind processes information) to social perception. Basic cognitive tendencies encourage us to perceive how groups differ, including groups based on sex. These cognitive tendencies may constitute the primary, innate factors that contribute to gender typing and gender stereotypes. One basic tendency is a desire to find meaning in the information that we have available and a second deals with our primary method of finding meaning—the creation of categories. It would be tremendously difficult to function in a world which contained no categories. How long would a child survive who could not comprehend the categories of "father" and "mother?" From each different visual angle the child's parents would appear to be new individuals. Placing human beings into distinguishable categories imposes a significant degree of meaning on our perceptions.

Our culture influences the categories that we create about people and teaches us to assign more importance to some categorizations than others (Tajfel, 1981). Such importance is conveyed when the culture attaches many associations to the category and assigns to it a functional significance, such as basing roles upon the categorization (Bem, 1983). Through these processes gender categories become "primary," while others, such as eye color, do not. No other dichotomy in human experience appears to have as many characteristics associated with it as does the distinction between female and male (Bem, 1983). Virtually every culture has perceived differences between men and women and assigned somewhat divergent roles to the sexes. Gender-related associations have been extended to nearly every aspect of life, including toys, jobs, hobbies, household tasks, inanimate objects (ships are female, the sun is male), and even animal species (dogs are male, cats are female).

Unfortunately, while categorization enables us to find meaning in stimuli, it also results in perceptual distortions (Tajfel, 1981). Thinking in terms of categories leads us to perceive greater differences between the groups than actually exist. Thus, we believe men and women have nothing in common. Thinking in terms of categories leads us to perceive greater similarity among the members of each category than actually exists. Thus, all men are assumed to be alike; all women are the same. In actuality, on virtually every characteristic the range of variation within men or within women exceeds the average difference between men and women (Hyde, 1985).

Rosabeth Moss Kanter (1977) wrote eloquently on women as tokens in male-dominated occupations and, in the process, identified perceptual patterns consistent with those just described. (Tokenism is discussed more fully in chapter 7.) Kanter defined skewed groups as those with a preponderance of one group over the other (85% versus 15%). Members of the smaller group were labeled tokens and were predicted to be treated as "representatives of their category, as symbols rather than individuals" (p. 208). Kanter argued that, in being perceptually salient, tokens would receive more attention. Awareness of the token group leads the majority to become more self-conscious and to focus on its own members' shared features. In the process, majority group members become more aware of their commonalities (all men are alike) and of their differences from the tokens (men and women have nothing in common). Thus the presence of the outsider creates a common bond among the majority; Kanter (1977) found that men emphasized topics of conversation at social events that differentiated themselves from women to a greater degree when women were present than in their absence.

Not every culture places as much importance on the gender dichotomy as ours. While the extent to which cultures exaggerate the differences and downplay the similarities between women and men may vary, one can expect the overall pattern of viewing men to be somewhat better than women to be consistent. While cultures have differed in what roles women and men are assigned, they have consistently assigned the most highly valued roles to men. If women grow potatoes and men grow yams, yams are served at the important ceremonials. Thus, a system of values has been included in cultural belief systems about gender, such that women and their roles are considered inferior to men and men's roles (Tavris & Wade, 1984).

The degree of perceptual distortion that results from categorization is somewhat predictable. If the dimension along which the categories are created is one highly valued in the culture, thus personally meaningful to its citizens, distortion is increased. Two examples related to racial bias make this point. Secord, Beven, and Katz (1956) found that prejudiced respondents exaggerated the physical differences between African Americans and whites, relative to non-prejudiced respondents. More recently, Oliver, Jackson, Moses, and Dangerfield (2004) showed that triggering the stereotype that African Americans are aggressive leads to more extreme judgments about facial differences. Participants read a news story about an individual in either a criminal setting (e.g., a story about a burglary-murder) or non-criminal setting (e.g., a story about a college professor winning an award). The news article included a photograph of an African American, who did not possess pronounced African American features. (Features had been previously scored in terms of how characteristic they were of African Americans.) In actuality, the same photograph was included for all stories and had been created using a computer program. The participants' task was to reconstruct the photograph by selecting from a series of facial features presented through the same computer program. For participants who had read the non-crime stories, the selected features did not differ significantly from the actual photograph, but for those who had read about a criminal the features chosen were more strongly characteristic of African Americans.

Just as cultures differ in what traits they associate with males and females, variations in socialization by race and ethnicity must be acknowledged. As one example, the markedly different family structures and role expectations within the African American community (Hyde, 1985) would doubtlessly lead to different patterns of socialization and, consequently, different gender-related associations. Smith and Midlarsky (1985) found whites to use more stereotypical concepts in their descriptions of women and men than African Americans. African Americans did not characterize women as passive, while many whites did. African Americans less often described men as competent and aggressive, and more often described men by their roles (e.g., father, truck driver, factory worker). Finn (1986) found that men agreed with more traditional sex role attitudes than women, and whites expressed more traditional beliefs than African Americans. Traditional was defined as agreeing with such beliefs as the husband should be super-ordinate in decision making power. Thus the gender-related concepts of African Americans tend to be more gender-neutral.

African American and Mexican American socialization practices were examined by Davenport and Yurich (1991). The patriarchal structure evident in Mexican American and Anglo cultures and on continental Africa was disrupted for African Americans in the United States by the practice of slavery (Davenport & Yurich, 1991). The slave owner took on the role of patriarch for both male and female slaves, resulting in an equal state of powerlessness for both. Post-slavery, African American women have combined the roles of employee and mother to a greater extent than other groups of women. Thus African American women and men have functioned in roles with more equality than is true of other races in the United States and, relative to other groups of women, the African American female is more often described as strong and resourceful.

In the traditional stereotypes of Mexican Americans, machismo describes males and hembrismo describes females (Davenport & Yurich, 1991). Machismo involves extreme manliness, with males avoiding all roles or activities associated with women and being aggressive, fearless, and dominating of women. Hembrismo involves extreme femininity, passivity, and self-denial. Davenport and Yurich present evidence that these traditional stereotypes are weakening, but are currently more supported by Chicano men than women. For example, Chicano men have been shown to be relatively neutral about traditional gender roles, while Anglo men, Chicano women, and Anglo women (in ascending order) express more disagreement with those roles (Gonzalez, 1982, as cited in Davenport and Yurich). Davenport and Yurich suggest that Chicano men may be resistant to changes in gender roles given their lack of access to the political and economic means of identity development available to men in other social classes.

International comparisons also show diversity in the roles to which men and women are socialized. Basow (1984) proposed that gender-typing might be less extreme in the South Pacific nation of Fiji, where sex-role socialization is less rigid. Child care is not thought to be the province of mothers but is shared in by many, and women actively participate in the agricultural activities which dominate their economy. Students in Figi were compared to those in the United States on a questionnaire which assessed femininity and masculinity. Relative to their United States counterparts, Figi males scored lower on masculinity and Figi females scored lower on femininity, Figi men and women did not differ significantly on either scale, and far fewer of the students from Figi qualified as sex-typed. Basow interpreted these findings as consistent with the more flexible attitude toward sex-typing present in Polynesian and Melanesian cultures and with the more even participation of both sexes in child rearing.

Virtually every aspect of our culture contributes to the teaching of gender roles. Parents are not the only models to which children attend. Teachers, neighbors, peers, and media images all contribute. Subtle (and not so subtle) messages may teach and perpetuate cultural ideologies. Condry and Condry (1976) showed men and women a videotape of a nine-month-old who responded to a jack-in-the-box first by staring and then by becoming agitated and crying. When the child was said to be a girl, adults described her as more fearful and less angry than when the same infant was said to be a boy. Will, Self, and Datan (1976) studied the play behavior of mothers with infants. The women claimed to believe that six-month-old boys and girls were alike and said that they would not treat their own sons and daughters differently. However, mothers who were presented an infant named "Beth" handed her a doll to play with more, and a train to play with less, than did mothers who thought the child was "Adam." Beth and Adam were actually the same child, a boy. Thus, the perceptions and behaviors of parents are biased by the sex of the child, and this may occur without conscious awareness.

More recent studies indicate that patterns of differential socialization continue. Idle, Wood, and Desmarais (1993) studied the play behavior of fathers and mothers with their sons and daughters, exploring feminine toys (e.g., baby dolls and kitchen sets), masculine toys (e.g., balls and trucks), and gender neutral toys (e.g., blocks and puzzles). The feminine toys were least preferred by both parents and children. Boys spent more time playing with the masculine toys than the neutral, while girls spent more time playing with the neutral toys. Fathers rated the masculine toys as most desirable for their sons, the feminine toys as least desirable. They rated the neutral toys as most desirable for their daughters, the masculine toys as least desirable. Mothers rated the neutral toys as most desirable for both sons and daughters, the feminine toys as least desirable for their sons and the masculine toys as least desirable for their daughters. Thus parents, particularly fathers, directed sons toward gender specific toys but daughters away from gender specific toys (and to neutral).

Gender differences in sex-typing were also identified in a study of science anxiety. Brownlow, Jacobi, and Rogers (2000) explored how often college students had heard sex-typed statements at home and if they believed that they would make similar statements to their own children. Male respondents indicated having heard more sex-typed statements in their home and also cited a greater probability that they would socialize their children in a sex-typed way.

Clearly each culture, and to some extent each racial and ethnic group, has expectations about the appropriate characteristics and roles for men and women. Those expectations will be conveyed to children through live and symbolic models and, given the basic cognitive tendencies all humans share, be readily perceived. Once those categorizations are established we move on to the second analytical process, in which children develop an internal motivation to conform to the characteristics assigned to their category.

Analytical Process 2: Establishing Preference. When addressing categories about groups of people, cognitive psychology replaces the term category with "scheme." A scheme is a cognitive structure, composed of a network of associations. Schemas organize and guide our perceptions, thus adding efficiency but also distortions.

Bem's gender schema theory (1981, 1983) proposes that given the importance of gender categories to all known cultures, we each have a set of gender-linked associations. The specific content of the schemas, however, is taught and thus can vary across cultures. States Bem (1981), "As children learn the contents of the society's gender schema, they learn which attributes are to be linked with their own sex and, hence, with themselves" (p. 355).

The gender scheme becomes a tool for self evaluation (Bem 1981, 1983). Children's feelings of self worth are developed through a variety of comparisons, one of which is how well they match the appropriate gender schema.

Thus, the male child is motivated to "act like a boy" to compare favorably with his masculine scheme and be able to feel good about himself. Out of a desire for high self esteem, then, comes a preference for gender-typed activities. Cultures teach the content of the gender schema, so external processes are involved in socialization. But internal, psychological processes are also involved as the gender scheme becomes a standard which the child is motivated to achieve.

Analytical Process 3: Gender-Typed Behavior. While gender schema theory suggests the motivating factor behind gender role acquisition, presumably the specifics of what is acquired will depend on the teachings of the culture. Mischel (1966; 1970) addresses the acquisition of sex-typed behaviors through observational learning. He defines sex-typed behaviors empirically as those that elicit different levels of reinforcement for the sexes. Thus, if boys are reinforced more when they shout on the playground, shouting on the playground is defined as a male-typed behavior; if boys are punished more when they play with dolls, playing with dolls is a female-typed activity.

Mischel[2] argues that boys and girls learn the behaviors of both sexes through the observation of models, but that they then perform the behaviors for which they anticipate being reinforced. Children are predicted to observe two types of models, those with whom they are in a nurturant relationship and those that are both powerful and willing to provide reinforcement. For girls and boys, the mother initially meets both of these criteria. Very quickly, however, children learn that males have the greater power in our culture and shift to imitating their fathers. Boys should make this shift quite readily. Girls are predicted to shift to male-typed behaviors to the extent that they are reinforced for doing so. Thus, girls will imitate males to the extent that they are allowed while also retaining many female-typed behaviors.

Bussey and Bandura (1999) suggest that gender is such an important social categorization that it takes on significance from birth. They cite examples of 7 month olds being able to differentiate male and female faces and voices, of 9 month olds looking correctly at a female face when listening to a female voice, and of 12 months looking at a male face for a male voice. They further suggest that through observational learning both sexes learn the male and female stereotypes.

In their earlier work, Bussey and Bandura (1984) discussed the models to which children will be most attentive. They suggested that children would observe and imitate models with whom they are similar and models that are powerful, then provided a test of their predictions based on children in a nursery school. For the power manipulation, children viewed a videotape of boys and girls playing. They established who was powerful by depicting one sex as in charge of a playroom, for some the girls owned the playroom and the boys had to ask permission to play, for others the boys owned the playroom. The nursery school children then viewed a film of three men and three women playing a game, which provided the opportunity to observe a same-sex (similar) other. The women players wore blue Mickey Mouse caps with the logo turned to the back, while the men wore green caps with the logo to the front; the women and men each displayed distinct sets of words and behaviors while playing the game. The children were then given a chance to select a hat, to determine how to wear it, and to imitate the words and actions of the adults. Boys were shown to have a strong preference for imitating the male model; girls imitated the female model more than the male but the preference was much less strong. Further, these patterns were moderated by the power of the models. When men were believed to be in power, boys showed a very strong preference for imitating the men, and girls imitated the men slightly (but non-significantly) more than the women. When women were in power, males showed only a non-significant preference for imitating the males (so statistically, no preference) and the girls showed a slight preference for imitating women. Thus the preference for same-sex imitation was greatly attenuated for both boys and girls when power differences were known.

Overall, theories based on observational learning explain that children will view models with whom they have a nurturing relationship (their parents), models with whom they feel similar (their same sex parent), and models who are perceived to be powerful (more often the father in patriarchal societies). The result is that boys will primarily imitate their fathers, while girls will imitate both mothers and fathers. Cultures and subgroups may differ in their tolerance for children displaying behaviors typed for the opposite sex. Hill (2002), for example, suggests that such tolerance on the part of African Americans may be dependent on socioeconomic status. Based on a qualitative analysis of interviews with African American parents, Hill argues that first-generation, middle class parents may be more ambivalent in their support for gender equality than parents with a stronger, more established socioeconomic base. Hill suggests that African Americans who recently have become successful seek acceptance by conforming to the norms of the dominant society, which at this time include equality at work but traditional gender roles at home.

If the content of gender schemas and the performance of gender-typed behaviors are influenced by learning, then change is possible. Bem (1983) suggests that our categories about men and women could be restricted to the areas that truly matter; anatomical and reproductive differences. If we did not teach children to extensively differentiate the world in terms of gender (strong boys play football, pretty girls play quietly and win beauty contests), then other aspects of behavior could remain gender neutral. Perhaps from conscious attempts to restrict the content of gender schemas we can begin to lessen our tendencies to see men and women as different and unequal.

CONTEXTUAL FACTORS

One of the primary descriptors of Americans today is "individualistic." We hold near to our hearts the beliefs that our individual efforts matter, that we can "be all that we can be," that we are responsible for our own fates. Individualism is embodied in the traditional American Dream and the traditional Protestant Work Ethic, both of which are central to the heritage of white, middle-class Americans. Our strong individualistic tendencies likely contribute to what is known in psychology as the fundamental attribution error. When asked to explain why individuals have achieved certain goals, or have failed to achieve their goals, we tend to focus on the relevant persons and to downplay the significance of their life circumstances. Thus we speak of people's lasting, dispositional characteristics (e.g., personality traits and innate capacities) and ignore the context in which they were observed. The fundamental attribution error predicts that we will attribute observed gender differences in behavior to the personal characteristics of the men and women involved and attribute differences in the behavior of racial groupings to their race. But what happens if a particular context, such as an occupational role, is experienced more often by the members of one group? That contextual factor may be confounded with the group-based characteristic (e.g., sex or race). The contextual factor and the group-based characteristic may be mixed together in our everyday casual observations, so that separating the context from the person is impossible.

Consider the sex of the person, the status of the person, and behaviors reflecting sensitivity to interpersonal cues as an example of confounded factors. Are women more sensitive to interpersonal cues, such that they discern and display emotions more readily than men? Are individuals in less powerful, subordinate roles more sensitive to interpersonal cues than those who possess greater power? Both relationships have received empirical support. What if women are more often found in subordinate roles and men in powerful roles? The sex of the person is confounded with level of power. What's needed to separate the two intertwined factors is to bring into the data set women who hold powerful roles and men who hold subordinate roles, but often those data are unavailable. If all four relevant groups could be compared, it would be possible to break the confound (Yoder, 1999). Table 6.1 depicts the data patterns needed to separate personal from contextual effects. If the data reveal the pattern in column two of Table 6.1, a gender difference would be sup-

Table 6.1. Relevant Comparisons Needed to Determine if an Observed Difference in Men's and Women's Behavior (Sensitivity to Cues) is a Result of Gender or Context

	Pattern supporting a gender difference	Pattern supporting a contextual difference
Subordinate women	Greater sensitivity to cues	Greater sensitivity to cues
Subordinate men	Less sensitivity to cues	Greater sensitivity to cues
Super-ordinate women	Greater sensitivity to cues	Less sensitivity to cues
Super-ordinate men	Less sensitivity to cues	Less sensitivity to cues

ported with women of any status level being more interpersonally sensitive than men; if the data reveal the pattern in column three, a contextual factor would be exposed with women and men with lesser status being more interpersonally sensitive than their same-sex but more powerful counterparts.

The premise that contextual (or situational) factors are a larger determinant of behavioral differences than gender, but that gender has been mistakenly emphasized, is a basic underlying premise in the writings of Barnett and Rivers (2004).

> In the past, gender was all-important. Whether you were male or female determined your role in society: the way you behaved and the work you did. Under these circumstances, it's easy to assume that the reason men and women were doing different kinds of work was biological. If you look around a community and see only women weaving and only men tilling the soil, you are apt to conclude that the "cause" of this difference is that women are suited for weaving and men for tilling. But that conclusion would be wrong. Being female doesn't automatically give you a talent for weaving. Rigid cultural norms, not biology, are operating here. As gender roles loosen—as they have done in the developed world—women's and men's behavior reflects many forces: their gender, their individual talents and preference, their personalities, and the situations in which they find themselves (pp. 5–6).

Among their many examples that context, not gender, determines behavior, is evidence regarding job-related motivations. Many of the early studies of gender differences in business were forced, given the available distribution of men and women in the work force, to compare women and men with very different levels of status within an organization. Thus male executives were often contrasted with female secretaries and males were found to be more ambitious and motivated. More recent studies comparing men and women in comparable positions of power find no differences in job motivation and satisfaction. Thus, when the contextual factors are the same, the sexes behave the same.

Janice Yoder (2002) values Kanter's (1977) writings on tokenism for helping to counter the bias of blaming women for the difficulties they encounter in the workplace (e.g., blaming women's fear of success). But she also criticizes Kanter for overlooking the importance of a variety of confounded, contextual factors. In particular, the token women professionals studied by Kanter differed from the men not just in being fewer in number, but also in that they were intruding into a male-dominated area. Occupational role deviance and subordinate status are contextual factors not acknowledged by Kanter. Are the effects of tokenism the same for men intruding into a female-dominated occupation? Males in a male-dominated occupation might fear a loss of status if their group is invaded by low status women, while women in a lower valued occupation may benefit from the inclusion of men. Indeed, male tokens in occupations dominated by women (e.g., male nurses) often find career advantages, such as easier paths to promotion. Yoder (2002) expressed concern that Kanter's work, in attributing women's negative occupational experiences to tokenism and suggesting solutions based on number-balancing, directed attention away from the real cause—sexism. Yoder argues that gender creates a different social context for women and men. Tokens differ from the dominants, producing perceptual distortions; if the tokens are also of lower status than the dominants, the dominants may intentionally work to keep the tokens subordinate. Women and men performing the same gender-skewed job, such as fire-fighting, do not experience the same context (Yoder, 2002). Further, gender is a status indicator, and it probably interacts with other status markers, such as race and ethnicity (Yoder, 2002).

THE MEANING OF "DIFFERENCE"

Fundamental to feminist reasoning about gender difference is the premise that individual variance greatly exceeds between-group variance (Barnett & Rivers, 2004; Hyde, 1985; Unger & Crawford, 1992). When a gender difference is discovered, what has actually been documented is a difference between the average scores for men and women. That difference does not imply that all men and all women differ and seldom translates into a discovery with everyday, practical significance. As stated by Unger and Crawford (1992), "On every trait or ability measured, there is more similarity than difference—that is, the areas where females and males overlap is larger (usually much larger) than those where they do not" (p. 68). Distributions typical of moderate to large gender differences are illustrated in Figure 6.1. While the average scores for the men and the women depicted might differ significantly, those averages differ by less than the range of scores for just men and by less than the range of scores for just women. Further, any two randomly selected individuals would probably differ by a greater amount than the group means.

Any two women or any two men (individual within-group variance) would likely differ more than women and men in general (between-group variance). Considering that most of the personality and cognitive differences between women and men are smaller than the difference depicted in Figure 6.1, assignment to roles based on average differences seem foolish at best. As stated by Barnett and Rivers, "Certain men and women may have personalities and talents that make them more suitable for a specific role, but personality and talent are individual, not gender based" (p. 6).

Perhaps our strongest stereotypes of gender difference relate to perceived differences in aggression, relating to our prior discussion of the hunter-warrior. Janet Hyde (1986) conducted a meta-analysis of 69 studies of aggression. Meta-analysis provides a statistical measure of the size of an effect, which can be interpreted in terms of its practical everyday importance. The effect sizes were in the small to moderate range. Small effects can be detected with psychological tests but are difficult to observe in everyday behavior; moderate effects can be observed but are not considered "grossly perceptible." (For comparison purposes, the average effect size for aggression was found to be $d = .50$ which is barely moderate; that for the sex difference in height is 2.0 which is considered large and grossly perceptible.) On average males behaved more aggressively on both physical and verbal tests, but the

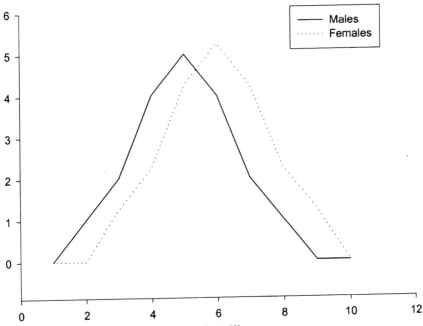

Figure 6.1. Depiction of a Moderate Gender Difference

pattern of gender difference is reasonably well captured by Figure 6.1. Stereotypes are not wrong in suggesting that men are more aggressive, but they imply a stronger and more consistent difference than actually exists. The scores on aggression for any two randomly selected men would likely differ by more than the average aggression scores for women and men. Perhaps more important, documentation of difference does not address the source of difference. Is it innate (hunter-warrior) or acquired (socialization) or a bit of both?

GENDER ROLE SOCIALIZATION AND WORK

Three different models relating gender and work are reviewed by Maria Martins-Crane, Michael Beyerlein, and Douglas Johnson (1995), including the "gender model" which argues for the role of early socialization, the "job model" which focuses on experiences encountered on the job itself, and an integrated model proposed by Astin (1984a), which considers both.

The gender model argues that early socialization leads men to view career development and support of family to be their primary roles and women to view family roles as preeminent (Martins-Crane, et al, 1995). Consequently women have a lower level of job involvement, are less motivated by job-related features such as pay and status, and have lower career expectations and aspirations. Rewards of the job such as social interactions and working conditions are expected to be more valued by women than men. Interest in part-time work, which would less interfere with family commitments, is also predicted for women. Clearly those who adhere to this model would advocate narrowly restricted work options for women.

The job model proposes that the work behavior of both men and women is determined by experiences encountered on the job. Martins-Crane and colleagues (1995) summarize this model by suggesting that "job aspects such as control, autonomy, and promotion are equally important to men and to women and have a positive relationship with job satisfaction. Since most jobs where women are employed have few of these features, women potentially will be less satisfied" (p. 33). They cite evidence that, under similar circumstances of low power, men and women show similar levels of commitment to organizations and similar focus on job considerations such as the social aspects of work.

Clearly the job model is more consistent with our prior discussion of gender differences and similarities and with our discussion of contextual factors. However the integrated approach advocated by Helen Astin (1984a) argues that sex-role socialization should not be ignored. Astin argues that psychological variables (work motivations and the effects of socialization), contextual sociological variables (structural opportunities in the work environment), and the interaction of the two determine job-related behaviors. Her argument suggests that "basic work motivation is the same for men and women, but that they make different choices because their early socialization experiences and structural opportunities are different" (p. 118). Figure 6.2 summarizes Astin's model (1984a; 1984b).

Astin (1984a) argues that *three basic needs* affect our motivations for work behavior. Survival needs are met through employment if it provides the income needed for food, shelter, etc., and through family work if, as within a marriage contract, one can expect reciprocation. Pleasure needs include the intrinsic pleasure that one may find in the work itself, including intellectual and emotional pleasure derived from accomplishing a task or achieving a goal. Contribution needs address our desire to contribute to the well-being of others, which may include one's family, friends, work group, community, or even nation. While service and helping occupations clearly relate to contribution needs, Astin argues that any occupation in which one produces useful

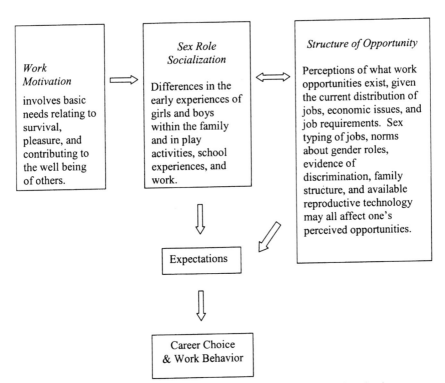

Figure 6.2.　Adaptation of Astin's Model of Career Choice and Work Behavior

goods and services has relevance to this need. Satisfaction of contribution needs is proposed to have relevance to one's sense of self-worth.

While the three motivating needs are thought to be the same for men and women, Astin (1984a) proposes that men and women differ in their *work-related expectations*. Expectations stem from beliefs about the types of work that are available and accessible to the individual and are thought to be shaped by both sex-role socialization and contextual factors such as the job market, family structure, discriminatory practices, and economic conditions — which Astin refers to as the *structure of opportunity*. Work expectations are proposed to begin developing in childhood, with play, involvement in household tasks, and early paid work all having an impact. Astin discusses early work by Janet Lever, which suggested that boys' outdoor play teaches more independence and provides more opportunity for recognition, that play in larger groups develops skills in dealing with groups and with a wider range of people, and that competitive games enhance competitiveness and desire to achieve; all have relevance to adult career roles. To the extent that play, household tasks, and early paid work are differentiated by gender, different skills are developed as are different expectations as to how to satisfy the three basic needs. In particular, early experiences might lead the sexes to differ in their expectations with regard to how to satisfy the contribution need. Different career choices and work behaviors are likely to follow.

Astin suggests that if gender socialization were the only factor shaping expectations, little change would occur. However, historical events and technological changes (which are part of the structure of opportunity) also affect expectations. For example, the experience of having an employed mother and the greater involvement of girls in sports as a result of Title IX of the Education Amendments of 1972 promise changes in expectations (1984a). Existing social norms about gender roles in work and family are also part of the structure of opportunity (Astin, 1984b). So gender socialization influences the structure of opportunity, which in turn influences gender socialization. Astin (1984a) argues that a wide range of factors is changing the structure of opportunity facing men and women, including (but not limited to) longer careers as a result of increased longevity, a declining birth rate and greater interest in careers as a source of need satisfaction, laws prohibiting employment discrimination and ensuring greater equality of opportunity, and an increased divorce rate and therefore an increased need for self-sufficiency. Thus, increased gender similarity in expectations is anticipated in the future.

Research Consistent with the Integrated Model. Just as women remain under-represented in upper management, they also remain disappointingly absent from political office. Certainly some of the same leadership and communication skills relevant to business apply to politics. A recent study on women and politics (Fox & Lawless, 2003) supports Astin's contention that both personal and contextual factors must be considered when predicting career-related behaviors. The "eligibility pool" hypothesis has been offered to explain the small number of women in top elective positions. Basically, that hypothesis suggests that most politicians come from the fields of business and law. Given that women have been under-represented in these areas, insufficient numbers of women have been eligible to run for office. Once women's representation in business and law equals men's, the number of women and men running for office should equalize. Overall, the eligibility pool hypothesis reflects the logic of the jobs model of gender and work, with men and women having similar interests but, in the past, unequal opportunity.

Fox and Lawless (2003) contend that the eligibility pool hypothesis fails to consider the effects of traditional sex-role socialization on the initial decision to run for office. They predicted that women from traditional family structures would both be less likely to run for public office and less likely to aspire to higher offices (such as governor and federal positions) than men from similar backgrounds. Working with a group of established professionals as respondents (lawyers, business executives, educators, legislative staffers, lobbyists, and heads of interest groups), they found that the women in their sample were less likely to come from traditional family structures; their professional female respondents were less likely to be married or to have children. Further, while female and male respondents were equally likely to consider running for office and to consider running for high office, the presence of children in the home decreased these likelihoods for women but not for men. Women who expressed nontraditional attitudes (e.g., support for the ERA and the belief that politics is not a male domain) were more likely to express interest in high level offices than similarly situated but more traditional women. Fox and Lawless conclude that historically socialized gender roles may continue to discourage women from seeking public office. To the extent that the differences were smaller than anticipated, their study supports the importance of contextual factors; women and men from similar careers showed much similarity in their career aspirations. To the extent that traditional family structures and belief systems moderated the results, the study supports Astin's argument that both sex role socialization and job structure must be considered.

Carol Watson's work (1994) supports the contention that personal and contextual factors must be considered when predicting negotiation behavior. Researchers in that area have depicted women as more cooperative, with cooperation in negotiations being interpreted as weak and ineffective. Women as "nice" negotiators has been explained through gender-role socialization (with women being nurturing and supportive and men tough and task-oriented), situational power (with the less powerful being more cooperative and the powerful more competitive), gender-plus-power (which fits with Astin's argument that both gender socialization and the structure of opportunity must be considered), and an expectation states theory (which also argues that gender and power are both important but may interact in mixed-sex pairs). From her review of the literature, Watson concludes that situational power is a better predictor of negotiation behavior than gender, but that gender must also be considered. While gender had little impact on negotiation behavior or outcomes, it related to confidence in performance; women were less confident. Further, powerless men and women sometimes behaved differently during negotiations. Schlueter, Barge, and Blankenship (1990) also found more differences in the influence strategies of lower level male and female managers than in those with more powerful positions.

Filiz Tabak (1997) provided evidence that expectations shape the structure of opportunity through an exploration of the career progress of women in Istanbul. Interviews with successful women indicated that in traditional families the husband's job came first, both men and women believed that wives were to give priority to home and children over work, and men were described as unaccustomed and not open to the idea of women in management.

Richardson and Freeman (1995), provided evidence that both women politicians and their constituents perceive gender differences in contribution needs. They reported differences in the amount of constituency service that is requested of male and female politicians and in the amount of service that they desire to provide. Compared to their male counterparts, female politicians reported receiving an average of two additional requests for constituency service per week, believed that they were providing more case assistance to constituents, and indicated more willingness to increase their level of service if given additional staff. Sex-role socialization may have created both women's greater interest in service, which parallels Astin's contribution needs, and the belief on the part of the public that women politicians are willing to provide such assistance.

RACIAL SOCIALIZATION PROCESSES

We noted earlier that many of the beliefs contained in the gender stereotypes are known to be unfounded, and yet they persist. Blaine Hudson and Bonetta Hines-Hudson (1999) contend that the same is true of racial stereotypes. They state that:

> . . . if one rejects the myth of genetically based racial inferiority, the reality of the present embodies a simple, but profound paradox: after the apparent repudi-

ation of racism and legal segregation a generation ago, racism and racial inequality should no longer exist—yet they do. How and why is this so? What is there about racism that renders it so resilient, so difficult to dislodge from the collective psyche of Americans and the structure of American culture and institutions? (p. 22).

Hughes (2003) contends that race-related attitudes, too, are a result of socialization, but this time racial socialization. She suggests that parents "transmit the world's views about race and ethnicity to children by way of subtle, overt, deliberate and unintended mechanisms" (p. 15).

Hudson and Hines-Hudson (1999) contend that, historically, whites have been socialized in ways which allowed us to enslave and then segregate African Americans, marginalize Latinos, exclude Asians, and dispossess Native Americans. One can only assume that growing up devalued within a culture has negative effects on the self image. Marie Ferguson Peters (2002) argues that African American parents have the responsibility of raising physically and emotionally healthy children in a society where being African American has negative connotations; children must be taught to survive in a world in which they will face prejudice and discrimination.

Hudson and Hines-Hudson (1999) provide evidence that little interaction among the races, or interaction of individuals in traditional white-dominant and African American-subordinate roles, relates to continued acceptance of biased beliefs. In a study of participants enrolled in race relations workshops, they found that most professional interactions of whites and African Americans involved the African American being at a similar or subordinate job level. When African Americans were in subordinate roles, white respondents expressed more stereotypical attitudes and African Americans expressed more self-stereotyping. With respect to career related characteristics, whites thought more criminal behavior, lower intelligence, and less leadership ability were characteristic of African Americans; African Americans thought more criminal behavior, less intelligence, but greater leadership ability were descriptive of their own group. African American women were more likely to perceive their group positively than were African American men. Greater familiarity with Africa and with African Americans helped to diminish negative views; lack of knowledge about the cultural/historical roles of African Americans was related to more biased perceptions. The authors concluded that familiarity with culture breeds tolerance, but familiarity gained through dominant-subordinate relationships breeds contempt. Further, whites' attitudes were described as polarized, with 15.9% scoring as highly biased and 36.6% as unbiased. Hudson and Hines-Hudson suggest that if 15.9% of individuals are patently racist, then the racial climate of one's workplace could be effectively poisoned.

While historically the term racial socialization has described the develop-ment of beliefs in white superiority and minority inferiority, many are now applying that same term to the development of healthy belief systems. The socialization transmission process can be used to develop world views about race and ethnicity which are beneficial to minorities. Minority parents have been found to encourage desirable beliefs in two areas (Hughes, 2003). The first relates to one's group's culture, history, and heritage and is termed cul-tural socialization; the second prepares children in ways to handle racial bias and is labeled preparation for bias.

Hughes (2003) compared parents of African Americans, Dominicans, and Puerto Ricans in terms of their emphasis on these two aspects of racial so-cialization. African Americans were thought to differ from the other two groups in having come to the United States involuntarily; Dominicans and Puerto Ricans were thought to share their voluntary status; African Americans and Dominicans were thought to be more racially distinctive than Puerto Ri-cans. All three groups were found to culturally socialize their children, with 95% of Puerto Ricans, 91% of Dominicans, and 100% of African Americans reporting having shared information of this sort with their children during the past year. The majority of each group emphasized preparation for bias to their children; 62% of Puerto Ricans, 68% of Dominicans, and 88% of African Americans reported having shared information of this sort with their children during the past year. Cultural socialization was valued by parents, regardless of their own perceptions of group disadvantage or personal experience with prejudice. The greater emphasis on preparation for bias by African American parents was attributed to the overwhelming persistence of discrimination against African Americans in the United States. Peters (2002) cites evidence that youth who are socialized about their heritage and about racial barriers show positive psychological and behavioral outcomes.

MEDIA AS SOCIALIZING AGENTS

A variety of authors have argued convincingly that television has an effect on our world view (e.g., Gorham, 1999; Pearl, Bouthilet, & Lazar, 1988). Gorham (1999) credits the media for the persistence of stereotypes in a world where people consistently disavow belief in them. He explains that "cultiva-tion research" focuses on how long-term, repeated exposure to media images affects social reality beliefs, and that researchers who study culture argue that media images convey the gender relations, race relations, and power relations within our society. The more dependent the individual is on the media for in-formation about the world, the greater the probability of erroneous world views. Gorham presents the case that those with power in the culture have the power to shape media conveyed messages. "Those who are in a dominant social position have the power to define the dominant understandings and thus have tremendous ability to make their definitions appear natural and unarguable" (p. 232). Peters (2002) reports that African American children view twice as much television as white children and that African Americans view television as a source of news and information more than whites do. Thus, though television has power to socialize all children, Peters suggests its power to socialize and influence the self-esteem of African American children is particularly strong.

African American women and men have been perceived in the eyes of the dominant culture as having nearly equal status, with women having a slight edge (Davenport & Yurich, 1991). This pattern has been clearly replicated in media images of African American and white characters in situation comedies (Reid, 1979). African American women were depicted as low on achievement but high on dominance and nurturance; white women were depicted as submissive and helpless; the depictions of the African American and white men did not differ in dominance. Reid argued that the portrayal of women was crucial to how men were viewed. White men appeared in films with white women; by contrast, white men appeared very dominating. African American men appeared in films with African American women; by contrast African American men did not appear dominating. The end result is the impression that white men are more dominant than African American men, even though their depictions did not differ. Further, the African American women appear dominating due to the relative passivity of the white female characters.

Pearl, Bouthilet, and Lazar (1988) summarized the effects of television programming on children's understanding of reality in a variety of areas, including sex-role socialization and race-role socialization. Marriage and family roles appear to be unimportant in the lives of television's men, but to dominate the lives of television's women. Married women tend to not have outside jobs and successfully employed women often have family problems. Not surprisingly, children who watch more television select more stereotypical roles for men and women. (Also noteworthy, programs which show counter-stereotypical roles are successful in shifting children's views of role appropriateness.) For white children, television serves as a prime source of information about minorities, though African American children and adults are more likely to view programs about African American characters. Minority children who view programs depicting positive minority images show enhanced cultural pride and self confidence.

Exploring sex roles and racial depictions, Eschholz, Bufkin, and Long (2002) conducted an analysis of the 50 top grossing films from 1996. Only 35% of the leading characters were women and 20% were African American or Hispanic. (Actually, only two leading characters were Hispanic; Native Americans and Asians were missing.) While 20% minority representation seems strong, African American characters appeared in films with primarily minority actors. When the films with only African American characters were removed from the sample, only 12% of the leading characters were African American. African American males and females were depicted as equally likely to be employed, but white males were more often employed than white females. Further, the African Americans had lower occupational prestige than their white counterparts, with this discrepancy being larger than it exists in actual employment statistics.

With respect to sex roles, Leaper, Breed, Hoffman, and Perlman (2002) examined gender-typing in cartoons. More characters were male than female, male characters were more physically aggressive (in cartoons with adventure and comedy themes), and female characters more often showed fear, acted romantic, were polite, and showed support. Arima (2003) found five gender-typed portrayals to be evident in Japanese television advertisements. Women dominated the roles of beautiful and wise housewives, young celebrities who tended to be office workers and sales people, and young ladies attracting people's attention, often by being depicted through close-ups of body parts or displayed in swim suits to advertise beauty products. The roles of middle-aged worker bee and middle and old-aged people enjoying private time were mainly filled by male actors. Arima concluded that these current media types corresponded to traditional gender stereotypes. Glascock (2001) found that, in American television, males outnumbered females both on and behind the camera, that the marital status or parental status of male characters was less likely to be known, and that male characters had significantly higher paying jobs, were twice as likely to be depicted as bosses, and were more likely to display physical aggression. Female characters were younger, more provocatively dressed, and more likely to be blonds and redheads. In addition, whites were over-represented at the expense of minorities.

If our world views are shaped by television, which continues to perpetuate many traditional stereotypical images, a distorted notion of reality results. Concerns also must be expressed about other types of media. For example, violent and misogynous rap music could similarly promote undesirable stereotypes (Rudman & Lee, 2002).

DISCRIMINATION, SOCIALIZATION, AND POWER

Gender-based socialization and racial socialization are powerful processes contributing to the development of and maintenance of stereotypes. Further, both socialization and stereotyping are strongly connected to power differences in our culture and relate to discrimination in the work place. Lott and Maluso (1995) argue for the separateness and inter-relatedness of two types of discrimination, personal and institutional. Slights from others and exclusion by others are examples of personal discrimination; barriers to jobs and promotions typify institutional discrimination. Both forms of discrimination, according to Lott and Maluso, stem from the tendency for persons of power to avoid and exclude persons from lower status social categories. This pattern is pervasive, such that people from a low status category may themselves discriminate against those from an even lower status social grouping. An example of this would be white women discriminating against women of color. Lott and Maluso "assume commonalities among racism, classism, heterosexism, ageism, and sexism that stem from the association of all with inequalities in social status and power" (p. 3) and agree with theorists who argue that discrimination is a result of ordinary social processes, including socialization.

In a very practical sense, women in management should not be naive and assume that others share their beliefs about women and men's equality or that the progress toward equality can be taken for granted. In one current example, some social and religious movements oppose the progress women have made, particularly progress toward equality within the family. The Promise Keepers is a conservative, Christian movement which originated in the 1990's. Though the Promise Keepers have rejected the racism that has sometimes been associated with evangelical Christianity and advocate men becoming more involved as fathers, they also advocate that men reclaim their roles as head of the family (Brannon, 2005). Promise Keepers do not support equal partnerships with women. We also live in a world where being called "girly men" is derogatory (as demonstrated by Arnold Schwarzenegger at the August 31, 2004 Republican National Convention). Women and minorities in management will be increasingly asked to interact with citizens of countries throughout the world, and thus will be affected by a varied set of stereotypes and prejudices.

Kanter (1977) thought solutions to organizational tokenism, whether experienced by women or by racial or ethnic minorities, rested in number-balancing strategies. She recommended such strategies as batch hiring and clustering under-represented groups. A minimum presence of 20%, moving women from token to minority status, would be necessary. Women were to be clustered in groups of sufficient number that they would not be identifiable as tokens, even if that meant that some work groups would include no women. Number-balancing would create organizations which were more tolerant of difference.

Yoder (1991; 2002) argues that the number-balancing solution ignores the role of status and argues that organizational policies which enhance the legitimate status of tokens must also be considered. In her research (Yoder, Schleicher, & McDonald, 1998) women were put into the position of being token leaders, token leaders with special training, or token leaders with special training and expertise recognized by a male experimenter. Groups led by trained, legitimated leaders outperformed the other two, showing that training alone did not lessen the effects of tokenism. Rather than placing the responsibility for change on the women, these results present an organizational strategy for change, in that high status members of organizations can legitimate women (Yoder, 2002). Yoder advocates changes in the proportion of men and women in a job (number-balancing), status enhancement, and redefinition of occupational roles by reducing stereotyping. Perhaps through such strategies the "structure of opportunity" can be modified to address the effects of the various "isms" on the careers of women and minorities.

SUMMARY

Socialization is the process through which we acquire an understanding of the differences in statuses, roles, and prescribed behaviors that exist within our culture and acquire an understanding of how we and others fit within the culture's social structure (Thornton, Chatters, Taylor & Allen, 1990). In this chapter, a feminist view of gender and racial differences was presented. Feminists believe that gender and racial variations are largely a result of socialization, and thus are both highly flexible and variable.

Issues explored included: gender-role acquisition, innate tendencies which contribute to our thinking in terms of discrete groups, conceptual and methodological factors that lead us to exaggerate the differences between groups, models connecting gender socialization to career expectations, and current attempts to employ racial socialization to promote positive identities. Throughout the chapter, the role of the media as an agent of socialization was emphasized.

NOTES

1. Much of the information on gender-based socialization processes was previously published in Karsten, 1994.

2. Learning theory assumes that the laws of learning apply universally, and thus Mischel does not address differences in the learning process based on race and ethnicity. However, if the races sex-type differentially, then the resulting sex roles would also differ.

REFERENCES

Arima, A. N. (2003). Gender stereotypes in Japanese television advertisements. *Sex Roles, 49*(1–2), 81–90.

Astin, H. S. (1984a). The meaning of work in women's lives: A Sociopsychological model of career choice and work behavior. *The Counseling Psychologist, 12*(4), 117–b26.

Astin, H. S. (1984b). In appreciation of the richness of the commentaries. *The Counseling Psychologist, 12*(4), 151–52.

Barnett, R. & Rivers, C. (2004). *How gender myths are hurting our relationships, our children, and our jobs.* New York: Basic Books.

Basow, S. A. (1984). Cultural variations in sex-typing. *Sex Roles, 10*(7/8), 577–85.

Bem, S. L. (1981). Gender schema theory: A cognitive account of sex-typing. *Psychological Review, 88*, 354–64.

Bem, S. L. (1983). Gender schema theory and its implications for child development: Raising gender-aschematic children in a gender-schematic society. *Signs, 8*, 598–616.

Brannon, L. (2005). *Gender: Psychological perspectives* (4th ed.). Boston: Allyn and Bacon.

Brownlow, S., Jacobi, T., & Rogers, M. (2000). Science anxiety as a function of gender and experience. *Sex Roles, 42*, 119–131.

Bussey, K. & Bandura, A (1984). Influence of gender constancy and social power on sex-linked modeling. *Journal of Personality and Social Psychology, 47*(6), 1292–1302.

Bussey, K. & Bandura, A. (1999). Social cognitive theory of gender development and differentiation. *Psychological Review, 106*(4), 676–713.

Condry, J. & Condry, S. (1976). Sex differences: A study of the eye of the beholder. *Child Development, 47*, 812–19.

Davenport, D. S. & Yurick, J. M. (1991). Multicultural gender issues. *Journal of Counseling and Development, 70*, 64–71.

Eagly, A. H. & Steffen, V. J. (1984). Gender stereotypes stem from the distribution of women and men into social roles. *Journal of Personality and Social Psychology, 46*, 735–54.

Eschholz, S., Bufkin, J., & Long, J. (2002). Symbolic reality bites: Women and racial/ethnic minorities in modern film. *Sociological Spectrum, 22*, 299–334.

Finn, J. (1986). The relationship between sex role attitudes and attitudes supporting marital violence. *Sex Roles, 14*(5/6), 235–44.

Fox, R. L. & Lawless, J. L. (2003). Family structure, sex-role socialization, and the decision to run for office. *Women & Politics, 24*(4), 19–48.

Glascock, J. (2001). Gender roles on prime-time network television: Demographics and behaviors. *Journal of Broadcasting and Electronic Media, 45*(4), 656–69.

Gorham, B.W. (1999). Stereotypes in the media: So what? *The Howard Journal of Communications, 10*, 229–47.

Hill, S. A. (2002). Teaching and doing gender in African American families. *Sex Roles, 47*(11/12), 493–506.

Hoffman, C. & Hurst, N. (1990). Gender stereotypes: Perception or rationalization? *Journal of Personality and Social Psychology, 58*(2), 197–208.

Hudson, J. B. & Hines-Hudson, B. (1999). A study of the contemporary racial attitudes of Whites and African Americans. *The Western Journal of Black Studies, 23*(1), 22–34.

Hughes, D. (2003). Correlates of African American and Latino parents' messages to children about ethnicity and race: A comparative study of racial socialization. *American Journal of Community Psychology, 31*, 15–33.

Hyde, J. S. (1985). *Half the human experience: The psychology of women* (3rd ed.). Lexington, MA: D. C. Heath & Co.

Hyde, J. S. (1986). Gender differences in aggression. In J. S. Hyde & M. C. Linn. (Eds.), *The Psychology of gender: Advances through meta-analysis* (pp. 51–66). Baltimore: Johns Hopkins University Press.

Idle, T., Wood, E. & Desmarais, S. (1993). Gender role socialization in toy play situations: Mothers and fathers with their sons and daughters. *Sex Roles, 28*, 679–691.

Kanter, R. M. (1977). *Men and women of the corporation.* New York: Basic Books, Inc.

Karsten, M. F. (1994). *Management and gender: Issues and attitudes.* Westport: CN: Praeger.

Leaper, C., Breed, L., Hoffman, L., & Perlman, C. A. (2002). Variations in the gender-stereotyped content of children's television cartoons across genres. *Journal of Applied Social Psychology, 32*(8), 1653–1662.

Lott, B. & Maluso, D. (1995). *The social psychology of interpersonal discrimination.* New York: The Guilford Press.

Martins-Crane, M. D. L., Beyerlein, M. M., & Johnson, D. A. (1995). In N. J. Struthers (Ed.), Gender in the workplace [Special issue]. *Journal of Social Behavior and Personality, 10*(6), 27–50.

Mead, M. (1935; 1963). *Sex and temperament in three primitive societies.* New York: William Morrow & Co.

Mischel, W. (1966). A social-learning view of sex differences in behavior. In E. E. Maccoby (Ed.), *The development of sex differences* (pp. 56–81). Stanford: Stanford University Press.

Mischel, W. (1970). Sex-typing and socialization. In P. H. Mussen (Ed.), *Carmichael's manual of child psychology* (Vol. 2, 3rd ed., pp. 3–72). New York: Wiley.

Oliver, M. B., Jackson, R. L. II., Moses, N. N., & Dangerfield, C. L. (2004). The faces of crime: Viewers' memory of race-related facial features of individuals pictured in the news. *Journal of Communication, 54*(1), 88–104.

Pearl, D., Bouthilet, L., & Lazar, J. (1988). Socialization and conceptions of social reality. In G. Handel, *Childhood socialization* (pp. 239–260). New York: Aldine De Gruyter.

Peters, M. F. (2002). Racial socialization of young Black children. In H. P. McAdoo (Ed.), *Black children* (2nd ed., pp. 57–96). Thousand Oaks, CA: Sage Publications.

Reid, P. T. (1979). Racial stereotyping on television: A comparison of the behavior of both Black and White television characters. *Journal of Applied Psychology, 64*(5), 465–71.

Richardson, L. E., Jr. & Freeman, P. K. (1995). Gender differences in constituency service among state legislators. *Political Research Quarterly, 48*(1), 169–79.

Rudman, L. A. & Lee, M. R. (2002). Implicit and explicit consequences of exposure to violent and misogynous rap music. *Group Processes and Intergroup Relations, 5*(2), 133–150.

Schlueter, D. W., Barge, J. K., & Blankenship, D. (1990). A comparative analysis of influence strategies used by upper and lower-level male and female managers. *Western Journal of Speech Communication, 54*, 42–65.

Secord, P. F., Bevan, W., & Katz, B. (1956). The Negro stereotype and perceptual accentuation. *Journal of Abnormal and Social Psychology, 53*, 78–83.

Smith, P. A. & Midlarsky, E. (1985). Empirically derived conceptions of femaleness and maleness: A current view. *Sex Roles, 12*, 313–28.

Tabak, F. (1997). Women's upward mobility in manufacturing organizations in Istanbul: A glass ceiling initiative? *Sex Roles, 36*, 93–102.

Tajfel, H. (1981). *Human groups and social categories: Studies in social psychology.* Cambridge: Cambridge University Press.

Tavris, C. & Wade, C. (1984). *The longest war: Sex differences in perspective* (2nd ed.). San Diego: Harcourt, Brace, Jovanovich.

Thornton, M. C., Chatters, L. M., Taylor, R. J., & Allen, W. R. (1990). Sociodemographic and environmental correlates of racial socialization by Black parents. *Child Development, 61*, 401–409.

Unger, R. & Crawford, M. (1992). *Women and gender: A feminist psychology.* New York: McGraw-Hill.

Watson, C. (1994). Gender versus power as predictor of negotiation behavior and outcomes. *Negotiation Journal, 10*(2), 117–27.

Weitzman, L. J. (1979). *Sex role socialization: A focus on women.* Palo Alto, CA: Mayfield.

Will, J. A., Self, P. A., & Datan, N. (1976). Maternal behavior and perceived sex of infant. *American Journal of Orthopsychiatry, 46*, 135–39.

Yoder, J. D. (1991). Rethinking tokenism: Looking beyond numbers. *Gender and Society, 5*(2), 178–192.

Yoder, J. D. (1999). *Women and gender: Transforming psychology.* Upper Saddle River, N. J.: Prentice Hall.

Yoder, J. D. (2002). 2001 Division 35 Presidential address: Context Matters: Understanding tokenism processes and their impact on women's work. *Psychology of Women Quarterly, 26*(1), 1–8.

Yoder, J. D., Schleicher, T. L., & McDonald, T. W. (1998). Empowering token women leaders: The importance of organizationally legitimated credibility. *Psychology of Women Quarterly, 22*, 209–22.

Chapter Seven

Power, Politics, Assertiveness, and Tokenism

OUTCOMES

After studying this chapter, you should be able to:

1. define power, influence, coercive, reward, referent, expert, and legitimate power, passive, assertive, and aggressive communication, coalition building, ingratiation, diminutives, disclaimers, glass elevator, occupational deviance, tokenism, merit principle, bureaucratic powerlessness, modal and affective tag questions, double deviate, self-efficacy, empowerment, empowerment paradox.
2. explain how influence strategies and political behavior may be used effectively in a real or hypothetical organization.
3. explain which, if any, of the suggestions for improving the political savvy of black executives also would apply to executives of other ethnic/racial backgrounds.
4. explain three influence strategies that can be used in a real or hypothetical organization.
5. explain gender differences in the use of influence strategies, according to two recent studies.
6. apply the scripting technique to a situation in which your communication should have been assertive but was either passive or aggressive instead.
7. explain why cultural differences must be considered when conducting training to improve assertive communication skills.
8. explain guidelines regarding nonverbal communication that female supervisors in the U.S. who want to enhance their power should consider following.

9. explain how tokenism harms women and minorities.
10. explain what organizations can do to empower tokens.
11. explain the methods R.M. Kanter suggests using to empower disenfranchised groups.
12. explain whether you agree or disagree with criticisms of empowerment, and state your reasons.
13. explain why women and minorities seem less likely than white men to acquire power in business organizations.

POWER, INFLUENCE, AND POWER SOURCES

Power has been defined as the potential ability to get people to change attitudes or behavior or the capacity to get others to do what they would not do otherwise (Bass, 1990). *Influence* is the actual ability to induce others to modify their behavior. The distinction between these terms resembles that between potential and kinetic energy; the former is dormant capacity, the latter, energy in motion.

According to French and Raven (1959), five general power sources are legitimate, reward, coercive, referent, and expert. The first three can be categorized as organizational and are derived from the positions individuals hold; the last two are personal and are derived from the characteristics and skills of individuals, regardless of their positions.

Legitimate power is based on one's position. For example, a corporate vice president has more of this type of power than a first line supervisor. An academic dean has more authority than a department head in a university.

Reward power is the ability to control the provision of tangibles or intangibles that specific individuals value, such as pay, promotions, appealing assignments, recognition, and praise. Managers' power increases if they control allocation of scarce resources. For example, if an already austere budget must be cut in a university, reward power of academic deans will rise to the extent they have access to and can distribute any remaining discretionary funds. They will have less reward power over faculty members who secure grants to support their own professional development, because such individuals depend less on deans for resources.

When using *reward power*, managers must ensure that their perceptions about what constitutes a reward agree with those of employees to avoid having it backfire. For example, a professor in an Organizational Behavior course with 500 students tried to apply principles taught in class by publicly commending a student for an outstanding test score. To provide positive recognition, intended as a reward, to the student, she invited him to the front of the classroom to participate in a demonstration. The student was embarrassed by the attention and did not consider it a reward. Making the situation worse, while he was in the front of the lecture hall, a jealous peer stole his notebook! (Karsten, 1994).

Control of technology, information, and knowledge also may enhance managers' reward power. The type of technology to which employees have access influences their productivity. According to Mann (1995, p.11), "the fact that technology has a major impact on power relations is an important reason why attempts to change technology often create major conflicts: the introduction of a new technology can alter the balance of power." The flow of information and knowledge greatly influences people's opinions of situations, as political "spin meisters" have aptly illustrated. Informal networks have been information sources that have been historically difficult for women and minorities to tap into; the consequences of their exclusion will be discussed in chapter 9.

Besides having formal authority based on job title, managers derive power from their ability to withhold desirable rewards or provide undesirable consequences to employees who do not meet job requirements. This is coercive power. Though operant theorists, such as B.F. Skinner, differentiate between withholding a positive and meting out a negative consequence and define only the latter as punishment, Schriesheim and Hinkins (1989) believe coercive power entails taking away tangible or intangible items that employees value and providing negative consequences. Negative results, or punishments, for failure to meet job requirements, should be provided as a last resort because of their potential for unintended consequences. Over-reliance on coercive methods is not recommended, because it may backfire. Punishing employees may extinguish one undesirable behavior, but another equally harmful behavior may replace it. Overall, coercive methods, which are perceived as "institutionally incorrect," are used rarely.

An inverse relationship exists between an authoritarian personality and the use of coercive power by men, but not women. Individuals with authoritarian personalities have been described as conventional, intolerant of ambiguity, resistant to change, and motivated by threat (Duncan, Peterson & Winter, 1997). They use a limited range of impersonal influence methods, comply with authority readily, and seek power. Rajan and Krishnan (2002) suggest that authoritarian men may have a high "external locus of control," which means that they attribute events to factors beyond their control. Authoritarian men "might prefer to put the onus of any coercive power on the institution to which they belong and on the rules of that institution rather than to accept responsibility for it" (Rajan & Krishnan, p.204).

Expert and *referent power* go beyond the hierarchy. People seek experts due to their knowledge, not their position. A positive relationship exists between an authoritarian personality and expert power for both women and men. Development of technical expertise is not only a prerequisite to legitimate power but also the most direct way to increase it. Authoritarian males seem to value legitimate power more than their female peers do (Rajan & Krishnan, 2002).

Besides increasing technical knowledge, managers can cultivate expertise in communication and interpersonal skills. Good communication skills will allow an understanding of the organization's vision to be transmitted to constituents; people skills will engender support for it (Rudolph & Peluchette, 1993).

Nurturing relationships inside and outside the organization can increase power as can gathering information about the way the organization works (Kotter, 1986) and priorities represented by competing constituencies' perspectives (Rudolph & Peluchette, 1993). Charisma is a power source that can be used or abused but may not be available to all leaders because of its association with distinct personal characteristics (Rudolph & Peluchette).

People are attracted to those with *referent power;* others enjoy their company and admire them. Former U.S. Secretary of State, Colin Powell, and Oprah Winfrey have referent power. Before their deaths in 1997, so did Mother Teresa of Calcutta and Diana, Princess of Wales.

FINITE OR INFINITE POWER AND ORGANIZATIONAL STRUCTURE

The amount of power can be considered fixed or infinite. Kanter (1977), a prominent contemporary management theorist, believes that power is unlimited. Her ideas are consistent with those of Mary Parker Follett, an important contributor to management thought who argued in the early twentieth century that power is infinite. In her words, "Our task is not to learn where to place power; it is how to develop power . . . Genuine power can only be grown" (Metcalf and Urwick, 1941).

Neither Kanter nor Follett believed that power should be used to "lord it over" others. Follett preferred "power with" to "power over" and thought one group's power could be increased without diminishing another's. In 1924, she said:

> There is an idea prevalent, which I think very harmful, that we give up individual power . . . to get joint activity. But first, by pooling power, we are not giving it up; and secondly, the power produced by relationship is a qualitative, not a quantitative thing . . . If we look at power as the power to do something, we shall understand this (Follett, 1924).

Kanter (1977) thinks that power should be based on expertise and special-ized knowledge, regardless of one's position in a hierarchy. From Follett's other statements about power, such beliefs also may have resonated with her.

Many of Follett's and Kanter's views are compatible with both the organic organizational structure (Burns & Stalker, 1961) and with what has been dubbed a "feminist approach" to management (Karsten, 1994). Features of organic, mechanistic, and proposed feminist organizations were presented in chapter 1.

POLITICS AND INFLUENCE IN ORGANIZATIONS

Sources of power, two theorists' views of them, and their compatibility with certain organizational structures have been discussed. Now the closely related topics of political behavior and influence tactics will be explained.

Engaging in organizational politics can be considered a way to increase in-fluence. Eiring (1999) defines politics as "getting what you want, the way you need it, when you want it." As recently as the 1990s, many women seemed to find politicking and power mongering" distasteful. Over half of successful executive women studied in the 1990s denied the value of politics, attributing their success to "hard work, tenacity, and determination." An additional 15% believed "luck" led to their success (White, Cox, & Cooper, 1992). None of the executive women mentioned political savvy as a factor that helped them advance, despite the fact that "Thinking hard work alone brings success brands you a political neophyte" (Kennedy, 1989).

As indicated in previous chapters, assumptions that women excel in inter-personal relations and men in analytic skills are dangerous because they ig-nore exceptions and individual differences and may limit opportunities for both sexes. This should be considered when evaluating the suggestion that "the qualities of intuition, sensitivity and a willingness to engage with feel-ings . . . stand women in good stead when embarking on developing political skill" (Mann, 1995, p. 17). The quote reflects stereotypical thinking, but Mann's notion that political skills can be learned and are not innate is useful.

African Americans are aware of the role of organizational politics in career progress. Seventy-two percent say politics are important, 79% understand how the political game works, and 69% say they deal with organizational pol-itics effectively (Livers & Caver, 2003). Livers and Caver are concerned about the 10% gap between the percent of blacks who understand politics and those who think they handle them well. They offer recommendations to blacks who wish to be politically astute. Many suggestions to African Amer-icans, such as building alliances, taking calculated risks, and evaluating strengths and weaknesses as related to their ability to influence others, seem applicable to anyone.

Blacks have been advised to determine how others perceive them by getting feedback (Livers & Caver, 2003). Those who are not black may focus on behavioral details in blacks that they would overlook in those with backgrounds more similar to their own. According to Livers and Caver (p. 150), "When blacks work with blacks in a white organization, their actions are scrutinized in a way seldom experienced by their white counterparts." Blacks need to realize that many whites have "an unconscious set of assumptions" that influence their perceptions of blacks and of themselves. Because such beliefs typically remain unspoken, dealing with them is difficult.

African Americans can try to manage others' perceptions by changing their own behavior *if* they feel comfortable doing so (Livers & Caver, 2003). Some do not mind consciously behaving differently at work than at home to be accepted; they view it as a game. Those who object to the idea of maintaining a different persona to "fit in" at work due to identity issues should not try it. Still others feel compelled to act differently than they would like due to others' perceptions. For example, black men in the Livers and Caver study left their office doors open when reviewing white women's performance due to concerns about "what others would think" if they were alone with a white woman.

Livers and Caver (2003) recommend that African Americans purposely cultivate positive relationships with other blacks because they create positive synergy. Such associations are "safe havens" where blacks can gain emotional support and converse openly regarding issues about which they may feel guarded in discussions with whites. Some blacks may have their own notions of the way a black leader should behave and view anything that deviates as deficient. Others may distance themselves from other blacks or create difficulties for them to preserve their own elect status. Such strategies resemble those some white women adopted when females began entering management, which earned them the label, "Queen Bee."

Besides acknowledging that diverse perspectives can be a source of political strength, non-blacks who are colleagues of African Americans should help coworkers understand organizational politics better by discussing political ramifications of behavior and decisions with them. They should consciously avoid misinterpreting behaviors that may be unfamiliar due to limited cultural knowledge. If the behavior of those from different backgrounds seems inappropriate or unwise, those who find it so should help them understand how it could be misread.

Though Livers and Caver (2003) direct their suggestions toward African Americans' non-black colleagues, some seems appropriate for all managers and employees. For example, all managers should heed their advice to make sure that formal, written organizational expectations are equitable and communicated to everyone. Likewise, managers should discuss informal expectations with all who are affected instead of keeping them secret.

Many articles that discuss gender, race, and organizational politics provide only anecdotal information. Research studies on differences in influence strategies based on racial or ethnic origin are rare. Those that discuss gender differences ignore experiences of women of color and do not necessarily focus on managerial women and men. Important influence strategies, which also may be considered political tactics, are bargaining, rationality, assertiveness, upward appeal, coalition-building, and friendliness, or ingratiation (Kipnis, Schmidt, & Wilkinson, 1980; Schriesheim & Hinkin, 1990).

Bargaining, or negotiating, involves exchanging favors. Wise negotiators ask for more than they need so they have something to "give up" when bargaining gets serious. Women may be less likely to do this (Babcock & Laschever, 2003). Because many have "interdependent self-schemas" that emphasize connection, they may be reluctant to ask for too much for fear of damaging relationships with superiors. Ironically, asking for too little may cause them to "sacrifice some of their employers' regard." As long as white males run most of the powerful companies in the U.S., females and minorities who want to boost their power must learn to ask directly for what they want—all of it—even if they feel uncomfortable making such requests due to gender socialization or cultural differences.

Rationality entails an appeal to logic or the use of data to convince others of the reasonableness of one's views. This may be more effective when dealing with executives who believe in employee participation than with those who are autocratic.

As an influence strategy, assertiveness is defined as "a direct and forceful approach" (O'Neill, 2004) and as "demanding compliance, ordering, setting deadlines, nagging, and expressing anger" (Rajan & Krishnan, 2002, p. 197). The definitions of assertiveness as an influence strategy differ from the notion of assertive communication, which will be discussed later in this chapter. "Demanding compliance" and "ordering" seem more like aggressive communication.

Upward appeal is enlisting the support of higher authority figures; coalition-building is developing alliances with others who share similar goals and obtaining their backing. For example, leaders of units A, B, and C, who are concerned about the future implications on their own unit of a top executive's action to eliminate an area of responsibility from unit D, might form an alliance with unit D. Though leaders of the first three units may have little else in common with unit D's leader, the four together can be powerful allies.

Alliance-building relies on the concept of "strength in numbers." Though rejection may still occur, refusing several units acting in concert to pursue a common goal is more difficult than turning down one unit's request.

Coalition-building also is crucial because isolates lack support for sound proposals. Managers must cultivate allies at all levels, including secretaries and maintenance workers, who often provide valuable support and information.

Ingratiation includes deliberate attempts to get in another's "good graces." Others call this strategy "friendliness," which means creating goodwill and establishing a pleasant relationship before making a request. Those asking for something may humble themselves or try to make those who can grant their requests feel important through flattery or praise.

The political and/or influence strategies of alliance-building and negotiation are helpful in obtaining monetary and other resources and in safeguarding one's turf. Eiring (1999) advocates attempting to "bond with everyone" including enemies and trying to convert them into allies by pointing out how "buying-in" could advance their own agenda. Mann (1995) recommends making a logical, public case for increased resources, stressing how obtaining them will benefit those who can provide them. This should be done after having built alliances with others who might be helpful.

Constant acquiescence and frequent or unnecessary confrontation are equally unwise. Managers must remember the importance of relationship maintenance to long range goal achievement.

Politically astute executives should be proactive and watchful. Otherwise, their information sources could dry up or parts of their responsibilities could be reassigned. Sure signs of trouble, such occurrences should be countered using previously mentioned influence strategies.

Even the most politically adept managers may experience "turf wars. These occur when one division's agenda starts to overlap another's. If dialogue can occur so that both units' underlying needs and goals can be identified, a "win-win" solution may be possible. If not, alliance building and negotiation may again be useful strategies.

Research regarding whether or not influence tactics vary based on gender have been mixed, but two recent studies (Rajan & Krishnan, 2002; O'Neill, 2004) show no difference. Consistent with Kanter's (1977) views, formal and informal power "embedded in the organization" (O'Neill, 2004), rather than gender, seem to affect influence activities used. These power factors include the gender ratio in the organization or job category, position in the hierarchy, organizational role, number of employees supervised, and participation in important networks and relationships with prominent mentors (O'Neill). In a national sample of female and male public relations practitioners who exhibit similar amounts of organizational power, those in higher positions are more likely to use assertiveness as an influence tactic (O'Neill). Hierarchical position relates positively to the use of assertiveness and coalition-building for men, but not women. In the same study, however, when the gender ratio in top management makes women tokens, men are less likely to use upward appeal, coalition-building, or assertiveness tactics. To explain this, O'Neill suggests that male public relations managers might feel very comfortable among senior managers who are nearly all men and, therefore, feel no need to use such tactics. Contrary to previous studies showing that less powerful individuals tend to adopt an ingratiation strategy out of deference to those with more clout, O'Neill's research found no power factors that were related to ingratiation.

The relationship between authoritarian personality type and the frequency of assertiveness and sanctions strategies as moderated by gender is the topic of Rajan's and Krishnan's 2002 study. Their findings reveal that authoritarian males use friendliness, bargaining, and assertiveness more often than female peers. Authoritarian men may act in a friendly manner to conform to their perceptions of "institutionally correct" behavior. Their female counterparts seem more likely to act in a way that is consistent with their personality.

As influence strategies, assertiveness and bargaining are compatible with traditional authority and stereotypically "masculine" norms. Authoritarian individuals are more likely than others to conform to stereotypical gender role expectations, which could explain why authoritarian males use assertiveness and bargaining strategies more often than authoritarian females do (Rajan & Krishnan, 2002).

ASSERTIVE COMMUNICATION

The dominant culture in the U.S. advocates that managers communicate assertively, rather than passively or aggressively. *Assertiveness* means stating needs and wants honestly, clearly, and directly in a manner that respects the needs and rights of others. It is a middle ground between passive and aggressive behavior. Assertive communicators are not rude but are willing to take the initiative if necessary. They recognize and accept their limits and express their views without apology or excess anxiety.

Those who communicate passively either fail to state their needs or mention them so indirectly or hesitantly that those to whom the messages are directed do not receive them. Passive communicators may allow themselves to be "used;" their deference allows others to treat them like doormats. Passive managers may become overburdened due to an inability to say "no" to their supervisors. They may tolerate substandard work to avoid confronting employees about performance deficiencies. Eager to please, they may fear rejection.

Aggressive communicators are at the opposite end of the spectrum. They fulfill their desires and needs even if they have to trample on the rights of others. They may be abrasive and domineering and seem to delight in verbally attacking or embarrassing others publicly or belittling their opinions. Aggressiveness can become workplace bullying and, in extreme instances, may constitute harassment.

Distinct nonverbal cues are associated with aggressive, assertive, and passive communication. Classic aggressive nonverbal signals include glaring at others with hands on hips, speaking in a loud, raspy tone, and wagging the index finger. Nonverbal cues consistent with assertive communication in the dominant culture include good posture, direct eye contact, a calm, clear voice, and a moderate tone of speech. In the majority culture, little eye contact or an averted gaze connotes passivity as does a whiny voice or slumped posture. In some cultures, however, making direct eye contact is considered rude behavior, a privacy violation, or failure to show proper deference.

The following responses illustrate the differences among aggressive, assertive, and passive communication. A managerial woman has just been asked to serve as secretary for a volunteer organization of which she is a member, and she does not want to assume that role.

Aggressive response: No way! I'm sick and tired of this organization always expecting a middle-aged woman to be the secretary. That's sexist!

Assertive response: I would prefer not to serve as secretary.

Passive response: Oh, I guess I can do it if no one else wants to.

Those recommending assertive communication as a power enhancer must realize that such a suggestion is controversial for several reasons. First, it represents an individual, behavioral solution to women's relative lack of power—a problem that may have structural causes. Secondly, assertiveness training that is limited to women reinforces gender stereotypes. Hite and McDonald (1995, p.9) explain that such a program

> . . . assumes that women as a group lack sufficient assertiveness and that men, as a group have this skill. By assigning this topic gender dependence, organizations deny males the opportunity to enhance their assertiveness abilities, while discounting women who have expertise in this area. . . When gender, rather than individual needs, is the primary rationale for training selection, gender bias is operating.

Third, assertive women are considered less likeable than nonassertive women (Rudman, 1998). Regardless of how well an assertive woman states her case, she risks decreasing her likeability and therefore her ability to influence the other side to agree with her point of view. In contrast, whether they are liked or not does not affect men's ability to influence others, and there is no connection between assertive behavior and likeability for men (Babcock & Laschever, 2003, p. 87–88).

A fourth reason why some question assertiveness training is because it needs to be modified when those trying to become more assertive have authoritarian personalities.

Such individuals tend to conform to "traditional" gender roles (Rajan & Krishnan, 2002). Authoritarian women might view assertiveness as "masculine" and resist it for that reason, whereas authoritarian men might link it with a "'soft' leadership style" compared to aggressiveness and might find it incompatible with typical stereotypes about men (Rajan & Krishnan, 2002).

Finally, the fact that assertive communication reflects culturally dependent norms for business communication that are consistent with the dominant group is a concern. It may be incompatible with cultural norms of Hispanics, Asian Americans, and Native Americans in the U.S. that emphasize collectivism and with other cultures worldwide in which achievement of group goals takes precedence over attainment of individual aims.

A study of low-income Hispanic, black, and white women shows little agreement on what constitutes passive, assertive, and aggressive behavior (Yoshioka, 2000). They reached consensus when assessing vignettes only when women of various races and ethnic origins interacted with unrelated children. Little agreement existed about whether communication in the vignettes was passive, assertive, or aggressive when interactions involved both sexes. Yoshioka (2000, p. 254) attributes such differences to cross-cultural distinctions in ways "women view their own social positions and roles vis-à-vis those of the fictitious men in the role play."

Compared to others in Yoshioka's (2000) study, Hispanic women attach great importance to the cultural concepts of *simpatia* and *personalismo*. Literally, *simpatia* means "nice" and enjoins personal conflict (Marin & Marin, 1991). *Personalismo* advocates cultivation of a personal quality in interactions (Comas-Diaz, 1984). Yoshioka (2000) says that these concepts create expectations for propriety, good manners, and deference that non-Hispanic whites do not encounter.

Other cultural differences that designers of assertiveness training in which Hispanics participate must be aware of are *machismo*, a behavior code that values virility for males, and *marianismo*, a code emphasizing female' alleged spiritual superiority. The traditional respect and strong loyalty for nuclear and extended family members also must be considered (Comas-Diaz & Duncan, 1985).

If dominant culture members view responses that seem appropriate to Hispanic women as passive, they may regard communication that seems assertive to African American women as aggressive and "masculine." According to Parker (2001, p. 45), "directness associated with Black women's communication may be viewed as deviant or not feminine, even though femininity and masculinity are socially constructed." Yoshioka (2000, p. 245) argues that in assertiveness programs that will succeed with African Americans, "Black linguistic styles not only must be taken into consideration but also must be valued as highly as white styles."

To deal with cultural variations in the context of assertiveness training, Yoshioka (2000) recommends "message matching," which is assessing the situation in terms of the amount of influence people have on one's livelihood and then deciding whether to communicate using a comfortable style or the dominant group's style, if it differs from one's own. Those who are not members of the dominant group must learn at least one additional communication style, which might seem like an extra burden, but doing so leads to increased flexibility, which will be prized as their careers progress.

Adding a "cultural component" to assertiveness training for dominant group members is another of Yoshioka's recommendations, but this could have drawbacks. Philosophically, an "add-on" is unappealing because it highlights the "outsider" status of executive women and minorities. Consideration of the fact that they may not fit the corporate mold comes across as an afterthought. Instead of adding a "cultural component," perhaps a discussion of the impact of cultural differences on views of assertiveness could be infused into the training.

Assertiveness is a communication skill that anyone can learn. Those who wish to advance to upper level management of major U.S. firms in the near future may want to become proficient in it, though it may seem uncomfortable at first. Aggressive communicators can modify their style to be more mindful of others' needs. Passive communicators can learn to speak up for themselves. This may involve a struggle for those whose cultures or gender roles have emphasized one style of communication over the other, but change is possible. Assertiveness also can help executives gain resources for their units, conduct honest appraisals of employees' performance, object to unfair assessments of their work in a professional manner, request pay raises, set limits and refuse unreasonable requests, and let their supervisors know the types of assignments or projects they would like.

Until recently, many men were socialized to avoid expressing positive feelings, and women were encouraged to suppress negative emotions. Men may have been uncomfortable voicing appreciation or telling loved ones how much they meant, whereas women may have felt guilty for becoming angry.

Women and men can benefit from learning to verbalize a wide range of feelings appropriately through assertiveness training that is sensitive to cultural differences.

Increasing assertiveness involves behavior change. Before modifying behavior, people must be aware of their current patterns. Just as those in smoking cessation programs identify circumstances in which they are most likely to have a cigarette and weight loss program participants keep track of when they eat and the type and amount of food they consume, would-be assertive communicators may benefit from logging situations in which they acted aggressively, assertively, and passively for about two weeks before trying to modify their behavior. They may reflect on and list their usual ways of reacting to employees who exhibit problematic behavior at work. They can then analyze typical reactions for signs of passivity or aggression and consider ways to respond assertively instead.

The Internet is another resource for finding tools to evaluate assertiveness levels. Searching for "assertiveness assessment" on google.com or other popular search engines can be productive.

THE SCRIPTING TECHNIQUE

James Waters developed the scripting technique, a method for analyzing behavior to identify signs of assertive, passive, or aggressive communication (Morgan & Baker, 1985). The four basic stages of scripting include a description of the situation, expression of feelings, a request for behavior change, and a statement of positive consequences to the party who modifies his or her behavior.

In the first stage, people objectively describe, in writing, a situation in which they used aggressive or passive communication and, with hindsight, realized assertive behavior would have been preferable. Then, in the second phase, people communicate their feelings, while carefully avoiding accusations or generalizations. Accusations typically start with the phrase, "You never . . ." or "You always . . ." and provoke recipient defensiveness.

A professor who asked students in a business class that also fulfilled a general education requirement in ethnic and gender studies to complete this exercise suspected a gender difference in statements they wrote to express feelings. In at least three consecutive semesters during the 1990s in which enrollment in this course was gender balanced, male students seemed more likely than female peers to write "I felt . . ." and then a cognitive rather than an affective response. They seemed to write the predicate as if the subject of the sentence had been "I thought" or "I believed." When the professor noticed this trend, she discussed it with the students and gave examples of words that expressed affective rather than cognitive responses. After that, the apparent gender difference in the use of words that reflected feelings and beliefs diminished. Further systematic study would be necessary before concluding that gender, and not some other factor, caused students to respond so differently to requests for statements describing feelings.

In the third phase of the scripting process, people ask the other party to make a specific, realistic behavior change. The request must be reasonable and represent something that can be accomplished within a particular time frame.

In the last stage, assertive communicators state positive consequences that will accrue to the *other party*, who is being asked to change his or her behavior. This answers the question, "What's in it for me?" from the perspective of the individual who must modify behavior. Readers should be able to identify each phase of the scripting process in the following example. Marla's supervisor, George, evaluated her performance as a secretary at a large New York firm annually. Paul, a member of George's staff, entered George's office while he was conducting an appraisal interview with Marla. George asked Paul if he agreed that Marla's performance should be rated "Outstanding." Paul said "no" because, in his view, only God was outstanding, and Marla's performance fell short of that impossible standard. George considered Paul's comments and then changed Marla's overall evaluation from "Outstanding" to "Above Average."

Marla: I feel angry about having the evaluation of my performance downgraded from "Outstanding" to "Above Average." I am upset that such an inappropriate comparison has caused my rating to be adjusted downward and that a staff member's intrusion into a private meeting was tolerated.

I am interested in your assessment of my performance. Please re-evaluate my work compared to established standards or to the performance of other secretaries with my education and experience who work in this organization. If you reassess my performance on that basis, I will believe that I have been treated equitably and will be motivated to continue to perform at a high level and be a valuable asset to this organization.

I also would feel more respected if future appraisal interviews were conducted without interruptions. Please do not let Paul or anyone else disrupt our next interview. An uninterrupted interview indicates that the organization takes the process seriously. It will allow me to focus on specific areas in which further development will benefit you and the organization (Lovas, 2004).

ASSERTIVE BEHAVIOR: THE CONSEQUENCES

Becoming assertive has positive and negative results. It provides an additional behavioral option and enhances people's sense of control but also may strain relationships. Significant others may not understand or may dislike the change if they have benefited from previous passivity. They may inaccurately label the new behavior as aggression to persuade newly assertive individuals to revert to old passive ways. This may be done based on fear of losing the old relationship in which they could dump extra work and emotional "garbage" on passive individuals. Those striving to become assertive should examine their behavior if accused of being aggressive. The claims may have no merit, but sometimes previously suppressed anger and frustration surface, causing formerly passive individuals to overshoot the mark.

As discussed in chapter 5, aggression is an intensified, proscribed behavior for females but is tolerated— and even expected—in males. This creates difficulties for executive women, as illustrated by an organization that required several managerial women deemed aggressive to attend a workshop for "bully broads" designed to encourage assertive behavior (*BBC News Online*, 2001). Attendance was mandatory if they wished to continue in their current positions, but no males—aggressive or otherwise—had to attend.

Livers and Caver (2003, p. 183) advise African American managerial women to continue to be confident and assertive but to realize that such behaviors "may be misinterpreted as pushy or threatening." They also suggest that socializing "is not a white thing" and that African American women should mingle to allow others to become acquainted with them. Interestingly, aspiring white women received similar advice in the 1990s when they were told that being considered "easy to be with" would help their careers (Catalyst, 1996).

SITUATIONS IN WHICH ASSERTIVE BEHAVIOR SHOULD BE USED

Those cultivating assertiveness skills do not have to use them in every situation. To decide whether it is worthwhile, they should consider tangible and intangible costs and ask themselves how important it is to be assertive in this situation and how they will feel later if they remain passive. This is illustrated by the inner conflict a woman with strong opinions on a controversial issue experienced when she attended a meeting at which the issue, which was not on the agenda, was discussed. She knew her views would be in the minority; perhaps no one in the group shared them. She also knew that she would pay a price in lost sleep and regret if she sat silently and did not state her beliefs. Speaking out was not cost-free; she might be socially ostracized or others might start withholding important information, thereby eroding her power. This woman decided that the costs of failing to state her opinion exceeded those of doing so and said what she thought. Though only one other person showed any support for her views, the discussion was respectful, and the woman was not ostracized or excluded from information networks because she stated her beliefs.

POWER AND COMMUNICATION

Increasing their assertiveness is one way in which people can become more powerful verbal communicators. Before discussing ways to improve oral communication, elements of the communication process will be reviewed and what is known and remains to be discovered about the impact of gender and race on communication and the interactions between those two factors will be explored. *Communication* is transmission of understanding or meaning. In two-way communication, senders transmit encoded messages to recipients, who decode them and give feedback to the senders. If no feedback is provided, one-way communication occurs.

Communication can be verbal, nonverbal, or written. Verbal, or oral, communication is spoken; gestures and facial expressions are examples of nonverbal communication, and written business communication includes e-mail and paper or electronic memos, letters, and reports. In verbal exchanges, the spoken word accounts for about 7% of the communication, the remaining 93% is based on nonverbal signals.

The role of gender and cultural communication differences is a contested area that requires more research. Though they disagree with the notion, Lakoff (1975) and Reardon (1995) suggest that the perception of women's communication styles as different from men's and, therefore, "deficient," may have partly explained their stymied career progress in the past. The proposed solution incorporates assertiveness training and other techniques to help women adopt more "masculine" styles of communication, which are regarded as the "norm." Tannen (1995) proposes that communication between women and men is "cross-cultural" because the sexes perceive the purpose of communication differently due to varying socialization experiences. In this view, males focus on the power dynamics of communication. They wish to raise their power profile or avoid having it diminished when interacting with others. When females communicate, they try to maintain equal status and are concerned about helping others "save face." If the sexes do, in fact, have such different perspectives, it is not surprising that misunderstanding occurs.

Herrick (1999), however, criticizes Lakoff's and Tannen's approaches to gender and communication. Neither considers the diversity among women in terms of factors such as social class, ethnic background, occupation, and age. Herrick believes that communication patterns vary and that biology and socialization are two of many elements including the power distribution and situational factors that influence them. Viewing women's and men's communication patterns as diametrically opposed is a mistake, according to Herrick (1999, p. 293), who concludes that "binary opposites, such as male and female language styles . . . limit our vision and can cause us to fall into stereotypical thinking that may reproduce the very situation we hope to rectify."

More research dealing with color and communication is needed. Leonard and Locke (1993) indicate that speech patterns of whites and blacks may be regarded as "polar opposites." Studies have shown that gender communication patterns are not dichotomous; future research may or may not draw the same conclusion based on race but is necessary to start to separate the effects of race and gender on communication (Popp, Donovan, et al., 2003).

POWERFUL SPOKEN, WRITTEN, AND NONVERBAL COMMUNICATION

Overall issues regarding race, gender, and communication have been presented briefly. The next section gives suggestions for dealing with more pragmatic issues involving the spoken word.

Skilled communicators avoid fillers, diminutives, excessive use of adjectives, and disclaimers. Fillers are speech segments like "uh," "um," or "y' know." If overused, fillers distract listeners, who pay more attention to them than to the message's content. Diminutives are words such as "merely," "simply," "tiny," "only" or "just." Their frequent use may indicate weakness or a low self-concept to members of the dominant culture. When accompanied by nonverbal signals such as a hesitating manner and slumped posture, those who approach the boss with, "I know you're busy, but this will *only* take a *little* time" may not be considered effective leaders. Besides diminutives, this example also contains a disclaimer, namely the phrase, "I know you're busy, but. . . ." Other examples of disclaimers are "You'll probably think this is a silly idea, but . . ." or "I really shouldn't say this, but . . ."

When apologies are in order, not receiving them can be annoying, but they can be overdone. Receivers' perspectives determine whether they are perceived as overused or as ritualized forms of communication that express concern. Tannen (1995) argues that some women use "I'm sorry" as ritualized communication in the same way that people ask "How are you?" as a greeting but do not expect—or want—to hear a litany of physical complaints. When both parties understand underlying assumptions, ritualized communication may be fine, but those who constantly apologize may seem less effective and more likely to be at fault than people who say they are sorry only when necessary (Tannen).

"Consider it done!" is more powerful than "I'll try," and top managers prefer subordinates who get the job done to those who agree to exert effort. Speaking tentatively detracts from powerful communication, though many admire those who put forth their best effort regardless of whether they achieve their goals.

Tag questions transform statements into queries and may be either modal or affective. "The meeting is tomorrow at 4 p.m., right?" or "You're going to be there, aren't you?" are examples of modal tag questions in which the speaker asks for confirmation. Some have speculated that less powerful individuals might use modal tag questions more often than powerful people because, as information requests, they connote dependency (Lakoff, 1975). Research support for this notion has been mixed, however. A 1980 study indicates that powerful people are more likely than others to use modal tag questions (Johnson), but a 1989 study (Cameron, McAlinden & O'Leary) shows the opposite. Modal tag questions are more common among meeting conveners than participants; Calnan and Davidson (1998) believe that roles and functions at work are more likely than gender to predict the use of tag questions.

Affective tag questions can be facilitative, in which the intent is to support those being addressed or give them a way to enter the conversation, or softening, in which those giving negative feedback "cushion the impact" by providing positive comments about another aspect of the individual's work. Evidence regarding whether women or men are more likely to use affective tag questions is inconclusive. Contradicting their previously stated hypothesis about modal tag questions, researchers, Calnan and Davidson (1998), show that men are more likely than women to use affective tag questions. Most males using affective tags in their study are in all-male groups, and they surmised that group composition influenced the results. Except for the difference just explained, Calnan and Davidson found little variation in the overall use of tag questions by gender. The organization's cultural norms and specific situational characteristics seemed more influential.

Suggestions about voice, pitch, and volume seem dependent on culture. Bias against high-pitched voices can harm careers based on an uncontrollable, non-job related factor. Some women have been socialized to speak quietly, but soft-spoken business executives risk having their message disregarded. On the other hand, loud, abrasive speech may be less acceptable in women than in men due to relaxed and intensified gender-related proscriptions on behavior, explained in chapter 5. Again, this puts women in a "double bind." If they speak too softly, their message will be considered unimportant; if they loudly advocate their views, their message may be overshadowed by a perception that they are obnoxious.

Though women and racial/ethnic minorities can change their speech patterns, cultural variations in style of speech should be accepted within a range. Some who speak one language and have little exposure to bi- or multilingual individuals may find it challenging to understand them initially, but effort by both parties usually overcomes this potential barrier. Diversity management programs also may assist in increasing comfort levels with variations in volume, pitch, and manner of speaking (Karsten, 1994).

Tolerance for differences in speech styles does not imply acceptance of ungrammatical language or slang. Livers and Caver (2003) advise African Americans who are concerned that they may be using non-standard English in the workplace to get feedback from someone whom they trust regarding their grammar and take steps to correct, it if necessary. Though these suggestions seem universally applicable, stereotypes about blacks' English usage that spawned such recommendations are, regrettably, not applied to whites, many of whom "routinely slaughter the English language" (Livers & Caver, 2003, p. 182). Whites' misuse of the language is not typically associated with lower intelligence, but blacks' verbal blunders may be judged harshly due to double standards (Livers & Caver).

Regardless of race/ethnicity, or gender, ungrammatical or non-standard English can cost managers promotions in the U.S. Some executives have hired "speech coaches" as consultants to assist employees who qualify for promotion except for their improper use of English on the job. (Lublin, 2004).

Whether or not people allow others to invade their personal space, how often and in which circumstances they smile, and the type of gestures they use affect others' perceptions of their power. Acceptable ranges for these forms of nonverbal communication vary based on culture, and an extensive discussion of cultural differences is beyond the scope of this book. Executives increasingly need knowledge of basic cultural variations and an awareness of individual differences to avoid misunderstanding.

In the U.S., female supervisors who want to enhance their power should not permit subordinates to invade their personal space. Women in the U.S. tend to be more comfortable with close physical proximity than their male peers. Allowing subordinates to get too close, physically, may signify low power. Those of other cultural backgrounds may feel comfortable with less personal space and may view those who prefer a larger personal "bubble" as cold or distant.

To smile or not is a dilemma for executive women in the U.S. Those who smile frequently may not be regarded as serious, but women who rarely smile may be considered aloof. Smiling is generally not an issue for male executives; those who smile are considered more approachable.

Small, close-to-the-body gestures connote weakness; large, expansive gestures indicate power. Large body size makes people seem more influential, which is a disadvantage for women, most of whom are physically smaller than most men. Similarly, allowing personal belongings to take up more, rather than less space, connotes power, but beyond some point, it may seem overbearing or connote disorganization (Karsten, 1994).

Potent written communication is concise and specific. Whether writing memos or reports to be distributed electronically or as hard copies, managers should get to the point, use simple, not complex, words, and choose the active voice more often than the passive (Karsten, 1994). Because sending e-mail messages is so easy, employees and managers alike have become lax regarding tone and grammatical and typographical errors. Such carelessness may reflect poorly on their organizations, especially since programs checking grammar and spelling are readily available. Managers and employees should be cautious when trying to interject humor in e-mail messages because of the possibility of misinterpretation. Without visual cues, comments intended to be witty could be interpreted as sarcastic or cynical. Re-reading e-mail messages before hitting the "send" key is always wise.

Organizations that wish to empower all employees should use inclusive, nonsexist terms in written and verbal communication. Gender-neutral terms to describe occupations, such as firefighter, mail carrier, and police officer, are widely accepted. In the past, when terms like "fireman" and "policeman" were used, children growing up may have visualized males in such positions. This imagery may have made some females less likely to consider those occupations.

TOKENISM

The definitions of power and influence at the beginning of this chapter and the discussion of power sources emphasizes the role of individuals in power acquisition; Kanter (1977) argues that features embedded in the structure of organizations and the context "stack the deck" against women and racial/ethnic minorities seeking to increase their power. One such feature is *tokenism*, the numeric imbalance that occurs when a group that is different than the majority constitutes 15% or less of the population being studied. Since more than 85% of top executives of major U.S. corporations are white males, theories of tokenism are relevant to women and racial/ethnic minorities aspiring to such positions.

Early articles on tokenism depicted men as the dominant group and women as tokens, but such notions extend to other groups (Kanter, 1977). For example, a person using a wheelchair in the midst of ambulatory individuals, a manager over age 65 whose colleagues are all in their 30s or 40s, and an Asian American individual in an otherwise white work group can be considered tokens.

Negative outcomes resulting from token status for women and racial/ethnic minorities include marginalization, confinement in stereotypical roles, devaluation, feelings of discomfort, and heightened visibility, leading to additional performance pressure (Kanter, 1977; Yoder, 2002). In the following passage, Ely (1995, p. 625) indicates that sex role stereotypes are more prevalent when few women have top positions.

> Women in these firms, when compared to women in firms with higher proportions of senior women, characterized men as more masculine and less feminine, evaluated feminine attributes and attributes they associated with women less favorably in relations to their firm's requirements for success, and had more difficulty enacting gender roles that were both personally satisfying and consistent with their firms' norms and expectations.

Interestingly, white males who constitute less than 15% of a group escape these negative outcomes. The term *glass elevator* describes the positive effects on promotional opportunities for token males in predominantly female workgroups within social work, elementary school teaching, nursing, and library science professions (Williams, 1992). Two male tokens in an otherwise female work group employed in a concession stand at a St. Louis zoo reported being very satisfied with their jobs, received favorable performance reviews, and were the only individuals in a group of first year workers to be promoted (Yoder & Sinnett, 1985). These findings made the researchers wonder whether other factors, such as status and selection of an occupation considered inappropriate for one's gender role, called *occupational deviance*, were confounded with numeric imbalance. Despite their desire for it to be otherwise, Yoder and Sinnett assumed, for study purposes, that in U.S. society, men's status is higher than women's and whites' is higher than blacks'.

Yoder and Sinnett (1985) wanted to know whether high status could protect *double deviates* from tokenism's harmful effects. These individuals differed once from the "norm" of maleness because they were women and a second time because they were employed in occupations generally regarded as "nontraditional" for females (Laws, 1975). Female leaders (non-tokens) in charge of an all female group were compared with a woman (gender token) leading a group of men, all of whom were of the same age and had the same level of education as the leader, and a woman (high status gender token) leading a group of men who were younger and had significantly less education than she did. The non-tokens and high status gender tokens were equally comfortable with the performance expected of them and with the leadership role, but the gender tokens who did not have higher status than their male followers were less comfortable and had greater anxiety about their performance than the non-token or high status token leaders (Yoder, 2002). Thus, enhancing the token woman's status seems to reduce the negative social costs she would otherwise experience. This also may explain why males, who are still thought to have higher status in the U.S. than women, seem immune from the "social costs" imposed on female tokens.

Yoder, Anaikudo and Berendsen (1996) extended this research to test the idea that occupational deviance, status, and numerical imbalance interact to produce tokenism's negative effects. They studied female black and white firefighters and created situations in which the former were "double tokens" based on race and gender as compared to white male firefighters. Firefighting was considered an ideal profession to study because it has been stereotyped as a more appropriate occupation for men than women, it requires social interaction, and only 5% of the incumbents are women.

Yoder, Anaikudo and Berendsen (1996) showed that a rise in the number of black female firefighters' white male peers was accompanied by a decrease in collegiality as evidenced by fewer informal discussions, less leisure time interaction, and less support and positive feedback for promotions. White female firefighters did not encounter these negative effects as the number of white male peers increased. Black and white female firefighters with an increasing number of black male colleagues felt a common bond with them due to shared experiences of discrimination. They also believed, however, that gender overshadowed racial/ethnic similarity among black men and women firefighters and caused black and white males to work together to isolate women (Yoder, 2002).

On the other hand, any connection the black and white female firefighters felt due to their shared problem of gender discrimination was insufficient to establish strong relationships. Only a few interacted with each other; the black female firefighters thought that race/ethnic differences overshadowed gender commonality. A few white women denied any influence of race on their interaction with black female peers, asserting their "colorblindness." McIntosh (1995) believes that only the privileged have the luxury of assuming that race is invisible and claiming to be colorblind.

Unlike Kanter's work, which assumed that numerical imbalance is neutral and causes negative consequences for tokens because majority group members do not know how to deal with them, Yoder's studies (2002) show that the dominant group engages in more active exclusionary tactics. Kanter's early work on tokenism, conducted when women's invisibility in management was attributed to personal factors such as "fear of success" (Horner, 1970), demonstrated the role of structural obstacles, rather than personal deficiencies, in hindering careers of executive women. Yoder's expansion on this work shows that numerical imbalance must be considered within the context of status and occupational deviance. Her research-based suggestions about ways in which organizations can disrupt the link between tokenism and its negative consequences are among her most important contributions to date.

In a study of three female token leaders' interactions with all-male work groups, only the trained leader whom a male experimenter introduced as an "expert" could influence her group. The individual introducing the female leader enhanced the group's perception of her status. Yoder (2002, p. 7) concluded that "the status enhancement of tokens, albeit competent tokens, rests in the hands of organizations whose high-status members can legitimate women."

Besides raising tokens' status, organizations should increase their numerical representation to 35% of relevant groups to minimize harmful effects, according to most tokenism researchers (Yoder, 2002; Collins, 1998). This is necessary because the dominant group may respond to an influx of tokens by intensifying discrimination against them.

The final way to empower tokens is to change the stereotypes about "appropriate" occupations based on gender. As explained in chapter 5, modifying engrained stereotypes is more difficult than it may seem.

The process through which individuals become tokens is interesting. Judith Long Laws' (1975) explanation emphasizes gender tokenism and defines males as the dominant group and all others as *primary deviates,* but her work could be applied to minorities as well. In Laws' scheme, *double deviates* are primary deviates (women) who are not content with their lot and aspire to equal treatment with the dominant group.

Before individuals can become tokens, dominant group members must sponsor them. In addition, both parties must agree on a role bargain, believe sponsors are unbiased, and expect tokens to defend sponsors (Kanter, 1977). The role bargain includes beliefs in exceptionalism, individualism, and the merit principle. The person who is to become a token is viewed as an exception and as superior to other "deviates." The belief that goals are accomplished due to individual effort alone, which is essential to the role bargain, may not be realistic. Honest people must concede that little is achieved without "standing on the shoulders" of those who have gone before. Industriousness is praiseworthy, but those who commend themselves for working hard should be thankful they have the health, strength, and stamina to do so. In most cases, they cannot take particular credit for such gifts. If success is due to individual effort exclusively, then those who are unsuccessful must blame themselves. This logic is unfortunate because factors embedded in society and in organizations can make it challenging for those who are not members of the dominant group to do well.

The merit principle is the idea that differentiation between superb and average job performance is possible and that better performers should be rewarded more handsomely than those whose work is average. According to the merit principle, exclusiveness is thought necessary to maintain high standards. Though justifiable in some instances, high standards that cannot be associated statistically with exemplary job performance may exclude deviates from an occupation or its higher echelons.

Are such rigorous standards essential for effective job performance? The rigorous two-day exam that must be passed to become a certified public accountant (CPA) is an example that can be considered before answering this question. A 14% pass rate on the first try is considered good. Perhaps the high standard is needed, but the bar may be set higher than required for job success to retain exclusivity and limit the supply of CPAs. This may raise compensation for those who pass the demanding exam, thereby demonstrating that they deserve to be accepted into the profession.

The process of creating tokens is complete when the dominant group integrates the tokens into their group in a way that guarantees they are not a threat and reinforces their second-class status. To do this, they may stereotype female tokens in familiar roles, such as the good mother, cheerful mascot, radical militant, or sex object. Tokens who are racial or ethnic minorities may be typecast as discussed in chapter 5. They may simultaneously be isolated socially and overloaded with work due to their visibility. Typecasting, isolation, and overload reaffirm the idea that they are second rate and allow the dominant class to retain control. Tokens cannot get away from their origins totally and are not permitted to be equal participants in dominant class activities (Laws, 1975).

Number balancing alone cannot overcome structural obstacles to power. As has been discussed, it must be accompanied by high-ranking managers' explicit statements that confer legitimacy on those who otherwise would be considered tokens and by attempts to dispel gender stereotypes about appropriate occupations. Other structural sources of power include flattened hierarchies, decentralized authority, and decision-making delegated to the lowest possible level (Kanter, 1977). Kanter recommends flattening hierarchies and decentralizing authority as ways to empower disenfranchised groups, such as women, who experienced bureaucratic powerlessness when larger numbers became managers in the 1970s and 1980s. This powerlessness was not due to personal deficiencies but was caused by features inherent in the structure of the large, impersonal organizations where many of them worked.

BUREAUCRATIC POWERLESSNESS

Managers experiencing bureaucratic powerlessness respond predictably. They control employees in attempts to retain the little power they have. Powerless managers have a reputation for being bossy and domineering. They are too concerned with enforcement of detailed rules and have been described as "nitpicky." Their excess territoriality harms the organization. Kanter (1977, p. 194) states:

> As each manager protects his or her own domain, the sense of helplessness and powerlessness of other administrators in intersecting units increases. They . . . respond by redoubling their domination over their territory and . . . workers. The result can be "sub-optimization": each subgroup optimizing only its own goals and forgetting about wider system interests.

Kanter's studies show that powerlessness, not gender, causes negative managerial behaviors. They counter the "bossy female manager" stereotype that was common in the 1970s and persisted, to a lesser extent, in the 1980s.

Factors in the business environment contribute to feelings of powerlessness. Rigid enforcement of rules and procedures remove employees' discretion and make them feel powerless; so do highly specialized tasks, which increase boredom. As work groups get larger, participation tends to drop and depersonalization rises.

In complex, contemporary organizations, executives must deal with more constituencies and greater interdependence and diversity in terms of values and goals than they did previously. They must manage more roles and relationships and deal with more conflict (Rudolph & Peluchette, 1993). A gap may exist between the amount of managers' position power and the quantity they need to do their jobs. Proposed remedies are to obtain or create more power or empower employees (Rudolph & Peluchette).

Hiring, promotion, and development decisions can affect power in organizations by reducing sources of bureaucratic powerlessness. This can be done by ensuring that women and minorities are hired for *line* rather than *staff* positions and do not linger in the lowest line position, that of first line supervisor. Staff positions, such as those of human resource managers within General Motors or other large corporations, are advisory. Those in staff positions have no power to tell employees how to run the production process, for example. Line managers, from manufacturing employees' immediate supervisor to the division vice president and the chief executive officer, have that power. Immediate, or first-line supervisor, is a common entry-level management position. Unfortunately, first level supervisors may have legitimate power but little else. They depend on employees to get the job done and on their own bosses for resources and may be unable to reward their employees without their supervisors' approval. For these reasons, upwardly mobile individuals should gain supervisory experience and move on to other positions.

Besides obtaining line positions above the lowest level, other ways to reduce bureaucratic powerlessness include involvement in liaison roles and in crucial activities that solve high priority organizational problems. In addition, organizations must commit to maintaining diversity in powerful departments.

Good performance of routine tasks is necessary but insufficient to increase power. Organizations seriously interested in raising the profile of previously disenfranchised groups must see that diverse employees are represented on task forces to address high priority organizational problems and unexpected crises. Individuals also can indicate an interest in serving on such groups as a means to boost their power.

Liaison activities are those that straddle organizational boundaries. Through their regular interactions with those in different organizational units, those engaged in such activities may increase their power by building alliances, as discussed previously.

Discerning which departments in an organization are most powerful is easy. Before accepting a position, wise job-seekers should find out how the department they are considering joining is viewed within and outside the organization. This will help avoid disillusionment and turnover that may result if new hires suddenly realize that their department is not currently engaged in activities that provide the organization with a competitive advantage.

EMPOWERMENT

Flattening hierarchies, decentralizing authority, delegating decision-making to the lowest level, supporting women and minorities' bid to obtain line positions in powerful departments, and considering diverse individuals for liaison and extraordinary activities and those that address top priorities are methods that Kanter (1977) suggested to empower disenfranchised groups. Since her initial recommendations, *empowerment* has become more popular. It is an ongoing process to facilitate employees' goal-setting, decision-making, and problem-solving in their areas of authority and responsibility and their sense of self-efficacy and organizational commitment.

Several parts of the definition merit further explanation. First, empowerment is an ongoing process, not a fad. Secondly, management is not "giving" anything to employees; they must assume power. If they wait for managers to provide it, the empowerment paradox is operative. True empowerment involves disenfranchised groups taking the power that should be theirs as valued partners in the enterprise. Members of disempowered groups must be regarded as equals of members of more powerful groups. If one group "shares" its excess power or confers it on the less powerful group, its power is reduced even more. This is the *empowerment paradox*. Empowering others in the sense of giving them power creates dependence. The relatively powerless must *assume* power.

For example, when mid- to upper-class citizens of developed nations wrote checks to assist hurricane victims in less developed countries, such as Jamaica, in September 2004 in response to humanitarian organizations' appeals, they provided needed assistance but did not empower them. More empowering was the global outpouring of tangible help and funds after the December 2004 tsunami in Asia. As the countries hit by the fall 2004 hurricanes recover, the power gap between more and less developed nations will narrow if citizens of the latter participate actively in their governments to decide what they need and make plans to get it. Tsunami-ravaged countries may be in no position to do that for awhile. Active involvement by the populace also assumes sufficient numbers of citizens with requisite knowledge and education to participate and governments that promote the common good. Whether or not the "hands-on" relief provided to nations devastated by the tsunami will reduce the power disparity between rich and poor countries remains to be seen. If less developed nations must continue to rely on developed countries for help, which seems inevitable for the foreseeable future, a power gap will persist.

Intuitively, it makes sense that employees should be involved in solving problems within their areas of responsibility and authority. Though they might bring new perspectives to units outside their usual spheres, their ideas might reflect lack of understanding of the culture and context of such units. If they are allowed to contribute only within their areas of responsibility, however, someone else is still in charge. Higher level executives are setting the parameters, which may detract from true empowerment.

The definition of empowerment proposed here has motivational and relational aspects. Open communication and inspirational goals, which are part of empowerment, can motivate people by increasing their organizational commitment and involvement (Conger & Kanugo, 1988).

Some employees may feel valued if asked for input, but the dwindling few who prefer directive, autocratic styles of leadership may view repeated requests for input as signs of managerial weakness. Autocratic leadership is linked to a masculine stereotype and democratic leadership to a feminine stereotype (Powell & Graves, 2003), but men and women may use either style depending on contextual factors (Yoder & Kahn, 2003). Nonetheless, if forceful, authoritarian leadership is stereotyped as masculine and a participative style is labeled feminine, managerial women face a dilemma. They will be viewed negatively if they forsake their expected gender role (Case, 1993), but if their behavior is consistent with the stereotypical feminine role, those who have mistakenly linked good management with the masculine stereotype will question female leaders' effectiveness. Perhaps democratic leadership will not be associated with the feminine stereotype in the future as much as it has been in the past. Any manager can learn to use this leadership style, and it is considered a highly appropriate behavior during turbulent times.

Open communication must be substantive; important information must flow freely. Mary Parker Follett advocated dialogue (Eylon, 1998) that transcended open communication and proposed conflict resolution that addressed underlying needs and goals of both parties, leaving them to feel that their basic needs had been met (Follett, 1924).

The motivational aspect of empowerment also stresses the importance of *self-efficacy*, the belief that a person will succeed at a task. Self-efficacy repeatedly has been associated with performance excellence (Conger & Kanugo, 1988). Four ways to increase self-efficacy are to design an initial task in a way that those who perform it will succeed, encourage employees to imitate successful role models, provide verbal encouragement, and generate positive emotional experiences (Rudolph & Peluchette, 1993).

Structuring a task to ensure initial employee success increases feelings of mastery and commitment and enhances self confidence if individuals believe they succeeded based on their own effort. For example, academic advisors of nontraditional students earning a college degree at a distance while balancing competing priorities strongly recommended a first course that provides an overview of their discipline and is perceived as relatively easy. In addition, the first assignment is deliberately made straightforward; its main purpose is to ensure initial student success, not to provide a venue to demonstrate intellectual prowess. These two actions enhance self-efficacy among nontraditional learners and increase their retention.

If role models are credible and similar to employees emulating their behavior, such imitation can enhance self-efficacy. Copying role models' behavior may have a downside if employees enact inappropriate behaviors along with those worthy of emulation.

Some view verbal persuasion as a less effective technique for promoting self-efficacy than other methods because it relies neither on employees' past performance nor on others' accomplishments. Further, if verbal coaching ignores a lack of skills needed to perform job tasks or is perceived as insincere, it can undermine employees' self-confidence (Rudolph & Peluchette, 1993).

Negative emotional experiences, such as being berated by a boss, may cause the self-esteem of employees who take such tirades seriously to plummet. Their performance also may be affected (Rudolph & Peluchette, 1993). Positive emotional experiences have the opposite effect; they spur greater passion for work and a drive for excellence. Organizations may sponsor a workshop or send employees to a conference to benefit from the emotional "high" they think will result. This strategy may backfire if speakers are not dynamic or if enthusiasm evaporates when employees return to the workplace and realize that they have neither the time nor the resources to implement the good ideas they gleaned from the conference.

The relational aspect of empowerment reduces dependency that is created when employees lack the power needed to do their jobs most effectively. It drives authority and responsibility for decision-making and problem-solving down to the most knowledgeable employees—those who do the work. Instead of performing tasks according to predetermined methods, employees decide what to do and how to do it to achieve organizational goals. They may also schedule their own work, decide on the best tools, equipment, and processes, and suggest ways to improve the entity's products or services.

Participation is an important part of empowerment, but the latter is more comprehensive. It is based on the premise that all employees should fully use their talents for the organization's good, regardless of their positions.

Employee empowerment is a lofty goal, but approximating it requires certain conditions. Empowerment is most effective when it exists within a compatible organizational culture and structure. An organization's culture consists of its core values that are taken for granted and communicated to employees through symbols and stories that define appropriate and inappropriate actions and influence employees' behaviors powerfully (Moorhead & Griffin, 2004).

Two common organizational structures that represent opposite ends of a continuum are organic and mechanistic (Burns & Stalker, 1961). Features of these structures, as well as a proposed structure consistent with a feminist perspective, appeared in chapter 1. An organic structure and the so-called feminist approach are compatible with a philosophy of empowerment; the rules-minded, external control-oriented mechanistic structure is not.

Besides a compatible culture and structure, organizations interested in increasing empowerment must provide training for employees who are unaccustomed to the new freedom to voice their opinions and have them taken seriously. Organizations must be committed to the changes that empowerment entails and must proceed slowly to avoid unintended negative consequences

(Moorhead & Griffin, 2004). Otherwise, Kizilos (1990, p. 56) suggests that the appropriate conclusion may be that organizations are "attracted to a fantasy version of empowerment and simultaneously repelled by the reality." "How lovely," Kizilos (p. 56) continues,

> to have energetic, dedicated workers . . . who solve problems on their own (but make no mistakes), who aren't afraid to speak their minds (but never ruffle any feathers), who always give their very best to the company (but ask no unpleasant questions about what the company is giving back). How nice it would be, in short, to empower workers without actually giving them any power.

Though empowerment promises to enable disenfranchised groups to overcome domination, it may, ironically, reflect Western male values. It emphasizes individuality, not inclusiveness, and seeks to help people progress from the third, or interpersonal, stage of adult development, to the fourth, or institutional, phase, according to psychologist, Robert Kegan (1995). In the third stage, individual and group identities are intertwined and inseparable. In the fourth phase, the self separates from the group and claims its own identity. Irwin (1999) believes feminists at mid-life favor empowerment because many make the transition from phase three to four at that point. Middle-aged white men, on the other hand, are more likely to be moving from stage four to five, the inter-individual phase. Separating as an individual is no longer their major task; instead, in phase five, they strive to re-connect the self with the larger world and may view empowerment as self-absorption.

Rajan and Krishnan (2002) maintain that personality and gender together affect power and that studies of the impact of only one factor are deficient. Mann (1995, p. 15) says that:

> under-representation of women in top management is due in large part to the fact that they [women] are less likely to acquire power than their male counterparts. Because they have access to less power, women are less likely to engage in, or make use of, organizational politics, preferring instead to rely on formal means to advance up the executive ladder.

If one accepts Mann's ideas, a logical next question is "Why are women less likely to acquire power?" Structural obstacles, which already have been discussed, prevent not only women but also racial and ethnic minorities from attaining power.

Most women want power, according to a recent Simmons College School of Management survey of mid- and top-level executive females, but these business women tend to use it differently than men. Nearly 85% of the 421 managerial women in the Simmons study desire power to make sure their organizations will be socially responsible; 70% want more clout so they can implement positive changes (Lewis, 2005).

Some women spurn overt power, however. Ebay CEO, Meg Whitman, ranked at the top of Fortune's list of 50 most powerful women in 2004, says power "has negative connotations" (Sellers, 2003, p. 86). Jenny Ming, president of Old Navy, reflects similar views when she says "Power is in your face and aggressive. I'm not like that" (Sellers, p. 86).

Gender parity at the top echelons of major U.S. firms—and the power that goes with it—will be possible in the next generation "only if that generation wants it" (Sellers, 2003, p. 96). Eighty percent of business women whom Simmons College surveyed do want it; they proactively seek powerful positions (Lewis, 2005). According to Catalyst (1996), 74% of professional women who have not yet reached top posts aspire to them; 26% are not interested. Sellers does not believe executive women "hang their egos on the next rung of the corporate ladder," however (p. 92). Instead, they prefer positions in which they can make a difference. Ann Fudge, CEO of advertising agency, Young and Rubicam, and former Kraft Foods executive, is a case in point. Between those positions, she collaborated with Harvard Business School to start a tutoring program for black children. As she says, "Women are consciously extending power to broader venues" (Sellers, p. 96).

Women and minorities may gain more power if those who have top jobs remember that all who succeed have received help along the way and return the favor. Consider a woman," urges Gail Evans (2004), author of *She Wins: You Win: The Most Important Rule Every Businesswoman Needs to Know*. She is emphatic that this means allowing them to compete, not giving them special advantages. Her advice also could apply to minorities. White male CEOs can assist in this effort, too. In a tight market for talent, progressive leaders know that fully using the abilities of all employees is imperative.

SUMMARY

This chapter distinguishes between power and influence and explains organizational and personal power sources. Guidelines for becoming more politically savvy, which were written specifically for African American managers, are presented, but some also apply to other groups. Influence strategies, such as bargaining, rationality, assertiveness, upward appeal, coalition-building, friendliness, and ingratiation, and gender variations in their use, are explained. Distinctions among passive, assertive, and aggressive communication are explored as are cultural issues that must be considered before recommending that managers become more assertive. The scripting technique for improving assertive communication is outlined, and situations in which it is worthwhile to try to develop assertive communication skills are discussed.

Basics of the communication process are described, as is the controversy over the extent to which gender differences in communication exist. Examples of powerful spoken, written, and nonverbal communication are provided.

The process by which double deviates become tokens, negative effects of tokenism on women and minorities, and actions organizations can take to enhance the power of tokens are explained. A discussion of empowerment, the empowerment paradox, and reasons why women and minorities may be less likely than white men to acquire power in organizations concludes the chapter.

REFERENCES

Babcock, L. & Laschever, S. 2003. *Women don't ask: Negotiation and the gender divide.* Princeton, N.J.: Princeton University Press.

Bass, B. 1990. *Bass and Stogdill's Handbook of Leadership.* 3rd ed. New York: The Free Press.

BBC News Online: Business. 2001, Aug. 8. Bitchy bosses go to boot camp.

Burns, T. & Stalker, G. 1961. *The management of innovation.* London: Tavistock.

Calnan, A.C.T. & Davidson, M.J. 1998. The impact of gender and the intersection with role and status on the use of tag questions in meetings. *Women in Management Review, 13*(1). 19–36.

Cameron, D. McAlinden, F. & O'Leary, K. 1989. Lakoff in context: the social and linguistic functions of tag questions. In J. Coates & D. Cameron. Eds. *Women in their speech communities.* London: Longman.

Case, S.S. 1993. Wide verbal repertoire speech: Gender, language and managerial influence? *Women's Studies International Forum, 16*(3). 271–90.

Catalyst. 1996. *Women in corporate leadership: Progress and prospects.* New York: Author.

Collins, L.H. 1998. Competition and contact: The dynamics behind resistance to affirmative action in academe. In L.H. Collins, J.C. Chrisler, & K. Quina, Eds. *Career strategies of women in academe.* pp. 45–74. Thousand Oaks: SAGE.

Comas-Diaz, L. 1984. Content themes in group treatment with Puerto Rican women. *Social Work with Groups, 7*(3). 75–84.

Comas-Diaz, L. & Duncan, J.W. 1985. The cultural context: A factor in assertiveness training with mainland Puerto Rican women. *Psychology of Women Quarterly, 9.* 463–76.

Conger, J.A. & Kanugo, R.N. 1988. The empowerment process: Integrating theory and practice. *Academy of Management Review, 13*(3). 91–112.

Duncan, L.E., Peterson, B.E. & Winter, D.G. 1997. Authoritarianism and gender roles: Toward a psychological analysis of hegemonic relationships. *Personality and Social Psychology Bulletin, 23*(1). 41–49.

Eiring, H.L. 1999. Dynamic office politics: Powering up for program success! *Information Management Journal, 33*(1). 17–25.

Evans, G.E. 2004, Oct. 7. Keynote address. Women's Executive Leadership Summit, Madison, WI.

Ely, R.J. 1995. The power of demography: Women's social constructions of gender identity at work. *Academy of Management Journal, 38*(3). 589–634.

Eylon, D. 1998. Understanding empowerment and resolving its paradox: Lessons from Mary Parker Follett. *Journal of Management History, 4*(1). 16+.

Follett, M.P. 1924. *Creative experience.* New York: Longmans, Green.

French, J. & Raven, B. 1959. The bases of social power. 150–67. In D. Cartwright, Ed. *Studies in social power.* Ann Arbor: University of Michigan.

Herrick, J. W. 1999. 'And then she said:' Office stories and what they tell us about gender in the workplace. *Journal of Business and Technical Communication. 13*(3). 274–97.

Hite, L.M. & McDonald, K.S. 1995. Gender issues in management development: Implications and research agenda. *The Journal of Management Development, 11*(4). 5–15.

Horner, M.J. 1970. Femininity and successful achievement: A basic inconsistency. 45–74. In J.M. Bardwick, E. Douvan, M.S. Horner, & D. Gutman. Eds. *Feminine personality and conflict.* Belmont, CA: Brooks/Cole.

Irwin, R. 1999. Gender psych 101: What is empowerment? *Everyman.* (38). 21.

Johnson, J.L.1980. Questions and role responsibility in four professional meetings. *Anthropological Linguistics. 22.* 66–76.

Kanter, R.M. 1977. *Men and women of the corporation.* New York: Basic Books.

Karsten, M.F. 1994. *Management and gender: issues and attitudes.* Westport: Greenwood Publishing Group, Inc.

Kegan, R. 1995. *In over our heads: The mental demands of modern life.* Boston: Harvard University Press.

Kennedy, M. 1989, Jan./Feb. Corporate politics can be dangerous and dirty: Here's how to come out alive and thrive. *Executive Female.* (63). 23–25.

Kipnis, D., Schmidt, S.M. & Wilkinson, I. 1980. Intra-organizational influence tactics: An exploration in getting one's way. *Journal of Applied Psychology, 65:* 440–52.

Kizilos, P. 1990. Crazy about empowerment? *Training, 27*(12). 47–56.

Kotter, J.P. 1986. Why power and influence issues are at the very core of executive work. In S. Srivasta, Ed. *Executive Power.* San Francisco: Jossey-Bass.

Lakoff, R. 1975. *Language and woman's place.* New York: Harper & Row.

Laws, J.L. 1975. The psychology of tokenism. *Sex Roles.1.* 51–67.

Leonard, R. & Locke, D.C. 1993. Communication stereotypes: Is interracial communication possible? *Journal of Black Studies, 23*(3). 332–43.

Lewis, D.E. 2005, April 10. Women like power, too, but wield it differently. *Wisconsin State Journal.* L13.

Livers, A.B. & Caver, K.A. 2003. *Leading in black and white: Working across the racial divide in corporate America.* San Francisco: John Wiley & Sons, Inc.

Lovas, M. 2004, October. Unpublished assertiveness script. Used with permission of author.

Lublin, J.S. 2004, Oct. 5. To win advancement, you need to clean up any bad speech habits. *The Wall Street Journal.* B1.

Mann, S. 1995. Politics and power in organizations: Why women lose out. *Leadership & Organization Development Journal, 16*(2). 9–15.

Marin, G. & Marin, B.V. 1991. *Research with Hispanic populations.* Newbury Park, CA: Sage.

McIntosh, P. 1995. White privilege and male privilege: A personal account of coming to see correspondences through work in Women's Studies. 76–87. In M. L. Anderson & P.H. Collins. Eds. *Race, class, and gender: An anthology.* 2nd ed. Belmont, CA: Wadsworth.

Metcalf, H.C. & Urwick, L. Eds. 1941. *Dynamic administration: The collected papers of Mary Parker Follett.* London: Pitman.

Moorhead, G. & Griffin, R.W. 2004. *Organizational behavior.* 7th ed. Boston: Houghton-Mifflin.

Morgan, P. & Baker, H. 1985, Aug. Building a professional image: Learning assertiveness. *Supervisory Management.* 15–20.

O'Neill. J. 2004. Effects of gender and power on PR managers' upward influence. *Journal of Managerial Issues, 16(1).* 127–145.

Parker. P.S. 2001. African American women executives' leadership communication within dominant culture organizations. *Management Communications Quarterly, 15*(1). 42–83.

Popp, D., Donovan, R.A., Crawford, M., Marsh, K.L. & Peele, M. 2003. Gender, race, and speech style stereotypes. *Sex Roles, 48*(7/8). 317–25.

Powell, G.N. & Graves, L.M. 2003. *Women and men in management.* 3rd ed. Newbury Park, CA: Sage.

Rajan, S. & Krishnan, V.R. 2002. Impact of gender on influence, power, and authoritarianism. *Women in Management Review, 17*(5/6). 197–206.

Reardon, K. 1995. *They don't get it, do they? Communication in the workplace: Closing the gap between women and men.* Boston: Little, Brown.

Rudman, L.A. 1998. Self-promotion as a risk factor for women: The costs and benefits of counter-stereotypical impression management. *Journal of Personality and Social Psychology, 74*(3). 629–46.

Rudolph, H.R. & Peluchette, J.V. 1993. The power gap: Is sharing or accumulating power the answer? *Journal of Applied Business Research, 9*(3). 12–21.

Schriesheim, C.A. & Hinkin, T.R. 1990. Influence tactics used by subordinates: A theoretical and empirical analysis and refinement of the Kipnis, Schmidt, and Wilkinson subscales. *Journal of Applied Psychology, 75*(3). 246–57.

Sellers, P. 2003. Power: Do women really want it? *Fortune, 148*(8). 80, 82, 86, 88, 92, 96, 100.

Tannen, D. 1995. The power of talk: Who gets heard and why. *Harvard Business Review, 73*(5). 138–48.

White, B., Cox, C. & Cooper, C.L. 1992. *Women's career development: A study of high-flyers.* Oxford: Blackwell.

Williams, C.L. 1992. The glass escalator: Hidden advantages for men in the 'female' professions. *Social Problems 39.* 253–67.

Yoder, J.D. 1991. Rethinking tokenism: Looking beyond numbers. *Gender & Society,* 5. 178–92.

Yoder, J.D. 2002. 2001 division 35 presidential address: Context matters: Understanding tokenism processes and their impact on women's work. *Psychology of Women Quarterly, 26.* 1–8.

Yoder, J.D., Aniakudo, P. & Berendsen, L. 1996. Looking beyond gender: The effects of racial differences on tokenism perceptions of women. *Sex Roles, 35.* 389–400.

Yoder, J.D. & Kahn, A.S. 2003. Making gender comparisons more meaningful: A call for more attention to social context. *Psychology of Women Quarterly, 27.* 281–90.

Yoder, J.D. & Sinnett, L.M. 1985. Is it all in the numbers: A case study of tokenism. *Psychology of Women Quarterly, 9.* 413–18.

Yoshioka, M. 2000. Substantive differences in the assertiveness of low-income African American, Hispanic, and Caucasian women. *Journal of Psychology, 134*(3). 243–59.

Chapter Eight

Career Planning:
A Model for a Diverse Workforce

OUTCOMES

After studying this chapter, you should be able to:

1. define career, self-efficacy, Myers-Briggs Type Indicator, Self Directed Search, Strong Campbell Interest Inventory, Occupational Outlook Handbook, informational interview, managerial microenvironment, builders, sustainers, subsisters, searchers.
2. explain what prompted the development of new career models that are more applicable to women and people of color than early career models that implicitly assumed that most managers were men.
3. explain how environmental and personal factors affect each other and the phases of the career planning process.
4. explain the four phases of the career planning process to someone with no knowledge of them.
5. explain how environmental factors, such as socioeconomic status, financial resources, quality of career counseling, and social support interact with gender and race/ethnicity to affect career preparation and initial career choice.
6. compare and contrast the usefulness of the Self Directed Search and Myers-Briggs Type Indicator as self-assessment tools to assist women and minorities in career planning.
7. assess the value of the career advancement advice presented in this chapter to you or to someone whom you know well.
8. explain the career change (last) phase of the career planning model for a diverse workforce.

DEFINITIONS AND EARLY CAREER MODELS

A *career* is a set of work-related activities in which a person is engaged throughout his or her lifetime. An individual may hold several *jobs* and may change *occupations* during his or her career. For example, a benefits manager may eventually be promoted to director of compensation and benefits. Both jobs are part of a specialty area within the human resource management occupation. A career change would occur if the director of compensation and benefits decides to go to law school to become an attorney.

Until recently, most career planning models were developed with white males in mind. They featured a linear, vertical career progression in which those who accepted increased responsibility could expect greater rewards. Careers were assumed to continue without interruption until retirement. Achievement was measured by vertical movement and salary increases. In an expanding economy, it was relatively easy for the white "man in the gray flannel suit" to develop self-knowledge through the use of interest inventories, obtain information about career opportunities, and match interests and skills to available positions.

Super's (1980) model associated ages with stages of career development, which are growth, exploration, establishment, maintenance, and decline.[1] These stages are summarized in a note following this chapter due to the author's belief that linking ages with stages is inappropriate and harmful to women and minorities. Until relatively recently, white women tended to leave and re-enter the workforce to deal with non-work responsibilities more than their male peers. Thus, their age may have placed them in the maintenance stage of Super's model, but they may have fit better in the establishment phase based on their developmental level. Because of prior discrimination that has lessened, the experiences of racial and ethnic minorities also may differ markedly from those assumed in Super's model. Career change has become so common that it seems misguided to think that it occurs primarily in the maintenance stage, or from ages 45–65. In addition, Super's final stage, "decline," has negative connotations. Though Super concedes that people increasingly start new careers in that stage, it has been associated with retirement and disengagement. Many individuals who are older than 65 would find the association of their age with a "decline" phase offensive. Alan Greenspan, Chair of the Federal Reserve System and, as of this writing, in his late 70s, is a notable example of someone who might feel that way.

A NEED FOR A NEW CAREER MODEL FOR A DIVERSE WORKFORCE

Assumptions underlying early career planning models including Super's did not consider the complexities of a diverse workforce. To address this short-coming, Astin (1984) and Larwood and Gutek (1987) developed career planning models that considered the reality that most employed white women face. Not until the 1990s did researchers start to incorporate issues that influence the careers of African Americans, Hispanics, and Native Americans in their models.

Though generalizations will be used to describe assumptions underlying career models tailored to women and ethnic and racial minorities, to avoid stereotyping, readers should be aware of individual differences and exceptions. In the past, women's career paths have been unplanned and nonlinear, but some researchers have noted that women have positioned themselves to benefit from serendipity. Others discount that idea, noting that women, more than men, tend to ascribe their success to external causes, such as luck. Serendipity, like luck, occurs when opportunity and preparation converge.

Historically in the U.S., the careers of white females, but not necessarily those of their black counterparts, have been interrupted more often than those of white males because the women have felt they needed to provide care for children or elders. African American women also have had such duties but may not have been able to take time off due to economic factors.

Because of its negative connotations, "interruption" may not be the appropriate word to describe career breaks needed to fulfill family or other obligations. Work, though important, is not the focus of existence for many women the way the dominant group in the U.S. has expected it to be for white males.

Many researchers and theorists including Gilligan (1982) and Woodd (2000) indicate that relationships and connections are important to women. Gilligan says that women struggle to balance self-actualization with relationship needs throughout their lifetime, and Woodd maintains that "the kaleidoscope of relationships that a woman sustains within her multiple roles contribute to her identity" (In Pringle, McCulloch & Dixon, 2003, p. 294). Interconnection characterizes careers of achievement-oriented black and white women (Richie et al., 1997). Their tendencies to deal with problems directly, persist despite challenges, and retain control over their work environment resemble behaviors of achievement oriented men, but several differences "demonstrate that one need not be a man to succeed in either traditional or nontraditional fields" (Richie et. al., p. 145). Neither black nor white women thought they had to "mute their femininity" to achieve, and they "displayed expressive characteristics (e.g. nurturance, relational orientation, and sensitivity) that contrast with the rugged individualism often depicted in traditionally masculine styles of achievement" (Richie et al., p. 145). There were no Queen Bees in Richie et al.'s study. Women supported other females and showed concern for the good of the community.

Women's tendency to define success as more than upward mobility and a fatter pay check also is typical of ethnic minorities such as Native Americans and Hispanics. Blacks, too, are likely to perceive a need to give back to the black community and help other blacks excel.

The four phases of career planning depicted in Figure 8.1 by the Arabic numerals 1, 2, 3, and 4 are career preparation, entry and progress, reassessment, and career change. Personal and environmental factors, some of which white males may not have had to consider, influence nearly every stage of the process. These factors are shown in Table 8.1, and their impact on each phase will be explained later. Readers may wish to refer to Table 8.1 and Figure 8.1 as they peruse this chapter.

IMPACT OF ENVIRONMENTAL AND PERSONAL FACTORS ON CAREER PREPARATION AND ENTRY

Environmental and personal factors may have an impact on each other, as may items within each classification. For example, the quality of prior education, an environmental factor, could be related to personal factors, such as knowledge and skills. Likewise, stereotypes and socialization, including information from family members, caregivers, friends, teachers, or counselors, may help shape values and beliefs. Within the category of personal factors, perceptions of knowledge, skills, and abilities can affect motivation.

The importance of environmental and personal factors to career planning may differ by gender and racial/ethnic group. Unlike individualistic values of many white males, values of Mexican Americans, a subset of Hispanics, American Indians, and African Americans emphasize collectivism. For example, Native Americans living on tribal lands may choose occupations based on the tribe's needs, not their personal interests (Jutunen et al., 2001). Because of this, asking them to complete interest inventories and other questionnaires designed to increase self-knowledge may be unwise.

American Indians tend to measure success according, not to economic standards, but to their contributions to others. They want to make a difference in their communities or tribes, families, or the lives of the next generation

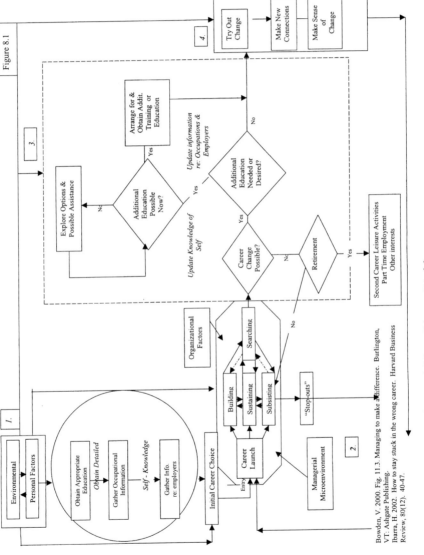

Bowden, V. 2000. Fig. 11.3. Managing to make a difference. Burlington, VT: Ashgate Publishing. Ibarra, H. 2002. How to stay stuck in the wrong career. Harvard Business Review, 80(12). 40-47.

Figure 8.1.   Career Planning Model for a Diverse Workforce

(Jutunen et al., 2001). Though money is deemed necessary, accumulation of wealth is less important than other values, such as happiness.

Black women have a strong sense of obligation to their families and communities (Pearson & Bieschke, 2001; Bell & Nkomo, 2000), and the family influences their career aspirations. Social support from family, especially parents, friends, and teachers, is associated with higher career commitment of black college students (Chung, Baskin & Case, 1999).

Discrimination can result in depression and anxiety among black women (Hackett & Byars, 1996), which has negative career consequences. A positive side effect of unequal treatment is that black women who experience discrimination become more determined to prove that they can succeed in nontraditional careers (Pearson & Bieschke, 2001).

The centrality of family to many Hispanic cultures has pros and cons in terms of career planning. Maintenance of traditional sex roles is stressed, particularly among first and second generation Mexican Americans. Women who step out of traditional sex roles may experience conflict with the Mexican American value of living in harmony. If they handle challenges and maintain harmony at home once, they may experience less external resistance and internal conflict the next time ((Rivera, Anderson, & Middleton, 1999). Those from different backgrounds might question why maintaining harmony at home is viewed as the woman's responsibility, but in that culture, it is.

Self-efficacy, or a belief that a person can perform a task successfully, seems important to the career development of women (Gomez, et al., 2001). Four factors that increase self-efficacy were described in chapter 7. Those particularly important to the self-efficacy of Hispanic women are vicarious learning, performance accomplishment, verbal persuasion, and physiological and affective states (Gomez, et al., 2001). Though Hispanic women's teachers and mothers verbally supported women's traditional roles, their actions often belied their words. The strength they displayed was not lost on their daughters and female students. Hispanic women learned vicariously from these role models that they, too, could succeed in nontraditional roles.

Socioeconomic status and financial resources may influence the occupational opportunities women and minorities consider appropriate and their choice of educational institutions. Though scholarships and financial aid for postsecondary education are available, dissemination of information about how to apply and encouragement to do so may differ based on factors such as socioeconomic status, quality of career counseling, and support from teachers and family members.

Some middle class families whose children are talented enough to be admitted to prestigious, costly universities may encourage them to attend more economical, less prestigious state universities to avoid saddling them with post-graduation debt. Since the next generation's business leaders and politicians often hail from elite institutions, this tendency, if widely followed, could hamper the career paths of prospective executives and limit leadership roles to children of those who are wealthy enough to simply write a large check.

Most elite institutions have large endowments that can reduce out-of-pocket costs for higher education to manageable levels for middle and working class families. For example, when determining financial aid, including scholarships, and grants, Harvard University does not expect a family with annual income of $40,000 or less to contribute anything to a prospective student's education (Ewers, 2004).

For some, the choice is not between elite schools or state universities but between attending a postsecondary institution and joining the workforce immediately after high school graduation. Compared to a decade ago, smaller percentages of students from lower income families attend college due to hefty tuition increases and financial aid that has not kept pace or a desire not to use financial aid loans, which are more readily available than grants (Rivedal, 2004).

Farmer (1997), however, cautions against assuming that the relationship between socioeconomic status and career success is always negative. She found a link between low socioeconomic status and the career aspiration and motivation among first generation immigrant males, who were ambitious to improve their economic standing. Depending on the situation, low socioeconomic status could either enhance or stifle career commitment (Farmer).

Table 8.1.   Personal and Economic Factors that Influence Career Planning

Personal Factors	
Knowledge, skills, abilities (KSAs)	Interests
Self-perception of KSAs	Values and beliefs
Self-concept	
Motivation	Self-efficacy
Race, gender, ethnicity and other unchangeable characteristics	

Environmental Factors	
Quality of prior education	Existence and quality of prior vocational/ career/guidance counseling
Socioeconomic status	
Financial resources	Cultural issues
Socialization	Discrimination
Stereotypes	Role models with whom person identifies
Family, caregivers, friends, teachers, counselors, spouses	Social support
	Care-giving responsibilities

The poor quality of career counseling that women received in high schools in the U.S. before the 1980s may have affected countless careers. A study of intellectually gifted women in the U.S. from 1910 to 1980 indicated that guidance counseling was woefully inadequate (Walker, Reis, & Leonard, 1992), and Reddin (1997) verified that finding in interviews of high-achieving women. Nevertheless, Farmer (1997) believes counselors, who had large workloads and entered the profession when it was not well-funded, should not be blamed. Female students in the 1970s and 1980s who had determination and other sources of support undoubtedly pursued their own career goals despite attempts to direct them toward traditional fields. Careers of others with fewer personal and outside resources may have been sidetracked due to poor advice.

CAREER PREPARATION: ENHANCING SELF-KNOWLEDGE

As has been discussed earlier with respect to Native Americans, interest inventories should not be used in the career preparation phase when dealing with subgroups that make career decisions based on the perceived benefit to or need of the community rather than on individual desires. Many self-assessment tools are available to others who wish to evaluate their strengths, interests, and areas that need improvement before making an initial career choice. Individuals may learn more about themselves indirectly through postsecondary education and by gathering information about occupations and potential employers. Participation in extracurricular and volunteer activities also may aid self-assessment.

A widely-used instrument to enhance self-knowledge about which questions have been raised is Holland's *Self-Directed Search*. Individuals completing it list the occupations they dreamed about as children and answer a self-scored set of questions about activities they like or dislike. This results in a three-letter summary code indicating their personal orientations from among six possibilities, which are artistic (A), conventional (C), enterprising (E), investigative (I), social (S), and realistic (R). The next step is to look up the summary code in a list of related occupations from the *Dictionary of Occupational Titles*. For example, some occupations listed for the code SAE (social, artistic, enterprising) are career counselor, music therapist, food and drug inspector, and foreign language teacher.

Some occupations identified through this process are of more interest than others; the purpose of the *Self-Directed Search* is not to pinpoint occupations that will fit individuals perfectly but to point out several that could be targeted for further exploration. As Farmer points out (1997, p. 4), however, "the number of persons who find the SDS results puzzling or unsatisfying is not insignificant." For example, a woman who is not particularly outdoorsy was puzzled by SDS results that indicated that "forest ranger" was among the jobs for which she would be well-suited.

A more troubling aspect is the tendency of females to score higher on social orientation and males to score higher on the realistic dimension, which results in channeling women toward "helping" professions and men toward "technical" occupations, thereby reinforcing the status quo (Holland, Fritschke, & Powell, 1994). Holland believes that this stereotypical interest pattern occurs because interests represent stable aspects of the personality that crystallize by adolescence (Spokane, 1996); others maintain that these variations reflect differing experiences based on gender.

Adults should be sure that their career vision is their own, not someone else's. Parents or caregivers may have expectations about appropriate careers for their children, which may be based on their own unfulfilled desires. Adults should not be swayed by others' ideas about the careers they should pursue. Rather, they should analyze childhood career fantasies before they accept them as relevant years later. Childhood career dreams may have reflected admiration for a role model rather than knowledge of a job's duties or a desire to use skills that it required. For example, when she entered college, Barb may have wanted to be a high school teacher simply because that was the occupation of her father, whom she admired greatly.

Developed by a mother-daughter team of psychologists, Katharine C. Briggs and Isabel Briggs Myers, the Myers Briggs Type Indicator is a forced-choice questionnaire that asks people how they prefer to act along four scales. The first, which measures introversion/extroversion, shows whether people relate more readily to the inner world of ideas or outer world of things. An intuiting/sensing scale tells whether people get information primarily through their senses or through intuition, and the next scale indicates whether decisions are made based on rational thought or feelings and emotion. The final scale indicates preference for an orderly, systematic way of gathering data and making decisions, which is known as "Judging," or a more spontaneous, relaxed approach, called "Perceiving." Scores on the four scales are combined to obtain a four-letter type for each respondent. Sixteen combinations of dimensions result, each of which has a descriptive profile. Descriptions of preferred management styles are provided for several possible combinations.

Though the Myers-Briggs Type Indicator shows individuals' preferences toward either the world of ideas or things, there are no correct or incorrect types. Adults must be competent in both spheres. About three-fourths of people in the U.S. are extroverted and gather information through their senses, and slightly more (55%) have a preference for "Judging" rather than

"Perceiving." A stereotypical gender difference exists in the thinking/feeling dimension, with 40% of U.S. women and 60% of U.S. men showing a preference for making decisions based on logical, rational analysis (Fox-Hines & Bowersock, 1995).

Most managers in the U.S. and Japan show preferences for sensing (S) and judging (J) on the Myers-Briggs Type Indicator, despite the fact that they occur together in only four of the sixteen possible personality types. Several strengths and weaknesses are associated with the SJ type. SJs are traditionalists who respect hierarchy and can be counted on in a crisis. Highly competitive achievers, such individuals may be criticized for taking themselves too seriously and may blame themselves when things go wrong, though they are not at fault (Fox-Hines & Bowersock, 1995).

The Myers-Briggs Type Indicator has been used extensively in industry to aid staff development and to establish teams that function optimally. Teams composed of individuals with varying "types" according to the Myers-Briggs instrument may have advantages compared to those made up of people of one "type" for the same reasons that diverse work groups may be more creative than those whose members are similar. The Myers-Briggs Type Indicator identifies people whose personality types are complementary and those whose less compatible types make working on improving their relationships important for them. Use of this questionnaire may help determine underlying causes of ongoing interpersonal conflict without blaming anyone. This, in turn, may start a process to resolve the problem.

This instrument also helps managers understand employees' strengths and reasons why they behave in certain ways. Armed with this knowledge, managers can discern how to motivate and reward their employees

Other resources that provide detailed information about how individuals might use the Myers Briggs Type Indicator to identify an appropriate career are readily available. One such source is *Do What You Are—Discover the Perfect Career for You Through the Secrets of Personality Type* (Tieger & Barron-Tieger, 1992).

Inventories besides the Self-Directed Search and the Myers-Briggs Indicator can be used in the self-assessment phase part of career preparation. Most private career consulting firms and college career planning centers administer them, and some are available on-line. They include the Strong-Campbell Interest Inventory and the Kolbe Conative Index (Kolbe, 1997), developed in the 1990s to evaluate what people will or will not do. Personality tests, on the other hand, indicate what people want to do, and intelligence tests show what they are capable of doing.

In the Strong-Campbell Interest Inventory, people compare their interests to those of successful individuals in different fields. They receive a profile comparing themselves to professionals in various occupations after responding to items about their interests. For example, the profile of one individual indicated that she was moderately different from a physical therapist, moderately similar to a pharmacist, and very similar to a mathematician (Karsten, 1994).

CAREER PREPARATION:
GATHERING OCCUPATIONAL INFORMATION

The next step in the preparation phase of career planning is to gather occupational information. The online *Occupational Outlook Handbook* is very useful. It explains common duties and skills necessary to perform various jobs in the U.S. economy, provides salary ranges, and indicates whether demand for jobs in specific occupations is expected to grow faster or slower than average in the next few years. At this writing, the URL for the *Occupational Outlook Handbook* online is http://www.bls.gov/oco/home.htm. If this stable URL changes, searching for "Occupational Outlook Handbook" on google.com or another common search engine should take the reader to that source. Other sources are widely available on-line, in reference sections of public and university libraries, and from career or placement centers in public educational institutions.

An informational interview can supplement research done to educate oneself about possible occupations and may be more valuable than a search of print or online information. It involves communicating with someone employed in an occupation of interest to learn more about its opportunities and challenges and can be conducted in person or via telephone or e-mail if a face-to-face session is impossible. Drawbacks associated with reliance on written communication with no chance to observe nonverbal cues, which would occur in a virtual interview, are significant and have been documented elsewhere. Those making an appointment to conduct an informational interview must remember that the purpose is to gather information, not to request a job. People requesting an interview must prepare questions in advance and respect the interviewee's time. Such a meeting should last a maximum of one hour.

Individuals who lack contacts in a field may experience challenges identifying an interviewee. They may need to contact officers or members of a professional organization in the occupation and ask for names of individuals who might agree to be interviewed. Professional organizations for various occupations are listed in *The Encyclopedia of Organizations,* and similar information is available on the Internet. Public or university librarians are usually helpful if additional guidance is needed. Those who are unaccustomed to interviewing people they do not know will have to take the initiative, be assertive, and make an appointment.

An informational interview may focus on the occupation of interest, but it also may deal with the opportunities at a particular company. Some potential questions follow (Karsten, 1994):

1. How did you get into this occupation?
2. What do you like best about this occupation? Why?
3. If you could change one aspect associated with this occupation, what would it be? Why?
4. What are the educational requirements for this occupation?
5. What types of skills and abilities should an applicant have to succeed in this occupation?
6. Tell me what you did on the job yesterday from the time you began work until you finished.
7. What are the general expectations regarding the amount of time spent working each week?
8. What is the salary range for this occupation?
9. What advice would you give to someone who is considering this occupation?
10. Why did you decide to work for this employer?
11. Describe this employer's approach to career planning assistance.
12. How does this employer help employees manage the work/life interface?
13. Describe this employer's approach to workplace diversity.
14. How would you describe this organization's culture?
15. Would you characterize the leadership in this organization as more autocratic (top-down) or more participative? Please give an example to illustrate your response.

After deciding on an occupation and determining that one has the required education and skills (or making plans to obtain them, realizing that this may be more challenging for certain populations), other questions must be addressed. For example, does the person want to work for a large or a small organization? In the public or private sector? Is geographic location important? Is there a preference for an urban, suburban, or rural lifestyle? What type of an organizational climate is desirable? Which of these preferences are negotiable, and which are not?

Sometimes compromises must be made. For example, large organizations may have formal, inclusive selection and training programs and specified career paths but can be bureaucratic and impersonal. Smaller organizations, though more flexible, may offer less career-planning assistance (Karsten, 1994).

Applicants for government positions typically must take standardized tests to qualify. Such procedures may provide a superficial guarantee of fairness to previously excluded groups, but government jobs have relatively low career ceilings. Some perceive public sector jobs as less prestigious than those in the private sector (Karsten, 1994).

The days of choosing an occupation for life are over. People can expect to change careers from six to ten times. For that reason, though still important, an initial career decision is not as crucial as it once was. This decision is influenced by all the previously described personal and environmental factors, and Cook, Heppner, & O'Brien (2002, p. 292) argue that most women carefully consider the impact on care-giving responsibilities. In their opinion, "the view that career decisions can be made without explicit consideration of home and family commitments is likely to seem naïve and shortsighted to many women today." It also might seem shortsighted to men who share child- or elder-care responsibilities.

Resources to aid in all aspects of the job search process are abundant; "sifting and winnowing" is a bigger problem. Suggestions for writing resumes that can be scanned and cover letters targeted to job specifications and for preparing winning answers to behavior-based selection interview questions are beyond this book's scope. Wise job seekers will get help in these areas.

CAREER ENTRY AND PROGRESS

Making the initial career decision takes the new employee to the threshold of the career entry and progress phase in Figure 8.1, which is an adaptation of Bowden's (1997) career states systems model. This model was developed to explain the careers of scientists but is more widely applicable. It proposes that four categories of factors influence careers and defines personal factors in a way that encompasses many of the factors that appear in Table 8.1. In addition to other environmental factors in Table 8.1, *macroeconomic factors* include the availability of alternative jobs, according to Bowden (2000).

Another relevant *macro-environment factor,* which Bowden did not discuss, is the *macro-societal opportunities structure.* This includes labor market trends in particular industries, relative stability of an industry, and the economic climate when people start their careers (Melamed, 1996, p. 238). White males "who worked in prosperous industries that offer good salaries and good salary progress opportunities were far more successful than men who worked in less prosperous industries." Conversely, women "were less likely to reach higher managerial levels in the more prosperous industries."

The managerial micro-environment is the individual/organization interface as personified by the first line supervisor. Due to a philosophy that emphasizes human resource management's support role and supervisors' direct responsibility to assist employees with career planning, the immediate supervisor plays a critical role in helping subsisters and searchers become sustainers and sustainers become builders. Supervisors' actions affect whether or not employees contribute their best efforts to the organization (Bowden, 2000).

Bowden refers to organizational factors in Figure 8.1 as the *organizational macro-environment*. Included here are career ladders and the other career planning support that human resource managers typically provide. The organizational environment sends messages regarding the worth and status of individuals and groups (Bowden, 2000).

An orientation period is associated with career launch, or entry. From there, newcomers become builders, sustainers, or subsisters, depending on personal, organizational, managerial, and macro-economic factors. Though they should not play a role, gender, race/ethnicity, and class sometimes do because of stereotypical assumptions.

Supervisors should try to prevent "launchers" from becoming "subsisters" by addressing their developmental needs. They should become familiar with substantiated differences in employees' needs based on race/ethnicity and gender and be knowledgeable about how best to fulfill them. If most factors that influence the career states model suddenly turn negative, launchers could move into subsistence mode despite managers' best efforts, but this should be an exception.

Subsisters work to satisfy financial needs. They may be disillusioned, alienated, or de-motivated due to real or perceived barriers to career growth. Bowden (2000) believes that some individuals striving for greater work/life balance may become subsisters temporarily, but they may be more likely to become sustainers. Subsisters who resign or are dismissed are called "drop-outs" in Bowden's original model, but they may be more accurately described as "stop-outs." The latter term recognizes the future potential of those who are temporarily unemployed. They may eventually become "searchers" and find employment in another organization or pursue other interests. Because of the possibility of a downward spiral, moving from "stopping out" to "searching" may be more challenging than it seems.

Sustainers are solid performers who excel in their positions. Though not currently interested in advancement, they may be in the future, in which case they would become "builders." Some who are part of dual career relationships may decide to be sustainers temporarily to allow the other party to focus on his or her career (Bowden, 2000). Managers should continue discussions with sustainers to make sure they receive assistance when they are ready to seek promotion.

Builders want to be promoted and have regular career discussions with supervisors. They also are likely to have mentors. Bowden identifies "would-be" builders as individuals who would be considered sustainers if not for frustrated career ambitions. They may not have received as much encouragement as builders or may lack training in key areas. Some consider their age an obstacle; others are not currently willing or able to change geographical location (Bowden, 2000).

Career advancement strategies and suggestions often are pitched to builders. Table 8.2 summarizes advice about what is needed to succeed in business in the U.S., where whites still hold most of the power. Because some suggestions assume much individualism and assertiveness, they may be difficult for those from cultural backgrounds characterized by collectivism to implement. As diversity at the top increases, this advice may need to be modified significantly. Obtaining a mentor and developing networks are notable by their omission from this list. They are discussed at length in chapter 9.

Though progressive firms provide career planning assistance, it is just that. Employees must assume primary responsibility for their own careers. The old "employment contract" in which the employer "took care of" employees for life in exchange for loyalty has been replaced by a new model that empowers employees and requires them to manage their careers actively. Employers are expected to motivate employees, and the latter must do their best work for an organization while on its payroll, but no long-term commitment exists on either side. If a better opportunity becomes available, it is understood that the employee will take it. If economic conditions necessitate a reduction in force, layoffs will occur. *Employability security*, which depends on the ability to constantly learn the new skills that the workforce demands, has replaced job security.

Table 8.2.   Career Advancement Advice

1. Assume responsibility for career planning.
2. Delight the "customer" repeatedly.
3. Be visible and be recognized.
4. Ask for what you want—all of it!
5. Develop specialized expertise, obtain the right credentials, and continue to learn.
6. Make others comfortable by applying the "platinum rule."
7. Preserve aspects of culture that are central to your identity.
8. Ask for performance feedback and receive it with openness.
9. Learn from mistakes and setbacks, but move on.
10. Be professional at all times.

Sources: (Stevenson, 2000; Wellington & Catalyst, 2001)

The second item relates to performance beyond expectations. A computer support services staff member in an organization epitomizes this approach. He listens intently to the computer needs of the managers who are his internal "customers" and suggests and implements changes that less-computer-savvy managers would not have thought to request. Improved service to the external customer often results from his extra efforts to help managers.

Since Jennings wrote *Routes to the Executive Suite* (1971), academics have touted the advantages of visibility and exposure for those who aspire to top executive positions. Increasing visibility poses added challenges for those whose upbringing or culture has taught them not to draw attention to themselves. For example, Asian Americans, Native Americans, and white women may be socialized not to stand out. Nevertheless, the unknown do not advance; those who aspire to lead organizations must get key decision makers to notice their good work. Women may face pitfalls when doing this that men do not encounter.

Bragging is most likely an intensified, proscribed behavior for women but a relaxed, proscribed behavior for men. As described in chapter 5, women who violate gender stereotypes against intensified, proscribed behaviors will be punished, sometimes severely. Also, one who is exposed is vulnerable to jealousy. If not handled carefully, this can cause support to erode when it is needed (Wellington & Catalyst, 2001). Carole St. Mark, Founder and President of Growth Management advises, "Don't underestimate the need to have good relationships with peers, subordinates, and superiors. You can have too much publicity, turning people off. If you build up resentment, they're anxious to trip you up" (Wellington & Catalyst, 2001, p. 99).

Getting credit for one's own work is important, but sometimes others try to claim it. This may result from differing perceptions, particularly when a team worked on a project. A woman recalled that after she had done 90% of the planning for a successful workshop, a male colleague claimed credit for it. In such a situation, publicly crying "foul" may be unwise. Relating the situation to one's mentor and asking for advice about how to avoid similar situations in the future is preferable (Stevenson, 2000). The mentor can discreetly tell other managers who deserved the credit.

Groups that are unaccustomed to communicating their needs and desires directly must overcome discomfort and do so to become top leaders. Babcock and Laschever (2003) maintain that women are reluctant to ask for money or resources because they do not want to harm their relationship with their boss, appear greedy, or have their request denied. When they ask, their requests, if meager, may not be taken seriously. An antidote may be to view negotiations over financial and other resources as a game and depersonalize rejection.

Refusing to negotiate for a larger salary increase is a mistake even if discomfort seems to outweigh the relatively small amount to be gained. According to Wellington and Catalyst (2001), "Money matters." Over a career, small raises add up and can make a huge difference in retirement income.

All who aspire to the executive suite must leave their comfort zones and ask for "stretch" assignments that may entail risk. Comfort should not be the goal; it can lead to stagnation rather than growth.

Developing expertise in an area of concern to an organization will distinguish a person positively. In addition to acquiring specialized knowledge, obtaining or maintaining the credentials expected in one's profession is important. Learning occurs in many ways, but it must be continuous for those who would lead today's global workplaces.

Advantages accrue to those who are "easy to be with," and a good way to make people comfortable is to focus on *them*. The golden rule, which advocates treating others the way one would like to be treated, should yield to the "platinum rule," which is more appropriate in culturally diverse workplaces. The latter urges people to treat others the way *they* want to be treated. Managers should make a point of getting acquainted with workers so they know how employees wish to be treated and must realize that their preferences may change.

Career mistakes are inevitable and should be viewed as steppingstones to the next success. Women should fight tendencies to attribute failure to internal causes, such as deficiencies in their effort or skills, learn from the situation, and let it go. Though valid, this advice is admittedly difficult to follow.

Stevenson (2000) acknowledges the importance of pride in one's cultural heritage but believes people must assimilate to some extent to succeed in the corporate mainstream in the U.S. Some may view such accommodation as "selling out." Nevertheless, Stevenson (2000, p. 13) contends that "while you are in your business environment, your values, attitudes, and behavior must be in alignment with those of your workplace—as long as that business mindset doesn't conflict with what you believe to be morally correct."

Constructive, honest feedback can help improve performance. Those who request it must receive it in the spirit in which it is given. Negative feedback that differs markedly from most other assessments, however, might not be properly motivated and should be questioned. Recipients of discouraging assessments may wish to get additional opinions or share the information with a mentor and ask for advice.

Professionalism in appearance and demeanor is a must for future CEOs. It is important to look and act the part and to realize that social gatherings outside the office are extensions of work. Wellington and Catalyst (2001) suggest that women eschew excess emotion to avoid reinforcing a stereotype;

perhaps men should be cautioned to spurn overt anger in the workplace for the same reason. Another recommendation is to overlook minor instances of boorishness and ignorance. Incidents of racism, sexism, or harassment must be confronted immediately, however, because they worsen if left unchecked.

Now that issues related to subsisters, sustainers, and builders have been discussed, the focus will shift to the remaining group in Bowden's (1997) model, the "searchers." Builders and sustainers with unmet needs may become searchers and seek opportunities in other organizations. Some may decide to change occupations as well as organizations. This may be a positive move if searchers eventually find a more suitable position elsewhere. Turnover, though costly, makes room for newcomers with fresh ideas. On the other hand, those who do not readily find new positions may spend more time searching than doing their current jobs, which may harm the organization.

Bowden (2000) suggests monitoring the percent of women and minorities who are subsisters, sustainers, and builders and taking action if they seem overrepresented as subsisters and underrepresented as builders. Subjective judgment is needed to determine, initially, the category into which each employee should be placed. Having a small, diverse group categorize employees could reduce potential for bias, but group members must be familiar with the employees and their job duties to make appropriate judgments.

REASSESSMENT AND CAREER CHANGE

Steps in the reassessment phase of the career planning model, which involve contemplating career change and perhaps cultivating new skills, are self-explanatory. The steps in the rectangle on the far right of Figure 8.1 are from Ibarra's model of career change (2002). She warns against relying on the three-step process of revisiting self-knowledge, gathering information about career opportunities, and seeking a match between an individual's skills and interests and available options. Ibarra (p. 42) is adamant that "the conventional wisdom on how to change careers is in fact a prescription for how to stay put" and maintains that successful career change follows "a first-act-then think sequence" to alter the intimate connection between "who we are and what we do" that has been forged over many years.

Trying to identify one's "true self" may be futile because people may have several "selves" depending on the circumstances (Ibarra, 2002). Instead, Ibarra advocates testing intriguing, new careers by freelancing, volunteering, or taking a sabbatical leave without quitting one's current position. Those in mid- to upper socioeconomic classes may be able to do this, but it might not be possible for others.

Rather than asking close friends or colleagues for advice, Ibarra (2002, p. 44) recommends developing new networks because friends and relatives "tend to reinforce—or even desperately try to preserve—the old identities we are trying to shed." Recreating one's life story based on a moment of insight about the career change will help clarify it and garner others' support. Such moments "helped people make sense of the changes that had long been unfolding" (Ibarra, p.47).

Career change may take up to three years; those who attempt short cuts may quickly end up where they started. Ibarra's unconventional approach that emphasizes doing over planning, favoring advice of people in newfound networks over that of long-time colleagues, and making sense of a change that has almost solidified is worth consideration. In her words, "what appears to be a mysterious, road-to-Damascus process is actually a learning-by-doing practice that any of us can adopt" (Ibarra, 2002, p. 47).

A final point about the proposed career planning model is that it must allow for career breaks. They can occur in any of the four career planning phases, and additional research is needed, not to determine the optimal timing of breaks, but to discover how to best integrate them into career plans of those who wish to take them, regardless of their gender or race/ethnicity. This will allow all employees to pursue their own definition of career success within their own time frames.

SUMMARY

This chapter explained the need for career models that recognize a diverse workforce and proposed a model combining the work of Bowden (2000) and Ibarra (2002) and adding elements original to the author. The four phases in the conglomerate model, all of which are influenced by environmental and personal factors described herein, are preparation, entry and progress, reassessment, and career change.

NOTE

1. The growth stage occurs until approximately age 14 when children's main way of learning about career options is through play and imitation of role models. In the exploration phase, which extends to about age 25, people tentatively choose an area of study and part-time work that ultimately result in an initial career decision, according to Super. Establishment (ages 25–45) involves either career advancement or frustration, and maintenance (ages 45–65) entails innovation and updating of one's skills or stagnation. Activities in the final stage, "decline," which occurs after age 65 according to Super, are explained in chapter 8.

REFERENCES

Astin, H. 1984 The meaning of work in women's lives: A sociopsychological model of career choice and work behavior. *Counseling Psychologist, 12*(1). 117–26.

Babcock, L. & Laschever, S. 2003. *Women don't ask: Negotiation and the gender divide.* Princeton, N.J.: Princeton University Press.

Bell, E. & Nkomo, S. 2000. *Our separate ways: Black and white women and the struggle for professional identity.* Cambridge, MA: Harvard Business School Press.

Bowden, V. 1997. The 'career states system model': A new approach to analyzing careers. *British Journal of Guidance and Counseling, 25*(4). 473–90.

Bowden, V. 2000. *Managing to make a difference.* Burlington, VT: Ashgate Publishing.

Chung, Y.B., Baskin, M.L. & Case, A.B. 1999. Career development of black males: Case studies. *Journal of Career Development, 25*(3). 161–71.

Cook, E.P., Heppner, M.J. & O'Brien, K.M. 2002. Career development of women of color and white women: Assumptions, conceptualizations, and interventions from an ecological perspective. *The Career Development Quarterly, 50*(4). 291–306.

Ewers, J. 2004, Aug. 30. Getting into college: What you need to know now about the admissions process. *U.S. News and World Report.* 74.

Farmer, H. 1997. Theoretical overview: The longitudinal study. 3–33. In H.S. Farmer & Associates, Eds. *Diversity and women's career development.* Thousand Oaks, CA: SAGE.

Fox-Hines, R. & Bowersock, R.B. 1995, Jan.-March. ISFJ, ENTP, MBTI: What's it all about? *Business & Economic Review.* 3–6.

Gilligan, C. 1982. *In a different voice.* Cambridge, MA: Harvard University Press.

Gomez, M.J., Fassinger, R.E., Prosser, J., Cooke, K., Mejia, B. & Luna, J. 2001. Voces abriendo caminos (Voices forging paths): A qualitative study of the career development of notable Latinas. *Journal of Counseling Psychology, 48*(3).

Hackett, G. & Byars, A.M.1996. Social cognitive theory and the career development of African American women. *The Career Development Quarterly, 44*(4). 322–40.

Holland, J., Fritzsche, B. & Powell, A. 1994. *Self-Directed Search (SDS): Technical manual.* Odessa: FL. Psychological Assessment Resources, Inc.

Ibarra, H. 2002. How to stay stuck in the wrong career. *Harvard Business Review, 80*(12). 40–47.

Jennings, E. 1971. *Routes to the executive suite.* New York: McGraw Hill.

Jutunen, C.L., Barraclough, D.J., Broneck, C.L., Seibel, G. A., Winrow, S.A. & Morin, P.M. 2001. American Indian perspectives on the career journey. *Journal of Counseling Psychology,48*(3). 274–85.

Karsten, M.F. 1994. *Management and gender: Issues and attitudes.* Westport: Greenwood Publishing Group, Inc.

Kolbe, K. 1997. *The conative connection: Acting on instinct.* Boston: Addison-Wesley.

Larwood, L. & Gutek, B.A. 1987. Working toward a theory of women's career development. In B.A. Gutek and L. Larwood, Eds. *Women's career development.* Thousand Oaks, CA: SAGE.

Melamed, T. 1996. Career success: An assessment of a gender specific model. *Journal of Occupational and Organizational Psychology, 69*(3). 217–42.

Pearson, S.M. & Bieschke, K.J. 2001. Succeeding against the odds: An examination of familial influences on the career development of professional African American women. *Journal of Counseling Psychology, 48*(3). 301–309.

Pringle, J.K. & McCulloch Dixon, K. 2003. Reincarnating life in the careers of women. *Career development international, 8*(6). 291–300.

Reddin, J. 1997. High-achieving women: Career development patterns. 95–126. In H.S. Farmer & Associates, Eds. *Diversity and women's career development.* Thousand Oaks, CA: SAGE.

Richie, B.S., Fassinger, R.E., Geschmay Linn, S., Johnson, J., Robinson, S. & Prosser, J. 1997. Persistence, connection, and passion: A qualitative study of the career development of highly achieving African-American-Black and White women. *Journal of Counseling Psychology, 44*(2). 133–48.

Rivedal, K. 2004, June 22. Finding aid a tough task in UW System. *Wisconsin State Journal.* A1.

Rivera, A.A., Anderson, S.K. & Middleton, V.A.1999. A career development model for Mexican-American women. *Journal of career development, 26*(2). 91–106.

Spokane, A. 1996. Holland's theory. 33–74. In D. Brown, L. Brooks & Associates, Eds. *Career choice and development,* 3rd ed. San Francisco: Jossey Bass.

Stevenson, O. 2000. *Career success is color-blind.* 2nd ed. Indianapolis: JIST Works.

Super, D. 1980. A life-span, life-space approach to career development. In D. Brown & L. Brooks. Eds. *Career choice and development.* 2nd ed. 197–261. San Francisco: Jossey-Bass.

Tieger, P.D. & Barron-Tieger, B. 1992. *Do what you are: Discover the perfect career for you through the secrets of personality type.* New York: Little, Brown, and Co.

Walker, B.A., Reis, S.M. & Leonard, J.S. 1992. A developmental investigation of the lives of gifted women. *Gifted Child Quarterly, 36*(4). 201–206.

Wellington, S. & Catalyst. 2001. *Be your own mentor.* New York: Random House.

Woodd, M. 2000. The move towards a different career pattern: Are women better prepared than men for a modern career? *Career Development International, 5*(2). 99+.

Chapter Nine

Mentoring and Networking Processes

OUTCOMES

After studying this chapter, you should be able to:

1. define mentoring, network, psychosocial support, instrumental behavior, marginalization, virtual mentoring, mentoring circles, negative mentoring, formal and informal networks, internal and external networks, virtual networking, dense or sparse networks, broad or narrow range of contact (in networks).
2. explain how mentoring functions that are provided differ based on the gender and race/ethnicity of the protégé and mentor.
3. explain whether or not you would prefer to be mentored by someone who shares your gender and/or race based on an analysis of the pros and cons of same-sex or race and cross-sex or race mentoring.
4. summarize advantages and disadvantages of informal mentoring to protégés and mentors.
5. explain issues involved in each of the four phases of the mentoring process identified by Kram.
6. explain the advantages to minority group members of networking with other minorities and with the majority group.
7. justify whether or not the advantages of networking to minorities and women outweigh the investment of time.
8. explain the mindsets that cause some women, members of racial/ethnic minority groups, and majority group members to avoid networking.
9. evaluate steps recommended for organizations that wish to improve the effectiveness of networking for women and minorities.

10. explain how you or someone whom you know well could apply the steps in the typical networking process from self-assessment to follow-up.

THE MENTORING PROCESS: AN INTRODUCTION

Career planning, discussed in chapter 8, mentoring, and networking are interrelated. *Mentoring* implies a close relationship in which a less experienced person learns and receives help and advice from a more experienced individual. A *network* is a group of people who provide advice and support. Networks can be invaluable in identifying leads for those who need to relocate or wish to advance or change careers.

In Greek mythology, Mentor was a trusted guide and advisor to Telemachus, the son of King Odysseus. While Odysseus was fighting the Trojan War, Mentor protected Telemachus' interests and introduced him to other influential rulers. The goddess of wisdom and war, Athena, would often disguise herself as Mentor and give advice to Telemachus. If one believes this legend, cross-gender mentoring may date from Greek mythology.

It is a long way from Greek mythology to the United States in the 1970s, but this discussion of mentoring will make that leap. Publications that focused much attention on the mentoring process in the 1970s were *The Seasons of a Man's Life* (Levinson et al.), a *Harvard Business Review* article titled, "Everyone Who Makes it Has a Mentor" (Collins & Scott), both published in 1978 and followed by "Much Ado About Mentoring," which appeared in the *Harvard Business Review* the next year (Roche, 1979). The first two sources emphasized that it was crucial for males who were interested in upper mobility to have a mentor; authors of all three sources focused on white men.

Kram (1985) was the first to analyze mentoring concepts systematically. She identified the main mentoring roles of psychosocial support and instrumental behavior, which later researchers demonstrated were independent dimensions. Psychosocial support enhances one's sense of competence and job effectiveness and consists of friendship, acceptance, counseling, confirmation, and role modeling (Kram). Instrumental behavior aids career advancement and includes coaching, sponsorship, protection, and help gaining visibility, exposure, and challenging assignments (Kram).

Earlier, a mentor was defined as a more experienced advisor who provides support and career advice to a less experienced individual. Crosby, Murrell, and Ely (1999) redefined mentoring as consisting only of psychosocial support. They distinguished it from sponsorship, which is instrumental behavior designed to help junior level managers advance. An emotional bond is not assumed to be part of sponsorship. Because subsequent researchers refer to psychosocial and instrumental functions when discussing mentoring, that convention will be continued here.

TYPES OF MENTORING

Mentoring relationships may be formal or informal, depending on whether an organization establishes them and assigns protégés to mentors or whether they develop spontaneously as managers and employees interact. Organizations should determine the purposes of a formal mentoring program in advance and must have a procedure for matching prospective mentors and protégés to avoid the "blind date" syndrome (Hale, 2000). So far, no "consistently reliable approach" (Hale) to the matching process has been identified, but Clutterbuck (2002) maintains that a systematic process is necessary. He argues that allowing mentees complete freedom to choose a mentor is as harmful as permitting no choice. Typically, prospective mentors and protégés complete biographical questionnaires to facilitate the matching process.

Formal and informal mentoring relationships differ in their duration. Formal programs last six months to one year, whereas informal relationships are more likely to last about three to six years (Allen & Eby, 2004). Informal mentoring is usually more effective than the formal arrangement in terms of the amount of career and socio-emotional support provided to protégés and positive effects on their pay and rate of promotion (Ragins & Cotton, 1999). In formal programs, mentors may be unwilling participants due to lack of time or other reasons, or mentor-protégé incompatibility may be a problem.

Due to the devastating effects on careers and the lives of mentoring partners when the process goes awry, Alleman and Clarke (2000, p. 64) insist that "a failed [mentoring] program is worse than no program at all." Indicators of negative mentoring are discussed later in this chapter, but to avoid failure, organizations should train participants in a formal program about what to expect from the mentoring process. They must devote adequate resources to the program, make sure "key people" are committed to it, and communicate openly with immediate supervisors so they do not feel as if they are being bypassed (Alleman & Clarke).

OBTAINING A MENTOR

Prospective protégés should take steps to increase their odds of attracting mentors instead of waiting to be selected. Waiting to be chosen may have negative connotations to some, reminding them of childhood concerns about being the last person picked for a team in a school sports game. On the other hand, calling attention to one's accomplishments might be difficult for those raised in collectivist cultures that eschew self-promotion.

Exceptionally high quality work, an excellent presentation, or success on a visible project plus positive interpersonal chemistry may cause senior managers to consider mentoring individuals whom they consider "rising stars." Besides doing superb work and becoming visible, prospective protégés should consider the types of people they would like to have as mentors. That may depend, in part, on their goals. If vertical career progression is their main objective, well-connected individuals who have the power to influence promotion decisions might be appropriate. If the goal is to increase career satisfaction and support, would-be protégés should consider someone they like and admire. In either case, prospective mentors should have good listening and interpersonal skills.

Though mentoring is a mutual relationship in which both parties learn from each other, the emphasis tends to be on the junior person learning from a more experienced individual. Procter & Gamble has successfully inverted that concept through its Mentor-Up program, which pairs junior level women with senior male executives. The women gain psychosocial and career benefits of mentoring, and senior male executives get the added benefit of seeing the organization through the eyes of aspiring women (Thomas, 2001). Mentoring those who are experiencing challenges due to factors beyond their control may make high level male executives more aware of and more likely to deal with such issues.

Mentoring is crucial to the career advancement, not only of white males, but also of female and male racial and ethnic minorities and white females. Nearly 75% of black women believe that having a mentor is critical to their career success (Catalyst, 2004.) Hispanic and Asian American women list the lack of a mentor as their top career obstacle (Catalyst, 2003a; 2003b). Studies of mentoring dealt almost exclusively with white males at first and then focused on women, who also were assumed to be white. Only recently has the mentoring literature incorporated experiences of women and men of color. To date, it has focused primarily on African Americans.

Many expect women and racial and ethnic minorities to have more difficulty than white males finding mentors, but most studies show no difference in the presence of mentors based on the protégé's gender (Fagenson, 1988; Ragins & Cotton, 1991, Baugh, Lankau, & Scandura, 1996; McGuire, 1999). Two studies (Thomas, 1990; Mobley, Jaret, Marsh, & Lim, 1994) indicate that women are mentored more than men, but research involving attorneys in a law firm confounded organizational level with gender. More women than

men are associates, rather than partners, and they are more likely to be protégés for that reason (Mobley et al., 1994). Though women perceive more
barriers to finding mentors than men do, they seem able to surmount them.

Evidence about whether or not whites and African Americans are equally
likely to have mentors is mixed. Studies in a financial services firm
(McGuire, 1999) and a public utility (Thomas, 1990) found no difference in
the prevalence of mentoring relationships between blacks and whites, but Viator's study (2001) revealed that African Americans did not have mentors to
the same extent as their white counterparts.

MENTORING FUNCTIONS BY GENDER AND RACE

Even if blacks and whites are mentored at the same rate, their experiences
may differ. Some hypothesize that mentors give more psychosocial support to
female (Burke & McKeen, 1995) and African American protégés than to male
and white mentees and provide more career assistance to latter than to former
groups (McGuire, 1999). Others believe female protégés seek more emotional than instrumental support (Ragins, 1989), but results on this point are
mixed. The function mentors provide most in informal relationships depends
on the race and gender of both the protégé and the mentor, and the mentor's
gender seems to be confounded with rank. Mentors of higher rank are more
likely to provide direct career advancement help, and white men hold more
high-level positions than women (O'Neill, 2002).

However, racially homogeneous male and female mentors give more socio-emotional support to female mentees but provide about the same amount
of instrumental help to mentees, regardless of gender (Allen & Eby, 2004).
Allen & Eby speculate that the mentors, due to their own gender stereotypes,
may feel "compelled" to give female protégés more psychosocial support or
feel more comfortable providing such assistance to women than to men.

Other variables besides the mentor's and the protégé's race and gender influence the mentoring relationship. These include the relationship's degree of
formality, its duration and current phase, the experience of the mentor, and
perceived similarity between mentor and protégé on other factors besides the
most observable (Allen & Eby, 2004).

WHO ARE MENTORS AND PROTÉGÉS?

Because whites remain powerful in organizations and are numerically dominant in the U.S., they are more likely to be mentors than are members of other

ethnic/racial groups. Though males may not be in the majority in the U.S. statistically, they are over-represented in top executive positions and are more likely than women to be mentors.

More women than men are in cross-gender mentoring relationships, according to three studies of private sector firms in the 1990s (Ragins & McFarlin, 1990; Ragins & Cotton, 1991, 1999) and research in governmental organizations (Javidan et al., 1995). Dyads with male mentors and protégés outnumbered those with female mentors and protégés by over two to one (Ragins & Cotton, 1991, 1999). The female mentor/male protégé is typically the least prevalent dyad, primarily because relatively few women occupy high-ranking positions.

Mid-level managerial women, who typically assume greater responsibility than men for personal and family duties, may not wish to become mentors because of the additional time and effort required (Ragins & Cotton, 1993). Higher ranked executive females have no such qualms about mentoring; they make time for it (Ragins & Scandura, 1994).

Concerns about perceived sexual involvement may cause some heterosexuals to approach cross-gender mentoring with caution. Though less discussed, sexual tensions also could be problematic in same-gender mentoring involving gays and lesbians. Mentors who avoid attending after-work social events with their protégés for fear of gossip could harm mentees' career prospects unwittingly, however, because many important contacts are made off the job. Estimates of the percentage of male mentor/female protégé relationships that involved sexual intimacy ranged from 10% to 25% in the early 1980s (Fitt & Newton, 1981; Collins, 1983); Crosby (1999) suggests that the percentage would now be lower given a different social climate.

Even if no sexual relationship exists, speculation can harm careers irreparably. For example, over a generation ago, Mary Cunningham, a Harvard graduate, was accused of having an affair with Bendix President, Bill Agee, when she was the highest ranking vice president of that firm. She vehemently denied the accusations, but the fact that Cunningham felt pressure to step down is an example of the sexual double standard that is just beginning to break down as illustrated by the New Jersey governor's resignation over a homosexual affair in 2004. Still, the governor's case differed markedly from Cunningham's, and despite widespread awareness of the problem of sexual harassment, a male executive having a heterosexual affair might not face such extreme pressure to resign. Though sexual transgressions remain proscribed to some extent, the prohibition may be relaxed for males but intensified for females (Prentice & Carranza, 2002).

The female mentor/male protégé is typically the least prevalent dyad. This reflects the fact that relatively few women have occupied high-ranking positions.

Same-race mentoring has advantages to ethnic and racial minorities. Attachment and trust are more likely to develop within same-race mentoring dyads, and such relationships

> have shorter and easier initiation periods, provide a greater sense of identification, increase levels of intimacy, enhance the balance in work life and social development, aid in grappling with the issues of inclusion and professional identity in early career phases, and help to frame and navigate the bicultural minority experience" (Kogler-Hill & Gant, 2000, p. 53).

Minority mentors who are marginalized may be at a disadvantage in providing other types of assistance, however.

Marginalization may explain why some African Americans prefer white mentors. Groups, such as African Americans, that have been devalued by a society and are highly visible may have marginalized status. That is, they feel isolated and misunderstood and may be ignored or stereotyped by dominant group members (Frable, 1993). Though they may have authority or position power, others may question their competence or repeatedly express surprise when informed of their accomplishments. The effects are to "render the mentor less powerful, less able to protect the protégé, and less able to access the informal networks that provide opportunity for the mentor as well as the protégé." (Murrell & Tangri, 1999, p. 222) Marginalization occurs based not only on race but also gender, disability, age, sexual orientation, and other factors beyond an individual's control.

The most-studied cross-race mentoring dyads involve whites and blacks, and most often, the mentors are male. Seventy percent of the African Americans whom Livers and Caver (2003) surveyed said that the mentor's race did not matter or that they would prefer to have two mentors, one black and one white; the percentages choosing each option were relatively equal. They expected the same-race mentor to "show them the ropes" and provide psychosocial support and the cross-race mentor to aid their career advancement.

Cross-race mentors and protégés typically share an interest that transcends race. For example, Wilson Davis, an African American, likes the same kind of jazz as his white mentor. That interest formed the basis for a solid friendship and Davis said his mentor, "did his best to make sure [people] understood that I knew a lot more than they gave me credit for" (Livers & Caver, 2003, p. 127). About 26% of the African-Americans in the Livers and Caver study said they would prefer a same-race mentor, whom they thought would have more empathy for the challenges they faced and warn them of potential career "land mines." The 4% who preferred a white mentor assumed that such an individual could better aid their upward mobility. Livers and Caver contend this notion is harmful. It insults the relatively few blacks who have gained the power and influence associated with high positions. On the other hand is the argument that "because whites hold most of the power in organizations, one is at a disadvantage in the distribution of rewards and opportunities if one lacks [a] developmental relationship with whites" (Thomas, 1999, p.158).

Some expect that women will serve as mentors for other females; similarly some may anticipate that African Americans and other racial minorities will become mentors for those of their ethnic/racial group. Such expectations can be frustrating, particularly if whites seem to have more latitude in choosing whether or not to be others' mentors. Racial and ethnic minorities may perceive mentoring as another uncompensated task. Some of the reasons African Americans do not wish to become mentors resemble those of individuals of any race: They are too busy, or the protégés are geographically distant. Like the dying breed of Queen Bees, a few African Americans believe that others should succeed on their own without help. Blacks with these views are rare; as explained earlier, most have a strong need to "give back" to the black community (Bell & Nkomo, 2000).

Other reasons why some African Americans prefer not to serve as mentors are more deeply rooted in their culture. They may not want to be seen as favoring others of their racial/ethnic group or may fear that close associations with other blacks will hamper their own chances for advancement (Livers & Caver, 2003).

Thomas (1999) explores conditions that encourage whites to mentor African Americans. He maintains that whites have more incentives to mentor blacks in organizations in which African Americans hold positions of power and authority. This creates a desirable incongruence between the power structure of U.S. society and that within the organization in which "more complex and less stereotypical race relations result, and people are both willing and able to engage more productively in cross-race relationships of all kinds" (Thomas, 1999, p. 161). In such situations, white managers might ask black peers for advice about how to deal with race issues as they mentor black protégés; the black managers serve as "sounding boards" (Thomas, 1999, p. 164). Black/white mentoring partnerships seem most productive and congenial when the mentor and protégé agree either to discuss race issues openly or not to speak of them (Thomas, 1993). The relationship does not proceed as smoothly when one party wants to talk about race and the other feels uncomfortable doing so.

Cross-race mentoring may be more likely when blacks hold positions of authority because black managers may urge white protégés or subordinates to become mentors for other blacks. Further, white managers may regard African American peers as role models of black success. Without such models, white managers may steer black protégés into technical or staff positions and away from management (Thomas, 1999).

One might wonder how having black managers serve as mentors for same race protégés could set the stage for whites to become mentors for black protégés later. Thomas believes same-race mentoring prevents black protégés from becoming isolated and withdrawing from the organization early in their careers. It also helps them create track records which make them more attractive to prospective white mentors (Thomas, 1999).

Thomas (1989) believes subconscious racial taboos reminiscent of the slavery era may hinder the development of cross-race/cross-sex mentoring relationships between blacks and whites, particularly from the viewpoint of black female protégés or black male mentors. They may worry that others will misconstrue their relationship as sexual in nature, calling to mind the white plantation owner's abuse of black women or the harsh treatment black males experienced at the mere suspicion that they looked at a white woman the wrong way. Though potentially difficult to discuss, these concerns must be aired openly so they do not poison working relationships.

Blake-Beard (1999) decries the fact that most studies of women and mentoring have implicitly assumed the perspective of white women. Her study of black and white female protégés shows that neither the amount of mentoring nor the career outcomes that result from the process differ by race. Those in line, rather than staff, positions receive significantly more mentoring, however. Compensation and promotion rates do not differ based on the protégé's race, but white women report significantly greater satisfaction with career progress and pay than their black peers. According to Blake-Beard, this shows that black women "still face a work environment that is psychologically challenging" (p. 34).

Unlike their white counterparts, African American female managers in Bell's & Nkomo's study (2000) had no "father figures" or mentors to provide psychosocial support. They did, however, have sponsors who, without forming an emotional bond, advocated for their upward mobility. These "super-bosses" also made sure that African American women received credit for their work. Their instrumental support was extremely valuable to the careers of black women, though Thomas (2001) indicates that professionals of color who receive only career and not socio-emotional support are more likely to experience career plateaus than their counterparts who receive both kinds of assistance.

Black men are effective mentors to same-race women. They help African American females understand the organization's culture and its informal rules. In addition, when African American males are promoted, they make sure that black women move to higher positions too (Blake, 1999). A *Cata-*

lyst study of nearly 1000 African American managerial women in Fortune 1000 firms shows that 54% of those with mentors are in same-race developmental relationships. Of those, 32% have male and 22% have female mentors (Catalyst, 2004).

Only 16% of the African American women in the *Catalyst* study have white female mentors; 29% have white male mentors (2004). The fact that white women are least likely to have developmental relationships with black women may stem, in part, from difficulties rooted in the history of the women's movement. In the past, black females distrusted their white female peers,

> who, while paying lip-service to revolutionary goals [of the radical feminist movement] were primarily concerned with gaining entrance into the capitalist patriarchal power structure. Although white feminists denounced the white male . . . they made women's liberation synonymous with women obtaining the right to fully participate in the very system they identified as oppressive (hooks, 1981 pp. 188–89).

Black women viewed white females as "cutthroat" and "competitive" (Blake, 1999) and as unlikely to spend time helping women of color advance for fear it would slow their own quest to gain power quickly.

African American women are more likely than their Hispanic or Asian American peers to have mentors and to get advice about race issues from them. Thirty-eight percent of African American females in a *Catalyst* study (2004) had mentors compared to 33% of Hispanic and 27% of Asian American women. Asian American females who either relocated to the U.S. before age 12 or were born in the U.S. were more likely to have mentors than those who immigrated after age 12 and spoke a second language at home. The former were defined as "more acculturated;" the latter as "less acculturated" (Catalyst, 2004).

Several reasons explain why Asian Americans are least likely to have mentors. Whites do not see a need to serve as their mentors because, overall, Asian Americans in the U.S. are successful. The "model minority" stereotype also obscures the need some have for assistance. Features of Asian Americans' collectivist cultures make them less likely to be part of western developmental relationships. They may worry about taking too much of the senior person's time and may not realize that mentors also benefit from the relationship.

Asian cultures tend to have more "power distance" between people and, therefore, are quite formal (Hofstede, 1984). They maintain strict status hierarchies in contrast to the mainstream U.S. culture, which emphasizes equality and has "low power distance." These tendencies challenge white managers trying to get to know Asian Americans well enough to serve effectively as their advocates.

OTHER DIVERSE MENTORING RELATIONSHIPS

So far, mentoring among individuals who differ in race and gender has been discussed. Developmental relationships may involve pairs of individuals who differ based on immutable or other important characteristics, such as socio-economic class or educational background. Challenges in establishing mentoring relationships increase with the number of dissimilar characteristics (Ragins, 2002). For example, perhaps gender is the only salient difference between two middle class white college professors at a university in the southeastern U.S., one of whom is a mentor to the other. Contrast that with the situation of an African American upper class, Muslim male who is assigned to be the mentor of a Hispanic, Protestant managerial woman from a working class background. Initially, one might expect mentoring in the second scenario to be more challenging, but that might not be the case if an overarching similarity in values or interests exists. When few similarities are apparent, more effort must be expended to identify those that are less obvious. Having to exert additional effort could stymie the relationship.

Commonalities between mentors and protégés are important because the former may be likely to choose mentees with whom they identify. These may be individuals who remind them of themselves at a previous time. Viewing the relationship from another angle, protégés may be more interested in developmental relationships with those whom they admire and view as role models.

Choosing protégés who are unlike themselves is risky for mentors. People have different comfort zones with diversity, but stretching that zone by purposely seeking positive interactions with people who are different is possible and potentially rewarding (Ragins, 2002).

Ragins (2002) argues that mentors and protégés who want effective relationships must understand, not deny, the meaning of privilege and of "outsider" status. They also must decide how to deal with difficult issues in a way that promotes dialogue to avoid either self-censorship or a lack of depth resulting from excess concern about offending the other party.

Ragins' (2002) ideas about diversified mentoring, some of which are summarized in the previous paragraphs, provide promising answers to issues other researchers have raised. For example, in response to the question of whether or not "women in positions of power . . . continue creating the experiences of 'isolation and invisibility' for junior women that they experienced themselves" through the mentoring process (Hansman, 1998, p. 58), Ragins probably would answer "no." Her concept of diversified mentoring rejects "an elitist patron system that excludes the socially different . . . and maintains a status quo based on accumulation of advantage and replication of exploitative hierarchical systems" (Carden, 1990, p. 276). Some women's studies scholars feared that mentoring would perpetuate such systems.

Though mentors often are immediate supervisors, an argument against having a supervisor as a mentor is that it will result in an unwise combination of developmental and judgmental roles. Behaving as a friend, counselor, or trusted advisor, as is required to perform the psychosocial function of mentoring, is inconsistent with the judgmental role required to evaluate performance. If protégés are concerned about how their supervisor will assess their performance, they may not engage as readily in open dialogue, which is essential to an effective mentoring relationship.

Mentors should be two or three levels above their protégés in an organization's hierarchy. A larger gap is inadvisable because mentees become too deferential and are reluctant to question mentors' advice. Top executives serving as mentors for entry-level protégés may dismiss or fail to understand their concerns or intervene in a situations inappropriately, thereby undermining the authority of the protégés' supervisors.

PHASES IN MENTORING RELATIONSHIPS

Kram (1985) identified initiation, cultivation, separation, and redefinition as the four phases of the mentoring process. Clutterbuck (2002) referred to the stages as rapport-building, direction-setting, progress-making, and winding down.

The major task in the first phase of mentoring is to establish an emotional connection. Similarity may facilitate this, but probing may be necessary to identify common values, interests, and hobbies, particularly in diversified relationships. Dissimilarity will cause the most difficulty in the first phase; later it may actually become beneficial (Clutterbuck, 2002). Developing trust and mutual empathy is important in the first phase. Without that foundation, it may be difficult for protégés to graciously accept frank assessments that mentors must provide in their role as "critical friends" (Clutterbuck). Mentors should help protégés clarify their career goals relatively early in the process; Clutterbuck includes clarification in the second phase but acknowledges that it is preferable for mentors and protégés to determine whether their goals are compatible in the first phase.

The cultivation stage, when the most psychosocial and career support occurs, is least likely to be plagued by disappointment and uncertainty. As this phase progresses, mentors and protégés start to learn from each other. It ends when mentors realize that they have helped as much as they can or when protégés are ready for more independence (Kram, 1985). The cultivation phase seems to resemble Clutterbuck's "progress making" stage most closely.

Emotional turmoil is not unusual in the separation, or "winding down" phase, and it is critical to manage this transition well in diverse relationships. Protégés may feel a sense of loss, or they may be more than ready to "spread their wings." If mentees become self-sufficient or if members of the dyad have achieved their goals, have no new issues to discuss, or are in danger of becoming too dependent on each other, it may be time to separate.

Redefinition occurs a few years after separation. Typically, the relationship becomes a friendship, but sometimes the parties simply lose contact with each other (Kram, 1985).

PROS AND CONS OF MENTORING TO PROTÉGÉS AND MENTORS

The informal mentoring process has advantages and disadvantages to the parties involved, which are outlined in Table 9.1. Some of the potential disadvantages listed may not exist in formal mentoring arrangements. For example, rumors of favoritism and sexual intimacy are less likely in formal programs (Hale, 2000). Other pros and cons of informal mentoring are self-explanatory.

Table 9.1. Advantages and Disadvantages of Informal Mentoring to the Protégé and Mentor

	To Protégé	To Mentor
Advantages	Learns about organizational politics & informal aspects of organizational life	Provides opportunities for continued learning
		Can train P to be successor, thereby becoming eligible for promotion
	Gains advocate who removes obstacles, makes sure P has a chance to prove him- or herself and gets credit for work, & provides honest feedback	Satisfies internal generative needs to develop others
	Enhances self-esteem	Gains support of P
	May aid career advancement	Gains trusted individual to whom s/he can delegate work
	Becomes aware of and avoids mistakes that M made, thereby saving time	
	Experiences career satisfaction	
	Obtains help setting realistic career goals.	

(continued)

Table 9.1. (*continued*)

	To Protégé	To Mentor

Disadvantages	May be difficult to leave mentor
	Risks career stagnation if
	  associated with non-mobile M
	May experience work overload
	  if M delegates too much to P
	May harm P's career if M fails
	May become isolated if
	  relationship with M is exclusive
	Maybe rumors of or actual
	  sexual involvement
	May depend on M too much
		May be accused of favoritism
		  toward P
		May have judgment questioned if
		  P's performance is lackluster
		May feel threatened by P
		May be rumors of or actual sexual
		  involvement

Adapted from Karsten, 1994, Table 9.2 p. 118. M = Mentor; P = Protégé

OUTCOMES OF MENTORING

If managed effectively, mentoring yields beneficial outcomes for organizations. These include greater productivity, minority advancement, retention, leader development and job satisfaction (Zaslow, 2003; Alleman & Clarke, 2000). The mentor's gender and race, but not the protégé's, strongly influence compensation that the protégé receives. Dreher and Cox (1996) found that MBAs who had white male mentors earned from nearly $17,000 to $22,000 per year more than those who had a mentor from any other group. MBAs whose mentors were women or men of color reaped no income advantage compared to those who had no mentors. Results were the same when Dreher and Chargois replicated this study (1998), and Ragins and Cotton (1999) reported that those with male rather than female mentors had higher pay and more promotions after controlling for other relevant variables.

Higher compensation and a greater number of promotions show a stronger association with instrumental than with psychosocial aspects of mentoring. Both aspects, however, are equally associated with subjective job and career satisfaction (Allen, Eby, Lenz, et al., 2004).

MULTIPLE MENTORS

Because no mentor is "perfect" and protégés learn different things from diverse people, individuals may consider having mentors who have divergent positions at various levels. Some advocate having one mentor who is employed in the same organization as the protégé and another from an outside organization to provide another perspective. Though having multiple mentors simultaneously may seem overwhelming to some protégés, having several mentors during one's career makes sense.

NEGATIVE MENTORING

Negative mentoring is distinct from the positive version described thus far. Negative factors include a mismatch in the personalities, values, or interests of the mentoring dyad, lack of technical or interpersonal expertise, distancing behavior, manipulation, and general dysfunctional behavior (Eby, Butts, et al., 2004). Distancing occurs when mentors neglect their protégés by failing to make appointments or breaking them, exhibiting a lack of interest in protégés, or excluding them from important meetings or developmental experiences. Bullying or behaving in an authoritarian or dictatorial manner, overloading protégés with work, and sabotaging or deceiving them or taking credit for their work are examples of manipulation. General dysfunctional behavior can range from a negative attitude to personal, family, or substance abuse problems. All forms of negative mentoring impede mentors' ability to provide guidance for their protégés (Eby, Butts, et al., 2004).

Not surprisingly, negative mentoring relates to reductions in the career and psychosocial support that mentees report receiving. Distancing seems most harmful to career support, but Eby, Butts, et al. (2004) failed to find a relationship between negative mentoring and protégés' decreased chances of getting a pay raise or promotion.

Those who perceive their mentors as manipulative believe they exhibit lack of expertise, distancing, and other, general dysfunctional behavior. The converse also is true.

The only forms of negative mentoring that seem associated with certain phases in the mentoring process are distancing and lack of expertise. Both occur more often in the separation phase when protégés believe they have learned as much as they can from the mentor and are ready for the next challenge (Eby, Butts, et al., 2004).

If studies on negative mentoring persuade one additional employer to avoid "forcing" senior employees to become mentors, they will have made a valuable contribution. Mentoring has many benefits, but it also has drawbacks, which are readily apparent when people who are unfit to be mentors are thrust into that role.

ALTERNATIVES TO ONE-ON-ONE,
FACE-TO-FACE MENTORING

Some organizations have a shortage of experienced employees to serve as mentors due to downsizing and international assignments. Others firms would like to have more high-ranking women and people of color become mentors, but have relatively few of them. They must not be pressured to assume additional uncompensated duties on top of a full work load. For these reasons, some organizations seek alternatives to traditional formal mentoring programs, namely mentoring circles and virtual mentoring. A *mentoring circle* includes one or two more experienced employees and four to ten less experienced individuals who meet regularly to discuss career related issues and provide support. Having two mentors is recommended to ensure that at least one will attend every meeting. The number of junior employees should not be too large; having a waiting list for participants may be preferable to having too many mentees.

Some mentoring circles become "learning circles" with the mentors as "learning leaders." These egalitarian arrangements should quell any concern about the supposed patriarchal nature of traditional mentoring relationships. Protégés in mentoring circles play an active role and may be given assignments to enhance their learning. Learning leaders perform many of the same roles as traditional mentors; they are allies, advocates, savvy insiders, guides, and catalysts (Kaye & Jacobson, 1995). They facilitate the professional growth of a small group of less experienced employees.

Technological advances have paved the way for virtual mentoring, in which much advice is provided via e-mail, voice mail, or chat rooms on the Internet. An introductory face-to-face meeting is valuable; after that regular communication via technology can be used to continue the relationship. In this way, geographical distance is no longer a barrier to mentoring.

Overman (2004) advocates mentoring between home country and expatriate employees, particularly if the individual in the home country expects an assignment in the nation where the expatriate is working. Such a mentoring relationship may facilitate a smooth cultural transition. In the U.S. and Canada, protégés commonly initiate contact with the mentor and play an active role in the relationship; in Europe and Asia, the mentor is expected to take the lead. Overman, however, indicates that it may be valuable for European and Asian executives to deal with assertive mentees (2004).

Mentor Circle in Canada is an example of a less personalized version of virtual mentoring. New business owners who have questions may post them in a chat room, and an on-line mentor will respond (Knouse & Webb, 2000).

Various professional organizations in the U.S. and elsewhere have similar services for members.

Peer and surrogate mentoring also may be helpful in certain instances. Peer mentors are usually assigned to facilitate an extended orientation for new employees. They make introductions, assist with the newcomer's socialization, help obtain resources, and may aid with relocation arrangements (Knouse & Webb, 2000). Retirees, such as members of the Service Corps of Retired Executives (SCORE), may serve as surrogate mentors. Knouse & Webb (2000, p. 50) suggest that retiring baby boomers might be particularly good at mentoring women and minorities and that "recent retirees may possess a significant portion of the company memory for locating scarce resources, solving problems, dealing with crises, and handling difficult customers."

Though mentors may be in short supply, guidelines to enhance the effectiveness of mentoring relationships are not. A full discussion is beyond the scope of this chapter, but a formal mentoring program must have a well-defined, clearly stated purpose that is tied to the organization's strategic objective, and results must be measured and evaluated against the purpose. Readers may wish to consult Clutterbuck's article (2002), "Building and sustaining the diversity-mentoring relationship," for additional mentoring guidelines. That piece provides suggestions for troubleshooting interpersonal problems in mentoring dyads and a list of behaviors that mentors should avoid.

Both networking and mentoring are developmental relationships, but networking does not usually result in relationships that are as close or as intense as mentoring. Because of that, people may have 250 to 300 others in their network at any given time but may have mentoring relationships with only a few over a lifetime.

Networking is a process of building and maintaining mutual relationships to give and receive job- and career-related help and social support. Dictionaries first listed the term as a verb in the 1960s, though people have engaged in networking far longer. The process gained attention as more women and racial/ethnic minorities began to enter management in the 1970s and realized that their careers seemed stymied for many reasons, not the least of which was exclusion from what was then called the "good old boy network," or interpersonal connections that white males instinctively relied on for career advice and social support.

According to the "six degrees of separation" principle, any given person is only about five or six people removed from anyone else in the world. Bjorseth (1996, p. 10) illustrates this principle by explaining how she was only one level away from knowing two of the three presidential candidates in 1992. In her words, "I went to college with someone who is a partner in

Hillary Clinton's former law firm; and, from my corporate days, I have a friend who had worked with Ross Perot several years before his candidacy [for president]."

Networks can be external or internal to an organization and formal or informal. Ibarra (1993) defines formal networks as prescribed task forces or committees established to accomplish certain tasks and informal networks as discretionary interaction patterns. She further categorizes informal networks as external, which include people outside the organization that employs the focal person, or internal, which include only those employed by the same organization as the focal person. Networks may be established based on demographic characteristics, such as race or gender, or one's position in a hierarchy. According to this definition, internal networks for women or for Hispanic employees at different organizational levels are informal, assuming participation is voluntary, even though the format of their meetings may be highly structured.

WHY IS NETWORKING IMPORTANT?

Business is conducted as the result of relationships, and those who wish to be successful managers must be parties to them. Wellington and Catalyst (2001) describe a newly minted white college graduate who believes so strongly in meritocracy that she turns down offers of introductions to valuable contacts and other career assistance, which she later regrets. Fresh out of school, she is certain that potential employers will immediately recognize her talent and place her appropriately. Proud and fiercely independent, her case is not atypical. More typical is the eventual realization that "waiting to be noticed" is not a viable success strategy.

"It's not what you know, it's whom you know" is an adage that addresses the importance of interpersonal relations in the achievement of career and other goals. If that is not reason enough to believe in the importance of networking, a variation, "It's not what you know, but who knows *you*" might be. This emphasizes the value of visibility and being known to those who can assist now or who might do so later. Networking helps people become known, and internal visibility is associated with increased total compensation and number of promotions for white males and to perceived career success among white females (Forret & Dougherty, 2004). Only 2% of the sample in the study was not white, so results may not generalize to other racial/ethnic groups.

Informal networking within an organization provides "intelligence" about the way the organization works and the political landscape; external, informal networking may supply information about career opportunities and trends affecting a field. Networking speeds the career advancement of women and racial/ethnic minorities (Ibarra, 1995) and helps African American managers who aspire to executive positions avoid premature career plateaus (Thomas & Gabarro, 1999). Livers and Caver (2003) contend that networking helps African-Americans overcome career obstacles and avoid pitfalls.

Fifty percent of Asian American (Catalyst, 2003a), 37% of Hispanic (Catalyst, 2003b), and over 33% of African American executive women (Catalyst, 2004) indicate that a lack of informal networks hinders their career progress (Catalyst, 2003b). An executive Asian American female reflects on the situation as follows: "I always feel like people who get promoted to management are kind of in-the-know somehow. They know the ropes. They know the way the company works. They understand about politics. I'm not exposed to that. . ." (Catalyst, 2003a, p.15). A bi-lingual managerial woman who is Hispanic explains how lack of interpersonal connections made her lose an opportunity for a key international position that specified fluency in Spanish and English: "A white female was hired. I was told that the only reason I didn't get the job was because I didn't have a big network in the company. . . The other person didn't speak Spanish at all, and she's taking classes at Berlitz" (Catalyst, 2003b, p.17). This example illustrates the fact that those who are not actively engaged in networking may be passed over for international assignments (Linehan, 2001), which are increasingly important for those aspiring to top management.

Those who are not networking may be less likely to have mentors. Often, mentoring relationships evolve from networking ties (Friedman, Kane, & Cornfield, 1998). Benefits of having a mentor were explained previously in this chapter.

Another advantage of networking is that it helps women and minorities overcome beliefs that their prospects for career success are limited (Friedman, Kane, & Cornfield, 1998). When people believe they have few opportunities, expectancy theory predicts that they will be less motivated to exert as much effort in the future. Further, they are likely to believe that the situation is unfair.

According to equity theory, when women and minorities perceive that the ratio of inputs to outcomes is unbalanced, they try to restore the balance. They may reduce their inputs by not working as hard or refusing to do anything "extra" for the firm, quit if that is economically feasible, psychologically withdraw, contribute to poor morale, or adjust their perceptions of the dominant group members' contributions to the organization upward. Most of these actions affect the organization negatively.

DIFFERENCES IN INFORMAL NETWORKS AND THEIR
BENEFITS BY GENDER AND RACE

Ibarra (1993) argues that organizational and social systems impose constraints on the networking process for women and minorities. Because of this, African American managers think they receive fewer benefits from networking than their white counterparts. To understand Ibarra's arguments that the work environment limits the ability of women and minorities to cultivate networks and restricts their make-up, one must comprehend concepts related to network composition and size, composition, and characteristics of networking relationships. The first set of concepts includes the demographic similarity of other network members to the focal person in terms of race, gender, and ethnicity, shared organizational affiliations, and the range of contacts in the network, which can be broad or narrow. For example, if members of a network are from areas far beyond the focal person's immediate work group, the network has a broad range. Conversely, if most members belong to the same work group, the network's range is narrow.

Relevant features of relationships include the strength of interpersonal ties and extensiveness of the connections of those in the focal person's network with each other. Interpersonal ties may be relatively weak or strong, and networks may have relatively dense or sparse connections. In *dense networks*, the members interact with each other often; in *sparse networks*, rarely. Because those in sparse networks seldom interact, it is efficient for the focal person to have them all in his or her network. The advice, information, and support they provide do not duplicate, as might occur in a dense network. The latter, however, provide more camaraderie and support to the focal person. For example, if a focal person's network includes members of a human resource department and unit heads throughout an organization, all of whom interact regularly, the focal person has a dense network. If, on the other hand, the focal person's network consists of people who rarely interact due to different occupations in various organizations that are located in diverse geographic areas, the focal person has a sparse network. Ibarra (1993) explains how dense networks reduce managers' power because members "cannot be played off each other in negotiations" as they could be in sparse networks.

Hispanics and African Americans have smaller networks than whites because fewer of them are in corporate management posts in the U.S. Thus, due to organizational constraints, managerial women and minorities may be less able than their white male peers to exercise the assumed universal preference to interact with similar others. To find demographically similar others, racial and ethnic minorities and women must have networks including a wider range of individuals. Knouse & Webb (2001) claim women and minorities do

not benefit as much from wide ranging networks as their white male colleagues because networks of the former tend to be sparse and members have
relatively low status and power.

Women are less likely than men to have contact with an organization's
powerful "dominant coalition;" such interaction is associated with future promotion (Ibarra, 1993). When women and minorities have connections with
those in power, the ties tend to be weak (Knouse & Webb, 2001). Weak ties,
though less persistent than strong bonds, are useful, because they link dissimilar organizational units, expose the focal person to new ideas, and can
have value in terms of career assistance. Weak connections benefit men more
than women, however, because, as relative "outsiders," "women needed
strong network relationships with strategic partners . . . to provide evidence
or cues of their legitimacy as key players" (Ibarra, 1993, p.73). Advantages
of weak ties "may be offset [for women] by the greater potential for bias and
stereotyping in superficial relationships," according to Ibarra.

It is easier to influence people with whom one has strong, close connections; studies measuring strong ties to powerful people show that those
links are "critical for centrality to organization-wide networks" (Ibarra, 1993,
p. 63). For these reasons, women and minorities without strong ties to influential people are at a relative disadvantage. Useful networks include those
with whom the focal person has both strong and weak ties; strong ties take
more effort to maintain, which may be another drawback for those with significant non-work responsibilities.

Though managerial women and men seem to receive the same amount of psychosocial support, the sources from which they obtain it varies. For women managers, it comes from networks of those with lower power and status, which
Rothstein, Burke, and Bristor (2001, p. 15) suggest contribute "to the difficulty
women experience getting promoted to senior management." Managers of both
sexes receive greater amounts of and more diverse types of psychosocial support
from males than from females in their networks (Rothstein, Burke & Bristor,
2001). Females in the networks of the managerial men and women seem to provide more support to the managerial women than to the men, however.

According to Smith-Lovin and McPherson (1993), unmarried career
women without children have similar social networks as men, regardless of
whether the men are married or have children. Ibarra (1993) suggests that
having children changes the composition of women's networks to the detri-
ment of their careers. Organizations and women should be aware of this tendency and should consider steps to compensate for women's loss of career
momentum that might otherwise result.

Friedman, Kane, and Cornfield (1998) show that involvement in voluntary,
intra-organizational African American network groups enhances the "career

optimism" of blacks by increasing their odds of obtaining mentors and by providing social support. Membership in such network groups does not increase the chances of getting more job-related feedback, nor does it reduce perceptions of discrimination. Some African Americans are concerned that participating in a network group with others of the same race/ethnicity could generate backlash from the majority group; this does not seem to be occurring (Friedman, Kane, & Cornfield).

Networking with both minorities and the majority group seems to distinguish successful minority executives from their white peers and from less effective minority managers. Minorities who network with one group exclusively will miss out on advising and support or career assistance. Pittinger (1996) says that minorities who avoid networking with others of the same racial/ethnic group because they think it will harm their careers ironically do themselves a disservice because white peers lack first-hand knowledge of obstacles blacks face and can not give as good advice about how to surmount them as their minority peers can. Thomas and Gabarro (1999) also stress that successful African American executives cultivate multiracial networks early in their career; their stalled counterparts do not. Black managers whose careers hit plateaus seem to have difficulty cultivating multiple relationships, and some lose career momentum when a close relationship with a mentor ends. The lesson for minorities is that "if minority managers want to be valued by their organizations, they need to value diversity in their own professional networks" (Pittenger, 1996, p. 63).

CULTURAL DIFFERENCES AND INFORMAL NETWORKING

Women and minorities in the U.S. face challenges developing and maintaining networks with others in their own nation. Because the workplace is global, special issues in cross-cultural networking also must be considered. For example, French employees generally prefer weak network ties; Japanese like strong connections (Monge & Eisenberg, 1987). Effective network members give and receive assistance, but cultural and gender differences exist in the willingness to ask for help. Those from Israel and the U.S. will ask for help more readily than Hungarian nationals, for example (Cohen, Guttmann, & Lazar, 1998).

Female managers, consultants, and professionals in the U.S., United Kingdom, and Spain who belong to informal, structured networks have different expectations and preferences regarding networks. Women from Spain emphasize social benefits of networking more than their peers in the U.S. or

United Kingdom and are less interested in its career advancement potential. U.S. women, on the other hand, engage in networking to develop skills and enhance career mobility. Interestingly, family obligations are more likely to prevent U.S. women from joining networks than to cause women from Spain or the U.K. to avoid participating. Women from the U.K. are more likely than their counterparts in other nations studied to list the cultivation of self-confidence and networking skills as goals for participation; they also express a stronger desire to join a network outside their organization than the other women (Travers, Stevens, & Pemberton, 1997).

NETWORKING IN PRACTICE: MISCONCEPTIONS

The discussion of networking has been theoretical so far. Practitioners have been touting advantages of networking for years, sometimes regardless of whether or not theories substantiate their claims. When they speak of networking, they may mean informal, unstructured interactions in which everyone engages, internal or external informal, structured associations based on demographic similarity, social identity, or professional affiliation. These distinctions are not as clear as they might seem; most networks based on demographic characteristics allow those who do not share that feature to join, but few do. For example, Wisconsin Women in Higher Educational Leadership (WWHEL) is an informal, external group consisting of individuals who have a common professional affiliation and demographic characteristic. Though it focuses on concerns of women who wish to advance managerial positions in colleges and universities, it does not exclude males.

Before people willingly participate in established networking groups, certain mindsets that may cause them to avoid such activity must be overcome. Foremost among them are that networking takes too much time, involves "using" others, or requires aggressive, pushy behavior that is anathema to those who consider themselves shy. Networking proponents counter the first argument by emphasizing the amount of time effective networking will save by facilitating future exchange of valuable resources and information. Entrepreneurs, especially, can ill-afford to shun networking. If done correctly and not rushed, a long-term side effect will be creation of new business at a far greater rate than "cold calls" would have yielded, but shortcuts must not be used, or the process will seem (and may be) self-serving. As an exchange of information and resources for mutual benefit, networking does not involve "using" people. Though it may eventually lead to an increase in clients or a sale, such developments must be considered byproducts of the successful establishment of a relationship. Otherwise, networking becomes a stealth technique for generating sales and deserves criticism for its dishonesty.

Fisher and Vilas (2000) describe those who are overly aggressive as "networking mongrels." Such individuals engage in networking at inopportune times and are concerned exclusively with their own agenda. An egregious example involved networking at the funeral of a family friend's relative in an attempt to identify job opportunities for an adult child.

Being pushy is unnecessary when networking. Patience and perseverance are more desirable. Though networking requires interaction with others, a low-key approach, which introverted personalities might favor, may be more successful than an aggressive manner. Those who are not particularly gregarious can adopt a networking style that works for them. The process should be approached as an opportunity to exchange information, not with a need to achieve a specific outcome. This may reduce the risk of rejection that is of greater concern to introverts than to extroverts.

Other misconceptions are that networking is a "code word" for selling and that it represents a "quick fix." As an information exchange that is facilitated through personal relationships, networking differs from selling. It "opens doors" and may eventually result in a sale if the product or service a person can provide meets the needs of another, but those who think building relationships wastes time and skip that stage to make a sale deserve any forthcoming negative reactions. Networking is a way of life, not a "thing to do." A long-term process, it involves cultivating and nurturing enduring relationships, which takes time (Fisher & Vilas, 2000).

Blacks and other racial/ethnic minorities may avoid networking because they do not want to maintain a bicultural façade any longer than necessary (Livers & Caver, 2003). It is stressful, and at the end of the work day, some are ready to remove the mask. Though it may help them find a mentor, networking exclusively with those who are demographically similar is not a good strategy for upwardly mobile individuals. Livers and Caver (2003) caution African Americans to understand the costs of not networking, but that advice applies to everyone. Nierenberg (2002) maintains that not networking is a "non-option" and that it is tantamount to "not working."

As the research of Ibarra and others has shown, however, it is not as easy for women and racial/ethnic minorities to develop networks that ultimately aid their upward mobility as it is for white males. They may be less likely to come in contact with "rainmakers," powerful people who make things happen, at work. Women still are more likely than men to have care-giving responsibilities, which reduce their time available for networking and other career enhancing activities.

PRIMER ON NETWORKING MECHANICS AND
SUGGESTIONS FOR INDIVIDUALS

Information about the mechanics of networking is widely available. Given the previously described vanishing link between maintenance of external contacts and number of promotions, compensation, and perceptions of career success (Forret & Dougherty, 2004), devoting much space to techniques focused on those contacts may be unwise. Popular books and Internet material dealing with networking usually refer to cultivation and continuance of external contacts. They typically suggest a five-step process of self-assessment, determination of the purpose and goals for networking, preparation, organization, and follow-up and provide suggestions regarding everything from avoiding a clammy handshake to writing memorable thank you notes.

Self-assessment is important to identify skills and talents that one has to offer and a preferred networking style (Fisher & Vilas, 2000). To be effective, one must decide if the purpose of networking is to gain psychosocial support, career assistance, feedback on ideas, or something else. Before attending a meeting or conference, clarifying specific networking goals is important. Is the aim to meet people who can provide support? To obtain advice? Or to meet individuals who might eventually be able to influence a promotion decision? Techniques will differ depending on the goals, but aims must be realistic. Having a goal of engaging in a meaningful conversation with two people is better than collecting the business cards of 25 through superficial, hurried encounters.

Preparation includes many things, such as not forgetting one's business cards, planning conversation starters and exit lines in advance, consciously thinking about focusing on the other person, and preparing an intriguing, yet clear self-introduction, which Nierenberg (2002) calls a 30-second "infomercial." Instead of a self-introduction that is nothing more than "name, rank, and serial number," those who are networking should prepare a tasteful introduction that leaves people interested. For example, instead of introducing himself as a hospital emergency room respiratory therapist, Joe could say, "I keep people breathing in life-threatening situations." Maureen, a human resource management professor, could say, "I teach future business leaders how to deal with every organization's most valuable resource—its people."

Preparation and organization are related; the former is important to benefit most from networking events. Practitioner-oriented books on networking invariably discuss the importance of developing a manual or electronic system to organize business cards so they will be most useful. Other tips include writing notes on the back of the card to jog one's memory about the person and about any promised follow-up action. Caution is advised when exchanging business cards with individuals of various cultures. Certain ways of accepting a card might be considered disrespectful in some cultures; writing on it might be perceived as defacement. This is true in China; also, a business card is to be received with both hands there as a sign of respect (Karsten, 2004).

Networking often breaks down at the follow-up stage. Many good intentions about remaining in contact fall apart after managers attending conferences return to the office. Sending a "nice meeting you" e-mail message takes only a few moments and is an appropriate way to thank the person for information or advice, suggest alternative future times to meet, and ask if contacting the person occasionally to stay in touch is acceptable. Practitioner oriented resources provide many suggestions for reinforcing a relationship including sending hand-written thank you notes, articles of interest, and appropriate gifts. It is important to understand various cultural norms regarding gift-giving in business. Some cultures expect it; others censure the gift-giver.

Nierenberg (2002) suggests prioritizing follow-up contacts into three tiers —close friends and family, business associates, and acquaintances who only need to be contacted every few months. Periodically, the contact list should be reviewed to determine changes in priority status or to cull names, as appropriate.

There is a point at which those who are persistent in the follow-up stage need to stop lest they be accused of stalking their contacts. To avoid this problem, Darling (2003) recommends limiting follow-up contacts to three if there has been no response.

Perhaps the most important follow-up activity involves keeping one's word. Those who say they are going to provide information or a referral must do so or risk having their credibility questioned. Credibility sets people apart positively because it is increasingly rare.

Livers and Caver (2003) present a list of networking suggestions for African Americans and admit that many are more widely applicable. One such guideline is to "speak so others can hear you." This means assessing and trying to match another's communication style and demeanor. It could involve communicating directly with someone who prefers such a style or injecting appropriate humor when interacting with someone who is light-hearted.

Other suggestions are to begin networking with those who are and are not demographically similar in early career phases and to avoid thinking that every apparent snub is intentional (Livers & Caver, 2003). Thomas and Gabarro (1999) emphasize the significance of the first point; black executives who establish close developmental relationships with others when they begin their careers seem less likely to experience career plateaus than minority managers without such connections. Networking increases the chances of developing close ties associated with a mentoring relationship. Regarding the second point, though ignorance does not excuse hurtful behavior, recipients may decide to distinguish between behavior motivated by maliciousness and that which is not and to tolerate the latter (Livers & Caver, 2003).

IMPROVING NETWORKING EFFECTIVENESS FOR WOMEN AND MINORITIES: RECOMMENDATIONS FOR ORGANIZATIONS

Steps individuals can take to improve their effectiveness in face-to-face networking situations have been discussed. Virtual networking is another option that is easy for employees and helps organizations overcome problems that occur when few "similar others" are at high enough levels to provide the assistance that women and minorities need. Most women and minorities have access to the Internet, if not at home, at work or at the local public library or community college. In addition, the National Science Foundation has provided funds to improve Internet access at colleges and universities that historically have had large populations of Hispanic, Native American, or African American students (Knouse & Webb, 2001).

Some decry the depersonalization of electronic networking, and that concern has merit. The most appropriate role of virtual networking may be to supplement, not supplant, face-to-face interaction. To that end, organizations can develop web pages and links to supplement face-to-face networks for women and minorities. Many networks have web pages; examples include Shell Oil's Black Networking Group based in Houston, TX, Women's Forum, and Women at the Top.

As part of their career and succession planning process, organizations can encourage women and minorities to explore informal networking opportunities on the Internet and simultaneously facilitate development of face-to-face networks of managers at senior levels. Senior levels must become more diverse so there are "similar others" with whom aspiring women and minorities can network. As mentioned previously, this means that organizations must recruit or promote more women and minorities. Nabi (2001) points out a need to enhance the quality of peer support for women at the top, who may be less likely than men to perceive their careers as successful as a result of peer support they receive. Though men get less peer support than women, it comes from more influential individuals. This suggests a power disparity favoring men (Burke & McKeen, 1995).

Organizations also should encourage colleges and universities to develop —or collaborate with them to produce—interactive, team-centered distance education degree programs and training and provide incentives for employees to participate. Knouse and Webb (2001) remind people that the Ivy League business schools can charge high tuition because of the opportunities to network with the nation's future business leaders. Premium tuition is considered an "investment" that will pay off handsomely. In distance education courses or training, students and managers worldwide can work together in teams to solve real or hypothetical problems in areas within electronic courses designed to facilitate interaction. Without discounting the importance of the work done as part of the training or on-line course, the contacts made with diverse others in various organizations at different levels might be even more valuable.

Though the four final recommendations for organizations are intended to improve face-to-face networking, two can be implemented in the on-line environment. A suggestion that is easy to implement on-line is to urge employees at all levels to welcome diverse others into the "inner circles" of existing networks. This can be done in chat rooms through a writing style that conveys acceptance of others. Because no visual cues may exist, determining demographic characteristics of participants in a virtual discussion or chat room may be impossible. For that reason, the on-line environment is conducive to the creation of a "level playing field" for all.

Nabi (2001) recommends making career counseling available as a means to provide extra personal support for women. This seems necessary because of the stronger link for females than males between personal support and reported feelings of career success. Though supplemental activities could occur on-line, initial face-to-face meetings with career counselors would be desirable. Nabi (p. 466) argues that career counseling might be more important to women currently "since women's careers tend to be more complex with regard to the balance between work and non-work life," but that it could benefit all employees as careers become more dynamic.

To the extent that they can influence informal networks, organizations should ensure that face-to-face networking meetings are held at locations that are psychologically comfortable for all. Though a country club may be open to women or minorities now, if it has a well-known history of racism or sexism, another meeting place should be selected.

In the 1970s and 1980s, if several women met informally, white males may have incorrectly concluded that they were "plotting" something. No such assumption was made at gatherings of white males. Livers and Caver (2003) indicate that the same false conclusion is still drawn with respect to African Americans and reminds managers that a few assembled minority employees should not be viewed with suspicion.

SUMMARY

Mentors give psychosocial and career support to less experienced employees, called protégés. Networking and mentoring serve many of the same functions, but relationships in social networks are typically less intense and occur among people at the same or different organizational levels. Chapter 9 distinguishes among formal and informal mentoring and networking, presents suggestions for obtaining a mentor, and discusses pros and cons of having mentoring pairs of the same or different races or sexes. Advantages and disadvantages of informal mentoring relationships to protégés and mentors are summarized, and alternatives to face-to-face mentoring and networking are defined. The second part of the chapter focuses on network composition and strength of interpersonal relationships among members. Myths causing people to avoid networking and the impact of cultural differences on the process also are described. Tips to help individuals improve networking effectiveness and recommendations for organizations that want to facilitate networking conclude the chapter.

NETWORKING INCIDENTS

Exclusion from the Golf Club

Jolene, a black female, accepted a position at the *Dallas Star* as News Editor. She was informed of a comprehensive employee benefits package, which included health insurance, life insurance, paid vacations and holidays, and sick leave, among other things. Later, she found out that her male colleagues also had a membership to the local, private golf and country club, which was worth $500. When she asked her white male boss about it, he told her that women typically had not been offered that benefit because two nights per week were "men's nights" at the golf and country club. His rationale was that giving her that benefit would not make much sense because the club's policy did not allow women two nights of the week anyway. Jolene's boss offered to extend the golf and country club membership to Jolene's husband. You are Jolene. What, if anything, should you do now? Explain.

A Networking Mongrel?

Ms. Lopez, a Hispanic woman, attended a conference on women and leadership and was especially enthusiastic about a presentation on mentoring. During a break following the presentation, Ms. Lopez warmly greeted the speaker, Ms. Greene, an African American woman, and told her how much she had enjoyed the presentation on mentoring. Ms. Lopez also asked Ms. Greene if she would be interested in contributing to a project that Ms. Lopez was working on regarding mentoring. This project would give Ms. Greene, who already had some national name recognition, additional exposure.

As the break drew to a close and participants began to leave to attend the next session, Ms. Greene said to Ms. Lopez, "Here, I'll give you my card," and the conversation ended. Ms. Greene gave Ms. Lopez what appeared to be a business card. As Ms. Lopez walked away, she glanced at the card and noticed that it said, "ABC Livery Service, Atlanta, GA" and had no contact information for Ms. Greene. Ms. Lopez had a sinking feeling, and then she was angry. She would have thought this was simply a mistake had she not recently read many articles about networking, some of which discussed *networking mongrels,* people who engaged in networking at inappropriate times or were more interested in "taking" than "giving." To her dismay, Ms. Lopez realized that Ms. Greene had considered her a "networking mongrel." What, if anything, should Ms. Lopez do?

REFERENCES

Alleman, E. & Clarke, D. L. 2000. Accountability: Measuring mentoring and its bottom line impact. *Review of Business, 21*(1/2). 62–8.

Allen, T.D. & Eby, L.T. 2004. Factors related to mentor reports of mentoring functions provided: Gender and relational characteristics. *Sex Roles, 30*(1/2). 129–38.

Allen, T.D., Eby, L.T., Lentz, E., Lima, L & Poteet, M.L. 2004. Career benefits associated with mentoring for protégés: A meta-analysis. *Journal of Applied Psychology, 89*(1). 127–36.

Baugh, S.G., Lankau, M.J. & Scandura, T.A. 1996. An investigation of the effects of protégé gender on responses to mentoring. *Journal of Vocational Behavior, 49.* 309–23.

Bell, E. & Nkomo, S. 2000. *Our separate ways: Black and white women and the struggle for professional identity.* Cambridge, MA: Harvard Business School Press.

Bjorseth, L. 1996. *Breakthrough networking: Building relationships that last.* Lisle, IL: Duoforce Enterprises, Inc.

Blake, S. 1999. At the crossroads of race and gender: Lessons from the mentoring experiences of professional black women. In F. J. Crosby, A. Murrell, & R. Ely, Eds. *Mentoring dilemmas.* 83–100. Mahwah, NJ: Lawrence Erlbaum Associates, Inc.

Blake-Beard, S.D. 1999. The costs of living as an outsider within: An analysis of the mentoring relationships and career success of black and white women in the corporate sector. *Journal of Career Development, 28*(1). 21–36.

Burke, R.J. & McKeen, C.A. 1995. Work experiences, career development, and career success of managerial and professional women. 81–96. In N.J. Struthers, Ed. Gender in the workplace [special issue]. *Journal of Social Behavior and Personality, 10*(6).

Carden, A.D. 1990. Mentoring and adult career development. *Counseling psychologist, 18*(2). 275–99.

Catalyst. 2003a. *Advancing Asian women in the workplace: Catalyst's new guide for managers.* New York: Author.

Catalyst. 2003b. *Advancing Latinas in the workplace: What managers need to know.* New York: Author.

Catalyst, 2004. *Advancing African American women in the workplace: What managers need to know.* New York: Author.

Clutterbuck, D. 2002. Building and sustaining the diversity-mentoring relationship. 87–113. In B.R. Ragins & D. Clutterbuck, Eds. *Mentoring and diversity: An international perspective.* Boston: Butterworth-Heinemann.

Cohen, B.Z., Guttmann, D & Lazar, A. 1998. The willingness to seek help: A cross-national comparison. *CrossCultural Research, 32.* 342–57.

Collins, E.G.C. & Scott, P. 1978, August-September. Everyone who makes it has a mentor. *Harvard Business Review.* 89–100.

Collins, N.W. 1983. *Professional women and their mentors: A practical guide to mentoring for the woman who wants to get ahead.* Englewood Cliffs, N.J.: Prentice-Hall.

Crosby, F.J. 1999. The developing literature on developmental relationships. 3–20. In F. J. Crosby, A. Murrell & R. Ely, Eds. *Mentoring dilemmas.* Mahwah, NJ: Lawrence Erlbaum Associates, Inc.

Crosby, F.J., Murrell, A. & Ely, R. Eds. 1999. *Mentoring dilemmas.* Mahwah, NJ: Lawrence Erlbaum Associates, Inc

Darling, D. 2003. *The networking survival guide.* New York: McGraw-Hill.

Dreher, G.F. & Chargois, J.A. 1998. Gender, mentoring experiences, and salary attainment among graduates of an historically black university. *Journal of Vocational Behavior, 53.* 401–16.

Dreher, G.F. & Cox, T.H. 1996. Race, gender and opportunity: A study of compensation attainment and the establishment of mentoring relationships. *Journal of Applied Psychology, 81*(3). 297–308.

Eby, L., Butts, M., Lockwood, A. & Simon, S.A. 2004. Protégés' negative mentoring experiences: Construct development and nomological validation. *Personnel Psychology, 57*(2). 411–48.

Fagenson, E.A. 1988. The mentor advantage: Perceived career/job experiences of protégés versus non protégés. *Journal of Organizational Studies, 13*(4). 309–20.

Fisher, D. & Vilas, S. 2000. *Power networking.* 2nd ed. Marietta, GA: Bard Press.

Fitt, L.W. & Newton, D. 1981. March/April. When the mentor is a man and the protégé is a woman. *Harvard Business Review.* 56–60.

Forret, M.L. & Dougherty, T.W. 2004. Networking behaviors and career outcomes: Differences for men and women? *Journal of Organizational Behavior, 25.* 419–37.

Frable, D.A. 1993. Dimensions of marginality: Distinctions among those who are different. *Personality and Social Psychology Bulletin.* 19. 370–80.

Friedman, R., Kane, M. & Cornfield, D. 1998. Social support and career optimism: Examining the effectiveness of network groups among black managers. *Human Relations, 51*(9). 1155–78.

Goto, S. 1999. Asian Americans and developmental relationships. 47–80. In F. J.

Crosby, A. Murrell, & R. Ely, Eds. *Mentoring dilemmas.* Mahwah, NJ: Lawrence Erlbaum Associates, Inc.

Hale, R. 2000. To match or mis-match? The dynamics of mentoring as a route to personal and organizational learning. *Career development international, 5*(4/5).

Hansman, C.A. 1998. Mentoring and women's career development. In L.L. Bierema, Ed. *Women's career development across the lifespan: Insights and strategies for women, organizations, and adult educators.* San Francisco: Jossey-Bass Publishers.

Hofstede, G. 1984. *Culture's consequences, international differences in work-related values.* Beverly Hills, CA: SAGE.

hooks, b. 1981. *Ain't I a Woman: Black Women and Feminism.* Cambridge, MA: South End Press.

Ibarra, H. 1993. Personal networks of women and minorities in management: A conceptual framework. *Academy of Management Review, 18*(1). 56–78.

Ibarra, H. 1995. Race, opportunity, and diversity of social circles in management networks. *Academy of Management Journal, 38*(3). 673–704.

Javidan, M., Bemmels, B., Devine, K.S. & Dasmalchian, A. 1995. Superior and subordinate gender and the acceptance of superiors as role models. *Human Relations, 48.* 1271–84.

Karsten, M.F. 1994. *Management and gender: issues and attitudes.* Westport: Greenwood Publishing Group, Inc.

Karsten, M.F. 2004, April. Students spend spring break in Beijing, Shanghai. *University of Wisconsin-Platteville Department of Business and Accounting Alumni Update.* 1–2.

Kaye, B. & Jacobson, B. 1995. Mentoring: A group guide. *Training & Development, 49*(4).

Kogler-Hill, S.E. & Gant, G. 2000. Mentoring by minorities for minorities: The organizational communications support program. *Review of Business, 21*(1/2). 53–8.

Knouse, S.B. & Webb, S.C. 2000. Unique types of mentoring for diverse groups in the military, *21*(1/2). 48–52.

Knouse, S.B. & Webb, S.C. 2001. Virtual networking for women and minorities. *Career Development International, 6*(4). 226–9.

Kram, K. 1985. *Mentoring at work: Developmental relationships in Glenview: Organizational life.* Glenview, IL: Scott Foresman.

Levinson, D.J., Darrow, C.M., Klein, E.G., Levinson, M.H. & McKee, B. 1978. *Seasons of a man's life.* New York: Knopf.

Linehan, M. 2001. Networking for female managers' career development: Empirical evidence. *The Journal of Management Development, 20* (9/10). 823–29.

Livers, A.B. & Cavers, K.A. 2003. *Leading in black and white: Working across the racial divide in corporate America.* San Francisco: John Wiley & Sons, Inc.

McGuire, G.M. 1999. Do race and gender affect employees' access to and help from mentors? Insights from the study of a large corporation. 105–20. In F. J. Crosby, A. Murrell, & R. Ely, Eds. *Mentoring dilemmas.* Mahwah, NJ: Lawrence Erlbaum Associates, Inc.

Mobley, M., Jaret, C., Marsh, K. & Lim, Y. 1994. Mentoring, job satisfaction, gender, and the legal profession. *Sex Roles, 31.* 79–98.

Monge, P.R. & Eisenberg, E.M. 1987. Emergent communication networks. 304–42. In F.M. Jablin L.L. Putnam, K.H. Roberts, & L.W. Porter. Eds. *Handbook of organizational communication: An interdisciplinary perspective.* Newbury Park, CA: SAGE.

Murrell, A.J. & Schwartz Tangri, S. 1999. Mentoring at the margin. 211–23. In F. J. Crosby, A. Murrell, & R. Ely, Eds. *Mentoring dilemmas.* Mahwah, NJ: Lawrence Erlbaum Associates, Inc.

Nabi, G.R. 2001. The relationship between HRM, social support, and subjective career success among men and women. *International Journal of Manpower, 22*(5). 457–75.

Nierenberg, A.R. 2002. *Nonstop networking.* Sterling, VA: Capital Books, Inc.

O'Neill, R.M. 2002. Gender and race in mentoring relationships: A review of the literature. 1–22. In B.R. Ragins & D. Clutterbuck, Eds. *Mentoring and diversity: An international perspective.* Boston: Butterworth-Heinemann.

Overman, S. 2004. Mentors without borders. *HRMagazine, 49*(3). 83–7.

Pittenger, K. 1996. Networking strategies for minority managers. *Academy of Management Executive, 10*(3). 62–3.

Prentice, D.A. & Carranza, E. 2002. What women and men should be, shouldn't be, are allowed to be and don't have to be: The contents of prescriptive gender stereotypes. *Psychology of Women Quarterly, 26.* 269–81

Ragins, B.R. 1989. Barriers to mentoring: The female manager's dilemma. *Human Relations, 41.* 1–22.

Ragins, B.R. 2002. Understanding diversified mentoring relationships: Definitions, challenges, and strategies. 23–53. In B.R. Ragins & D. Clutterbuck, Eds. *Mentoring and diversity: An international perspective.* Boston: Butterworth-Heinemann.

Ragins, B.R. & Cotton, J.L. 1991. Easier said than done: Gender differences in perceived barriers to gaining a mentor. *Academy of Management Journal, 34.* 939–51.

Ragins, B.R. & Cotton, J.L. 1993. Gender and willingness to mentor in organizations. *Journal of Management, 19.* 97–111.

Ragins, B.R. & Cotton, J.L. 1999. Mentor functions and outcomes: A comparison of men and women in formal and informal relationships, *Journal of Applied Psychology, 84.* 529–50.

Ragins, B.R. & McFarlin, D.B. 1990. Perceptions of mentor roles in cross-gender mentoring relationships. *Journal of Vocational Behavior, 37.* 321–39.

Ragins, B.R. & Scandura, T.A. 1994. Gender differences in expected outcomes of mentoring relationships. *Academy of Management Journal, 37.* 957–71.

Roche, G.R. 1979, Jan.-Feb. Much ado about mentoring. *Harvard Business Review.* 17–28.

Rothstein, M.G., Burke, R.J. & Bristor, J.M. 2001. Structural characteristics and support benefits in the interpersonal networks of women and men in management. *International Journal of Organizational Analysis, 9*(1). 4–26.

Smith-Lovin, L. & McPherson, M.J. 1993. You are who you know: A network approach to gender. In P. England. Ed. *Theory on gender/feminism on theory.* New York: Aldine.

Thomas, D.A. 1989. Mentoring and irrationality: The role of racial taboos. *Human Resource Management, 28.* 279–90.

Thomas, D.A. 1990. The impact of race on managers' experiences of developmental relationships. *Journal of Organizational Behavior, 11.* 479–92.

Thomas, D.A. 1993. Racial dynamics in cross-race developmental relationships. *Administrative Science Quarterly, 38.* 169–94.

Thomas, D.A. 1999. Beyond the simple demography-power hypothesis: How blacks in power influence white-mentor-black-protégé developmental relationships. 157–70. In F. J. Crosby, A. Murrell & R. Ely, Eds. *Mentoring dilemmas.* Mahwah, NJ: Lawrence Erlbaum Associates, Inc.

Thomas, D.A. 2001. The truth about mentoring minorities: Race matters. *Harvard Business Review 79*(4). 99–107.

Thomas, D. & J. Gabarro. 1999. *Breaking through: the making of minority executives in corporate America.* Boston: Harvard Business School Press.

Travers, C., Stevens, S. & Pemberton, C. 1997. Women's networking across boundaries: Recognizing different cultural agendas. *Women in Management Review, 12*(2). 61.

Viator, R. 2001. An examination of African-Americans' access to public accounting mentors: Perceived barriers and intentions to leave. Manuscript submitted for publication.

Wellington, S. & Catalyst. 2001. *Be your own mentor.* New York: Random House.

Zaslow, J. 2003, June 5. Moving on: Don't trust anyone under 30: Boomers struggle with their new roles as mentors. *Wall Street Journal.* Eastern Edition. D1.

Chapter Ten

Work/Life Integration

OUTCOMES

After studying this chapter, you should be able to:

1. Define dual earner couple, dual career couple, work/life balance, work/life integration, long-term care insurance, dependent care reimbursement account, resource and referral program for child- or eldercare, telecommuting, job sharing, compressed work week, employee assistance program, intermittent leave (under the Family and Medical Leave Act), elder care, California's Family Temporary Disability program.
2. explain reasons for increased interest in work/life initiatives since 1990.
3. explain the factors to which black women's relatively high workforce participation rate, historically, can be attributed.
4. summarize the effects of race on work/life issues that black corporate managers and their families face.
5. compare work/life issues faced by southeast Asian women or women from Hong Kong with those encountered by Hispanic women in the U.S.
6. evaluate the pros and cons of using various alternative work arrangements/flexible schedules to facilitate work/life integration in an organization with which you are familiar.
7. develop and justify a proposal for work/life initiatives in an organization with which you are familiar, considering economic factors and the need to recruit and retain a diverse workforce.
8. explain provisions of the federal Family and Medical Leave Act (FMLA), which employees are entitled to benefits provided by the

FMLA, and which employers must comply with it to a new U.S. citizen who has no knowledge of the law.

9. explain how contextual factors, such as job design characteristics and support from supervisors and top managers, affect outcomes of work/life initiatives.
10. explain suggestions for dealing with issues that arise in the implementation of work/life initiatives.
11. explain research-supported positive and negative consequences of work/life initiatives to employers.

WORK AND PERSONAL LIFE: SYNOPSIS OF ORGANIZATIONAL CONCERN

Work and personal life in the U.S. have not been as separate as some would like to think. During national emergencies, the government and/or employers have run temporary programs to assist with child care. This happened during the Civil War, World War I, and World War II so women, who were generally regarded as having primary responsibility for raising children at that time, could work outside the home to support the wars. Feminist researchers Glenn (1996) and Collins (1994) maintain that women of color have been less likely than white women to view paid employment and family obligations as separate spheres. Rather, employment provided the means for them to ensure the survival and growth of their children.

The current concern about integrating work and life seems a product of white middle class culture. It was preceded by angst about balancing work and family, which emerged after women's influx to the workforce as a result of equal rights laws passed in the 1960s and the women's movement. Because females were assumed to be caregivers and a majority had children, a need for additional child care arose. Some began to question the mindset that women, by nature, were more suited than men to caring for children and wondered why men did not share child rearing tasks more equally. Socialization and reinforced stereotypes provide part of the answer, but the issue continues to be discussed.

In the meantime, organizations began to respond to the need for more child care by running their own centers. In 1971, Stride Rite Corporation was the first U.S. firm to open a child care center. Despite its efforts and that of a few "scattered" employers, Friedman (1990) claims that "serious activity" related to child care assistance did not occur until the 1980s. In her view, the Reagan administration played a role in employers' heightened interest in supporting child care in the 1980s:

> The former president made it both necessary and fashionable for the business community to play a larger role in the child care delivery system. By cutting back on social services, the nonprofit community was forced to look to other funding sources. At the same time, public-private partnerships encouraged by a Republican White House sanctioned business investments in social programs. Between 1983 and 1985, the White House sponsored 33 breakfasts for corporate CEOs to educate them about child care. During that period, the number of employers providing child care support tripled (Friedman, 1986, p.172).

The number of organizations funding child care services grew from 600 in 1982 to 5400 in 1990 (Friedman, 1990), and 1200 of the 5400 provided on- or near-site centers. In the 1980s, less costly variations of centers, including care for mildly ill children, resource and referral services, and child care consortia developed. Consortia consisted of firms that pooled resources to set up centers where employees of any of the cooperating companies could send their children (Arthur & Cook, 2004). By the end of the decade, some employers had added counseling and elder care to their work/life initiatives (Arthur & Cook).

REASONS FOR THE GROWTH OF WORK LIFE INITIATIVES

Downsizing and consequent corporate restructuring, the predicted labor shortage among skilled and technical employees at the end of the 1990s, and a workforce that increasingly preferred extra time to more money contributed not only to the growth of flexible scheduling but also to an increased emphasis on work/life balance or integration.

Layoffs and downsizing in the late 1980s led to an emphasis on "doing more with less." Employees who kept their jobs often were expected to accomplish as much, collectively, as they did when their units had more staff. The way work was done had to change, and employee participation and total quality management were stressed as ways to remain competitive in a workplace that was starting to become global. Change spurred the growth of work/ life initiatives in the late 1980s according to the Ford Foundation Study, *Relinking Life and Work: Toward a Better Future* (Rapoport & Bailyn, 1996).

In the 1990s, predictions about a shortfall of skilled workers materialized and forced employers to attend to retention as well as recruitment. Sandholtz, Derr, et al. (2002) indicated that the top career motivator of Fortune 500 firm employees in the 1990s was balance between work and life. Nearly twice as many selected balance as their main career priority as chose security, a distant second. Addressing balance became a business necessity for employers who wanted to retain a qualified workforce.

As "rust bowl" manufacturing jobs yielded to service sector positions, more households found two incomes essential to maintain their standard of living. According to Schmidt and Duenas (2002, p. 294), "working family income has never really recovered from recessionary problems of the 1980s and 1990s." For years, many African American and other minority households relied on two pay checks, but that trend was publicized only when it began to affect a large number of white households.

Attitudes of employees have made work/life programs more important. Members of Generation X, born between 1965 and 1980, are more likely to believe they are entitled to such programs than were their Baby Boomer predecessors, born between 1946 and 1964.

Since the 1970s, demographic trends have led to greater interest in work/life initiatives. Women's labor force participation rate in the U.S. continued to rise. The work force was 47% female in 2002 and is projected to remain at that level through 2012 (Labor Force, 2003–04). The percent of households composed of married couples with their own children dropped from 40% in 1970 to 23% in 2003 (Fields, 2003). In the same time frame, the proportion of families headed by single mothers jumped from 12% to 26%, and the percentage headed by single fathers rose from 1% to 5% (Fields). The percent of single parent families moderated in the 1990s, increasing to 13% from 1990 to 1997 after having grown from 6% to 12% of all families from 1970 to 1990 (U.S. Census Bureau, 2001).

The percentage of mothers of children under age one in the workforce declined from a high of nearly 58% in 1998. This drop has attracted media attention, but more than half of all mothers with children younger than 12 months old remain in the labor force. In 2003, the figure was 53.7% (U.S. Department of Labor, Bureau of Labor Statistics, 2004a). Nearly 78% of mothers of school aged children (6–17) and of unmarried mothers of children from birth through age 17 were in the workforce in 2003. Almost 69% of married women with children under age 18 whose spouses were present were in the labor force in that year (U.S. Department of Labor, Bureau of Labor Statistics, 2004b).

Changing work force demographics and the skilled labor shortage ushered in an era of corporate concern for diversity. In turn, responsiveness to the needs of a diverse work force led to greater emphasis on workplace practices to help employees deal with work and life issues effectively.

Many U.S. employees re-examined their priorities in the aftermath of the 2001 World Trade Center bombings in New York. Some career-absorbed individuals looked for employer support to make changes to allow them to spend more time with family and friends. Again, this was largely a mid- to upper class phenomenon; those at lower income rungs did not have the luxury of being able to refocus.

GENDER AND RESPONSIBILITY FOR DOMESTIC AND CHILD CARE DUTIES

Among middle to upper middle class whites, women have historically assumed most responsibility for domestic duties and child care, as Hochschild and Machung (1989) point out in *The Second Shift.* Its thesis is that women are overburdened because after working at a "paid job" for eight hours, they must work an unpaid "second shift" at home. Gradually, men, of necessity, are assuming more responsibility for household duties. Those who have children want to be more involved parents than their fathers or grandfathers were. Nevertheless, a 1995 study shows that employed women with more than one child work a total of 90 paid and unpaid hours compared to their male peers' total of 60 hours (Clay, 1995). Married men do about 45% of household chores and spend two-thirds as much time with their children as do their spouses (Sandholtz, Derr, et al., 1999). A U.S. Department of Labor time use survey indicates that employed women work on household tasks an additional hour each day compared to employed men. Among full-time employees, men spend slightly more than 30 minutes per week in paid employment than women (Working women, 2004).

Gender parity in child care and household tasks seems elusive at higher organizational levels. A study of high-achieving parents based on annual earnings shows marked differences. Sixty-one percent of the women but only three percent of the men organize activities for their children; fifty percent of the women but only nine percent of the men prepare meals, and thirty-seven percent of the women but just nine percent of the men help their children with homework (Hewlett, 2002).

Is an increased percent of women in the workforce or executive ranks associated with greater organizational response to work/life concerns? Some studies support this assumption (Goodstein, 1994; Konrad & Mangel, 2000; Dreher, 2003), but others contradict it. Inconsistencies may mean that other factors besides the percentage of women in organizations influence their responsiveness to work/life issues (Milliken, Martins, & Morgan, 1998). A national survey of human resource managers at large firms in the service industry that are responsive to work/life issues reveals that "the growth in the percentage of women in an organization's workforce tends to be negatively related to responsiveness"(Milliken, Martins, and Morgan, p. 589). This seems counterintuitive, but Milliken, Martins, and Morgan suggest that women entering the organization may have little influence on corporate policies. Their studies show no link between an increased percent of women or employees with care-giving responsibilities in the top ranks and organizational responsiveness. Perhaps those who became top managers in the 1990s internalized the notion that career supersedes family or personal life and, therefore, are not strong advocates of work/life initiatives (Milliken, Martins & Morgan).

Dreher's (2003) study of the connection between work/life initiatives and the proportion of women in management contradicts the findings of Milliken, Martins, and Morgan (1998). In his research of 72 large Fortune 500 firms representing a cross-section of industries, Dreher (p. 553) found that "after controlling for industry and annual sales, the percentage of female managers in the 1980s and early 1990s was positively associated with the presence of work life HRPs [human resource practices] in 1994." He attributes this to resource dependency theory, to be explained in the next paragraph, and to Kanter's ideas (1977) that as sex ratios equalize, powerful executive women will form coalitions to introduce practices that address work/life issues. The underlying assumption that work/life concerns are women's issues is as disturbing as it is inaccurate.

Konrad's and Mangel's (2000) national survey of large public and private sector employers also shows a link between the percent of women employed and a firm's work/life initiatives. This is consistent with findings of Goodstein (1994), who believes companies employing high proportions of women become dependent on their labor. Therefore, such firms provide work/life initiatives to accommodate them. Though women are responsible for over 50% of domestic and care-giving duties, the idea that work/life initiatives should be implemented to help women perform *their* dual roles reinforces the status quo.

Similar logic unleashed criticism against Felice Schwartz (1989), former president of *Catalyst*, for ideas expressed in a *Harvard Business Review* article. Schwartz suggested that organizations acknowledge that it is more expensive to employ women than men at top levels and advocated "cutting waste" by categorizing business women into one of two categories early in their careers. Women, but not men, were to be classified as "career primary" or "career secondary." Barriers were to be removed to catapult "career primary" women into top posts. "Career secondary" women were to have interesting work but would voluntarily opt off the "fast track" to have time for non-work pursuits, most notably family duties. Schwartz never used the term "mommy track," but it was applied to "career secondary" women.

Critics contended that 1) the suggestion that women, but not men, be divided into two tiers discriminated against females; 2) it was unrealistic to expect women to know at the outset whether they wanted to be "career primary" or "career secondary;" and 3) no mechanism existed for switching "tracks." Further, they did not believe it was necessary for women to trade career involvement for family time. The idea of a mandatory tradeoff rests on the notion that enacting multiple roles results in a net drain in scarce human energy. Barnett and Baruch (1987), on the other hand, suggest that multiple roles replenish an abundant store of energy. Despite criticisms, Schwartz' article prompted organizations to think about innovative ways to retain employees when the skilled labor supply was dwindling in the 1990s (Kaplan, 1989).

When concern about successfully combining work and personal life surfaced, the focus was on a phenomenon that was new for the white middle class—the *dual earner couple* in which both adults were employed. Dual earner couples, in which both partners worked mainly for economic reasons, were distinguished from *dual career couples*, in which both had high levels of education, expected increasing responsibility on the job, and desired professional development and self-fulfillment. Authors wrote about advantages and disadvantages of dual career lifestyles and coping mechanisms to consider when they became stressful. Dual earner and dual career lifestyles are now the norm, and such material seems passé.

WORK/FAMILY BALANCE VS. WORK/LIFE INTEGRATION

An emphasis on work/life initiatives evolved from a concern for balancing work and family responsibilities. The fact that the term "work/life initiative" is more inclusive is not lost on employees without children, some of whom feel like "second class citizens" as companies add benefits specifically tailored to employees with children.

Whether work and personal life should be "balanced" or "integrated" also is an issue. Balance may imply separation, and at the extreme, that may not be possible or desirable. It would mean refusing to take personal telephone calls during working hours even in an emergency or declining to speak to a supervisor who calls an employee's home with an urgent question. Though exceptions exist, Kossek, Noe, & DeMarr (1999, pp. 110–111) maintain that "women are more likely to have more permeable and flexible boundaries between work and family roles, due to increased demands related to workload (paid and unpaid), need for multi-tasking of roles, and differing styles in managing boundaries between work and home."

Males or females with permeable boundaries between work and personal life may be more likely to integrate than to separate the two. Total separation may seem unnatural. On the other hand, eliminating boundaries between work and personal life could lead to increased stress and chaos for some. The subtitle of Hochschild's book, *The Time Bind: When Work Becomes Home and Home Becomes Work* (1997) is germane. She argues that organizational commitment comes at the expense of personal life and detracts from balance. As will be discussed later, researchers Berg, Kalleberg & Appelbaum (2003) disagree.

"Balance" in terms of emphasizing work and non-work activities equally and allocating approximately equal time to both may be an achievable long-term, but not short-term, goal. Flexibility is the key. Major projects occasionally demand significant effort beyond normal working hours; perhaps professional employees can take compensatory time off during less busy times. Hourly workers or those in dual earner relationships may not have this luxury, however. Sandholtz, Derr, et al. (2002) call planned periods of intense work followed by time to pursue other activities *alternating* and recommend it as one of several strategies to avoid the burnout that may be caused by constant juggling of career and family or personal responsibilities.

WORK/LIFE INTEGRATION: EXPERIENCES OF RACIAL AND ETHNIC MINORITIES

As mentioned, work-family balance became an issue when it affected white mid- to upper-class women, some of whom may have considered paid employment optional. Many women of color did not have that luxury. In African American families, adult females and males both had to work outside the home. A "family wage" never existed (Mullings, 1986), and the ban on women's employment did not apply to them. Paid employment was a necessity, and society was unconcerned about how African Americans managed to combine work and family. The topic was not considered worthy of serious research.

When African American women tried to withdraw from the labor force after emancipation and demanded that a wage to support the entire family be paid to their husbands, they were accused of being lazy. An official of the Freedmen's Bureau attributed financial problems black families had in that era to the "evils of female loaferism" (Gutman, 1976).

Ironically, the slavery legacy created greater equality between the sexes among African-Americans. In a family of slaves, one gender had no effective way to dominate the other (Mullings, 1986). Apparently, there is still some carryover. Wilson and her colleagues (1990) report that the socialization of blacks creates an expectation that women and men both will make decisions within the family and contribute to its financial support. Black men generally know that they will be expected to assist with domestic chores and child care within a marriage and accept that arrangement. Blair-Loy (2003) states that black men do more house work and child care than white men, but black women still perform the majority of household tasks.

In 1890, 40% of black women were in the labor force compared to 16% of white women (Richardson, 1986). Only 3.2% of married white women earned wages in 1900, but 26% of married black women did (Tucker & Wolfe, 1994). By 1944, 44% of black married women but less than 30% of their white counterparts were in the labor force (U.S. Commission on Civil Rights, 1990). Those percentages rose to 66% and 60%, respectively, in 1994 (Bureau of Labor Statistics, 1995). By the late 1990s, the work force participation rate of black women exceeded that of white, Hispanic, Asian, or Native American women (Toliver, 1998). In 2004, 61.5% of black women were employed compared to nearly 59% of white women, nearly 58% of Asian women, and 56% of women of Hispanic origin (U.S. Department of Labor, 2005). Data regarding work force participation of Native American women are not as readily available.

Black women's relatively high work force participation may be explained, in part, by the fact that black men's unemployment rate exceeds that of their female peers; in the 1990s nearly twice as many black as white men were out of work. Black men have a lower participation rate than their white counterparts. Also, women's wages make up a greater percentage of total household income in black families with dual earners than in similar white families (Toliver, 1998).

Black women accept the breadwinner role as central to good parenting. Unlike many white women, they have been socialized to view work and family life as complementary (Blair-Loy, 2003). Their socialization and experience emphasizes the importance of self-sufficiency and independence, and they tend to have a strong work orientation (Blair-Loy). Though about half of black families have two heads of household (Toliver, 1998), black women who are raising children are more likely than white females to be divorced or never married. These facts are not lost on black professional women, who identify their mothers as important role models. The message they gave to their daughters was that they must be able to support themselves (Blair-Loy).

Few studies of work/life issues have focused on black professional women, but Blair-Loy's (2003) research on black female attorneys shows no negative effects of marriage and children on their salaries. Those who are married have higher salaries than their single peers, and child bearing does not affect their incomes. Studies on women in the workforce in general, based primarily on whites, are strikingly different. Economists have calculated that white women face a six to seven percent wage penalty for each child (Hewlett, 2002).

Challenges blacks experience in the workforce cannot all be attributed to socioeconomic class. Blaming problems on class, rather than race, is more palatable to U.S. citizens, who may believe class-based issues are more easily remedied (Toliver, 1998).

In the late 1990s, however, black families in the U.S. remained concentrated in the lowest 40% of the population based on income. They made strides into the middle class, but only one-third of all black families reached that level (Toliver, 1998). An erosion of support for affirmative action in employment promoted "the false notion" among whites "that there no longer is a race problem and that those blacks who have made it have worked hard, and those who have not are lazy, criminal, less gifted or suffer from deficient values" (Toliver, p. 5).

Race is still salient to upper middle class black managers, who are considered "elite" within the black community. "It affects the work lives of African Americans, their mate selection opportunities, their parenting behaviors, their roles as husbands and wives, and a variety of other areas of social living" (Toliver, 1998, p. 10). Thus, race has an impact on work life issues for blacks in the U.S.

All families experience stress, but Toliver (1998) argues that black families have more than whites in the U.S. due to vestiges of racism. Spillover of strain from work to family is greater for black than white managers because the former must be "culturally ambidextrous," or bicultural. They must develop strengths that allow them to survive and thrive in sometimes hostile work and societal environments.

Black upwardly mobile professionals and managers who have children are beginning to experience a challenge that is a side effect of their success. They fear that their children, who grew up in the mainstream (white) culture, will lose their black identity, will be ill-prepared to deal with racism as adults, or both. They want their children to know about the heritage, struggles, and successes of blacks, to develop a positive black identity, and to be prepared for the possibility of isolation when they enter the workforce so it will not be a "rude awakening." Thus, blacks have additional concerns beyond those that all parents face.

Relocation within the same organization due to promotion or lateral move disrupts any family, but Toliver (1998, p. 169) maintains that the potential for negative consequences is magnified for blacks and other minorities. She says:

> the problems of uprooting children from cultural connections essential for their healthy development as black youngsters . . . and distancing black individuals

and families from community, civic, social, and religious organizations and institutions including the black church—in light of the special significance of
these in black life and, indeed, black psychosocial survival [create] the case for
. . . concern.

Though many firms offer relocation assistance, it is not usually described as
a work/life initiative. Perhaps it should be.

Practical issues that whites need not consider affect black families who
must relocate. For example, an African American manager says, "You can't
presume as a black family, moving into that neighborhood, that someone's
going to be willing to watch your little black children as [they] may be to
watch little white children" (Catalyst, 2004, p. 7).

Like black women, female Asian Americans tend to view paid employment
and job training as extensions of their responsibility to their families when the
motivator is economic necessity. They have a long history of employment in
agriculture and family owned firms. Twenty percent of Asian Americans live
in families with more than three wage earners, more than any other ethnic/
racial group. The comparison figure for whites is 12% (Grahame, 2003). Multiple breadwinners are necessary for economic survival due to the low wages
recent Asian immigrants earn.

Literature about the way Asian American women deal with work and domestic responsibilities is sparse. So much diversity exists among Asian Americans based on their nation of origin and whether or not they are recent immigrants that trying to generalize from isolated studies is futile. Nevertheless,
three such studies will be summarized.

A study of Chinese American married women who recently emigrated from
Hong Kong shows that they contributed a greater share of household income
after they came to the U.S. Their husbands' wages in the U.S. are lower than
they were in Hong Kong, but their own incomes are higher. These women
participate in job training, care for children and a household, and are employed part-time. Some of their husbands help, in a limited way, with child
care and domestic chores mainly because no network of female extended
family members and friends is available. Despite being overburdened according to objective assessments, the women seem satisfied and view job
training as a means to attain positions that will provide health insurance and
other benefits which are important to their family's well-being (Grahame,
2003).

Asian American women have more responsibility for elder care than their
black or Hispanic peers. Twenty-three percent assist with care of elderly relatives compared to 15% of black and 20% of Hispanic females (Catalyst,
2003a). "Less acculturated" Asian American women, defined as those who

speak a language other than English in the home and who immigrated as teens or adults (Catalyst, 2003b), are more than twice as likely to have elder care duties than their "more acculturated" counterparts, who were born in the U.S. or arrived before age 12 and do not speak a second language at home.

The next two studies of managerial and professional women outside the U.S. provide a glimpse of cultural factors that create challenges for women from Hong Kong or southeastern Asia who may later immigrate to the U.S. The environment may be different, but moving to another country does not immediately change socio-cultural factors associated with the nation of origin.

Married managerial women in Hong Kong report nearly universal exhaustion due to sex-based division of domestic work and child care and long working hours (Lo, 2003). They have little support in dealing with demands of employers and families; unlike Western men, Hong Kong males generally have not assumed household tasks or child care duties. In addition, Lo believes attempting to change the workplace culture is unrealistic because most organizations operate in the "command and control" mode. The change managerial women in Hong Kong want most is a flexible schedule, which would give them greater control over when they work (Lo).

Southeast Asian women employed as professionals and managers in the United Kingdom say that their nuclear and extended families are their greatest obstacles to career advancement. Their weekends are especially tiring due to pressure to entertain extended family members. The status of Southeast Asian women at work does not relieve them of social and familial responsibilities, and their extended family, rather than being a source of help and support, creates additional strain (Rana, Kagan, Lewis & Rout, 1998).

Assertive individuals could think of many solutions, the first of which might be to say "no" to unreasonable demands by relatives and the second of which might be to hire additional help. These suggestions would, however, be perceived as culturally insensitive and could result in more pressure and blame directed toward the southeastern Asian women. Instead, Rana, Kagan, et al. (1998) suggest that superiors actively listen to each employee's work life concerns as a first step to empowering them.

Like Asian Americans, Hispanics are diverse. Literature about their work/life concerns emphasizes the importance of family. Their inclusive definition of the term goes beyond the nuclear family to include aunts, uncles, cousins, and grandparents. Raphael (2001a) describes the extended family as the Hispanic culture's "social center." A multinational oil firm in Mexico discovered how important the family is to its employees after it stopped a monthly parking lot fiesta for employees and their families due to costs. Boston consultants hired to determine the cause of a 20% productivity drop blamed the event's cancellation. Employees apparently thought that the company no longer cared about their families (Raphael) and became demoralized. A spike in productivity and morale accompanied re-establishment of the fiesta.

Latinas' family responsibilities extend to their elders. They are not quite as likely as Asian American women to have such duties, but 52% of those who do indicate that organizational support for work/family balance is extremely or very important (Catalyst, 2003b).

A study of a sample of 192 Hispanic workers, from data collected by the Families and Work Institute, shows that 58% experience conflict between employment and their personal lives. Job pressure and lack of supervisory support relate to conflict between work and family or personal life for this sample. The younger the child(ren) in the home, the greater the amount of conflict that exists between work and personal life. A supportive work environment overall and high levels of time and leave benefits correlate negatively with high work/personal life conflict (Delgado, Canabal, & Serrano, 2004). Many families with young children face challenges finding affordable, high quality care for them. These issues are compounded for poor families, those that face discrimination, and those who have special language needs, such as some Hispanics who are new arrivals to the U.S. (Delgado, Canabal, & Serrano).

Family and social ties can provide support or increase strain for Hispanics. In addition, recent Hispanic immigrants encounter stress when adapting to a new culture. They are more likely to be less educated and poor than whites and are less likely to have Hispanic role models in management (Delgado, Cannabal & Serrano, 2004). Issues of concern include discrimination based on skin color and illegal immigration. Mexicans, Cubans, and Puerto Ricans constitute the largest groups of Latino immigrants, and geographical proximity of Mexicans to their country of origin may make the acculturation process more difficult (Delgado, Cannabal & Serrano).

Female Puerto Rican professionals, many of whom immigrate to the U.S. mainland, are undergoing a transformation in sex role expectations related to career and family obligations. They graduate from college at a higher rate than Puerto Rican males, are more likely than other Hispanic women to hold professional or technical positions, and are increasingly participating in careers in business administration and the natural sciences, which were previously male dominated occupations in their country (Cofresi, 1999).

The traditional Puerto Rican cultural ideal of submissive, self-sacrificing women clashes with the reality of professional women's lives. Thirty women in the professions, several of whom are mid- to top tier managers, want to expand their roles, according to a 1990s study. Ninety-seven percent define themselves in terms of their professional identity or their ability to combine work and family duties. They stress the importance of intelligence, assertiveness, self-confidence, and goal directedness rather than values more traditional for women in their culture (Cofresi, 1999). Sixty percent say the role of mothers in Puerto Rico is changing; 47% believe the same about the role of wives. Women want to share parenting and domestic tasks with men; though getting assistance can be challenging, most expect cooperation from spouses or partners (Cofresi). Puerto Rican female professionals studied believe that both daughters and sons must be raised to be goal oriented and independent.

Due to their small absolute numbers, finding information on issues of concern to Native Americans related to balancing or integrating work and personal life is nearly impossible. The work force participation rate of Native American women from ages 18–64 grew from 35% to 64% from 1970 to 1990 (Population Reference Bureau, 1993), but they have been referred to as "the lowest paid, lowest ranked, most unemployed segment of the national work force" (Witt, 1979). Nonetheless, Native Americans' emphasis on wholeness and unity with nature suggests that they may favor integration, rather than separation, of work and personal life. They may have much to offer to other cultures in terms of ways to achieve such integration.

Tucker and Wolfe (1994) identify several issues that women of color identify as work/family concerns which corporations rarely categorize as such. These include housing subsidies, transportation assistance, health insurance, and retirement assistance. Such items are crucial to facilitate labor force participation of low-income employees. Ellen Bravo, co-chair of the Economic Sufficiency Task Force of the Wisconsin Women Equal Prosperity Project, puts it bluntly: "Money is a work-family issue. If you don't have money, you can't afford the [child] care you need" (Gross, 2004).

WORK/LIFE INITIATIVES: CATEGORIZATION OF BENEFITS

Nearly all employee benefits fit in the category of Work/Life Initiatives. Three breakdowns are dependent care, alternative work options, which include flexible scheduling and a flexible work place, and job characteristics. Benefits addressing health and wellness and safety and security are sometimes considered work/life offerings. Safety and security benefits, which are omitted from Table 10.1, include retirement and financial planning assistance, life, legal, and long-term care insurance, tax-deferred retirement savings plans, such as 401(k) plans, pensions, and self-defense training.

A relatively new benefit, long-term care insurance pays partial costs of home health or nursing home care for employees and their spouses. Some

Table 10.1.   Categorization and Explanation of Work Life Initiatives

A.	**Dependent Care Assistance**

A.1.   Dependent care reimbursement account 73%
A.2.   Resource & referral for child- or elder care; 19%-child care; 21% -eldercare
A.3.   Dependent care subsidy; child care 4%, elder care 2%
A.4.   On-site child care center 4%
A.5.   Consortium for child care
A.6.   After/before school child care
A.7.   Summer programs for school-age children
A.8.   Dependent life insurance 62%
A.9.   Well-baby program 44%
A.10. Lactation program 21%
A.11. Extended family leave-beyond fed. FMLA-39%; beyond state FMLA-28%
A.12. Paid family leave 24%
A.13. Paid maternity leave (beyond short term disability) 13%
A.14. Paid paternity leave 15%
A.15. Dependent grandchildren health insurance 38%
A.16. Foster children health insurance 29%
A.17. Ability to bring child to work in emergency 28%
A.18. Emergency /sick child care-9%
A.19. Emergency elder care-2%
A.20. Scholarships for dependents 20%
A.21. School selection/referral help 8%
A.22. Educational loans for family members 5%
A.23. Tutoring for school-age children
A.24. Adoption assistance 18%
A.25. Foster care assistance 6%
A.26. Parenting, care-giving seminars, workshops
A.27. Parenting, care-giving support groups

B.   Alternative Work Arrangements/Flexible Schedules
B.1.   Flextime (flexible start/stop/break times) 57%
B.2.   Telecommuting-part time 36%; full-time 19%
B.3.   Compressed work week 34%
B.4.   Job sharing 17%
B.5.   Voluntary part-time work

C.   Work Redesign & Management Practices
C.1.   Advancement opportunities
C.2.   Autonomy
C.3.   Challenge

Table 10.1. (*Continued*)

C.4.   Control
C.5.   Job security
C.6.   Participation
C.7.   Teams—increased use of
C.8.   Technology use

D.   Health/Wellness/Leisure Programs (other than health insurance)
D.1.   Employee Assistance Program 70%
D.2.   Wellness program 56%
D.3.   On-site vaccinations, such as flu shots 60%
D.4.   CPR/First aid training 54%
D.5.   Health screening 43%
D.6.   Prenatal program 29%
D.7.   Weight loss program 26%
D.8.   Stress reduction program 19%
D.9.   Massage therapy at work 14%
D.10. Fitness center subsidy/reimbursement 30%
D.11. On-site fitness center 20%
D.12. Paid tickets to cultural & sporting events 37%
D.13. Club memberships 33%
D.14. Organization-sponsored sports teams 33%
D.15. Food service-cafeteria 29%
D.16. Travel planning service 20%

E.   Other
E.1.   Domestic partner benefits-34% female-/male partners; 27% same-sex partners
E.2.   Paid personal days (besides sick, floating, vacation) 34%
E.3.   Time off for community service 19%
E.4.   Sabbatical leave-unpaid 18%; paid 4%
E.5.   Postal services 32%
E.6.   Dry cleaning pick-up 11%
E.7.   Pre-prepared carry-out meals 3%
E.8.   Concierge services 3%
E.9.   Grief recovery program 15%
E.10. Support groups (various types) 10%

Sources: Percentages are from Society for Human Resource Management. 2004. SHRM benefits survey report. M.E. Burke, Survey Program Coordinator. Alexandria, VA: SHRM. Items without percentages are from various sources.

policies also cover employees' parents and in-laws. The annual premium for long-term care insurance easily exceeded $2000 per couple in 2004; those obtaining coverage before age 50 usually pay lower rates. Premiums typically rise, but some policies guarantee no rate increase for a specified period after issuance. Long-term care insurance is recommended for those with assets between $200,000 and $2 million. Those with fewer assets may need to rely on government-provided medical assistance; those with more than $2 million may be able to self-insure. Additional information on long-term care is available from major insurers. Other safety and security benefits are fairly self-explanatory.

A more inclusive view of work/life initiatives than that presented in Table 10.1 might encompass life-long learning. Benefits in this category are tuition reimbursement, opportunities to attend workshops and conferences, and training/education on topics ranging from a foreign language or English as a second language to specific computer software or systems. The decision to include cardiopulmonary resuscitation (CPR) and first aid training with health and wellness in Table 10.1 is arbitrary; it would also fit under life-long learning as defined here.

Those desiring a detailed description of all the benefits listed in Table 10.1 and a summary of current issues may wish to consult compensation textbooks or web sites of professional organizations such as the Society for Human Resource Management (SHRM), the Employee Benefit Research Institute, or the American Compensation Association. A few benefits in each category will be discussed; those selected are notable because a high percentage of employers provide them or because they have been widely publicized despite the fact that few firms offer them.

Benefits in Table 10.1 are listed under the categories Dependent Care Assistance (A), Alternative Work Options/Flexible Scheduling (B) Health/Wellness/Leisure (D), and Other (E). Benefits offered by the greatest percent of employers responding to a 2004 SHRM survey appear first and are followed by related benefits, as determined by the author. An exception occurs among benefits listed under the heading, "Health/Wellness/Leisure." In that category, the on-site vaccination, offered by 60% of employers, is listed after wellness programs, which are offered by 56% of employers. Wellness programs include offerings and information related to physical and emotional health, so including vaccinations in that category seems more appropriate than listing them separately. Items under Work Redesign (C) appear in alphabetical order. The classification scheme in Table 10.1 is somewhat arbitrary. Others may categorize the same benefits differently.

Dependent Care Assistance

A dependent care reimbursement account is a subset of flexible spending accounts. The Economic Recovery Tax Act of 1981 permitted employees to set aside up to $5000 pre-tax in these accounts for reimbursement for qualified child- or elder-care expenses in the next calendar year. The percentage of employers who responded to the SHRM survey and offer benefits categorized as dependent care assistance has remained fairly constant since 2000. New benefits added to the survey in 2004 were dependent life insurance and health insurance for dependent grandchildren and foster children.

Underestimating qualified expenses is recommended because unspent money is not refunded but used to cover administrative costs. Employees obtain a tax identification number from qualified child- or elder-care providers, get signed receipts after the care has been provided, and submit them with other required documentation to their employer's designee, usually a benefits consulting firm. They receive a reimbursement check for these expenses. Typically, receipts for one calendar year must be turned in during the first few months of the following calendar year to qualify for reimbursement. The percentage of employers providing this reimbursement account has grown from 60% in 1993 to 73% in 2004, making it the most widely used work/life benefit (SHRM, 2004b).

A general flexible spending account allows reimbursement for medical and other qualified expenses besides dependent care. It is a work/life initiative that potentially can help all employees. Pretax dollars can be set aside to reimburse employees for costs of prescribed medications, health insurance premiums, and other qualified expenses.

The trend in dependent care assistance is to offer relatively inexpensive benefits that provide tax advantages to the employer and employee. Organizations that provide dependent care benefits try to balance employees' needs for child and eldercare with a responsibility to contain costs (SHRM, 2004b). For that reason, significantly more firms offer resource and referral programs that help identify appropriate caregivers and other services than provide on-site or subsidized dependent care. From 2000 to 2004, a mean of four percent of employers offered the following benefits: company-supported, subsidized, or on-site child care centers (SHRM).

Percentages were even lower for elder care. A mean of 2% subsidized its costs and 1% provided company-supported elder care. The SHRM benefits survey began tracking this benefit in 2002, and the mean percent of employers offering it from 2002–04 is less than 1%.

"Businesses can no longer afford *not* to provide child care options" for employees according to Whigman-Desir (1993, p. 88). An estimated 5600 U.S.

employers offer some type of child care assistance, and costs range from $20,000 to $1 million (Arthur & Cook, 2004). Employees appreciate resource and referral options, which provide valuable information and identify caregivers, but they are insufficient, given the cost of child care. In 2004, the cost of sending a child to a center averaged over $7000 per year, and placing a child in licensed care at someone else's home ranged from $80. to $300. per week. Expenses continue to rise; increases have run from three to eight percent per year for the past few years when inflation, and, in many cases, pay raises, have been lower than average (Shellenbarger, 2004).

Few employers offer on- or near-site child care centers due to high start-up and operating costs and potential liability. Hoffman-LaRoche started a center in a home in a residential neighborhood after two years of contracting for such service in the early 1990s (Whigham-Desir, 1993). Abbott boasts that its *Early Discoveries* child care center is the largest in Illinois at 46,000 square feet (Work/Life Fact Sheet, 2004). Mentor-Graphics and SAS, Inc. are examples of two other firms that provide on site child care facilities.

A small California employer started a two-room child care center in 2000 for children from birth through age three and charged employees $150 per month in a market in which they could easily have paid $1000 per month for private child care. The ratio of staff to children was one to four. Those directly affected seemed happy with the arrangement, but the center had to be closed. It was operating illegally because its urban location did not provide an outdoor play area of 75 square feet per child (Raphael, 2001b). Nevertheless, children got fresh air regularly because their parents took them outdoors to play at lunch time. This situation highlights another reason why companies hesitate to start centers. Besides expensive start-up and operating costs and staffing and food related regulations, other strict regulations exist, including those covering the types of space and amount of light in play areas (Raphael). Health and zoning regulations and fire codes are extensive, and liability due to possible injury or abuse is a huge concern.

The number of child care centers has not risen dramatically since the 1990s, when 80,000 care centers were available to serve 13 million children under age seven who needed care while their parents worked (Whigham-Desir, 1993). This excludes school-age children who need care at the beginning and/or end of the day. Despite the shortage of high quality child care and the government's 25% tax break for companies that set up centers (Arthur & Cook, 2004), the percent of on-site child care centers will not skyrocket anytime soon.

The need for assistance caring for elderly or disabled family members will rise as the work force ages and the life expectancy increases. By 2020, 40% of U.S. employees will spend about 15 hours per week assisting elderly loved ones

(Gregg, 1998). Previous studies predicted that 37% of U.S. employees would be more concerned about elder care than child care by 2005 (Prince, 1996).

Assistance that older or disabled individuals require varies. It ranges from running errands, housekeeping, accompanying them to medical appointments, and helping them with finances, to assisting with activities of daily living, such as dressing, eating, or bathing. Caring for elderly or disabled family members may involve frequent, psychologically taxing medical emergencies. In addition, those caring for parents must deal with role-reversal. Elder care may include dealing with the medical establishment and the social service bureaucracy—therapists, in-home health aides, and medical equipment providers. Familiarity with the morass of conflicting health insurance regulations may become important as may evaluation of nursing home options.

The emotional health of care-givers declines and depression symptoms increase as the number of hours of care provided rises. Women providing elder care, whether employed or retired, exhibit more depression symptoms than men (Lee, Walker, & Shoup, 2001).

Forty percent of those who assist with elder care simultaneously care for children (Labor Project, 2002). These individuals, roughly between the ages of 45 and 55, have been called the "sandwich generation" because of their dual care-giving roles. Champion-Hughes (1998, p. 299) says, "it is quite apparent how such responsibilities can become overwhelming, particularly when an employee is caring for an ill, elderly parent, his or her own children; and trying to pursue a career." Without any elder care assistance, lost productivity due to absenteeism alone ranged from $250,000–$400,000 for medium sized firms in the late 1990s and "into the millions" for large companies (Champion-Hughes).

The remaining type of benefit under the category of dependent care assistance to be discussed is the leave of absence for family and medical reasons. Table 10.2 summarizes major provisions of the federal Family and Medical Leave Act of 1993 (FMLA). An analysis of state leave laws will not be attempted here. When state and federal family and medical leave laws conflict, the statute that is more beneficial to the employees applies.

Detailed information about the FMLA appears on the web site of the Wage and Hour Division of the Employment Standards Administration of the U.S. Department of Labor at www.dol.gov/esa/. This chapter clarifies points in Table 10.2, summarizes an important U.S. Supreme court case dealing with FMLA, and discusses California's new paid leave law, which became effective in 2004.

Contrary information has been disseminated, but the frequently asked questions section of the Wage and Hour Division web page within the Department of Labor web site indicates that, under the FMLA, "parent" does not

Table 10.2.   Summary of Major Provisions of the Family & Medical Leave Act of 1993

Basic Provisions:

12 weeks of unpaid, job-protected leave per 12-month period for birth of a child, adoption or foster child placement, the employee's serious health condition or that of a spouse, child, or parent

Employers who must comply:

All public agencies—local, state, federal employees, educational institutions. Private sector employers at locations in the U.S., its territories or possessions with 50 or more full- or part-time employees within 75 miles of a particular work place. Fifty or more employees must have worked each day during each of 20 work weeks in the current or prior calendar year

Employees who are covered:

Those who worked for a specific covered employer for at least 12 months total and worked at least 1250 hours during the 12 months before the leave was requested

Employer notification requirements:

1. Poster approved by Secretary of Labor;
2. Employee handbook if employer maintains one;
3. Written notification to employee that absence is being designated FMLA leave based on information provided by employee.

Other employer obligations:

1. Continue employee's health benefits during FMLA leave (Employee must pay his/her share of costs.)
2. Restore employee who takes FMLA leave to the same or equivalent position with equivalent wages, benefits, terms & conditions of employment (unless the employee is designated as a "key" employee and certain provisions are met.)
3. Allow employee to have intermittent leave or reduced work schedule to deal with his/her own or covered family member's serious health condition. (Intermittent leave not required for birth or adoption or foster care placement.)

Obligations of employees:

1. Provide 30-day advance notice for foreseeable covered events including expected birth or adoption or foster care placement or planned medical treatment for self, child, spouse, parent. Give as much notice as possible for unforeseeable, covered events;
2. Obtain medical certification of employee's or covered family member's serious health condition from health care provider;
3. Schedule intermittent leave so it does not disrupt the employer's schedule unduly.

Enforcement:

Wage and Hour Division, Employment Standards Administration, U.S. Department of Labor

Penalties for employer violation:

1. Lost wages and benefits plus interest;
2. Actual damages if no lost wages (such as cost of hiring caregiver plus interest);
3. Injunction.

Sources: (Davis, 2003; SHRM, 2004a: U.S. Department of Labor, Employment Standards Administration, Wage and Hour Division. 2004)

include a spouse's parents (U.S. Department of Labor, 1995). Children are covered up to age 18; longer coverage is possible if they are unable to care for themselves due to physical or mental disabilities. This means they cannot independently perform at least three "activities of daily living," such as eating, bathing, dressing or "instrumental activities of daily living," such as paying bills, shopping, or cooking (U.S. Department of Labor).

A 2002 Department of Labor opinion clarified the applicability of the FMLA to military reservists. Time they spend on active military duty must be counted as time worked for FMLA purposes when they return to their previous employer.

Employer criticism about the perceived expansion of the definition of "serious health condition" notwithstanding, minor ailments such as colds, stomach upsets, or ear infections are not covered under the FMLA unless complications occur. Examples of situations that trigger FLMA leave include in-patient care in a hospital or other residential medical facility, a three-day absence from work plus treatment by a health care provider, chronic or permanent, long-term conditions requiring supervision, and pregnancy.

The FMLA has specific posting requirements. If a significant percent of the work force cannot read English, posters must be written in a language in which the employees are literate. Sample posters are available from the Department of Labor web site; posting violations result in a $100. fine for each incident.

Besides obligations listed in Table 10.2, employers must inform employees of their right to substitute accumulated paid leave for unpaid FMLA leave. Employers may require them to do so but must inform them and explain other conditions they must fulfill to substitute paid for unpaid leave. *Key employees*, defined as salaried workers who are in the highest paid 10% of employees within 75 miles of a work site, may not be entitled to reinstatement in their prior positions following FMLA leave, as are other covered employees. Employers who refuse to reinstate non-key employees to an equivalent position or retaliate against them for exercising their FMLA rights face penalties.

Employers' groups, such as SHRM, oppose mandated benefits including any expansion of the FMLA in principle. *Intermittent leave* provisions, which allow employees to take leave in less than full day increments, have led to difficulties pertaining to attendance policies. These provisions particularly disturb employers, because they must track intermittent leave in very small increments. To remedy this situation, employer groups have proposed legislation requiring employees eligible for intermittent leave to take at least four hours of leave at a time.

With hindsight, employer concerns that the FMLA would be unduly burdensome and costly and would stifle their flexibility seem exaggerated. The percent of employers who believe that complying with the FMLA is easy declined from 85% to 63% from 1995 to 2000 (Commission on FMLA, 1996; Waldfogel, 2001), but a majority still concur. In 2000, 90% said the law, has had either a positive impact or no effect on growth and profitability, 83% said the same regarding productivity. Nearly 94% said intermittent leave had no effect on profits; 81% claimed it did not affect productivity (Waldfogel, 2001).

A bipartisan Commission on Family Leave report (1996) indicates that the FMLA generally had a positive impact on employees in the first three years following enactment. The percent of employees who took leave for medical or family reasons held nearly constant from 1995 to 2000 at 16% and 16.5%, respectively. In the same five years, the percent of employees who took FMLA-covered leave rose from 1.2 to 1.9 % according to employee data and from 3.6% to 6.5% based on employer data (Cantor et al., 2001). A small percent of employees surveyed (3% in 2000 and 2.4% in 1995) needed leave but did not take it; 66% cited financial reasons in 1995, and 77% did so in 2000 (Cantor et al.).

Representing a small percent of the total, surveyed employees who wanted a leave but could not afford it encountered significant difficulties. At a time when they would have extra expenses associated with care-giving, they would also lose income by taking FMLA authorized leave (Amason, Gibson et al.,2000). Nine percent of those who could not afford unpaid leave but took it anyway wound up on public assistance; for women, the figure was 12% (Amason, Gibson, et al.).

Grahame (2003) complains that the FMLA is predicated on the norm of a North American, white, middle class family and is nearly worthless for those who do not fit that mold. Employees in lower socioeconomic classes and recent immigrants may need incomes of all wage earners in their households to make ends meet. Having an adult in their household take an unpaid leave is not a viable option.

Other reasons employees do not take leave relate to stereotypes and the organizational climate. Despite the fact that FMLA-covered employers must offer leave to women and men, women are more likely to use it. Twenty percent of employed women and 12.7% of employed men took FMLA leave in 1995. By 2000, the figures were 19.8% and 13.5%, respectively (Cantor et al., 2001). Men's reluctance to take leave is not because the law is relatively new nor does it seem to be a phenomenon unique to the U.S. Amason et al. (2000) report that few men in Sweden take leave even though it is a longstanding entitlement and they receive 90% of their pay for up to 18 months.

Care-giving and nurturing children have been stereotyped as more appropriate for females; males, particularly those who were mid- to upper class and white, were assumed not to have such responsibilities. Recalling the Prentice and Carranza model explained in chapter 5, until recently, domestic and caregiving duties have been intensified prescribed behaviors for women and relaxed prescribed behaviors for men. To combat these stereotypes, Congress passed the FMLA "to eliminate the stigma associated with family leave as being an insupportable burden on the workplace associated with women and remove the ability of employers to avoid leave responsibilities by hiring only men" (Zachary, 2003, p. 26).

Organizational climate can affect decisions about taking a leave of absence. Without support from supervisors, it can be career suicide. Because leave-takers' work is commonly divided among remaining employees while they are gone, coworkers may apply strong peer pressure to avoid being burdened.

Two important milestones regarding family and medical leave occurred in 2003. California was the first state in the U.S. to pass a paid family leave law, which became effective in 2004. The Family Temporary Disability Insurance program requires employers to offer six weeks of paid leave for reasons similar to those in the FMLA. Coverage is notably different from the FMLA. Employees may take advantages of its provisions immediately; employers are covered regardless of size, but those employing fewer than 50 employees do not have to provide job-protected leave. The latter provision may be subject to a court challenge (Shuit, 2003). Funding for California's FTDI comes from a payroll tax. Employee and employer advocacy groups in other states will undoubtedly monitor California's situation to determine their strategies.

In 2000, President Clinton tried to encourage paid family leave through a Department of Labor regulation allowing states to tap unemployment insurance funds to provide it. That rule was repealed in 2003, however, due to dwindling state unemployment reserves and lobbying by employers' groups (U.S. Department of Labor, 2003). No state had started using unemployment funds for paid family leave by the time the regulation was rescinded (U.S. Department of Labor).

Another significant event in 2003 occurred as the result of a U.S. Supreme Court case, *Nevada Department of Human Resources v. Hibbs.* The Court decided that the FMLA applies to the states and that they may be sued for its violation. In an analysis of legislative history of the FMLA, the Court concluded that Congress intended it to apply to the states.

Alternative Work Options/Flexible Scheduling

Though not designed to deal with the need for lengthy absences, flexible schedules are inexpensive and may help employees cope with "routine" elder and child care needs. Because anyone can use them, alternative work options overcome an objection from childless employees that work/life initiatives discriminate against them because the initiatives are directed toward families with children. Single and childless employees like flexible schedules, and, because they are not costly, so do employers.

Managers' concerns about most alternative work options are similar. How must supervision change? How will managers ensure that communication and coordination occur? Those accustomed to evaluating direct reports based on "face time" will need to adjust to an outcomes based system for flextime and other alternative work options. They also may need to set guidelines regarding attendance at any required face-to-face meetings. Assuming it is possible to participate via conference call or teleconferencing software, employees need to know if that will suffice or if their physical presence is required.

Flextime represented the first major change from a 40-hour, five day work week in the U.S. *Gleitende arbeitzeit*, which means "gliding work time" when translated literally, was imported from Germany in the early 1970s. Hewlett-Packard pioneered flextime in the U.S. in 1972 (Schmidt & Duenas, 2002). It features flexible starting and ending work times within a range. Flextime varies according to company needs. Some organizations specify "core time," during which all employees must be present at the workplace; employees typically have leeway in deciding when to take lunch or other breaks. This flexibility helps them better manage their lives by giving them time for personal tasks that are difficult to schedule on weekends or in the evenings.

Widespread availability of personal computers starting in the 1980s increased the popularity of *telecommuting*, also called flex-place or telework. Under this arrangement, employees work part- or full-time at home or a remote location while connected to the office electronically. Telecommuting allows employers to hire a workforce that is geographically dispersed, which may be helpful in increasing diversity, and to better serve customers who are spread across various time zones. Some full-time telecommuters may feel isolated or detached from the organization, however. Drawbacks to employers include costs of buying and maintaining equipment employees will use at remote sites and liability in case of job-related injury.

Like flextime, the compressed workweek gained favor in the 1970s as a means to reduce commuting and resulting traffic congestion and pollution. It typically involves working 10 hours per day four days per week. Modifications are possible; one involves nine-hour workdays Monday through Thursday and a four-hour day on Friday. Compressed workweeks give employees an extra block of time for personal or family activities; potential employee drawbacks include fatigue and, for some, difficulty obtaining care for dependents during extended work hours.

Job sharing occurs when two employees split one full-time position. They earn half of the full-time salary but, depending on the organization's policies, may both receive employee benefits, such as health care. If both receive benefits, employer costs will be higher than if one person were hired for a full-time position. A job sharing arrangement may allow an employer to retain two talented employees it would otherwise lose, however. Coordination and communication between the two employees sharing a job are crucial for this arrangement to be effective.

In 2001, 28% of the 945 employers Hewitt & Associates surveyed regarding work/life benefits offered voluntary part-time employment (Roberts, 2002). A study of 82 managers and professionals from 42 firms in the U.S. and Canada who opted to work less than full-time shows that 91% were happier with the balance between home and work than they were when employed full-time. "They felt good about both being able to place high priority on the quality of their family lives and still have a career" and said they felt "less exhausted, more creative, more focused, and fresher at work" (Lee, MacDermid, et al., 2002, p. 213).

Managers seem more satisfied than professionals with reduced workloads. Forty-three percent of managers and 22% of professionals were promoted while they worked less than full-time. Sixty nine percent of professionals and 11% of managers thought they were doing more work than they were being paid to do when they had reduced workloads (Lee, MacDermid, et al., 2002).

Work Redesign and Management Practices

Batt and Valcour (2003) believe that flexible schedules alone are insufficient to help employees achieve work/life integration. The best results occur when organizations combine flexible scheduling, human resource incentives, and work redesign and when supervisors and top managers are supportive. Beneficial aspects of work redesign and management practices are discussed in an upcoming section of this chapter dealing with contextual factors that affect the outcomes of work life initiatives.

Health, Wellness, and Leisure Activities

All employees, whether or not they have dependents, should be able to use items categorized as health, wellness, and leisure activities in Table 10.1. A Conference Board survey indicates that wellness programs are popular among employees who do not have children; 73% of them use that benefit (Picard, 1997). Seventy percent of all employees take advantage of employee assistance programs; they are the most used benefits in this group. Employee assistance programs typically have an in-house coordinator who refers employees with marital, financial, family, or personal problems to appropriate social service agencies for professional counseling or other help. Started to deal with substance abuse problems, these programs have expanded. For this type of program to be successful, employees must feel confident that they will face no stigma if they contact the EAP coordinator and be assured that conversations are confidential.

Other Work Life Initiatives

In addition to their high use of wellness programs, childless employees favor benefits in the last category of Table 10.1. Of those who have the following items available, 73% use domestic partner benefits and 42% take sabbaticals (Picard, 1997). Seventy-one percent also use tuition assistance, but educational benefits were excluded from Table 10.1.

CONTEXTUAL FACTORS AFFECTING OUTCOMES OF WORK LIFE INITIATIVES

Employers who implement work/life initiatives should experience some of the positive consequences listed in Table 10.3. Not all will accrue to every employer; desirable effects are moderated by supervisory support, top management support, perceived usability of work/life benefits, the workplace environment, nature of jobs, and implementation procedures.

Until recently, the focus of work/life initiatives was on employees' individual traits. With respect to work/family programs, a subset of work/life initiatives, Berg, Kalleberg, and Appelbaum (2003) argue that features of the job and organization also must be considered. Being in a "high performance work system," characterized by employee participation, formal and informal training, opportunities for promotion, intrinsic rewards from work, and pay-for-performance, should make the "spillover" of attitudes and behaviors from work to family life more positive. This occurs because employees perceive greater control and efficacy and experience more job challenge and variety in high performance systems (Berg, Kalleberg, & Appelbaum).

As job variety and challenge rise, married sailors perceive family and work roles as increasingly compatible (Jones & Butler, 1980). Examples in the following paragraphs also indicate that job characteristics affect employees' psychological wellbeing, and, hence, their ability to effectively manage off-the-job family responsibilities. Having challenging work and taking part in decision-making not only can alleviate the effects of a stressful family life but also "may have a positive effect on employees' assessments of the company's family friendliness" (Berg, Kalleberg, & Appelbaum, 2003, p. 175).

A study of 4400 employees in steel, apparel, or medical electronics manufacturing firms, shows that features of jobs and organizations have a significant impact on employees' ability to effectively manage work and family roles. Specifically, "job demands such as long weekly hours, involuntary overtime, and conflict with coworkers all reduce workers' ability to balance work and family responsibilities. In contrast, intrinsically rewarding, challenging jobs that require workers to be creative and to use their skills increases the ability of workers to balance these demands." (Berg, Kalleberg, & Appelbaum, 2003, p. 184). The only gender difference in this study is the fact that working more involuntary overtime detracted from men's, but not women's, ability to cope with work and family demands effectively.

Batt and Valcour (2003) show that job design characteristics affect the management of work/family demands in their study of 557 white collar employees in dual earner relationships. Their findings indicate that autonomy and team collaboration are associated with more control in managing work and family life and are consistent with studies reporting that "parents who felt they had greater autonomy in their jobs, more control over their work schedules, less hectic and demanding jobs, and/or more job security reported appreciably less conflict, less stress, and better coping than other parents" (Galinsky, Bond, & Friedman, 1996, p. 131).

Unlike Berg, Kalleberg & Appelbaum, Batt and Valcour (2003) show gender differences in results. Work-family conflict, and turnover intentions are negatively related to supervisor support for women, but not men. Flexible schedules are associated with reduced turnover intentions for men, but not women. Having coordination responsibility predicts work-family conflict for men, and flexible work hours and technology use does the same for women. Though technology use contributes to greater control over work and personal life regardless of gender, because it "invades" the home, it may interfere with personal life, particularly for women.

Batt and Valcour include job security, salary, and career development assistance as human resource incentives. They cite a link between job security and both reduced work/family conflict and turnover intentions. High salaries relate to greater control and a diminished desire to leave an organization. For men in the study, but not women, higher salaries are linked with greater work-family conflict. Career development assistance predicts turnover intentions for men and women. It is associated with higher intent to quit for males but lower intent to leave for females.

IMPLEMENTATION OF WORK LIFE INITIATIVES

The quality of execution of work/life initiatives varies widely. A prescriptive approach suggests linking implementation to both strategic human resource management and the organization's strategic planning process. This resembles the recommended approach for putting diversity initiatives into place.

Having policies that allow employees to successfully combine work and non-work roles is important, but sincere support from immediate supervisors and top management is crucial. Supervisory and top management support and perceived usability of work/life programs are interrelated. Before they will use such programs, employees must be convinced that their careers will not be jeopardized as a result. They must see that qualified employees who choose flexible schedules get promoted. Supervisors and top executives who "walk the talk" by modeling integration in their lives are more credible than those who do not.

Sometimes immediate supervisors focus too much on the short term costs of accommodating employees' reasonable requests to use work/life benefits and forget about long-term positive consequences. Short-run challenges for immediate supervisors may increase if employees take leaves of absence and use flexible work options. Supervisors may or may not be allowed to hire temporary replacements; if not, they may need to pick up the slack or ask remaining workers to fill in. If not handled carefully, those employees could become resentful. If supervisors assume too much additional work, they may experience burnout, which will create additional burdens for *their* bosses.

The solution, in addition to involving supervisors and employees in planning work/life initiatives so their concerns can be addressed, entails thinking about how to change the way work is done to achieve the same goals with less effort and stress. Potential advantages of redesigning jobs to enhance work/life integration were explained earlier in this chapter.

Top executives also must support lower level managers in their implementation of work/family initiatives. Their backing is necessary for symbolic reasons and to provide resources. Diversity researchers have recommended that managers be held accountable for the success of diversity efforts. Similarly, Casner-Lotto (2000), of the Work in America Institute, suggests that executives evaluate their subordinate managers' support of work/life initiatives when reviewing their performance.

Besides gaining the support of management from first line supervisors to the CEO, organizations must scrutinize job design, organizational practices and policies, work group functioning, and the corporate culture to make sure they are not inadvertently sabotaging work/life integration efforts. Casner-Lotto (2000) says that "grassroots employee involvement" is the key to effective implementation of work/life initiatives and recommends building on a program to which employees already are committed so new efforts are not dismissed as "the flavor of the month." She cites Bank of America's connection of work redesign, begun as part of a work/life initiative, to a "Service Profit Chain." In that chain, associates' satisfaction represents the first link on the way to enhanced "customer loyalty, revenue growth, and profitability" (Casner-Lotto, 2000, p. 39).

As part of an ongoing evaluation process, employee feedback should be obtained systematically when implementing work-life initiatives. Organizations must be willing to change, if warranted, based on a collaborative assessment involving employees and management (Casner-Lotto, 2000).

POSITIVE CONSEQUENCES OF WORK/LIFE INITIATIVES TO EMPLOYERS

Employers undertake initiatives to help employees manage work and personal life for sound business reasons. Work/life benefits initiatives may be offered initially due to a sense of social responsibility or to attract and retain skilled, managerial, or professional employees, for whom demand exceeds supply. The "business case" for work/life initiatives is the same rationale that supports diversity management, which was discussed in chapter 4.

Results of research examining the impact of flexible schedules on employer outcomes, such as absenteeism, are mixed. Thomas and Ganster (1995) find no impact, but six of eight studies of flextime done by Baltes et

Table 10.3. Positive Consequences to Employers of Work/Life Initiatives (Supported by Research Evidence)

Increased:	Decreased:
Profit and sales growth	Absenteeism
Market performance	Turnover
Perceived organizational performance	Stress related illness
Productivity	Work family conflict
Ability to recruit employees with needed skills	Substance abuse
Motivation	Aggression
Organizational commitment	
Organizational citizenship	
Job satisfaction	
Effort (beyond minimum needed to retain job)	
Shareholder return	
Loyalty	
Percent of senior management positions held by women	

al. (1999) show reduced absenteeism. Schmidt and Duenas (2002) demonstrate that flextime cuts paid absences and idle time on the job. However, only two of five studies of the compressed work week indicate lower absences (Baltes et al.).

Flextime has several positive consequences. A study of 3381 U.S. workers shows that flexible time schedules relate to organizational loyalty among women and men at all life stages with and without children under age 18 (Roehling, Roehling, & Moen, 2001). Among small biotech firms employing a gender-balanced workforce composed of about 50% professionals, flexible work policies perceived as usable are linked to productivity among women and men. Eaton (2003) generalizes further by saying that flexibility forecasts performance and commitment among all workers.

Besides enhancing employee morale, flextime usually aids recruitment and retention. Rau and Hyland (2002), however, show that flextime attracts prospective employees only if they are already facing role conflict and has no effect otherwise.

Flextime enhances employers' ability to respond to customer demand for rapid response and to operate 24/7 without increasing employee burnout. Because of differences in time zones, business may literally be conducted at any time in a global marketplace.

Flexible schedules lower work/family conflict, and, in doing so, may cut absenteeism (Arthur & Cook, 2004). Increased work/family conflict is negatively associated with job- and life satisfaction (Kossek & Ozeki, 1998) and vice versa (Thomas & Ganster, 1995). Work/family conflict may rise due to dissatisfaction with care-giving options, particularly if couples disagree about how to resolve challenges associated with care-giving roles. Dissatisfied employees may withdraw from work or exhibit aggression or distress (Kossek, Noe, & DeMarr, 1999).

Flextime's advantages generally outweigh its disadvantages. Nonetheless, its implementation may increase expenses for utilities, security, and some services, such as a company cafeteria, which may need to stay open for extended hours (Schmidt & Duenas, 2002).

In some cases, a positive outcome is associated with a particular type of work/life initiative. Three types of work/life programs, namely longer leaves of absence than required by law, supportive supervisors, and flex-place, are linked to new mothers' greater job satisfaction. These benefits enhance retention of women who have recently become mothers (Holtzman & Glass, 1999). Other studies indicate lower turnover or reduced absenteeism among employees who take advantage of one or two work/life benefit options. Data from interviews of over 2000 managers and 947 trade union workers and questionnaires that more than 28,000 employees in Great Britain completed show a 12% turnover rate in organizations that allow employees to work from home compared to an 18% rate in those that do not (Felstead, Jewson et al., 2002). At Johnson & Johnson, a U.S. firm, absenteeism dropped 50% among employees using leaves or flexible work options (Gottlieg, Kelloway & Barham, 1998).

An analysis of data from 527 U.S. organizations in several industries shows a connection between a "work-family bundle," defined as "a group of complementary, related, and sometimes overlapping human resource policies that may help employees manage non-work roles" (Perry-Smith & Blum, 2000, p. 1107), and sales and profit growth, perceived organizational performance, and perceived market performance. The age of a firm and its proportion of women are linked to profit and sales growth but not to the other two measures, leading Perry-Smith and Blum (p. 1114) to suggest that "gender should receive less attention in work-family research." They recommend that a "work/family bundle" should be included as "best practices" among organizations that adopt a strategic approach to human resource management.

Arthur (2003) demonstrates a relationship between an announcement of a new work/life initiative and increased shareholder value of Fortune 500 firms in any given year from 1971–1999. The association is more pronounced in high tech firms than in other organizations. Since the 1980s, certain work/life initiatives have become so common that their adoption indicates conformity to social expectations and is a source of legitimacy, which helps them obtain other resources. Arthur calls for studies of the relationship between work-family practices, not just announcements, and shareholder value. As evidence that companies are actually implementing the "family friendly" practices they have announced, she points out that 61% of firms she analyzed appeared in *Working Mother's* annual list of 100 Best Companies for Women in 1999 (Arthur).

Work/life initiatives reduce costly absenteeism and turnover (Grover & Crooker, 1995; Greenhaus & Parasuraman, 1997). Aetna's director of work-life strategies says that such initiatives saved her company over $1 million each year by increasing retention (Fyock, 1998). On a list of 16 factors that would make them want to remain employed by the firm, IBM employees rate work/family initiatives number six (Landauer, 1997). Expenses associated with recruiting and hiring a new employee are as much as 200% of the previous employee's annual earnings (Eaton, 2003).

Though development needs are ongoing, lower turnover can reduce initial orientation and training costs. A larger applicant pool is associated with firms that have work/life initiatives. Hannon and Milkovich (1996) believe this will result in higher quality employees being hired, assuming the use of valid, reliable selection procedures.

Employees in organizations with work/life programs may be more likely than workers at firms without them to exert more effort than required to keep their jobs (Osterman, 1995). Those who use work-life programs at DuPont "were 45% more likely to agree strongly that they will 'go the extra mile' and are least likely to feel overwhelmed or burned out" (Landauer, 1997, p. 3).

Lockwood (2003) presents another reason for adopting work/life initiatives that dovetails with opinions of DuPont employees. She says they help cut health care claims, particularly those that are stress-related.

Champion-Hughes (2001) maintains that organizations can improve productivity by instituting work/life initiatives and illustrates this point by considering the Los Angeles Department of Water and Power. In that unit, every dollar invested in work/family programs generates $10. She argues that a "totally integrated benefits system" including work/family benefits helps employers motivate employees. Lockwood (2003) also indicates that workers' productivity and motivation are linked to their employer's dedication to and support of work/life initiatives.

Some believe the extensiveness of work/life offerings affects productivity, but Konrad and Mangel's (2000) study of large public and private sector organizations qualifies that conclusion. Their research reveals that a wide array of work/life benefits is associated with productivity only for organizations employing high percentages of women and professional employees.

Grover and Crooker (1995) indicate that employees who have more work/life programs available have higher organizational commitment, defined as the extent to which workers are involved in and identify with an organization (Champion-Hughes, 2001). Berg, Kalleberg, and Appelbaum (2003) take a different approach to organizational commitment in their study of manufacturing firms in the apparel, medical electronics and imaging, and steel industries in the 1990s. They maintain that non-supervisory employees in firms that have participative work systems are likely to be more committed to their organizations and that commitment itself has a positive impact on employees' ability to balance work and family commitments.

Work-life initiatives are related to organizational citizenship, which means employees' willingness to help an organization achieve its goal by, for example, assisting coworkers or dealing with temporary irritations, such as having to move to a different building to accommodate remodeling, without grumbling (Champion-Hughes, 2001). In a manufacturing firm, workers' evaluation of the worth of work/life programs also is linked to increased organizational citizenship behaviors (Lambert, 2000).

A gap between the availability and use of work/life initiatives may exist, however. Some organizations that adopt programs seem more concerned about improving their reputations than creating a culture responsive to employee needs to deal effectively with non-work and work issues (Kofodimos, 1995).

REMAINING EMPLOYER CONCERNS ABOUT
WORK LIFE INITIATIVES

Most employers realize that work life initiatives are beneficial for previously discussed reasons. Remaining concerns about implementing such practices may be based on fear of creating "either a sense of entitlement or feelings of resentment" (Friedman, Christensen & DeGroot, 1998). As an antidote, employers are urged to clarify business priorities, treat each employee as a "whole person," and constantly question the approach to work to "enhance the organization's performance while creating time and energy for employees' personal pursuits" (Friedman, Christensen & DeGroot, p. 120). Employees who know the organization's goals and are known as multi-faceted individuals with varied interests will develop loyalty to organizations that give them latitude regarding when and where work is done. Friedman, Christensen and DeGroot argue that greater loyalty overcompensates for any increased sense of entitlement.

Resentment occurs when employees feel they have been disadvantaged or treated unfairly. As alluded to earlier, single employees without children may feel this way if they are repeatedly asked to work holidays so coworkers can spend time with their families or expected to assume extra uncompensated duties to help the organization when another employee takes FMLA leave. If this happens, single employees have legitimate concerns that should be addressed.

Single employees without children also may have an issue under the Equal Pay Act if the value of their total compensation including benefits is less than that of coworkers with children because providing health insurance for a single person is less expensive for the employer. Employers might argue that they cannot afford to offer the equivalent of a cash "rebate" to employees who have no dependents and, thus, need no family health plan. Further, they may be reluctant to cut benefits of employees with children because they need to recruit and retain them, too.

A solution for large employers involves offering flexible, or "cafeteria" benefits. In this arrangement, employees choose desired benefits from various options up to a specified dollar amount (or number of points). This assumes organizations make available benefits that appeal to employees with diverse lifestyles and needs. Because employees have the same dollar amount or point value, equal pay concerns become moot. Organizations that adopt this system may incur extra administrative costs, but these may pale by comparison to expenses associated with lawsuits. Unfortunately, small employers may not be able to afford the range of benefits needed to make flexible plans appealing.

Many firms include domestic partner benefits among their offerings as part of a plan to attract and retain a diverse workforce. Discussion has occurred about whether or not proposed state Defense of Marriage Acts, defining marriage as relationships between one woman and one man, or a constitutional amendment to that effect, would invalidate such benefits. Rather than becoming embroiled in the controversy that is inevitably part of such a discussion, employers might consider allowing employees to cover one other adult and all dependents under health insurance plans. To contain administrative costs, employees might be permitted to change the covered adult only at specified times, perhaps once every two years. By taking this approach, employers could keep the focus on business issues.

SUMMARY

Whether paid employment should be integrated or balanced with the rest of life became an issue when the percent of women in the workforce began to increase in the 1970s. Though females and males both are able to care for children and elders and perform domestic chores, women still do more of that type of work.

Work/life balance or integration was not a concern until it affected large numbers of white, middle-class women. Black women historically have participated in the labor force to a greater extent than white women and regard paid employment and parenting as complementary. Asian American women have more responsibility for elder care than black, Hispanic, or white women; Hispanic women report that their family ties may either provide support or increase strain.

The main categories of work/life initiatives sponsored by U.S. firms are dependent care assistance, alternative work arrangements including flexible schedules, work redesign and management practices, and health, wellness, and leisure programs excluding health insurance. These topics were discussed in chapter 10, and provisions of the FMLA were covered in the discussion of dependent care assistance. Research-supported positive consequences of work/life programs were explained as were suggestions for implementing these initiatives.

CASE STUDY: TROUBLE AT TMC? BY MARK S. HAMEL

TMC, Inc. is a global marketer of cleaning and sanitizing products directed to a variety of markets including restaurants, hotels, and the food-processing industry. To support its worldwide distribution of cleaning products, the company operates an equipment manufacturing plant in Chicago, which manufactures and distributes dispensing equipment. The Chicago plant supports all nine of the firm's operating divisions, each of which has unique requirements and dictates unique service requirements to the operation.

TMC has some conservative philosophies. White males who have worked for the company for several years are very well-represented in upper and middle management. In the past few years, one female and one black male have been named to the board of directors, but they are nearly the only minorities. Though human resource policies have been updated to reflect the increasing diversity among nonexempt workers at the plants, many decisions are still influenced by informal networks in the organization. All managers attend required diversity training, but little daily application of the principles covered seems to occur.

Due to the huge growth in the number of products served and the need to integrate the shipments of dispensing equipment with those of cleaning products from its chemical plants, TMC decided to put a state-of-the-art warehouse management system into the Chicago facility and to eventually roll the distribution software into its worldwide network of chemical plants. After the corporate-level team chose the product, the local Chicago management team would oversee the implementation. Implementation would take eight to nine months and would be followed by a four to five month period of fine-tuning the software for optimum performance. The total cost of the project would be over $2 million.

The person who led the product selection process was a female information systems manager who had been hired recently. Shortly after the selection process ended, she left the firm amid rumors of disagreement with her supervisor, the vice president of global operations.

TMC had a less-than-stellar track record of technological improvements and was determined to see this one succeed. The Chicago equipment operation was chosen for this project partly because of its higher degree of technical expertise compared with most of the chemical plants worldwide. The distribution operation had earned corporate recognition for high quality and service levels over the past two years, which was expected to continue after project implementation. It is a complex, high-volume operation that ships over 1500 orders a day to its global customers. Most orders are shipped the same day they are received. Because the software is scheduled to be rolled into the chemical distribution system over the next two years, on-time implementation is very important.

The software product chosen was a user-configurable database system that would direct the flow of material through the warehouse from the time of order entry until shipping. One task for the local implementation team was to configure the software to meet the business objective of maintaining good service, while enabling Chicago to integrate its orders with those of the chemical plants. Minimizing the number of modifications to the software code was crucial to limit complexity, thereby containing future costs of maintaining and upgrading to other versions.

Assembling a team to configure and set up the software was one of the first responsibilities of Don Brown, the plant manager, and Marty Delgado, the warehouse manager. Besides Don and Marty, four other team members would be chosen from the nonexempt distribution workers. Among the qualifications would be computer literacy, familiarity with the details of the daily distribution operations, and the time and ability to travel. Three stays of up to three weeks at the software company's headquarters would be required, during which the details of the software would be taught. Additionally, trips to the sites of several existing software users would provide ideas about how other firms used the system. All team members would receive laptop computers with remote access to all of TMC's network resources. Those who could read between the lines could figure out what that meant in terms of the time commitment expected on this project.

Don, the plant manager, who also was the project manager, had worked at TMC for 25 years. He was used to making decisions with a minimum of input from his subordinates and could not always be described as being contemporary in his thinking. Because the team members would periodically interact with corporate staff, Don was very concerned about who would be on the implementation team and the political ramifications that their contact with corporate staff would have.

Marty, the warehouse manager, would recommend the team of four people who would be charged with configuring the software to direct the flow of materials throughout the warehouse. Don would make the final decision on these recommendations. As word of the upcoming project spread through the Chicago plant, it became obvious that inclusion on the team was desirable. Many people viewed this as an opportunity to travel—something unique for this type of position—as well as to get away from the physical labor of the warehouse. One problem Marty faced was a conflict between two skills required: computer literacy and familiarity with details of the distribution operation. While looking at the list of available individuals, Marty found some with one skill or the other, but few with both. For the most part, people familiar with the operation had not improved their computer skills much over the years. Conversely, recent hires had very good computer skills but did not understand the operating details as well as more experienced employees.

A notable exception, however, was Kristi Henry. She had worked in the warehouse for over seven years and had gradually accepted more responsibility. She had worked in all functional areas filling and shipping orders to all the divisions that the plant serviced. Two years ago, she had assumed responsibility for many daily computer tasks needed to make sure that orders were processed properly and on a timely basis. When the project and implementation process were announced, Kristi had immediately expressed a strong desire to take part. Kristi was assertive and did not hide her aspirations, which Marty admired.

There was another fact that Kristi had not hidden. She had recently become pregnant for the first time. Her due date was four months before the tentative "go-live" date, and she intended to take a six-week maternity leave.

Marty had always thought highly of Kristi's abilities and was responsible for her advancement in the department. He often had called on her when special customer needs required someone who knew how to get things done or when someone who could work well with very little supervision was needed. When analyzing problems in specific areas, he often had gone to Kristi because of her detailed understanding of the department's daily operations and her ability to find the root cause of problems. And he was the one who had urged Kristi to pursue formal training on several specific computer applications.

When Marty began to formally interview interested individuals for team membership, he did not have many questions about Kristi's qualifications. He did have questions about her ability to contribute to the team's efforts not only immediately after the birth of her child, but also during the weeks before the birth. "What if you have to take time off for bed rest?" he asked. "What about medical check-ups?" "How will you handle this if you are traveling to Milwaukee for three weeks at a time?"

Marty also expressed concern that Kristi's due date fell during one of the most critical times of the project—-the time during which final testing would be conducted and when the final "go" or "no go" decision would be made. Having attended diversity training and the corporate interaction management program, Marty also realized the importance of pointing out to Kristi that his main concern was for her and her ability to prepare for the upcoming birth and attend to her own welfare and that of the child.

As was typical, Kristi had anticipated many of the questions that Marty asked. "What if another team member gets sick and must take time off?"

Kristi responded. She also mentioned that her health maintenance organization (HMO) had doctors in Milwaukee whom she could see if necessary while she was staying there. Kristi noted that with the laptops and network access team members would be given, she could keep in touch and work on the project while at home. She anticipated being back in time for the crucial "go-live" period and fine-tuning afterward.

Kristi also pointed out that the entire team would have to prove its competence in the initial months of the project and that other team members should be able to fill any voids created by her absence. Part of the team's responsibilities would be to train others to become proficient with the new system. By the time Kristi took her leave of absence, another person should have emerged who would be able to take her place temporarily. This could only make the team's efforts more successful in the long run.

"Just because I'm starting a family doesn't mean I'm a different person," said Kristi. "If a man had to take a leave because of a sudden illness, would you deny him the position if he were most qualified?"

Marty found it hard to argue with Kristi. He knew that because of her dedication to her job, she had often worked extra hours and had taken work home in the past without being directly compensated. Sometimes he had counseled Kristi to back off for fear of burnout. In the end, Kristi's adamant stand only reaffirmed Marty's desire to include her on the team. Being overruled by Don was what Marty feared most. He knew Kristi well enough to know that if she were not included, he might lose her.

In a weekly meeting with Don, the two scheduled a follow-up meeting in two days when Marty would make his recommendations. At the weekly meeting, Don told Marty that he had heard of Kristi's pregnancy.

"It's just too bad that we can't include Kristi Henry on the team," said Don.

"Why not?" asked Marty.

"I thought you knew," said Don, acting surprised. "Kristi's pregnant. There's no way she can do the work that will be required of team members. Even though she said she only wants to take a six-week leave, we both know that she'll be tempted to go part-time or make other career sacrifices to spend more time with her new child. She just won't be the same person after the baby is born."

Marty was unprepared for this. Don's opinion didn't particularly surprise him; he knew that he would face a tough battle with Don if he wanted Kristi on the team.

"Have you considered Jim?" Don continued. "He's expressed interest. I heard he's thinking of retiring and wants to raise his income over the next few years. Serving on this team might make him eligible for some plum assignments."

Jim Franken, an African-American male, had worked for the firm for nine years and was quite familiar with the details of the distribution operation. He was taking advantage of opportunities that TMC offered to improve his computer skills. Also, TMC's retirement plan weighed the last three years of employment heavily when determining benefits.

Marty had not taken time to formulate his arguments to include Kristi on the team and honestly had not considered Jim. He knew that he had a lot of thinking to do before the next meeting with his boss, Don.

Analyze this case by responding to the following:

1. Identify the most critical current problem.
2. Identify the most crucial underlying problem. (What is the root cause of the most critical current problem?)
3. Provide three non-overlapping alternatives to either the most critical current problem or the most crucial underlying problem. Indicate which problem you are addressing.
4. State at least two criteria on which you will evaluate all of the alternatives. Criteria are factors on which you can compare the alternatives, such as cost, advancement potential, etc. If evaluating an alternative based on one criterion does not make sense, then a different criterion should be used instead.
5. Select one alternative (not a combination) as the solution to the problem. Explain your reasons for choosing one alternative rather than the others.

REFERENCES

Amason, P., Gibson, D.M., Webb, L.M. & Allen, M.W. 2000. Family and medical leave act: Its communicative impact on families and employers. *Communication Law Review, 4.* Retrieved Oct. 15, 2003 from http://www.uark.edu/depts/comminfo/CLR/amason.html

Arthur, M. 2003. Share price reactions to work-family human resource decisions: An institutional perspective. *Academy of Management Journal, 46.* 497–505.

Arthur, M. & Cook, A. 2004. Taking stock of work-family initiatives: How announcements of "family-friendly" human resource decisions affect shareholder value. *Industrial & Labor Relations Review, 57*(4).

Baltes, B.B., Briggs, T.E., Huff, J.W., Wright, J.A. & Neuman, G.A. 1999. Flexible and compressed workweek schedules: A meta-analysis of their effects on work-related criteria. *Journal of Applied Psychology,84*(4). 496–513.

Barnett, R. & Baruch, G. 1987. Social roles, gender, and psychological distress. 122–41. In R. Barnett, L. Biener & G. Baruch. Eds. *Gender and Stress.* New York: The Free Press.

Batt, R. & Valcour, P.M. 2003. Human resource practices as predictors of work-family outcomes and employee turnover. *Industrial Relations, 42*(2). 89–220.

Berg, P., Kalleberg, A.L. & Appelbaum, E. 2003. Balancing work and family: The role of high-commitment environments. *Industrial Relations, 42*(2). 168–185.

Blair-Loy, M. 2003. Family and career trajectories among African American female attorneys. *Journal of family issues, 24*(7). 908–33.

Bureau of Labor Statistics. 1995. *Statistical abstract of the United States.* Washington, D.C.: U.S. Department of Commerce.

Cantor, D., Waldfogel, J., Kerwin, J., McKinley Wright, M. et al. 2001. *Balancing the Needs of Families and Employers: Family and Medical Leave Surveys. 2000 Update.* Rockville, MD: Westat.

Casner-Lotto, J. 2000, Summer. Holding a job, having a life—the next level in work redesign. *Employment Relations Today.* 29–41.

Catalyst. 2003a. *Advancing Latinas in the workplace: What managers need to know.* New York: Author.

Catalyst. 2003b. *Advancing Asian women in the workplace: What managers need to know.* New York: Author.

Catalyst, 2004. *Advancing African American women in the workplace: What managers need to know.* New York: Author.

Champion-Hughes, R. 2001. Totally integrated employee benefits. *Public Personnel Management, 30*(3). 287–91.

Clay, R.A. 1995, November. Working mothers: Happy or haggard? *APA Monitor.* 1, 37.

Cofresi, N.I. 1999. Gender roles in transition among professional Puerto Rican women. *Frontiers, 20*(1). 161–77.

Collins, P.H. 1994. Shifting the center: Race, class and feminist theorizing about motherhood. In E.N. Glenn, G. Chang & L.R. Forcey. Eds. *Mothering, Ideology, and Experience.* New York: Routledge.

Commission on FMLA. 1996. *A Workable Balance: Report to Congress on Family and Medical Leave Policies.* Washington, D.C.: U.S. Department of Labor, Women's Bureau.

Davis, G.M. 2003, July-Aug. *The Family & Medical Leave Act: 10 Years Later.* Alexandria, VA: SHRM. Retrieved on November 12, 2004 from http://www.shrm.org/hrresources/lrpt_published/CMS_005127.asp

Delgado, E.A., Canabal, M.E. & Serrano, E. 2004. Work and family balance among Latinos in the U.S.: Barriers and facilitators. *Journal of Family and Consumer Sciences, 96*(3). 26–34.

Dreher, G.F. 2003. Breaking the glass ceiling: The effects of sex rations and work-life programs on female leadership at the top. *Human Relations, 56*(5). 541–51.

Eaton, S.C. 2003. If you can use them: Flexibility policies, organizational commitment, and perceived performance. *Industrial Relations, 42*(2). 145–67.

Felstead, A., Jewson, N., Phizacklea, A. & Walters, S. 2002. Opportunities to work at home in the context of work-life balance. *Human Resource Management, 12*(1). 54–76.

Fields, J. 2003. *America's families and living arrangements: 2003.* Current Population Reports, P20-553. Washington, D.C.: U.S. Census Bureau.

Friedman, D.E. 1986, June. Elder care: The benefit of the 1990s? *Across the Board.*

Friedman, D.E. 1990. Work and family: The new strategic plan. *Human Resource Planning, 13*(2). 79–89.

Friedman, S.D., Christensen, P. & DeGroot, J. 1998. Work and life: The end of the zero-sum game. *Harvard Business Review, 76*(6).

Fyock. C.D. 1998, Winter. Retention tactics that work. *Employment Management Today.*

Galinsky, E., Bond, J.T. & Friedman, D.E. 1996. The role of employers in addressing the needs of employed parents. *Journal of Social Issues, 52*(3). 111–36.

Glenn, E.N. 1996. Split households, small producer and dual wage-earner: An analysis of Chinese American family strategies. In S. Coontz, M. Parson, & G. Raley, Eds. *American Families: A Multicultural Reader.* New York: Routledge.

Goodstein, J.D. 1994. Institutional pressures and strategic responsiveness: Employer involvement in work/family issues. *Academy of Management Journal, 37.* 350–82.

Gottlieg, B.H., Kelloway, E.K. & Barham, E. 1998. *Flexible work arrangements: Managing the work-family boundary.* New York: John Wiley & Sons.

Grahame, K.M. 2003. "For the family": Asian immigrant women's triple day. *Journal of Sociology and Social Welfare, 30*(1). 65–88.

Gregg, L. 1998. Humanity in the workplace: When work/family becomes an HR issue. *Credit Union Executive Journal, 38*(5). 32–6.

Greenhaus, J.H. & Parasuraman, S. 1997. The integration of work and family life: Barriers and solutions. In *Integrating Work and Family: Challenges and Choices for a Changing World.* S. Parasuraman & J.H. Greenhaus. Eds. Quorum: Westport, CT.

Gross, E.V. 2004, Nov. 19. Problems and solutions for working women. *Wisconsin State Journal.* C10.

Grover, S. & Crooker, K.J. 1995. Who appreciates family-responsive human resource policies: The impact of family-friendly policies on the organizational attachment of parents and non-parents. *Personnel Psychology, 48.* 271–88.

Gutman, H. 1976. *The black family in slavery and freedom.* New York: Pantheon.

Hannon, J.M. & Milkovich, G.T. 1996. The effect of human resource reputation signals on share prices: An event study. *Human Resource Management, 35*(3). 405–24.

Hewlett, S.A. 2002. Executive women and the myth of having it all. *Harvard Business Review, 80*(4). 66–74.

Hochschild, A.R. 1997. *The time bind: When work becomes home and home becomes work.* New York: Metropolitan Books.

Hochschild, A.R. & Machung, A. 1989. *The second shift.* New York: Viking.

Holtzman, M. & Glass, J. 1999. Explaining changes in mother's job satisfaction following childbirth. *Work and Occupations, 26.* 365–404.

Jones, A.P. & Butler, M.C. 1980. A role transition approach to the stress of organizationally induced family role disruption. *Journal of Marriage and the Family, 42.* 367–76.

Kaplan, E. 1989, Spring. The mommy track: A new fact of life? In S. Nkomo, Ed., *Newsletter of the Women in Management Division of the Academy of Management.*4–5.

Kanter, R.M. 1977. *Men and women of the corporation.* New York: Basic Books.

Kofodimos, J. 1995. *Beyond work-family programs: Confronting and resolving the underlying causes of work-personal life conflict.* Greensboro, NC: Center for Creative Leadership.

Konrad, A.M. & Mangel, R. 2000. The impact of work-life programs on firm productivity. *Strategic Management Journal, 21*(12). 1225–34.

Kossek, E.E., Noe, R.A. & DeMarr, B.J. 1999. Work-family role synthesis: Individual and organizational determinants. *International Journal of Conflict Management, 10*(2). 102–127.

Kossek, E.E. & Ozeki, C. 1998. Work-family conflict, policies, and the job-life satisfaction relationship: A review and directions for organizational behavior human resources research. *Journal of Applied Psychology, 83.* 139–49.

Labor force. 2003–04, Winter. *Occupational Outlook Quarterly.* P. 43.

Labor project for working families. 2002. Retrieved on November 9, 2004 from http://isst-socrates.berkeley.edu/iir/workfam/home.html.

Lambert, S.J. 2000. Added benefits: The link between work-life benefits and organizational citizenship behavior. *Academy of Management 43.* 801–15.

Landauer, J. 1997. Bottom-line benefits of work/life programs. *HR Focus, 74*(7). 3–4.

Lee, J.A.,Walker, M. & Shoup, R. 2001. Balancing elder care responsibilities and work: The impact on emotional health. *Journal of Business and Psychology, 16*(2). 277–88.

Lee, M.D., MacDermid, S.M., Williams, M.L., Buck, M.L. & Leiba-O'Sullivan, S. 2002. Contextual factors in the success of reduced-load work arrangements among managers and professionals. *Human Resource Management, 41*(2). 209–23.

Lo, S. 2003. Perceptions of work-family conflict among married female professionals in Hong Kong. *Personnel Review, 32*(3). 376–91.

Lockwood, N.R. 2003. Work/life balance: Challenges and solutions. *2003 SHRM Research Quarterly.* Retrieved on Oct. 19, 2004 from http://www.shrm.org/research/quarterly/0302worklife_essay.asp.

Milliken, F.J., Martins, L.L. & Morgan, H. 1998. Explaining organizational responsiveness to work-family issues: The role of human resource executives as issue interpreters. *Academy of Management Journal, 41*(5). 580–93.

Mullings, L. 1986. Uneven development: Class, race, and gender in the United States before 1990. 41–57. In E. Leacock & H. Safa. Eds. *Women's work: Development and the division of labor by gender.* South Hadley, MA: Bergin & Garvey.

Osterman, P. 1995. Work/family programs and the employment relationship. *Administrative Science Quarterly, 40.* 681–702.

Perry-Smith, J.E. & Blum, T.C. 2000. Work-family human resource bundles and perceived organizational performance. *Academy of Management Journal, 43*(6). 11–7–17.

Picard, M. 1997. No kids? Get back to work! *Training, 34*(9). 33–8.

Population Reference Bureau. 1993, Nov. *What the 1990 census tells us about women.* Washington, D.C.: Population Reference Bureau.

Prentice, D.A. & Carranza, E. 2002. What women and men should be, shouldn't be, are allowed to be, and don't have to be: The contents of prescriptive gender stereotypes. *Psychology of Women Quarterly, 26.* 269–81.

Prince, M. 1996. Elder care benefits valued. *Business Insurance, 30*(31). 3–4.

Rana, B.K., Kagan, C., Lewis, S. & Rout, U. 1998. British South Asian women managers and professionals: Experiences of work and family. *Women in Management Review, 13*(6). 221–32.

Raphael, T. 2001a. Savvy companies build bonds with Hispanic employees. *Workforce, 80*(9). 19.

Raphael, T. 2001b. Business can make child care work. *Workforce, 80*(12). 88.

Rau, B.L. & Hyland, M.A.M. 2002. Role conflict and flexible work arrangements: The effects on applicant attraction. *Personnel Psychology, 55*(1). 111–37.

Rapoport, R. & Bailyn, L. 1996. Re-linking life and work: Toward a better future. Ford Foundation. Retrieved Nov. 2, 2004 from http://www.fordfound.org/publications/recent_articles/life_and_work/relink_toc.cfm?print_version=1.

Richardson, L. 1986. *The dynamics of sex and gender.* 3rd ed. Boston: Houghton-Mifflin.

Roberts, S. 2002. Companies slow to employ alternative work options. *Business Insurance, 36*(4). T3–4.

Roehling, P.V., Roehling, M.V. & Moen, P. 2001.The relationship between work-life policies and practices and employee loyalty: A life course perspective. *Journal of Family and Economic Issues, 22*(2). 141–70.

Sandholtz, K., Derr, B. Buckner, K. & Carlson, D. 2002. *Beyond juggling: Rebalancing your busy life.* San Francisco: Berrett-Koehler.

Schmidt, D.E. & Duenas, G. 2002. Incentives to encourage worker-friendly organizations. *Public Personnel Management, 31*(3). 293–308.

Schwartz, F.N. 1989, Jan.-Feb. Management women and the new facts of life. *Harvard Business Review.* 65–76.

Shellenbarger, S. 2004, Oct. 21. As cost of child-care rises sharply, here's how some families are coping. *The Wall Street Journal.* D1.

SHRM 2004a. *Briefly stated: Family and Medical Leave Act.* Alexandria, VA: SHRM. Retrieved on November 9, 2004 from http://www.shrm.org/research/briefly_published/Family%20and%20Medical%20Leave%20Act%20(FMLA).asp

SHRM. 2004b. *SHRM 2004 Benefits Survey Report.* M. E. Burke, Survey Program Coordinator. Alexandria, VA: SHRM

Shuitt, D.P. 2003. Are you ready for paid family leave? *Workforce, 82*(1). 38–42.

Thomas, L.T. & Ganster, D.C. 1995. Impacts of family-supportive work variables on work-family conflict and strain: A control perspective. *Journal of Applied Psychology, 80*(1). 6–15.

Toliver, S.D. 1998. *Black families in corporate America.* Thousand Oaks, CA: SAGE.

Tucker, J. & Wolfe, L.R. 1994, Sept. *Defining work and family issues: Listening to the voices of women of color.* Washington, D.C.: Center for Women Policy Studies.

U.S. Census Bureau, Public Information Office. 2001. Family composition begins to stabilize in the 1990s, Census Bureau Reports. *U.S. Department of Commerce News.* Retrieved on November 10, 2004 from http://www.census.gov/Press-Release/cb98–88.html.

U.S. Commission on Civil Rights. 1990, Oct. *The economic status of black women: An exploratory investigation.* Washington, D.C.: U.S. Commission on Civil Rights.

U.S. Department of Labor, Bureau of Labor Statistics. 2004a. Table 6. Employment status of mothers with own children under 3 years old by single year of age of youngest child and marital status, 2002–03 annual averages. Retrieved Nov. 18, 2004 from http://www.bls.gov/news.release/famee.t06.htm

U.S. Department of Labor, Bureau of Labor Statistics. 2004b. Table 5. Employment status of the population by sex, marital status, and presence and ages of children under 18, 2002–03 annual averages. Retrieved Nov. 18, 2004 from http://www.bls.gov/news.release/famee.t05.htm

U.S. Department of Labor, Bureau of Labor Statistics. 2005, May. Report 985. Table 3: Employment status by race, age, sex, & Hispanic or Latino ethnicity, 2004. Annual averages.

U.S. Department of Labor, Employment Standards Administration, Wage and Hour Division. 1995, Jan. 6. 29 CFR 825.113 – What do "spouse," "parent," and "son or daughter" mean for purposes of an employee qualifying to take FMLA leave? Retrieved Nov. 12, 2004 from http://www.dol.gov/dol/allcfr/ESA/Title_29/Part_825/29CFR825.113.htm.

U.S. Department of Labor, Employment and Training Administration. 2003, Oct 9. Rules: Birth and adoption unemployment compensation: CFR part removed. *Federal Register online via GPO access.* Washington, D.C.: U.S. Government Printing Office. 58539-49. 03–25507.

U.S. Department of Labor, Employment Standards Administration, Wage and Hour Division. 2004. *Sheet #28 Family and Medical Leave Act.* Retrieved Nov. 12, 2004 from http://www.dol.gov/esa/regs/compliance/whd/whdfs28.htm

Waldfogel, J. 2001. Family and medical leave: Evidence from the 2000 surveys. *Monthly Labor Review, 124*(9). 17–23.

Whigham-Desir, M. 1993. Business and child care. *Black Enterprise.* 86–93.

Wilson, M., Tolson, T., Hinton, I. & Kiernan, M. 1990. Flexibility and sharing of childcare duties in black families. *Sex Roles, 22.* 408–23.

Witt, S.H. 1979. Native women in the world of work. In T. Constantino, Ed. *Women of color forum: A collection of readings.* Madison, WI: Wisconsin Department of Public Instruction.

Work/life fact sheet. n.d. Abbott Laboratories. Retrieved November 20, 2004 from http://www.abbott.com/news/facts/worklife.cfm.

Working women lead men in housework. 2004, September 16. *Wisconsin State Journal.* C4.

Zachary, M.K. 2003. Labor law for supervisors: Supreme court rules FMLA applies to states. *SuperVision, 64*(8). 23–26.

Chapter Eleven

Stress and Managerial Women and Minorities

OUTCOMES

After studying this chapter, you should be able to:

1. define stress, eustress, stressor, maternal wall, institutional racism, decision latitude, inter-role conflict, intra-role conflict, ambiguity, interpersonal stressor, diversity stress, boundary flexibility, boundary permeability, work-family conflict, family-work conflict, stress contagion (crossover), agentic traits, instrumentality, negative affectivity, challenge- and hindrance-related stress, ethnic identity, hardiness, internal and external locus of control, expansion theory, perfectionism, workaholism, organizational justice, cognitive restructuring, problem-focused and emotion-focused coping methods, primary, secondary, and curative stress management interventions, burnout.
2. explain the stress model presented in Figure 11.1, and evaluate its usefulness.
3. explain additional stressors single parents who are managers face compared to those that parents who are part of dual career couples encounter.
4. explain the unique stressors that Native Americans have experienced historically.
5. explain differences in the major stressors that black and white executives face.
6. give examples of the main categories of work related stressors identified in the stress model depicted in Figure 11.1.
7. evaluate the adequacy of major life events checklists in measuring stressors affecting women and blacks.

8. explain how five individual characteristics or behaviors moderate the effects of stressors on perceived stress and on its consequences.
9. explain gender-based differences in self esteem, locus of control, negative affectivity, perfectionism, and Type A behavior that can be supported by research.
10. explain the interrelationships among perfectionism, Type A behavior, and workaholism as moderating variables.
11. explain how specific environmental factors moderate the effects of stressors on strain in a real or hypothetical organization.
12. explain gender and race/ethnicity differences in the methods used to cope with adverse consequences of stress.
13. justify which types of preventive stress interventions would be most beneficial to you or to someone whom you know well.

COST AND PREVALENCE OF WORKPLACE STRESS

Stress costs billions of dollars each year in the U.S. A National Institute of Occupational Safety and Health approximates expenditures of $145 billion due to injuries, many of which are stress-related (National Institute for Occupational Safety and Health [NIOSH], 2000). The American Institute of Stress (2002) estimates that total stress-related costs are $300 billion annually. Costs alone indicate that workplace stress is a serious problem; the toll on human lives makes the issue even more important.

In 2001, 5649 cases of stress, anxiety, or neurotic disorders caused employees to miss work (NIOSH, 2004). This rate of .6 per 10,000 full-time employees represents a 25% drop from 1992, but it still results in additional employer expenses and extra work for remaining employees who have been relatively unaffected by stress-related disorders.

Table 11.1. Stress-Related Absences and Employment in Private Sector Firms, 2001

Race/Ethnicity	Absences due to stress, anxiety, or neurotic disorders[1,2]	Employment[3]
American Indian/Alaskan Native	negligible	.6%
Asian/Pacific Islander	5%	4.4%
Black, non-Hispanic	10%	14%
Hispanic	21%	11%
White, non-Hispanic	55%	70%

[1]Percentages may not sum to 100 due to rounding. [2]NIOSH data—includes private employers with < 100 employees [3]EEOC data—includes only private employers with 100 or more employees
Sources: EEOC (2001); NIOSH (2004).

Who misses work due to stress, anxiety, or neurotic ailments? Employed women account for the majority of cases (NIOSH, 2004). Table 11.1 shows a breakdown of stress-related absences and private sector employment by race/ethnicity in 2001.

STRESS: A DEFINITION

Two definitions of stress will be mentioned but will not be used here. Stress can be regarded as a physiological state of the individual, but that definition is vague. Defining stress as a response of individuals to a perceived gap between demands and resources (Barnett & Baruch, 1987; Cooper, Sloan, & Williams, 1988) emphasizes its negative aspects. Though consistent with the historical use of the word, which meant distress or hardship in the 1600s (Davidson & Cooper, 1992) and force or pressure in the 1700s (Hinkle, 1973), the second definition ignores the positive effects, or motivating value, of stress, called *eustress*. *Distress* refers to the negative consequences of stress.

The definition of *stress* used in this chapter combines those developed by Ivancevich and Matteson (1996) and Stockdale, Murphy, Cleveland, et al. (2000). It is *a physiological, emotional, and mental state that occurs in response to special demands of an event, situation, or action, moderated by individual differences*. Stress is the response, not the event or action that provoked it. The latter is called a *stressor*. According to DeFrank and Ivancevich (1998, p. 56), "only significant or unusual situations, rather than the day-to-day minor adjustments of life, can really be said to produce stress." Perhaps repeated, chronic minor irritations might rise to the level of "special demands" in this definition.

Individuals seem to have an optimal stress level, which varies based on personality and other factors. Task performance is usually highest when stress is at a moderate level. Boredom sets in at low stress levels; people start to feel overwhelmed if stress is too high.

A GENERIC STRESS MODEL

Many researchers have developed stress models. The details and assumed interrelationships of the variables differ, but most follow a similar format. Stressors are related to tasks, roles, relationships, the physical environment, careers, and organizational structure, culture, or practices. They may be categorized, more generally, as work-related and non-work-related. Their effects are moderated by individual or environmental factors to produce perceived stress, which leads to positive or negative outcomes for individuals and organizations. Primary and secondary appraisals affect stress perceptions. The former is an evaluation of "what's at stake" (Portello & Long, 2001) to determine the degree to which a situation poses a threat, could lead to loss or harm, is irrelevant, or represents a positive challenge (Utsey, Ponteretto et al., 2000). The latter is an assessment of the availability of resources to deal with a situation in a way that reduces its threat potential (Lazarus & Folkman, 1984).

Most research focuses on negative stress outcomes, also called *strains*. Adverse outcomes for individuals can be classified as physiological, psychological, and behavioral. Organizational outcomes relate to commitment, performance, and withdrawal behaviors. Individual and organizational outcomes may be inter-related. Individual coping mechanisms vary based on the nature, intensity, duration, and time of onset of stressors, and the nature of moderating factors. They are generally categorized as problem- or emotion-focused approaches. Stressors related to the job, organizational culture, or work environment that seem to result in adverse consequences may indicate a need for serious, long-term organizational change. Figure 11.1 is a general model of the causes and consequences of perceived stress.

The generic stress model's straightforwardness should not obscure its complexity. The same factors may be both moderating variables and stressors. Stressors may interact with each other, as may moderating variables, to worsen or ameliorate perceived stress. Coping methods also may serve as moderating variables, and social support is an example of a factor that may be either.

STRESSORS

Stressors may be related to gender, race/ethnicity, or both. Some stressors seem to affect most managers, regardless of gender or race/ethnicity. For example, black and white managerial women in Davidson's (1997) study both rank work overload as the top stressor. Women may be more likely than men to perceive organizational politics as a stressor (Nelson & Burke, 2000). Minorities and females experience the glass or concrete ceiling, harassment, tokenism, isolation, stereotypes, work-family conflict, the "maternal wall," and prejudice and discrimination as stressors. Most have been discussed in previous chapters.

Work-family conflict and the "maternal wall" seem more problematic to whites than blacks. As mentioned in chapter 10, black couples may have more

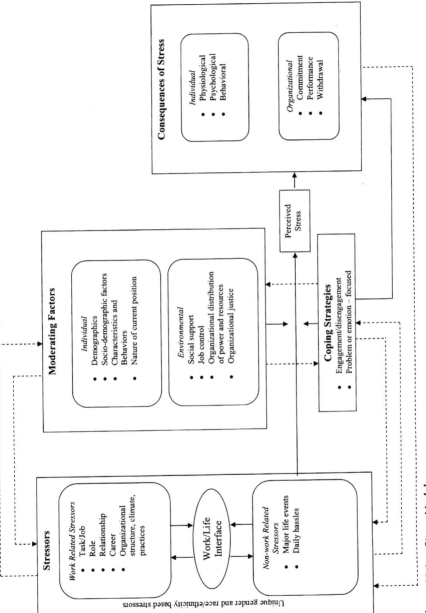

Figure 11.1. Stress Model

egalitarian relationships and black women may view the provider role as integral to their role as parents. The *maternal wall* is a manifestation of stereotypical attitudes toward women with children. They are assumed to be more committed to their children than to their careers and therefore do not receive as many development opportunities as they would otherwise (Nelson & Burke, 2002). Failing to equally consider qualified women and men for positions is illegal, but proving that gender was the underlying reason may be difficult. A "wage penalty" per child, explained in chapter 10, does not seem to be assessed on black women as it is on white women. For that reason, the maternal wall may be a greater obstacle for the latter.

Single parent managerial women face special stressors. Compared to those with spouses or partners, they may have greater work overload, less social support, and more financial strain (Gill & Davidson, 2001). Their career advancement opportunities and job choice may be limited due to difficulties arranging for child care when attending evening functions, working extended hours, or traveling overnight is necessary. Executives may be expected to attend evening meetings and be able to travel. Single parent managerial women believe they are sometimes excluded from events because other women view them as a threat (Gill & Davidson). This perception of executive women who are single parents represents their reality, but the extent to which it reflects a stereotype is unknown.

Compared to two-career couples, male and female single parents have less discretionary income. They must spend a larger percentage of total household income on necessities such as housing, utilities, and food. A child's illness is a major stressor for any parent, but single parents may not have another adult available to take turns caring for the sick child. Extended family members may not live nearby or may be unavailable to help. Care centers that accept mildly ill children are not prevalent and may not exist in rural areas.

Male single parents in management face similar challenges except that they may be less likely to be excluded from social groups due to marital status. They still must cover basic expenses from one income, but that income may be higher than that of similarly situated women due to the persistence of a gender-based wage gap. Anecdotal information indicates that those who believe the stereotype that parenting is easier for women due to nurturing abilities regarded as innate may hold male single parent managers in higher esteem than their female counterparts.

Individual and institutional racism, prejudice, and discrimination are particularly salient for minority managers. All subjects in a study of blacks (Landrine & Klonoff, 1996) experienced racial discrimination at some point in their lives; 98% had encountered it within the previous year. Seventy-five percent of a sample of 156 African Americans had experienced racial stress as compared to 44% of a sample of 376 U.S. citizens of western European descent (Plummer & Slane, 1996). Of the one-third of survey respondents who reported having dealt with discrimination in another study (Thompson Sanders, 1996) 61% characterized it as "moderate" or "severe." Examples include inequities in pay, promotion, or job assignments, denial of housing, and refusal of service.

Though many experience "everyday unfair treatment" regardless of their race/ethnicity, it also may be a manifestation of individual racism. For example, blacks report receiving poorer service in stores and restaurants and less courteous treatment than others and being followed in stores due to a suspicion of shoplifting (Williams, Spencer, & Jackson, 1999). Cornel West, a noted Princeton scholar who formerly taught at Harvard, recounts being unable to hail a taxi in New York City. Though he acknowledges the minor nature of this incident compared to experiences of other blacks, West (1993, pp. x–xi) says "the memories cut like a merciless knife at my soul as I waited on that godforsaken corner"

Institutional racism is defined as "policies that exclude [minority group members] from full participation in the benefits offered to other members of society" (Utsey, Ponterotto, et al., 2000). It may entail imposing harsher penalties on illegal activities when engaged in by minority than majority group members. For example, Utsey, Ponterotto, et al. cite federal drug laws that apply a less onerous penalty for possession of powdered cocaine, which whites are more likely to use, than crack cocaine, which is more available to blacks. In addition, the root cause of the higher job loss rate among blacks than whites may relate to underlying institutional racism.

Asian Americans of Japanese and Filipino ancestry are more likely than those of Korean or Chinese heritage to believe that a greater percent of Asian Americans than whites who violate the law are punished due to a double standard in law enforcement (Kuo, 1995). All four groups agree that Asian Americans with identical qualifications hold worse positions than whites and that Asians must perform better than whites to succeed (Kuo).

Other stressors unique to racial/ethnic minorities include biculturalism, acculturation, and minority status. These will be presented in turn, followed by a discussion of stressors that occur for those who are "doubly disadvantaged' based on race/ethnicity and gender.

"Soul wound" and "historical trauma" are stressors for American Indians (Walters & Simoni, 2002), but those terms also may apply to other minority groups that have encountered racism and discrimination. Forced migration to urban areas, seizure of land, often without proper compensation, and stays at boarding schools designed to indoctrinate them as children in the majority culture have contributed to trauma. The involuntary sterilization of 40% of

American Indian women of childbearing age in the 1970s under the direction of the Indian Health Service (Jaimes & Halsey, 1992) is another example of an action causing "soul wound." Forced internment of Japanese Americans during World War II also may qualify as "historical trauma." Forced splitting of families, physical abuse, and rape of black women by white plantation owners created as much—or more—"soul wound" and "historical trauma" for blacks, but a debate over which group's pain is worse is fruitless. Rather, it is better to take steps toward the elusive goal of rooting out racial and ethnic intolerance and its negative consequences wherever it occurs.

Violence is a stressor for targets, bystanders, and perpetrators, and Native Americans have experienced more than their share. The violent crime rate in which American Indians are victims is 2.5 times higher than the national average. At 98 per 1000, the violent crime rate among Native American women is greater than for females of any other ethnic group. They are affected by violence at a rate nearly 50% higher than that which affects black men (Walters & Simoni, 2002).

Women and minorities both deal with social isolation, but its effects may be more pronounced for minorities, particularly blacks. Besides isolation on the job, blacks may experience the same in their neighborhoods or communities, especially if they relocate to areas where no strong black community exists (Toliver, 1998).

Biculturalism has been defined previously; it creates stress for minorities in a majority dominant work culture because they must behave, speak, and dress differently. Toliver (1998) identifies a positive side of biculturalism in her study of black managers. She maintains that it may be beneficial for blacks to be able to draw on the strengths of two different communities on and off the job. Further, Toliver suggests that marginalization, rather than being a stressor, encouraged the sample she studied to believe that they were part of an elite group while growing up. They had advantages that others of similar ethnic and racial backgrounds lacked, and they were expected to succeed in future careers and in life.

American Indians typically do not view biculturalism as an advantage. Colonization forced them to adapt to a majority culture that espoused values in conflict with their own. Though the cultures of specific tribal nations differ, they invariably emphasize cooperation, group identification, responsibility for friends and extended family members, and tradition (LaFromboise, Heyle, & Ozer, 1990). These characteristics contrast with the majority culture's emphasis on competition, individual achievement, and consumerism.

Acculturation is the process through which people, particularly immigrants or racial/ethnic minorities, adapt to the dominant culture or choose not to do so. As was discussed in chapter 4, *assimilation* is an acculturation strategy involving immersion in and acceptance of the mainstream culture. *Integration* means being immersed in both the dominant and minority cultures; *marginalization*, linked with the highest stress levels, implies a rejection of both cultures. *Separation* involves a focus on the minority and rejection of the majority culture (Sutton, undated).

Whether or not the acculturation process is a stressor has been debated. It seems to be for Mexican American women, who risk losing support of their ethnic group, and for Native American women. According to Zambrana, Scrimshaw et al. (1997, p. 1024), "risky health behaviors, stress levels, and medical risks all seemed to increase with greater acculturation and decreases in social support of the Hispanic community." LaFromboise, Heyle, and Ozer (1990) report that acculturation has led some male Native Americans to try to dominate female Native Americans and has eroded the complementary relationship that previously existed between the sexes. Other studies, however, show more stress among less acculturated individuals (Tran, Fitzpatrick, et al, 1996). Native American women seem to deal with acculturation better than their male peers. LaFromboise, Heyle, and Ozer (1990) suggest this is due to Native women's traditionally greater role flexibility, which made them willing to assume roles that Native men would have spurned.

Minority status is a social stressor for Asian American refugees and immigrants, but Kuo (1995) laments that little research has systematically analyzed its impact. Racial/ethnic minority and socioeconomic status combine with institutional role expectations to form a social stratification system, or hierarchical "pecking order." Having "low status" in this system is a stressor (Kuo).

"Negative synergy" may explain why stressors associated with being female and a member of a racial/ethnic minority group may be more harmful than an additive model implies. It may place their career progress in "double jeopardy." Few studies have been done on such individuals, but Davidson's (1997) comparison of black and white managerial women shows that both groups rank being undervalued or underutilized among their top three stressors. Beyond that, stressors differ between the two groups. In addition to work overload, mentioned earlier, performance pressure, powerlessness, and a need to be three times as qualified to get the same job as whites complete the top five stressors for executive black women. For their white counterparts, the top five stressors included being the boss, having to acquire and use managerial styles considered "masculine," and being assertive and confident.

Some work and non-work-related stressors, such as the threat of terrorism and workplace violence and the effects of immigration on racial/ethnic minorities, are beyond the scope of this book. They are real concerns, but because volumes could be written about either, they will not be addressed here.

Work-Related Stressors

Work-related stressors appear in Figure 11.1. Change and resulting lack of control may be overriding factors that affect each category of stressor (Stockdale, Murphy, Cleveland, et al., 2000). Job stressors may be quantitative, such as work overload or under-load, or qualitative. Either a lack of skills to accomplish a task or repetitive, boring work could be qualitative stressors. The quality of the job experience, not just the quantity of work, helps determine whether it challenges incumbents or provokes strain. Jobs featuring energizing work on diverse tasks, an opportunity to learn, a sense of achievement, and a match between the incumbent's interests and abilities and job requirements have beneficial effects on women's health (Barnett & Baruch, 1987). Similarly, women who perform "substantively complex" jobs independently and feel valued have "the highest levels of well-being" (Lennon, 1987).

Decision latitude and psychological demands influence whether jobs are considered challenging or too taxing. *Skill discretion*, the opportunity to use different skills on the job, and *task authority*, the ability to make decisions affecting one's work, comprise decision latitude (Karasek & Theorell, 1990). Jobs are placed in one of four quadrants of a grid based on whether psychological demands and decision latitude are relatively low or high. Those featuring high psychological demands and high control are no more stressful than average. Attorneys' and accountants' jobs fit in this category (Stockdale, Murphy, Cleveland, et al., 2000); perhaps higher level managerial jobs also could be placed in this quadrant. Lower level managerial jobs may be characterized by high psychological demands but low control; such jobs are most stressful. Mail carrier and restaurant server fit in this quadrant (Stockdale, Murphy, Cleveland, et al.), as may administrative assistant, or secretarial, jobs. Smith (2001) includes manager, nurse, and teacher among the most stressful in the economy due to high demands and low control.

Inter- or intra-role conflict, ambiguity, and role incongruity are examples of role demands. *Inter-role conflict* occurs when demands of two different roles clash. For example, if the job requires attendance at a reception outside normal working hours at the same time an employee plans to have dinner with her daughter to celebrate a special occasion, that employee may experience inter-role conflict between the roles of parent and employee. *Intra-role conflict* may occur when competing priorities exist at work and synergy is not possible. Spending time on one priority means less is available to devote to the other. *Ambiguity* means uncertainty about tasks to be accomplished or the best ways to complete them. First-time managers typically must deal with much ambiguity.

Because the percentage of women and men in management, overall, is nearly equal in the U.S., women in leadership roles should no longer be viewed as incongruous. Nevertheless, those who have rigid notions of prescribed and proscribed gender-related stereotypes still may perceive role incongruity when they see women in top leadership roles. They also may perceive role incongruity among men whose active involvement with their families necessitates leaving work early or being unavailable for work-related travel.

Challenges associated with maintaining relationships with bosses, coworkers, and subordinates are interpersonal stressors. Harassment, discussed in chapter 3, is an extreme example of a maladaptive approach to such sources of stress. Managers, by definition, must get things done through others, so their jobs are susceptible to relationship stressors. They must reward, motivate, discipline, and gain cooperation from employees, listen to their concerns, mediate disagreements, and evaluate performance. Interpersonal or personality conflicts may occur during any of those activities. If they are *functional conflicts*, in which people ultimately resolve differences, they may be productive. *Dysfunctional conflicts*, the goal of which is to attack and discredit those with opposing views, are counterproductive and create distress (Karsten, 1994).

Conflicts with supervisors tend to induce more distress than those with coworkers (Kelloway, Sivanathan, et al., 2005), and women may be more upset than men by interpersonal conflict (Almeida & Kessler, 1998). However, this tendency may not exist for managerial women who have adopted leadership styles similar to those of male peers. Managers' relationships with colleagues may induce stress. Peers may create tension by exerting group pressure to punish workplace nonconformists.

Advantages of diversity management were described in chapter 4, but if a workforce characterized by gender, ethnicity/race, age, and lifestyle diversity is not handled well, relationships may become strained. In that context, *diversity stress* is defined as difficulty caused by uncertainty about the nature of a multicultural situation and appropriate responses (DeFrank & Ivancevich, 1998).

Stressors associated with the physical environment on the job are self-explanatory. They include inadequate ventilation, extreme temperatures, and noise (Karsten, 1994). Hazards from malfunctioning equipment, potential dangers due to lax security measures, and problems associated with new technology use also may be included in this category. Technological change and use of new equipment may lead to negative consequences in some; others will react positively. Proper ergonomic techniques are important to avoid strain; in addition, appropriate lighting and periodic exercise will help avoid physical strain associated with overuse of video display terminals.

Common career stressors are job insecurity, obsolescence, lack of promotion and inadequate mobility. Fear of losing one's job is visceral, but in the labor market of the early 21st century, the best guarantee of future employability is lifelong learning to sharpen existing skills and develop new ones. Though career ladders are much shorter than they were in the mid 20th century, some still mistakenly equate success with the number of promotions received. With such a mindset, disappointment is inevitable. Employees should be encouraged to adopt a more realistic view of career progress and may need to broaden their concept of success.

Aspects of an organization's structure, culture, and practices may become stressors. For example, spreading responsibility for accomplishment of a major project to many units without assuring coordination could be a structural stressor (Stockdale, Murphy, Cleveland, et al., 2000). A closed, authoritarian culture would be a stressor for many. Failure to define performance criteria, development of vague criteria after an evaluation period ends, rather than at the outset, or distribution of rewards based on "politics" or "popularity" rather than on clear contributions to the organization's goals also are stressors (Gamse, 2003).

WORK LIFE INTERFACE

The work-life interface is labeled as such to emphasize the fact that boundaries or borders exist between work and home regardless of whether or not employees currently have responsibilities toward members of a nuclear or extended family. Single employees who live alone may have parents, stepparents, or other relatives who may need their assistance in the future. As Boyar, Maertz, et al. (2003, p. 177) state, "All employees have the potential to experience work-family conflict and should not be excluded because they are unmarried, do not have children living at home, or their spouse [assuming they have one] does not work."

The focus of this section is on conflict that occurs at the work-life or work-family interface. Two distinct variables have been identified: *work-family* and *family-work* conflict. They are both types of inter-role conflict that occurs when demands of one role make fulfilling requirements of the other difficult (Bellavia & Frone, 2005). In the 1990s, 25%-50% of individuals in the U.S. from ages 25 to 54 who did not live alone and were employed at least 20 hours per week faced work-family conflict (WFC). In contrast, only about 10–14% experienced family-work conflict (FWC) (Bellavia & Frone).

Two features of work-family boundaries or borders affect conflict and integration levels and ease of transition in either direction, namely flexibility and permeability. Those working from home have greater *boundary flexibility*, which means they have more discretion regarding where and when they work. *Permeability* refers to the degree to which work interferes with personal or family life and vice versa (Clark, 2000). Flexibility and permeability promote integration and ease work-home transitions (and vice versa) but also may be associated with increased conflict. Employees retain some control over boundary permeability, however. Those working at home can establish rules to minimize interruptions from other household members while they are engaged in job-related tasks.

Interestingly, WFC relates positively to FWC, but the latter is inversely related to the former (Boyar, Maertz, et al., 2003). This could be because family boundaries are easier than work boundaries to infiltrate. When work prevents employees from performing their family roles adequately, a spillover of negativity may result. Conflict that originates in the family is less likely to spill over to work because "employees make adjustments in their home lives rather than their work lives, since the immediate effect is less damaging to [their] livelihood" (Boyar, Maertz, et al., p.180).

Certain factors increase the odds of WFC, FWC, or both, and others have a protective effect. Negative affectivity, list-making, and use of avoidance or resignation as coping techniques are linked to WFC and FWC. It seems reasonable that negative moods and perceptions and passive responses could increase these types of conflict, but their association with list-making seems counterintuitive initially. People habitually underestimate the amount of time it will take to complete tasks, however (Buehler, Griffin & Ross, 1994). When they see many remaining tasks on "to-do" lists, they feel as if they have lost control, which may increase perceptions of work-family conflict or vice versa (Adams & Jex, 1999). A preference for being organized negatively associates with WFC and FWC (Bellavia & Frone, 2005). Preoccupied attachment styles, in which people think of one domain while physically in the other, increase the chance of FWC (Sumer & Knight, 2001) as do marital tension, number of children, unavailability of childcare, and criticisms or burdens imposed by family members (Grzywacz & Marks, 2000).

Psychological involvement in the job, low levels of supervisory support for those who are highly involved with their work, job dissatisfaction, and work overload increase the risk of WFC (Grzywacz & Marks, 2000). Factors such as "hardiness," supervisory support, and "informal accommodation of work to family" reduce the risk of WFC (Bernas & Major, 2000). Conscientiousness (Bruck & Allen, 2003) lessens the chances of FWC as do perceptions of instrumental and emotional support (Bernas & Major).

Among other criticisms of studies on WFC and FWC, Boyar, Maertz et al. (2003, p. 177), indicate that "measurement of family responsibility has been deficient." They advocate examining the number of people residing in a household rather than number of children to avoid underestimating the effects of providing in-home care for an elderly relative or the children of a sibling (Boyar, Maertz et al.). Perhaps extent of physical and/or mental disabilities of those living in the home also should be considered.

Little evidence supports the role of gender as a mediating variable between predictors and outcomes of WFC or FWC according to Bellavia and Frone (2005). That may be true in the U.S., but a study of over 12,000 employees in the Netherlands shows that predictors of WFC differ by gender. Overtime, amount of commuting time, physical demands, and the presence of dependent children increase the likelihood of WFC for women there. Job insecurity, shift work, full responsibility for household duties, and accountability for the care of a chronically ill child in the home predict WFC for men (Peeters, M.C.W., de Jonge, J., et al., 2004).

Joint outcomes of FWC and WFC are marked with an asterisk on Table 11.2. In addition, WFC is negatively related to organizational commitment (Anderson, Coffey, & Byerly, 2002); FWC is inversely related to self-reported performance and positively linked to absenteeism (O'Driscoll, Ilgen, & Hildreth, 1992).

The last work-life interface issue to be addressed is *stress contagion*, or crossover. Unlike spillover, in which distress in one role, such as work, causes stress associated with personal or family roles to rise within one person, *crossover* occurs when increased distress in one spouse or partner leads to higher distress in the other (Westman, 2002). For example, a managerial woman whose spouse is a health care professional experiences distress when her husband is called to the hospital where he is employed after normal working hours to assist in life-threatening situations.

Westman (2002) indicates that crossover is somewhat more likely to go from husband to wife than vice versa, perhaps because women are more likely to provide social support and to empathize with their husbands' stress. It is premature to suggest that women who have been socialized to accept the "feminine" gender role and internalized gender stereotypes might be more susceptible to stress contagion, but future research to prove or disprove this idea might be productive.

Non-work Related Stressors

Categorizing "major life events" and "daily hassles" as non-work related stressors may be inaccurate, because some of each may be job-related. This section, however, will focus primarily on life events and daily irritations that occur off the job.

Major life events that are stressors are typically evaluated on checklists or scales. One example is the Holmes and Rahe Social Readjustment Rating

Scale (SRRS), developed more than 35 years ago to assess the amount of life stress in a year. Most stressors listed in the SRRS relate to personal, not organizational, factors. Scale items include a spouse's death, a major personal accomplishment, or the birth or adoption of a child. Unlike some checklists, the SRRS assigns a weight to each event. For example, a speeding ticket counts 11. A spouse's death is weighted 100 (Holmes & Rahe, 1967 as reported in Karsten, 1994).

As Craeger (1991) reported, Witkin, a researcher, added some items to the SRRS and considered the fact that some stressors may have a different impact on women than men. Responsibility for preparation for major holidays was added as a stressor. Until recently, women typically made special foods, bought gifts, and prepared to entertain, regardless of their employment status. Such duties can be time-consuming for anyone who assumes them. Other stressors added to the SRRS in the late 1980s or early 1990s are single parenthood, crime victim status, chemical dependence, and the process of parenting teens.

The likelihood of becoming ill or being injured in the next two years is linked to the overall SRRS score if people do not alter their stress responses. Those who score at least 300 have an 80% chance of becoming seriously ill in the future if they continue their current response pattern to stressors. If effective coping mechanisms are used, high SRRS scores may not necessarily result in sickness or injury, however (Karsten, 1994).

The adequacy of major life events checklists in measuring stressors has been debated since the 1970s (Turner & Avison, 2003). After acknowledging that the "massive" stress literature supports a connection between social stress, as evaluated by a major life events checklist, and mental problems, Turner and Avison question whether results would differ based on gender, race/ethnicity, and socioeconomic status. Their examination of recent life events, chronic stressors, total lifetime major events, daily discrimination, and total stress in a sample of 900 young black and white males and females shows that reliance on "recent life events systematically and dramatically underestimates the significance of social stress for the mental health of young adults" and that "checklist scores yield substantially biased estimates of total stress exposure across gender, race/ethnicity, and socioeconomic status" (Turner & Avison, p.498).

Measuring exposure to recent life events alone with no consideration of chronic stressors implies that men experience slightly more total stress (Turner & Avison, 2003), but this may not be true. Stress components tend to offset one another. For example, though men witness more violence and are more likely to report exposure to traumatic events, they seem to have less social stress than women. Because women are more likely than men to be affected by stressful events that happen to friends, coworkers, and relatives, they tend to report more strain-producing major and recent life events and more deaths on the SRRS (Turner & Lloyd, 1995).

In Turner & Avison's study, blacks' reported levels of nearly every type of stress analyzed exceeded those of whites. An inverse relationship occurred between reported stress and socioeconomic status. Respondents in the lowest third based on socioeconomic status showed higher levels of every stress measure than those in the middle or top third (Turner & Avison, 2003). "Limiting stress measurement to a checklist of recent events significantly overestimates total stress exposure among women relative to men and systematically underestimates such exposure among African Americans relative to whites and among persons of lower socioeconomic status relative to their more advantaged counterparts," according to Turner and Avison (p. 496).

Some disagree with the idea that major life events are the most crucial determinants of dysfunctional stress. They contend that the cumulative effect of small, repeated irritations such as traffic congestion or minor disagreements can be more harmful (Schaefer, Coyne, & Lazarus, 1981). Consistent with this view are the ideas that the "mental health effect of chronic stress can be stronger than acute stress" (Mossakowski, 2003, p. 320) and minor instances of racial discrimination may "have greater effects on health outcomes than their magnitude may suggest" (Meyer, 2003, p. 264). Further, Meyer questions the value of scales measuring daily annoyances because they may be influenced by people's moods at the time and notes that many researchers refuse to use them. Perceptions of daily hassles as stressors may differ based on race/ethnicity. Non-managerial Asian American women report higher levels than people of any other ethnic group (Thompson, 2002).

MODERATING FACTORS

Individual characteristics and behaviors that may moderate the effect of stressors on perceived stress and its consequences to be discussed are agentic and instrumental characteristics, self-efficacy and self-esteem, ethnic identity, hardiness, locus of control, negative affectivity, perfectionism, Type A behavior, and workaholism. Available literature will be summarized, but readers are cautioned that imprecise definitions may lead to overlap or confounding of moderating factors. Further, the literature has many gaps. A few studies examine the effects of individual characteristics and behaviors on stress among managers; some look at the impact on employees in general. Research on stress and managerial women has typically focused on white women; research on executive women of color related to factors that have a buffering effect on the impact of stressors on perceived stress is rare.

Agentic and instrumental characteristics are similar and are related to efficacy. Though the word does not appear in common collegiate dictionaries,
"agentic" is most likely a modification of *agency*, derived from *agere*, a Latin
verb meaning "to act." Optimism, self-efficacy, and instrumentality have
been called "*agentic traits*" (Long, 1998). One definition of *instrumentality* is
"agency or means;" assertiveness and confidence are examples of instrumental characteristics according to Portello and Long (2001). Efficacy is the
power to produce a desired effect; *self-efficacy* is one's belief that he or she
can carry out a task or behavior successfully (Bandura, 1982). All three terms
imply action and accomplishment. Managerial women have stronger agentic
qualities than female clerical workers, according to Long (1998). Such characteristics are associated with more positive views of the work environment
and fewer reported daily annoyances (Long, Kahn, & Schutz., 1992).

Contrary to expectations, Portello and Long (2001) indicate that executive
women who score high on instrumental qualities evaluate interpersonal conflict as more troubling than those scoring lower after effects of *negative affectivity*, or negative moods, are removed. This may stem from a belief that,
as managers, they should be able to deal effectively with interpersonal relations and frustration when doing so is difficult (Portello & Long).

The impact of self-efficacy as a moderating variable is mixed. It reduces
effects of role overload on anxiety and tension among military staff (Jex,
Bliese, et al., 2001) but does not mitigate the effects of stressors on strain
among educational employees (Jex & Gudanowski, 1992).

Self-esteem, the extent to which people value and like themselves, decreases the chance that stressors will result in distress. Low self-esteem is
linked to anxiety, depression, (Pierce, Gardner, et al., 1993) reduced self-efficacy, and an increased desire to please others (Jex, Cvetanovski & Allen,
1994). Compared to men in the workforce, employed women are more likely
to believe that others hold them in high regard. Because managerial women
typically occupy lower ranked positions than male peers and get relatively little recognition, however, they may have lower self-assessments and therefore
may not benefit from the buffering effect of high self-esteem to the same degree that men do (Fielden & Cooper, 2002).

Racial discrimination affects self-esteem, especially among African Americans. In a study of non-managerial African Americans, Simpson and Yinger
(1985) show a negative relationship between discrimination and both self-
esteem and life satisfaction. Nonetheless, 60% of Davidson's (1997) female
executive interviewees seem satisfied with their levels of self-confidence.

The situation is different for Chinese non-managerial women in Toronto
who have experienced discrimination. They are more likely to have reduced
self-esteem as compared to Chinese women who have not encountered

discrimination. Interestingly, weak evidence indicates that Chinese men who have been discriminated against have higher self-esteem than those who have not (Pak, Dion, & Dion, 1991).

For Filipino Americans (Mossakowski, 2003), urban Native American women (Walters & Simoni, 2002), and perhaps other groups, a strong ethnic identity buffers the effects of racial discrimination and prejudice on negative outcomes, such as depression. *Ethnic identity* is a high degree of commitment and strong connection to one's ethnic group as evidenced by knowledge of and pride in its heritage and culture and significant participation in its cultural events and practices (Mossakowski, 2003). Mossakowski suggests that it may be difficult for discrimination to affect the self-esteem of those with a strong ethnic identity because they immediately dismiss negative racial stereotypes as false. *Enculturation*, or the process through which minorities develop ethnic identity, helps Native American women avert depression and avoid psychological distress and alcoholism (Walters & Simoni). It also improves their self-esteem.

Hardiness is a characteristic attributed to managers which involves resilience, stress-resistance, and a positive view of change as a challenge to be mastered rather than something to be feared. Because it entails a sense of control over one's life, hardiness may be confounded with locus of control, to be discussed later. It includes a commitment to an important goal or activity (Beehr & Glazer, 2005). Evidence about whether or not hardiness mitigates the effects of stressors on strain is mixed, however.

Locus (literally "place") of control may be internal or external and is on a continuum. People with *an internal locus of control* believe their efforts have an impact on outcomes. They are achievement-oriented, responsible individuals who take the initiative to accomplish tasks (Cherrington, 1991). Those with an *external locus* believe they are without influence; events that are beyond their control simply occur. Managers are more likely than non-supervisory employees to have an internal locus of control (Kapalka & Lachenmeyer, 1988). As a result, they experience fewer psychological complaints (Weiten, 1989). Managerial women are less likely to have an internal locus of control than male counterparts, which puts them at heightened risk of developing psychological maladies (Hochwater, Perrewe, & Dawkins, 1995). Studies of managerial women which produced these results are based mainly on white women and may or may not generalize to women of color. In addition, executive women do not seem to have higher anxiety, hostility, or depression than non-managerial employees (Beatty, 1996.)

Negative affectivity is a tendency to view events pessimistically and is characterized by anger, anxiety, and depression. It colors perceptions of stressors and strain and is linked to frequent use of ineffective coping techniques among white executive women (Portello & Long, 2001). Whether negative affectivity is a moderator that should be factored out of studies analyzing the relationship between stressors and strains or a variable whose impact on strain is mediated by stressors is being debated. Removing it may only be appropriate if people with high negative affectivity report higher stress levels than those that actually exist (Cavanaugh, Boswell, Roehling, & Boudreau, 2000). Determining when this occurs seems nearly impossible because self-reported perceptions of strain are subjective by nature. Another unresolved question regarding negative affectivity that is measured via self-reports is whether those who have a high degree perceive additional stressors that others fail to see or choose work environments characterized by above average stress levels (Jex, Adams, & Ehler, 2002).

Women generally have more negative affectivity than men, but women in positions of low control are especially susceptible (Nelson & Burke, 2002). This may indicate that negative affectivity has less impact on executive females than on other female employees because management positions, particularly at higher levels, are characterized by a high degree of control.

Several studies show gender differences in depression and unhappiness with women reporting higher levels than men (Nolen-Hoeksema, 1987). These are based primarily on whites in various occupations and may or may not generalize to women and men in management. Perhaps women report more negative affectivity because it is more socially acceptable in the U.S. for women than for men to have intense emotions and express them openly (Jex, Adams, & Ehler, 2002). Though executive women may differ from the norm, women, with some exceptions, tend to mull over negative emotions and events more than men do, and rumination prolongs depressed moods (Almeida & Kessler, 1998). This inclination also may contribute to higher reported negative affectivity.

The next three moderating factors, perfectionism, Type A behavior, and workaholism, have some similarities. An inner compulsion to avoid error or accomplish as much as possible may be at the root of each.

Perfectionism, as a mindset, tolerates no mistakes. Three types of perfectionism are self-oriented, other-oriented, and socially prescribed. *Self-oriented perfectionists* expect themselves and their performance to be flawless; *other-oriented perfectionists* demand impeccable behavior of others and are harsh critics of anything less. *Socially prescribed perfectionists* believe that others require faultless behavior of them. Socially prescribed and self-oriented perfectionism have been linked to depression in studies of university students and psychiatric patients (Sherry, Hewitt et al., 2003). Women are more likely than men to have self-imposed standards of perfectionism (Nelson & Burke, 2002), but whether or not this finding generalizes to managerial women and men of various ethnicities remains unknown.

Type A behavior has been described as time-conscious, competitive, aggressive, and hard-driving. The "free floating hostility" associated with Type A behavior may be its most damaging characteristic; that part has been linked to increased coronary heart disease (Adler & Matthews, 1994).

Some studies show that women in management exhibit higher levels of Type A behavior than men (Rees & Cooper, 1990), but this may reflect differences in organizational environments. Environmental stressors and challenges that managerial women often face in environments numerically dominated by men may precipitate Type A behavior (Fielden & Cooper, 2002).

The coping method used moderates the effects of Type A behavior on strain. Executive women who employ *problem focused styles*, in which they attempt to resolve the difficulty directly and actively, reduce symptoms of strain. Those who resort to emotional approaches, in which they vent feelings, seek social support, and blame themselves, have more strain (Fielden & Cooper, 2002).

Three components characterizing *workaholics* are an inner compulsion to work and high involvement in and low enjoyment of work. In a study of primarily white female MBAs, Burke (1999) compares workaholics to "work enthusiasts," formerly dubbed "extra-effort people," and "enthusiastic workaholics." *Work enthusiasts* have high involvement and joy in work but do not feel driven; *enthusiastic workaholics* rate high on all three dimensions. Workaholic managerial women are less optimistic about future careers and less satisfied with their communities and friends than their counterparts who are work enthusiasts; they have less job, career, and family satisfaction than either work enthusiasts or enthusiastic workaholics (Burke). A direct relationship exists between feelings of being driven to work and poor physical and emotional well-being and between enjoyment in work and positive well-being (Burke).

Enactment of multiple roles simultaneously may buffer the negative effects of stress according to those who subscribe to the *expansion theory*. This is the idea that human energy is not "scarce" but is a renewable resource (Barnett & Baruch, 1987). Instead of draining energy, multiple roles replenish it. People gain resources from each of their roles. When career disappointments occur, employees can draw strength from their relationships. Becoming addicted to work due to personal problems is not recommended, but focusing on work temporarily may provide the perspective needed to objectively evaluate a personal situation.

Remaining moderating variables categorized as "other" include financial resources, management level, and dissolution of a marital relationship through death, divorce, or separation. Portello and Long (2001) present evidence that executive women who are married, have children, and have relatively high incomes evaluate stress more positively. How much of the favorable assessment is due to income level and how much is due to additional roles of wife and mother is unknown. Smith (2001) reports that stress rises as employees' salaries increase, but other studies contradict this. Female managers with relatively low financial resources who perceive the work environment as more demanding and less supportive are more likely to perceive relationship stressors as threats to their competence (Portello & Long, 2001).

As executive women are promoted, they are more likely to have jobs that encourage good health and positive environments. Female CEOs seem to have less global job stress than managerial women at lower levels (Nelson & Burke, 2000).

Dissolution of a marital relationship may be linked to stress long after it ends. A greater proportion of those who are widowed, separated, or divorced report high stress compared to those who are not (Smith, 2001). Smith's study does not report stress variations among single (never married), partnered, and currently married individuals.

Environmental factors

Environmental factors that may moderate the effect of stressors on strain include social support, job control, and organizational justice. The absence of any of these factors also may be considered stressors, and an organization may decide to provide them or increase their levels to help employees cope with stress. Social support may come from friends or relatives off the job, coworkers, or supervisors. Good supervisors provide task-related, emotional, informational, and appraisal support (Kelloway, Sivonathan, et al., 2005).

Perceived and actual support may differ. Perceived organizational support is a feeling that that the employer is concerned about workers and appreciates their contributions. This variable is negatively related to role conflict and role ambiguity among individuals with liaison, or boundary spanning, positions (Stamper & Johlke, 2003).

Black women's strong belief in responsibility to the black community may increase the social support available to aspiring black females. Bell and Nkomo (2000, p. 183) call the "geographic, social, and psychological space where African Americans lived, shared a collective history, and held a common understanding of the way of life in a black community" their "homeland." Successful black women are expected to "give back" to those in the homeland, and managerial black women's families have done so when they "joined with people in the homeland to give these women unconditional love, armored them to go out into the world and do their best, and told them stories of black people's painful struggles to achieve racial equality" (Bell &

Nkomo). The families and "homeland" community provided aspiring black women with emotional support that may have been lacking in the workplace.

Emotional support from a supervisor can reduce negative stress consequences that otherwise might result from a job in which employees have little control over the pace of work or the way in which tasks are done. This illustrates an interrelationship between two variables, each of which could serve as stressors or moderators depending on the circumstances. In this instance, lack of job control is the stressor, and support is the moderator. A high degree of job control may moderate high job demands to lessen stress. For example, managerial jobs are generally considered less stressful than clerical positions because managers have more job control.

Three types of *organizational justice*, defined as perceived fairness, are distributive, procedural, and interactional. *Distributive justice* refers to perceived equity in the allocation of outcomes, including the organization's resources and power. *Procedural justice* is related to the process through which resources are assigned, and perceived fairness of treatment and information provided in an interpersonal exchange or transaction is *interactional justice* (Cropanzano, Goldman, & Benson, 2005). When low job control is a stressor, perceived organizational justice may cushion its negative impact (Cropanzano, Goldman, & Benson). When one type of organizational injustice is a stressor, another type may buffer its negative effects. For example, perceived distributional justice may lessen the adverse effects of procedural injustice.

CONSEQUENCES OF STRESS

Though negative outcomes of stress are widely recognized, some organizational consequences may be positive, especially if the stress is "challenge-related" rather than "hindrance related." *Challenge-related stress* occurs when individuals perceive a positive net gain from potentially distress-provoking demands, such as work overload or a high degree of responsibility. In *hindrance-related stress*, the net result is negative.

A study of 1886 primarily male executives in large U.S. firms reveals that challenge-related stress is positively associated with job satisfaction and negatively linked to job search. The associations between hindrance-related stress, on one hand, and job satisfaction and job search, on the other, are in the opposite directions. An inverse relationship also exists between hindrance-related stress and voluntary turnover (Cavanaugh, Boswell, Roehling, & Boudreau, 2000). Both types of stress are negatively linked to extroversion and positively associated with neuroticism. The relatively small percentage of women in the sample report more challenge-related stress than the men do (Cavanaugh, Boswell, Roehling & Boudreau, 2000).

Another study of over 450 mainly white female non-managerial employees at a university again shows that challenge- and hindrance-related stress associate in opposite directions with certain work outcomes. Challenge-related stress is inversely related to job search, intent to quit, and work withdrawal behaviors, such as absenteeism and tardiness. It is positively associated with loyalty. Hindrance-related stress is negatively linked to loyalty and positively related to work withdrawal behaviors, job search, and voluntary turnover (Boswell, Olson-Buchanan, & LePine, 2004). Both types of stress seem related to anxiety and emotional exhaustion, two dimensions of psychological strain (Boswell, Olson-Buchanan, & LePine).

Prior to the research on challenge- and hindrance-related stress, empirical studies attempting to link work stress with negative organizational outcomes, such as job dissatisfaction, intent to quit, and job search, often failed to do so (Bretz, Boudreau, & Judge, 1994; Leong, Furnham & Cooper, 1996). Cavanaugh et al. (2000) maintain that this happened because both challenge- and hindrance-related stress were measured on the same scale. Since they have the opposite impact on work outcomes, they cancel each other out.

Women generally report a higher level of distress than men but have thus far maintained a longevity advantage of nearly eight years (Nelson & Burke, 2000). Though they are more willing to say they experience pressure, women do not report worse mental health than men unless they are employed in male-dominated industries and use an interpersonal leadership style (Gardiner & Tiggerman, 1999). They are, however, two to three times more likely than male peers to report a "history of affective disorders" (Almeida & Kessler, 1998). With some exceptions, women report more chronic maladies; those which men mention tend to be life threatening. Due to socialization, women may be more willing to report stress symptoms; men may be less likely to discuss health issues (Stockdale, Murphy, Cleveland, et al., 2000).

Stockdale, Murphy, Cleveland, et al. (2000) reject a biological explanation for varying reactions to work stress among women and men and offer a "structural" explanation instead. They say responses differ due to the extent that women have dissimilar organizational roles. More managerial women than men report stress as a consequence of their experience both on and off the job. When the unpaid "second shift" (Hochschild & Machung, 1989) of domestic and childcare duties, for which women are more likely to be responsible, is considered, women work longer than men. Long work hours affect both mental and physical health. Compared to non-managerial employed women, executive women seem to have better health outcomes, however. The association of multiple roles with a lowered risk of cardiovascular disease is especially strong among females in high status positions but has been noted for all employed women (Nelson & Burke, 2000).

Table 11.2 illustrates one possible way to categorize stress outcomes. Some items included may be both individual and organizational consequences; classifying them as one or the other is admittedly arbitrary. For example, an increased number of accidents or errors could have been categorized as an "individual behavioral consequence" instead of a consequence to the organization pertaining to performance quality and quantity. Similarly, job dissatisfaction could have been considered an organizational, rather than an individual, outcome.

As mentioned previously, until recently most studies of managerial stress were based on white males, and most research on executive females and stress did not consider women of color. For that reason, a shortage of research on outcomes of perceived stress on minorities and women of color exists. Table 11.2 summarizes negative consequences of perceived stress based on studies of various groups such as managers, employees, female employees, executive women, women of color, and specific minority groups, such as blacks, black executive women, Native American women, and Asian Americans. Unfortunately, empirical studies on stress outcomes are not readily available for each major racial/ethnic group by gender and occupation. For that reason, the summary in Table 11.2 is sketchy. Fontana (1989) enumerates negative outcomes that are commonly attributable to stress but does not cite empirical studies to verify the connection. They are included in Table 11.2, but readers are cautioned that supporting evidence for these consequences may or may not exist.

Notable by their absence from the table are studies pertaining to the effects of stress on Hispanics. A study of Hispanic immigrants was not used because issues they encounter are beyond this book's scope. The few other existing studies are not readily available.

Most items in Table 11.2 are self-explanatory; a few require elaboration, and an explanation is appropriate for some items that have been omitted. For example, *psychogenic disorders*, listed as adverse physical consequences of perceived stress to individuals, are physical illnesses that begin with a psychological problem (Stockdale, Murphy, Cleveland, et al., 2000). Reduced morale is listed as a stress outcome for managerial women in Table 11.2 but is believed to be an adverse consequence for employees generally. So is *burnout*, which does not appear in Table 11.2 but can be defined as extreme physical and mental exhaustion that hinders, or may prevent, effective job performance. Minor aches and pains, muscle twitches, excess perspiration (Beehr & Glazer, 2005), and digestive problems (Stockdale, Murphy, Cleveland, et al., 2000), though not listed in Table 11.2, are considered effects of stress on employees.

State workers' compensation laws were originally designed to provide prompt compensation for work-related physical injuries without assigning fault. Their coverage expanded to cover stress-related illness including emotional distress caused by workplace conditions. Because the number of claims due to on-the-job stress rose by the 1990s, over 30 states adopted more stringent standards which led to a reduction in such claims. For example, in Oregon, stress must be the "major contributing cause" of an injury or illness to be compensable (DeFrank & Ivancevich, 1998). Employee stress from justifiable human resource actions such as performance appraisal and discipline up to and including discharge are not compensable, even if they are handled poorly (DeFrank & Ivancevich). To prevail, stress-based workers' compensation claims increasingly must be related to unusual situations. DeFrank and Ivancevich give an example of a woman employed as a secretary in a major U.S. city who experienced ongoing psychological trauma, but no physical injuries, after a steel beam fell into her office. That was deemed extraordinary enough to warrant compensation.

COPING MECHANISMS

Coping mechanisms are methods to deal with stress at the individual or organizational level or at the interface between the two. This section will discuss positive, rather than dysfunctional, coping mechanisms. The latter may result in increased daily hassles (Portello & Long, 2001) or adverse stress consequences which appear in Table 11.2. *Individual coping* is the management of internal or external demands that are judged to exceed one's resources via cognitive or behavioral means (Lazarus & Folkman, 1984). *Organizational level coping* methods may include job redesign, adoption of alternative work schedules, or provision of benefits to help employees integrate or balance work and life, all of which were discussed in chapter 10.

Though different coping approaches can be identified, the process is complex, dynamic, and situation-specific (Fielden & Cooper, 2002). Personality, demographics, other individual characteristics, the context, and subjective evaluation of the situation greatly affect the effectiveness of the selected method(s). Coping also involves primary and secondary appraisal, which were described earlier in this chapter.

As previously indicated, coping methods are commonly classified as problem- or emotion-focused (Billings & Moos, 1981). Stockdale, Murphy, Cleveland, et al. (2000) add a third category of "appraisal-focused" methods, which others include as a subset of emotion-focused strategies.

Problem-focused methods address the issue directly. They involve planning, thinking positively, seeking information and advice, confronting others, and contacting civil rights organizations if the stressful event entails discrimination. These approaches are considered more effective than emotion-focused coping, but no method is appropriate in all situations. Problem oriented

Table 11.2.   Adverse Consequences of Stress

To the Individual:	To the Organization:
Physical	**Withdrawal**
Elevated blood pressure-6,7, 11	Increased absenteeism
Coronary heart disease-7,11	Increased tardiness
Headaches-10	Increased voluntary turnover
Psychogenic disorders-12	
Relatively short menstrual cycles-12	
Physical illness (skin disease, cancer)-3	
Raised risk of miscarriage, pre-eclampsia during pregnancy-2	
Low energy levels-9	
Decline in physical health*	
Psychological/Emotional	**Commitment**
Depression-3,5,6,8,10,11*	Reduced loyalty
Anxiety-3,5, 10, 11*	(hindrance related stress)
Anger/Frustration-3,10,11	Increased job search
Sleep disturbances-3,10,11	(hindrance related stress)
Exhaustion-3	Increased intent to quit
Mental fatigue-11	*(hindrance related stress)
Disappointment-10	Decreased job involvement
Increased psychological distress*	Decreased organizational commitment
Reduction in mental well-being*	
Suicidal thoughts-3	
Job dissatisfaction-3*	
Reduced morale-2	
Changes in personality characteristics-9	
Worsened existing personality problems-9	
Weakened emotional and moral constraints-9	
Decline in interest and enthusiasm-9	
Increased cynicism about clients, colleagues-9	
Life dissatisfaction*	
Decreased family satisfaction*	
Cognitive-9	**Performance Quality and Quantity**
Decreased concentration	Reduced productivity
Increased distractibility	Increased accident rate
New information is ignored	Increased error rate
Deterioration of long- and short-term memory	
Deterioration of long term planning ability	

Table 11.2. (*continued*)

To the Individual:	To the Organization:
Behavioral Increased substance abuse-4, 11* Increased conflict-4 Eating disorders-12 Smoking-2 Increased shifting of responsibility to others-9 "Bizarre" behavior patterns-9	**Legal and Medical Costs** Increased health care consumption Increased workers' compensation claims Increased number of lawsuits **Other** Increased employee theft Increased aggression Increased workplace violence

*Outcomes of Family-Work and Work-Family Conflict

Key for Table 11.2

1 = Managers	7 = Blacks
2 = Executive women	8 = Filipino Americans
3 = Black executive women	9 = Source-Fontana (1989) [may not be empirically based]
4 = Native Americans	10 = Asian Americans
5 = Native American women	11 = Non-managerial employees
6 = Women of color	12 = Employed women

strategies can be used only when people can take control; if that is impossible, emotion-oriented coping may be the only option. In general, men seem to use problem-focused strategies more than women (Vingerhoets & Van Heck, 1990), but there are exceptions. When dealing with racial discrimination, Asian American women are more likely than male counterparts to use problem-focused coping (Kuo, 1995).

Overall, *emotion oriented coping*, particularly readjustment of one's thoughts, is a dominant strategy among Asian Americans (Kuo, 1995). When facing discrimination, a majority in Kuo's (1995) study believe "things could be worse" and think that Asian Americans "are less victimized" than other minorities.

Use of problem- and emotion-based strategies also differs by nationality and education level among Asian Americans. Chinese Americans are less likely to use problem oriented approaches than Koreans; Koreans are more likely to use emotion based approaches than Filipinos, who have a propensity to use problem oriented strategies. Kuo (1995, p. 124) concludes as follows: "These inter-group differences suggest that despite their common Confucian heritage, ethnicity still has a role in influencing coping choices."

Contrary to popular belief, education, not socioeconomic status, relates to increased problem-focused coping (Kuo, 1995). Among Asian Americans, family income, another component of socioeconomic status, associates negatively with problem oriented strategies.

Ethnic identity is linked to problem-oriented coping among Hispanics. Those with higher levels deal with discrimination by refuting racist stereotypes and discussing it; those with lower levels try to ignore it (Mossakowski, 2003).

Emotion-focused coping tries to change emotions arising as a result of stressors. It may include "venting" (expressing feelings to trusted confidantes as a release), wishful thinking, self-blame, or meditation. Appraisal-oriented coping, defined as a separate category of coping by Stockdale et al. (2000) but included under emotion-focused methods here, may entail redefining the meaning of the stressful event or situation or avoidance techniques, such as directing energy elsewhere.

As indicated earlier, support-seeking may be either a moderating variable or a coping mechanism in the stress model. When regarded as the latter, it is usually categorized as an emotion-focused strategy. Greenglass (2002) identifies two types of support: emotional, which provides a forum for "venting" and empathic reaction to distress, and instrumental, which consists of advice and practical help. The latter seems similar to advice-seeking as a problem-focused strategy.

Nelson and Burke (2000) maintain that women are at a disadvantage in terms of social support because they experience added challenges finding mentors and role models and being accepted in informal networks. Workplace support seems to reduce work stress for men more than women even when both receive equal amounts (Nelson & Burke, 2000). Other research contradicts this finding, however. Research on federal employees links coworker support to instrumental and preventive coping among women, but not among men. Greenglass (2002), reporting on her study with Fiksenbaum, maintains that women's use of negative coping, such as wishful thinking, diminishes when coworkers support them. Female managers who are single parents have less support than peers in two-parent households. They are less likely to receive support from ex-spouses or partners and may obtain little from extended families. Nevertheless, they tend to make good use of support they do have, primarily provided by female friends (Gill & Davidson, 2001).

Unemployed managerial women engage in activities to provide both emotional and instrumental support to a greater degree than their male counterparts. They are more likely to work for volunteer organizations, which not only provide an outlet but also may lead to valuable contacts to aid the job search process. Unemployed male managers, on the other hand, "tend to actively refuse situations in which they would have access to social support, thereby denying themselves an effective means of coping" (Fielden & Cooper, 2001).

Social support was among the top coping methods female Native American college students used to deal with bicultural conflict in the late 1980s.

They also engaged in positive self-talk, worked harder, exercised, obtained professional counseling, and recalled beliefs about spirituality (LaFromboise, Heyle, & Ozer, 1990).

Overall, emotion-oriented approaches are linked to increased emotional distress (Fielden & Cooper, 2002), but specific methods may elicit such a response more than others. Obtaining social support through cultivation of close relationships, discussed here as an emotion-focused strategy, may have positive organizational and personal consequences. Women seek significantly more instrumental and emotional support than men (Greenglass, 2005), which may be advantageous in coping with stress. Requesting help also is more consistent with gender role socialization commonly experienced by women.

Approaches that Asian Americans employ to deal with the stress associated with racial discrimination have been discussed. Because of the shortage of easily accessible information on other racial/ethnic groups, only the experiences African Americans have had coping with the stress of discrimination will be mentioned. African Americans rely on different strategies to confront *individual racism*, which affects them personally, *institutional racism*, previously defined as policies that exclude them from full participation in society and enjoyment of societal benefits, or *cultural racism*, the belief in the "superiority" of the cultural practices of the dominant group (Jones, 1997).

African American women are more likely than men to seek social support in response to individual racism but prefer avoidance strategies to either problem-solving or social support (Utsey et al., 2000.) The preferred coping method for African American men is unstated. An earlier study shows that African Americans who have experienced discrimination adopt an avoidance strategy (Krieger & Sidney, 1996), but other research contradicts this. Feagin (1991) indicates that African Americans respond to individual racism with resigned acceptance or verbal counterattack; Lalonde, Majumder, and Parris (1995) suggest that black Canadians' preferred method of dealing with institutional racism is to seek social support.

Why do some African Americans prefer avoidance to more active coping strategies? They and other racial/ethnic minorities find direct confrontation costly in terms of time and energy, even when discrimination is serious. In an individualistic culture such as the U.S., which emphasizes competition and personal responsibility for success or failure, it is increasingly difficult to gain support for the idea that a negative outcome was caused by discrimination, rather than a personal shortcoming. Because discrimination is more subtle than it once was, white mid- to upper classes in the U.S. may be more likely to blame the person alleging discrimination for its existence than to consider the context or other societal factors contributing to the problem (Utsey et al., 2000).

ORGANIZATIONAL COPING:
STRESS MANAGEMENT INTERVENTIONS

Criticisms of stress management interventions are nearly as widespread as their use. Though they require a commitment of organizational resources and prospective consultants tout their advantages, "surprisingly little" (Hurrell, 2005) is known about their effectiveness due to methodological and other problems including inconsistent terminology. Systematic, rigorous evaluation of the effectiveness of stress management is lacking.

Arthur (2002, p. 556) indicates that many interventions "fail to deliver because they are superficial," and Dewe and O'Driscoll (2002) decry the fact that they are often administered on an "ad hoc" basis. Other concerns are that stress management programs are too narrow or invite legal liability (Bellarosa & Chen, 1997). Dewe and O'Driscoll (p. 161) raise relevant questions about liability. They ask:

> What thought, for example, has been given to such ethical issues as informed consent, anonymity and confidentiality, potential harm and the individual's right to withdraw or not attend? Where in the intervention process has attention been given to the individual's right to access information collected during the intervention and their right to know how that information may be used, not to mention the legal risks organizations face by failing to pay attention to such issues?

Some organizational interventions, such as equitable development and reward systems, workplace programs to provide social support and networking opportunities, zero tolerance for harassment, and concern for work-life integration, are recommended for organizations that wish to provide a welcoming environment for executive women (Nelson & Burke, 2000). These simply reflect good management practice, assuming they are the result of an analysis of needs of a particular workforce, not instituted as "one size fits all" measures. Finally, lack of top management support and employees who are unwilling to participate will quickly derail stress management. Support from the top is crucial to the success of stress management, as it is for most organizational processes.

Preventive (proactive) or *curative* (reactive) *stress management* interventions may be implemented at the individual, work group, or organizational level. Individual level techniques are used most often, perhaps because some managers believe that reinforcing the mindset that stress is an individual problem absolves them from responsibility for dealing with it. In the long run, this idea may cause problems because the context seems to influence employees' stress perceptions (Long, 2001). Individual level interventions may be more effective than those implemented organization-wide, however (Van der Klink et al., 2001).

Primary preventive approaches are intended to reduce the risks of damage from stressors or eliminate them, whereas *secondary preventive measures* help employees manage their responses to stressors. *Curative interventions* promote healing after employees have been harmed by strain. They have been called tertiary preventive measures (Nelson & Burke, 2000), but due to their after-the-fact nature, this seems a misnomer. Preventive interventions may include one or several of the following: relaxation, physical fitness, exercise, biofeedback, cognitive restructuring, meditation, assertiveness training, and time management. Stress awareness/ education is another preventive measure (Bellarosa & Chen, 1997: Cartwright & Cooper, 2005).

Progressive relaxation involves systematically tensing and relaxing muscle groups to obtain a calming response. For high control employees, cognitive restructuring seems more effective in stress reduction than relaxation, however, according to a meta-analysis of 48 studies of stress interventions (Van der Klink et al., 2001). Interventions that include relaxation seem to be most effective in combating negative physiological or psychological effects of stress, and ninety-six stress management experts rank relaxation as most practical, easiest to implement, and least costly (Bellarosa & Chen, 1997).

Physical fitness entails monitoring, exercise, and good nutrition to increase cardiovascular and respiratory endurance. Previously mentioned stress management experts rank physical fitness most effective in achieving five of seven objectives including individual fitness and physiological indices, reduction of negative symptoms, enhancement of psychological well-being, reduction of health care cost, and organizational effectiveness and image (Bellarosa & Chen, 1997). Exercise may be viewed as part of physical fitness or considered a separate stress management technique. It is generally thought to be helpful in reducing stress. For example, Atchiler & Motta (1994) show that anxiety levels dropped after one session of aerobic exercise. Even exercise is not recommended in all circumstances, however. In group settings, certain types of exercise can increase competitiveness and aggression, particularly among those with Type A tendencies (Cartwright & Whatmore, 2003).

Biofeedback is included in fewer than 5% of stress management programs. It measures physiological changes in muscle and skin to provide information about the physical effects of stress interventions and is typically used along with relaxation methods (Cartwright & Cooper, 2005).

Cognitive restructuring involves changing perceptions of stress to build resilience. Unwarranted negativity is systematically replaced by more rational thoughts. This strategy seems most effective among individuals whose jobs have a high degree of decision latitude, such as managers (Van der Klink, et al., 2001). Sixty-seven percent of stress management experts use cognitive restructuring "always," "constantly," or "often" compared to 59% who say the same about physical fitness, 56% for relaxation, and 35% for meditation (Bellarosa & Chen, 1997).

Meditation is focusing on one repetitive stimulus to prevent distraction and induce calmness. It is similar to physical relaxation but employs mental exercises to achieve the same end (Van der Klink et al., 2001).

Assertiveness training, discussed in chapter 7, is fairly widely used. Nevertheless, stress management experts do not consider it a very effective intervention (Van der Klink et al., 2001).

Stress awareness/education incorporates preventive techniques such as relaxation, exercise, and biofeedback. Factual information, such as that presented in this chapter regarding the pervasiveness of stress, its causes, positive and negative consequences, and coping mechanisms, is provided.

Managing time more effectively sounds easy but can be challenging. After re-assessing priorities, those who wish to use time wisely might benefit by asking themselves these questions:

1. Must these duties be done? Are they necessary?
2. If they are necessary, can they be done less often?
3. Regardless of whether or not they can be done less often, can they be delegated?

If activities are essential, doing them less frequently saves time. For example, a professor whose department thought it was desirable to publish an alumni newsletter decided to do so only twice per year instead of three times, saving both time and funds. If work-related duties can be delegated, it is wise to abandon perfectionism and assign them to others. Professionals who can afford to hire help to do household and other chores should do so. In many cases, the time gained is well worth the money spent.

Employee assistance programs (EAPs) are invariably part of curative stress interventions, but Bento (1997) quips that doubt exists about whether they help employers or employees. To control costs, "gatekeepers" of employee assistance programs may be reluctant to refer individuals to social workers, psychologists, and psychiatrists, whose help, more than that of professionals with less training, benefits employees experiencing the negative consequences of stress (Seligman, 1995). Among the few studies assessing the effectiveness of EAPs is one that attributes reduced absenteeism, fewer health claims, and savings to their use (Landy, Quick, and Kasl, 1994). In another, a life insurance company reports $4.23 in claims savings for every dollar invested in an EAP (Intindola, 1991).

So far, stress management interventions have been discussed for employees in general, not necessarily managers let alone executive women or racial/ethnic minorities in management. Nelson and Burke (2000) outline suggestions for executive women who are interested in primary and secondary stress prevention and in curative measures. They suggest cognitive restructuring, self-analysis to identify personal stressors and develop plans for alleviation, and acceptance of positions with high visibility and developmental opportunities to reduce the risk of dysfunctional stress. Palliative measures recommended include meditation, conversations with trusted individuals to reduce the tendency to obsess or ruminate, and daily exercise. As a precaution, Nelson and Burke (2000) also urge executive women to develop relationships with physicians, psychologists, and other professionals before their services are needed in much the same way as they would develop contacts with tax lawyers or accountants on the job.

SUMMARY

This chapter begins with an overview of the prevalence and cost of workplace stress. A comprehensive model of stress is presented to explain how work- and non-work related stressors and those related to the work/life interface lead to perceived stress, which has individual and organizational consequences. The process is affected by moderating factors and coping mechanisms, which may interact to reduce or worsen stress. The same factor may be a moderating variable and a coping mechanism; for example, social support can be both. Moderating factors may be individual characteristics and behaviors or organizational variables such as the amount and type of social support, job control, and organizational power. Individual coping methods may be problem-focused or emotion-oriented; organizational coping includes stress management interventions that may be preventive or curative.

Stress-related issues relevant to ethnic and racial minorities and women are integrated throughout the chapter. For example, racism, discrimination, and biculturalism are stressors of particular concern to minorities; racism also may affect self-esteem, a moderating factor. Ethnic identity may buffer the negative effects of stress. Gender issues related to negative affectivity, another moderating variable, are discussed. Managerial women in low or middle level positions report more stress than men; executive females at top levels seen to experience less than women at lower levels.

REFERENCES

Adams, G.A. & Jex, S.M. 1999. Relationships between time management, control, work-family conflict, and strain. *Journal of Occupational Health Psychology, 4.* 72–77.

Adler, N. & Matthews, K. 1994. Health psychology: Why do some people get sick and some stay well? *Annual Review of Psychology, 45.* 229–59.

Almeida, D.M. & Kessler, R.C. 1998. Everyday stressors and gender differences in daily distress. *Journal of Personality and Social Psychology, 75*(3).

American Institute of Stress. 2002. *Job stress.* New York: Author.

Anderson, S.E., Coffey, B.S. & Byerly, R.T. 2002. Formal organizational initiatives and informal workplace practices: Links to work-family conflict and job-related outcomes. *Journal of Management, 28.* 787–810.

Arthur, A.R. 2002. Mental health problems and British workers: A survey of mental health problems in employees who receive counseling from employee assistance programs. *Stress and Health,18*(2). 69–75.

Atchiler, L. & Motta, R. 1994. Effects of aerobic and non aerobic exercise on anxiety, absenteeism, and job satisfaction. *Journal of Clinical Psychology, 50*(6). 829–40.

Bandura, A. 1982. Self-efficacy mechanism in human agency. *American Psychologist, 37.*122–47.

Barnett, R. & Baruch, G. 1987. Social roles, gender, and psychological distress. 122–41. In R. Barnett, L. Biener & G. Baruch. Eds. *Gender and Stress.* New York: The Free Press.

Beatty, C.A. 1996. The stress of managerial and professional women: Is the price too high? *Journal of Organizational Behavior, 17*(3). 233–51.

Beehr, T.A. & Glazer, S. 2005. Organizational role stress. 7–34. In J. Barling, E. K. Kelloway & M.R. Frone, Eds. *Handbook of Work Stress.* Thousand Oaks, CA: Sage.

Bell, E. & Nkomo, S. 2000. *Our separate ways: Black and white women and the struggle for professional identity.* Cambridge, MA: Harvard Business School Press.

Bellarosa, C. & Chen, P.Y. 1997. The effectiveness and practicality of occupational stress management interventions: A survey of subject matter expert opinions. *Journal of Occupational Health Psychology, 2*(3).

Bellavia, G.M. & Frone, M.R. 2005. Work-family conflict. 113–48. In J. Barling, E.K. Kelloway & M.R. Frone, Eds. *Handbook of Work Stress.* Thousand Oaks, CA: Sage.

Bento, R.F. 1997. On the other hand. . . The paradoxical nature of employee assistance programs. *Employee Assistance Quarterly, 13*(2). 83–91.

Bernas, K.H. & Major, D.A. 2000. Contributors to stress resistance: Testing a model of women's work-family conflict. *Psychology of Women Quarterly, 24.* 170–78.

Billings, A. & Moos, R. 1981. The role of coping responses and social resources inattenuating the stress of life events. *Journal of Behavioral Medicine, 4.* 157–89.

Boswell, W.R., Olson-Buchanan, J.B. & LePine, M.A. 2004. Relations between stress and work outcomes: The role of felt challenge, job control, and psychological strain. *Journal of Vocational Behavior, 64.* 165–91.

Boyar, S.L., Maertz, C.P., Jr., Pearson, A.W. & Keough, S. 2003. Work and family domain variables and turnover intentions. *Journal of Managerial Issues, 15*(2).

Bretz, R.D., Boudreau, J.W. & Judge, T.A. 1994. Job search behavior of employed managers. *Personnel Psychology, 47.* 275–301.

Bruck, C.S. & Allen, T.D. 2003. The relationship between big five personality traits, negative affectivity, type A behavior, and work-family conflict. *Journal of Vocational Behavior, 63.* 457–72.

Buehler, R., Griffin, D. & Ross, M. 1994. Exploring the "planning fallacy": Why people underestimate their task completion times. *Journal of Personality & Social Psychology, 67.* 366–81.

Burke, R.J. 1999. Workaholism among women managers: Work and life satisfactions and psychological well-being. *Equal Opportunities International, 18*(7). 25–35.

Cartwright, S. & Cooper, C. 2005. Individually targeted interventions. 607–22. In J. Barling, E. K. Kelloway & M.R. Frone, Eds. *Handbook of Work Stress.* Thousand Oaks, CA: Sage.

Cartwright, S. & Whatmore, L. 2003. Stress and individual differences: Implications for stress management. In A. Antoniou & C.L. Cooper. Eds. *New perspectives in the area of occupational health.* London: Wiley.

Cavanaugh, M.A., Boswell, W.R., Roehling, M.V. & Boudreau, J.W. 2000. An empirical examination of self-reported work stress among U.S. managers. *Journal of Applied Psychology, 85*(1). 65–74.

Cherrington, D.J. 1991. Needs theory of motivation. In R.M. Steers & L.W. Porter, Eds. *Motivation and work behavior.* New York: McGraw-Hill.

Clark, S.C. 2000. Work-family border theory: A new theory of work/family balance. *Human Relations, 53.* 747–70.

Cooper, C.L., Sloan, S.J. & Williams, S. 1988. *Occupational stress indicator: Management guide.* Windsor, Berks.:NFER-Nelson.

Craeger, E. 1991, October 8. Women and stress. *Wisconsin State Journal.* 1C.

Cropanzano, R., Goldman, B.M. & Benson III, L. Organizational justice. 63–88. In J. Barling, E. K. Kelloway & M.R. Frone, Eds. *Handbook of Work Stress.* Thousand Oaks, CA: Sage.

Davidson, M.J. 1997. *The Black and Ethnic Minority Woman Manager: Cracking the Concrete Ceiling.* London: Paul Chapman.

Davidson, M.J. & Cooper, C.L. 1992. *Shattering the glass ceiling: The woman manager.* London: Paul Chapman.

DeFrank, R.S. & Ivancevich, J.M. 1998. Stress on the job: An executive update. *The Academy of Management Executive, 12*(3). 55–67.

Dewe, P. & O'Driscoll, M. 2002. Stress management interventions: What do managers actually do? *Personnel Review, 31*(1/2). 143–62.

Equal Employment Opportunity Commission. 2001. Employment in private industry by race/ethnic group/sex and by industry, U.S. Retrieved December 14, 2004 from www.eeoc.gov/stats/jobpat/2001/national.html.

Feagin, J.R. 1991. The continuing significance of race: Anti-black discrimination in public places. *American Sociological Review, 56.* 101–16.

Fielden, S.L. & Cooper, C.L. 2001. Women managers and stress: A critical analysis. *Equal opportunities international, 20*(1/2). 3–16.

Fielden, S.L. & Cooper, C.L. 2002. Managerial stress: Are women more at risk? 19–34. In D.L. Nelson & R.J. Burke, Eds. *Gender, Work, Stress, and Health.* Washington, D.C.: American Psychological Association.

Fontana, D. 1989. *Managing Stress(Problems in Practice)*. Oxford: The British Psychology Society and Routledge.

Gamse, P. 2003. Stress for success. *HRMagazine, 48*(7). 101–04.

Gardiner, M. & Tiggemann, M. 1999. Gender differences in leadership style, job stress and mental health in male- and female-dominated industries. *Journal of Occupational and Organizational Psychology, 72*(Part 3). 301–16.

Gill, S. & Davidson, M.J. 2001. Problems and pressures facing lone mothers in management and professional occupations—a pilot study. *Women in Management Review, 16*(7/8). 383–400.

Greenglass, E. 2002. Work stress, coping, and social support. 85–114. In Nelson, D. L. Nelson & R.J. Burke, Eds. *Gender, Work, Stress, and Health*. Washington, D.C.: American Psychological Association.

Grzywacz, J.B. & Marks, N. 2000. Family, work, work-family spillover and problem drinking during midlife. *Journal of Marriage and the Family, 62*(2). 336–48.

Hewlett, S.A. 2002. Executive women and the myth of having it all. *Harvard Business Review, 80*(4). 66–74.

Hinkle, L.E. 1973. The concept of stress in the biological and social sciences. *Science, medicine, and man, 1*. 31–48.

Hochschild, A.R. & Machung, A. 1989. *The second shift*. New York: Viking.

Hochwater, W.A., Perrewe, P.L. & Dawkins, M.C. 1995. Gender differences in perceptions of stress-related variables. Do the people make the place or does the place make the people? *Journal of Managerial Issues, 7*. 62–74.

Hurrell, J.J., Jr. 2005. Organizational stress interventions. 7–34. In J. Barling, E. K. Kelloway & M.R. rone, Eds. *Handbook of Work Stress*. Thousand Oaks, CA: Sage.

Intindola, B. 1991. EAPs still foreign to many small businesses. *National Underwriter, 95*. 21.

Ivancevich, J.M. & Matteson, M.T. 1996. *Organizational behavior and management*. 4th ed. Chicago: Irwin.

Jaimes, M.A. & Halsey, T. 1992. Native American women. 311–44. In M.A. Jaimes, Ed. *The State of Native America*. Boston: South End Press.

Jex, S.M., Adams, G.M. & Ehler, M.L. 2002. Assessing the role of negative affectivity in occupational stress research: Does gender make a difference? 71–84. In D.L. Nelson & R.J. Burke, Eds. *Gender, Work, Stress, and Health*. Washington, D.C.: American Psychological Association.

Jex, S.M., Bliese, P.D., Buzzell, S. & Primeau, J. 2001. The impact of self-efficacy on stressor-strain relations: Coping style as an explanatory mechanism. *Journal of Applied Psychology, 86*. 401–09.

Jex, S.M., Cvetanovski, J. & Allen, S.J. 1994. Self-esteem as a moderator of the impact of unemployment. *Journal of Social Behavior and Personality, 9*. 69–80.

Jex, S.M. & Gudanowski, D.M. 1992. Efficacy beliefs and work stress: An exploratory study. *Journal of Organizational Behavior, 13*. 182–91.

Jones, J.M. 1997. *Prejudice and racism*. 2nd ed. New York: McGraw-Hill.

Kapalka, G.M. & Lachenmeyer, J.R. 1988. Sex-role flexibility, locus of control, and occupational status. *Sex Roles, 19*. 417–27.

Karasek, R. & Theorell, T. 1990. *Healthy work: Stress, productivity, and the reconstruction of working life.* New York: Basic Books.

Karsten, M.F. 1994. *Management and gender: Issues and attitudes.* Westport: Greenwood Publishing Group, Inc.

Kelloway, E.K., Sivanathan, N., Francis, L. & Barling, J. Poor leadership. 2005. 7–34. In J. Barling, E. K. Kelloway & M.R. Frone, Eds. *Handbook of Work Stress.* Thousand Oaks, CA: Sage.

Kuo, W.H. 1995. Coping with racial discrimination: The case of Asian Americans. *Ethnic and racial studies, 18*(1). 109–27.

Krieger, N. & Sidney, S. 1996. Racial discrimination and blood pressure: The CARDIA study of young black and white adults. *American Journal of Public Health, 86.* 1370–78.

LaFromboise, T.D., Heyle, A.M. & Ozer, E.J. 1990. Changing and diverse roles. *Sex Roles, 22*(7/8). 455–75.

Lalonde, R.N., Majumder, S. & Parris, R.D. 1995. Preferred responses to situations of housing and employment discrimination. *Journal of Applied Social Psychology, 25.* 1105–19.

Landrine, H. & Klonoff, E. A. 1996. The schedule of racist events: A measure of racial discrimination and a study of its negative physical and mental health consequences. The Journal of Black Psychology, 22, 144–168.

Landy, F., J. Quick & Kasl, S. 1994. Work, stress, and well-being. *International Journal of Stress Management, 1*(1). 33–73.

Lazarus, R.S. & Folkman, S. 1984. *Stress, appraisal, and coping.* New York: Springer.

Lennon, M.C. 1987. Sex role orientation, coping strategies, and self-efficacy of women in traditional and nontraditional occupations. *Journal of Health and Social Behavior, 28.* 290–305.

Leong, C.S., Furnham, A.Y. & Cooper, C.L. 1996. The moderating effect of organizational commitment on the occupational stress outcome relationship. *Human Relations, 49.* 1345–63.

Long, B.C. 1998. Coping with workplace stress: A multiple group comparison of female managers and clerical workers. *Journal of Counseling Psychology, 45*(1).

Long, B.C., Kahn, S.E. Kahn & Schultz, R.W. 1992. Causal model of stress and coping: Women in management. *Journal of Counseling Psychology, 29.* 227–39.

Meyer, I.H. 2003. Prejudice as stress: Conceptual and measurement problems. *American Journal of Public Health, 93*(2). 262–64.

Mossakowski, K.N. 2003, September. Coping with perceived discrimination: Does ethnic identity protect mental health? *Journal of Health and Social Behavior, 44.* 318–31.

National Institute for Occupational Safety and Health. 2000, July 28. *National occupation research agenda: 21 priorities for the 21st century.* Retrieved December 16, 2004 from www.cdc.gov/niosh/00–143g.html.

National Institute for Occupational Safety and Health. 2004. *Worker Health Chartbook, 2004.* NIOSH Publication 2004–146. Retrieved November 24, 2004 from http://www2a.cdc.gov/NIOSH-Chartbook/imagedetail.asp?imgid=47.

Nelson, D.L. & Burke, R.J. 2000. Women executives: Health, stress, and success. *Academy of Management Executive, 14*(2). 107–22.

Nelson, D.L & Burke, R.J. 2002. A framework for examining gender, work stress, and health. 3–14. In D.L. Nelson & R.J. Burke, Eds. *Gender, Work, Stress, and Health.* Washington, D.C.: American Psychological Association.

Nolen-Hoeksema, S. 1987. Sex differences in unipolar depression: Evidence and theory. *Psychological Bulletin, 101.* 259–82.

O'Driscoll, M.P., Ilgen, D.R. & Hildreth, K. 1992. Time devoted to job and off-job activities, interrole conflict, and affective experiences. *Journal of Applied Psychology, 77.* 272–79.

Pak, A.W.P., Dion, K.L. & Dion, K.K. 1991. Social psychological correlates of experienced discrimination: Test of the double jeopardy hypothesis. *International Journal of Intercultural Relations, 15.* 243–54.

Peeters, M.C.W., deJonge, J., Jansen, Jansen, P.P.M. & van der Linden, S. 2004. Work-home interference, job stressors, and employee health. *International Journal of Stress Management, 11*(4).

Pierce, J.L., Gardner, D.G., Dunham, R.B. & Cummings, L.L. 1993. Moderation by organization-based self-esteem of role condition-employee response relationship. *Academy of Management Journal, 36.* 271–88.

Plummer, D. L. & Slane, S. 1996. Patterns of coping racially stressful situations. *The Journal of Black Psychology, 22,* 302–315.

Portello, J.V. & Long, B.C. 2001. Appraisals and coping with interpersonal stress: A model for women managers. *Journal of Counseling Psychology, 48*(2).

Rees, D. & Cooper, C.L. 1990. Occupational stress in health service workers in the U.K. *Stress Medicine, 8.* 79–80.

Schaefer, C., Coyne, J. & Lazarus, R. 1981. The health-related functions of social support. *Journal of Behavioral Medicine, 4*(4). 381–406.

Seligman, M.E.P. 1995. The effectiveness of psychotherapy: The *Consumer Reports* study. *American Psychologist, 50.* 965–74.

Sherry, S.B., Hewitt, P.L., Flett, G.L. & Harvey, M. 2003. Perfectionism dimensions, perfectionistic attitudes, dependent attitudes, and depression in psychiatric patients and university students. *Journal of Counseling Psychology, 50*(3).

Simpson, G.E. & Yinger, J.M. 1985. *Racial and cultural minorities: An analysis of prejudice and discrimination.* 5th ed. New York: Plenum.

Smith, A. 2001. Perceptions of stress at work. *Human Resource Management Journal, 11*(4). 74–86.

Stamper, C.L. & Johlke, M.C. 2003. The impact of perceived organizational support on the relationship between boundary spanner role stress and work outcomes. *Journal of Management, 29*(4). 569–88.

Stockdale, M.S., Murphy, K.P., Cleveland, J. et al. 2000. *Women and men in organizations: Sex and gender issues at work.* Mahwah, N.J.: Lawrence Erlbaum Associates.

Sumer, H.C. & Knight, P. A. 2001. How do people with different attachment styles balance work and family? A personality perspective on work-family linkage. *Journal of Applied Psychology, 86.* 653–63.

Sutton, L. *Feed a cold, starve a fever: An exploration into the relationship between culture, belief, and health.* N.d. Retrieved November 24, 2004 from http://www .members.tripod.com/random_sage/part2b.htm.

Thompson Sanders, V. L. 1996. Perceived experiences of racism as stressful life events. *Community Mental Health Journal*, 32.223–233.

Thompson, V.L.S. 2002. Racism: Perceptions of distress among African Americans. *Community Mental Health Journal, 38*(2). 111–19.

Toliver, S.D. 1998. *Black families in corporate America.* Thousand Oaks, CA: Sage.

Tran, T. V., Fitzpatrick, T., Berg, W.R. & Wright, R., Jr. 1996. Acculturation, health, stress, & psychological distress among elderly Hispanics. *Journal of Cross Cultural Gerontology 11.* 149–65.

Turner, R.J. & Lloyd, D.A. 1995, December. Lifetime trauma and mental health: The significance of cumulative adversity. *Journal of Health and Social Behavior, 36.* 360–75.

Turner, R.J. & Avison, W.R. 2003, December. Status variations in stress exposure: Implications for the interpretation of research on race, socioeconomic status, and gender. *Journal of Health and Social Behavior, 44.* 488–505.

Utsey, S.O, Ponteretto, J.G., Reynolds, A.L. & Cancelli, A.A. 2000. Racial discrimination, coping life satisfaction, a nd self-esteem among African Americans. *Journal of Counseling and Development, 78*(1).

Van der Klink, J.J.L., Blonk, R.W.B., Schene, A.H. & van Dijk, F.J.H. 2001. The benefits of interventions for work-related stress. *American Journal of Public Health, 91*(2). 270–76.

Vingerhoets, A.J. M. & Van Heck, G.L.1990. Gender, coping, and psychosomatic symptoms. *Psychological Medicine, 20.* 120–35.

Walters, K.L. & Simoni, J.M. 2002. Reconceptualizing Native women's health: An "indigenist" stress-coping model. *American Journal of Public Health, 92*(4). 520–24.

Weiten, W. 1989. *Psychology themes and variations.* Pacific Grove, CA: Brooke/ Cole.

West, C. 1993. *Race Matters.* Boston: Beacon Press.

Westman, M. 2002. Gender asymmetry in crossover research. 129–50. In Nelson, D.L. & R.J.Burke. *Gender, Work, Stress, and Health.* Washington, D.C.: American Psychological Association.

Williams, D.R., Spencer, D.I.S. & Jackson, J. 1999. Race, stress, and physical health: The role of group identity. In R.J. Contrada & R.D. Ashmore, Eds. *Self, Social Identity, and Physical Health: Interdisciplinary explorations.* London: Oxford University Press.

Zambrana, R. E., Scrimshaw, S.C.M., Collins, N. & Dunkel-Schetter, C. 1997. Prenatal health behavior & psychosocial risk factors in pregnant women of Mexican origin: The role of acculturation. *The American Journal of Public Health 87*, 1022–26.

Index